Same-Sex Relationships, Law and Social Change

This edited collection provides a forum for rigorous analysis of the necessity for both legal and social change with regard to regulation of same-sex relationships and rainbow families, the status of civil partnership as a concept and the lived reality of equality for LGBTQ+ persons.

Twenty-eight jurisdictions worldwide have now legalised same-sex marriage, and many others some level of civil partnership. In contrast, other jurisdictions refuse to recognise or even criminalise same-sex relationships. At a Council of Europe level, there is no requirement for contracting states to legalise same-sex marriage. Whilst the Court of Justice of the European Union now requires contracting states to recognise same-sex marriages for the purpose of free movement and residency rights, unlike the US Supreme Court, it does not require EU Member States to legalise same-sex marriage. Law and Sociology scholars from five key jurisdictions (England and Wales, Italy, Australia, Canada and the Republic of Ireland) examine the role of the Council of Europe, European Union and further international regimes. A balanced approach between the competing views of critically analytical rights-based theorists and queer and feminist theorists interrogates the current international consensus in this fast-moving area. The incrementalist theory, whilst offering a methodology for future advances, continues to be critiqued. All contributions from differing perspectives expose that even for those jurisdictions which have legalised same-sex marriage, still further and continuous work needs to be done.

The book will be of interest to students and scholars in the fields of human rights, family and marriage law, and gender studies.

Frances Hamilton and **Guido Noto La Diega** are Senior Lecturers in Law, both at Northumbria University.

Same-Sex Relationships, Law and Social Change

Edited by Frances Hamilton
and Guido Noto La Diega

Routledge
Taylor & Francis Group
LONDON AND NEW YORK

First published 2020
by Routledge
2 Park Square, Milton Park, Abingdon, Oxon OX14 4RN

and by Routledge
52 Vanderbilt Avenue, New York, NY 10017

Routledge is an imprint of the Taylor & Francis Group, an informa business

A glasshouse book

British Library Cataloguing-in-Publication Data
A catalogue record for this book is available from the British Library

Library of Congress Cataloging-in-Publication Data
A catalog record for this book has been requested

ISBN: 978-0-367-07609-2 (hbk)
ISBN: 978-0-429-02158-9 (ebk)

Typeset in Galliard
by Apex CoVantage, LLC

Contents

Contributors

Erez Aloni is an Assistant Professor at the Peter A. Allard School of Law, University of British Columbia. Aloni's primary research interests lie in the legal regulation of adult relationships and complex family structures. His work examines the diverse laws that together affect a family's composition and well-being, and explores how those laws create effects – socioeconomic and otherwise – on society at large. Prior to joining UBC in 2017, he served as an assistant professor at Whittier Law School, where he taught contracts and domestic relations. Previously, he was an academic fellow at the Center for Reproductive Rights and Columbia Law School. He received his LL.M. and S.J.D. from the University of Pennsylvania Law School, where he also taught a seminar on law and sexuality.

Frances Burton, PhD, is a Senior Lecturer in Law, Buckingham University. She began to read Law at St Anne's College, Oxford, before transferring to the University of London for her first degree, to which she has added a Masters degree in Employment Law and Industrial Relations from Leicester University, a Masters degree in Education from the School of Education of the Open University and a PhD from LJMU on the basis of a comparative study of Cohabitants' Rights in both common law and civil law jurisdictions. She was initially called to the Bar by Middle Temple (from which she received a Harmsworth Major Exhibition) and then proceeded *ad eundem* to Lincolns Inn, where she is a member of leading Chancery Chambers at 10 Old Square, and now practising from there as a Mediator and Family Law Arbitrator, MCIArb. Her research interests are mainly in Family Law and Property, but also in the English Legal System, Legal Method and Skills, Access to Justice, and particularly Dispute Resolution. She has published widely in these fields, including textbooks, articles in academic journals and professional publications, conference papers and professional newsletters, in hard copy and online.

Lauren Clayton-Helm, PhD, is a Senior Lecturer in Law at Northumbria University at Newcastle. Upon completing her PhD within the Conflict of Laws, she has continued to research and publish in this area. Other areas of interest include International Family Law and Family Law more generally.

Catherine Donovan, PhD, is Professor of Sociology at Durham University. She has spent nearly thirty years researching the intimate and family lives of lesbians, gay men and, more recently, bisexual and transpeople. After her early work on family and parenting relationships, her most recent work has included the first comparative study of love and violence in same-sex and heterosexual relationships and the first multi-method study exploring the use of violent and abusive behaviours in the relationships of LGB and/or T people. Other research interests have included LGB and/or T child sexual exploitation, austerity and the emotional impacts of austerity for practitioners. She led on a project developing a bystander intervention initiative, Be the Difference,' based on a campus survey of students' experiences of violence, abuse and harassment. Currently she is also developing work on hate crime/incidents with a project exploring the usefulness of 'hate relationships' to explain some experiences of hate that involve on-going experiences from one or more perpetrators; and a project exploring 'cuckooing', whereby offenders inveigle themselves into the homes of situationally vulnerable individuals in order to use them as a base for their nefarious activities.

Douglas Ezzy, PhD, is Professor of Sociology at the University of Tasmania, Australia. He is editor of the *Journal for the Academic Study of Religion*. His research includes both health sociology and contemporary religious diversity. His books include *Lesbian, Gay, Bisexual and Transgendered Christians* (2018, with Bronwyn Fielder), *Reinventing Church* (2016, with Helen and James Collins), *Sex, Death and Witchcraft* (2014), *Teenage Witches* (2007, with Helen Berger) and *Qualitative Analysis* (2002).

Bronwyn Fielder, PhD, is a postdoctoral researcher at the University of Tasmania. Her research focuses on the reproduction of inequalities in society and ways in which these inequalities can be addressed. She has presented at numerous conferences on the ways LGBT Christians negotiate seemingly disparate identities and seek to live a life that is both authentic to their sexuality and/or gender, as well as their religious selves. Her book, *Lesbian, Gay, Bisexual and Transgendered Christians: Queer Christians, Authentic Selves* (co-authored with Douglas Ezzy), was published in 2018.

Frances Hamilton, PhD, is a Senior Lecturer in Law at Northumbria University. She holds an MA from the University of Cambridge together with an LLM from Trinity College Dublin. She is also a qualified solicitor. Her research interests involve the difficulties facing individual countries and international courts in recognising same-sex relationships. She takes a comparative law approach, as well as looking at human rights law and an EU free movement perspective. She is also interested in the necessary interaction between legal and social change in this area. She has worked as a Senior Lecturer in Law at Northumbria University since 2009 and prior to this worked as a solicitor in London firms Reed Smith Richards Butler LLP and Hogan Lovells LLP.

Andy Hayward, PhD, is an Associate Professor at Durham Law School. He is also Co-Director of a research centre, *Gender and Law at Durham* (GLAD) that coordinates research activities in relation to law and gender studies. His research interests lie in family law, property law and legal history. His research critically analyses the legal regulation of formalised and non-formalised adult relationships, and in particular, the property consequences generated by their breakdown. He has published widely on domestic and comparative civil partnership reform.

Alexander Maine is a Lecturer in Law at the University of Leicester. His socio-legal research focuses on Family Law and Gender; Sexuality and Law, in particular relationship recognition; and the effect of law on the lived experiences of LGBTQ people. He holds an LLB from Newcastle University and is a PhD candidate at Northumbria University School of Law. His PhD thesis is entitled *Same-Sex Marriage and the Sexual Hierarchy: Constructing the Homonormative and Homoradical Legal Identities*, and he is Co-Editor of a forthcoming Edward Elgar *Research Handbook on Gender, Sexuality, and Law.*

Guido Noto La Diega, PhD, is Senior Lecturer in Law at Northumbria Law School, where he is International Research Partnerships Coordinator and co-convenor of NINSO Northumbria Internet and Society Research Group. After a PhD in Private Law (Unipa) and a Postdoc in Cloud Computing Law (QMUL), he developed an expertise in LGBTQ+ rights that led to a Santander-sponsored visiting professorship in Rio de Janeiro, where he taught 'Sexualities, Genders, and Laws.' He is co-chair of Northumbria LGBTQ* Network, and scientific committee member of Mediterranea International Center for Human Rights Research.

Louise Richardson-Self, PhD, is a Lecturer in Philosophy and Gender Studies at the University of Tasmania. She has published extensively on LGBTQ+ rights, including her book *Justifying Same-Sex Marriage: A Philosophical Investigation* (2015). She was recently awarded a Discovery Early Career Researcher Award by the Australian Research Council (2019–2021) for the project *Hate Speech Against Women Online: Concepts and Countermeasures* and was the recipient of the Australian Academy of the Humanities' R. M. Crawford Medal in 2016.

Fergus Ryan, PhD, is an Associate Professor in Law at Maynooth University, part of the National University of Ireland. He has many years of experience teaching and researching law, with a particular focus on family law, gender, sexual orientation, and human rights. From 1998–2013, he taught at the Dublin Institute of Technology (now TU Dublin), at which he served as Head of the Department of Law from 2003 to 2009, and again in 2013. He has also been a visiting lecturer, visiting scholar, and external examiner at a number of universities and third-level institutions. From 2002–2018, he served as internship director for the University of Tulsa College of Law summer abroad programme in Dublin. He has written and spoken extensively on various legal topics, with a particular emphasis on the family, constitutional law and LGBTQ+ rights. He has published several texts, academic articles and book chapters, and has advised multiple state agencies on issues of family law and human rights. He has assisted members of the Irish Senate in drafting legislation and legislative amendments. He twice served as President of the Irish Association of Law Teachers and was, formerly, chair of One Family.

Alexander Schuster, PhD, is a Post-Doc Researcher at the University of Verona. He has a proven track record of research in the area of family law and sexual orientation. He holds a dual doctorate from Trento and Strasbourg University with a thesis on gender-neutral family institutions. Important EU level funded projects include acting as a coordinator of the RightsOnTheMove.eu project on the freedom of movement of families in the EU, co-funded by the European Union since January 2013. He has also conducted major interdisciplinary researches, including one for the Italian government on LGBT discrimination in the South of Italy. Dr Schuster is also an Italian attorney and the member for Italy, European Commission Sexual Orientation. He has also acted as an advocate in key case law before the European Court of Human Rights, including the well-known *Oliari and Others v Italy* case. Dr Schuster has published widely in this area in several different languages and currently holds the position of post-doc researcher at the University of Verona.

Angioletta Sperti, PhD, is an Associate Professor of Comparative Public Law at the University of Pisa, where she teaches comparative constitutional law and human rights law. Her main research interests include constitutional justice, comparative legal systems, LGBT rights. She has also conducted extensive research on presidential accountability and impeachment in the Italian system of government. She holds an LLM from UCLA (USA) and a PhD from Scuola Superiore S. Anna (Italy). She is the author of *Constitutional Courts, Gay Rights and Sexual Orientation Equality* (Hart, 2017) and of three monographs (in Italian) on the Italian constitutional court (Corti supreme e conflitti tra poteri, 2003) the presidential accountability (La responsibilità del Presidente della Repubblica, 2010) and the dialogue among constitutional courts on LGBT rights (Omosessualità e diritti, 2013). She regularly contributes to articolo29.it, a legal website focusing on the advancement of LGBTQ+ rights in Italy, and is managing editor of *GenIUS*, an Italian law review on gender and sexual orientation equality.

Brian Tobin, PhD, is a Lecturer in Law at the National University of Ireland, Galway (NUIG), where he teaches and researches primarily in the areas of Family and Child Law. His particular research focus is on emerging family forms and the law, marriage equality and the legal position of children born via donor-assisted human reproduction and surrogacy. Dr Tobin has published articles on these areas of law in leading peer-reviewed journals such as the *International Journal of Law, Policy and the Family*, *Journal of Social Welfare and*

Family Law, *Child and Family Law Quarterly*, *Australian Journal of Family Law*, *European Human Rights Law Review* and the *Irish Jurist*. He has previously appeared before UK and Irish parliamentary committees advising on the legal and constitutional issues pertaining to surrogacy and donor-assisted human reproduction. He is a frequent media commentator on these issues in Ireland. Dr Tobin has just completed a sabbatical year as a Visiting Researcher at the Dickson Poon School of Law, King's College London.

Alina Tryfonidou, PhD, is Professor of Law at the University of Reading. She joined Reading as a Lecturer in September 2011, after being a Lecturer in Law at the University of Leicester from 2007 to 2011. Prior to that, she was teaching European Law as a Visiting Tutor (2005–2007) at King's College London whilst pursuing her PhD studies at the same institution. Professor Tryfonidou obtained her LLB (2001), LLM (2002) and PhD (2008) from King's College London and is an Associate of King's College (AKC) since 2008. She is a non-practising member of the Cyprus Bar since 2003, a Fellow of the Centre of European Law at King's College London since 2007, and a Fellow of the Higher Education Academy (FHEA) since 2016. In 2004, Professor Tryfonidou completed a traineeship (*stage*) at the European Commission, at the Internal Market Directorate General, and in 2010–2011 she was an IALS Visiting Fellow.

Introduction

This edited collection results partly from a conference entitled 'Same-Sex Relationships: A New Revolutionary Era and the Influence of Legal and Social Change' organised by Dr Frances Hamilton, Dr Guido Noto La Diega and Laura Graham of Northumbria University and hosted at Northumbria University on 10 September 2018. The continued and generous sponsorship of the Society of Legal Scholars made this conference possible, despite the cancellation and re-organisation of the conference following the 'Beast from the East' snowstorm. The input of all valued chapter contributors, anonymous peer reviewers, colleagues, research assistant Cameron Giles and editorial advice from Routledge is fully recognised and gratefully received by the editors.

The chapters in this volume rigorously analyse the necessity for both legal and social change with regard to regulation of same-sex relationships and rainbow families, the status of civil partnership as a concept and the lived reality of equality for LGBTQ+ (used to denote 'lesbian, gay, bisexual, transgender and queer). The area studied can be regarded as an illustration of social change in action. It was only fifty years ago that same-sex sexual acts between males were partly decriminalised in England and Wales.[1] There has been rapid change worldwide. Twenty-eight states have legalised same-sex marriage.[2] Recent international judgements from the US Supreme Court,[3] Inter-American Court[4] and the Court of Justice of the European Union (CJEU) have accelerated progress. Taiwan has recently become the first Asian country to legalise same-sex marriage. Yet difficulties remain. Globally, over seventy countries still retain criminal sanctions for same-sex sexual activities[5] and many other countries do not legally recognise same-sex relationships. Whilst the European Court of Human Rights (ECtHR) has used an incremental case-based approach driven by an evolutive and dynamic interpretation of human rights to advance LGBTQ+ persons and same-sex couples' rights, at present there is no requirement for contracting states to legalise same-sex marriage.[6] This book includes contributions from legal experts and sociologists, utilising an exciting mix of doctrinal, empirical and theoretical methods to interrogate the current international consensus. A compelling international and comparative law perspective is demonstrated by contributions from authors from five jurisdictions including England and Wales, Italy, Australia, Canada and the

Republic of Ireland. Critical rights-based theorists and those espousing queer and feminist theory debate throughout.

For the sake of consistency through all chapters, this edited collection has adopted a common terminology. The common acronym LGBTQ+ has been used in order to avoid multiple possible such acronyms, although individual authors have drawn upon different specific uses where these are necessary in specific contexts. Other commonly adopted terminologies include 'same-sex' rather than 'same-gender,' cisgender (used to denote persons whose sense of personal identity and gender correspond with their birth sex) and transperson (used to denote persons whose gender identity or gender expression is different from their assigned sex). Donovan usefully defines 'heteronormativity' as:

> convey[ing] the multiple ways in which society is organised – structurally and culturally – to (re)produce a particular ideal of heterosexual living as the preferred way of living against which everybody else (including heterosexual women and men) can be compared and found wanting.[7]

Part 1: the role of the European Court of Human Rights and the European Union in relation to the treatment of same-sex couples' relationships

An essential aim of the edited collection in a Brexit era, is to critically consider the role, which the ECtHR and the European Union (EU) can play in the treatment of same-sex couples' relationships. The ECtHR's position awaiting a consensus to develop before requiring contracting states to legalise same-sex marriage[8] is contrasted with the possibilities for the EU in this area. Hamilton's chapter argues that greater co-ordination between the EU and the ECtHR,[9] and further understanding of the concept of EU citizenship encompassing far reaching free movement and non-discrimination provisions, can be advantageous to the advancement of LGBTQ+ persons' and same-sex couple's rights. Noto La Diega and Clayton-Helm's chapters both consider the field of conflict of law in grappling with the difficulties faced by countries internationally when concerned with the recognition of foreign same-sex marriages and civil partnerships. Noto La Diega's chapter identifies a tripartite analysis, categorising European states into countries which recognise, downgrade and erase same-sex marriages celebrated abroad. Clayton-Helm's chapter proceeds by comparative analysis with the US approach and considers the role which the EU can play in moving towards a harmonised choice of law rule on same-sex marriage.

Part 2: differing paths towards legalisation of same-sex marriage

Part 2 analyses debate concerning the relative merits of different paths towards legalising same-sex marriage. Whilst the court-based method adopted by the US

Supreme Court in *Obergefell v Hodges*[10] was opportune due to a lack of consensus in Congress at the time,[11] this method has been heavily criticised as resulting in a 'naked usurpation of the legislative function.'[12] Others recommend the legislative method as allowing recognition to happen 'democratically rather than judicially.'[13] Sperti's chapter demonstrates that the 'apparent contrast'[14] between legislative and court-based methods should not be exaggerated. She concludes that in fact the 'similarities in the synergy between national legislators and constitutional courts needs to be acknowledged.'[15] Tobin and Richardson-Self et al. comment on introduction of same-sex marriage by means of nation-wide referendums and postal votes in the Republic of Ireland (ROI) and Australia respectively. Whilst Tobin recognises the achievement of same-sex marriage in ROI, a country traditionally morally conservative society[16] which had previously constitutionally guaranteed marriage as taking place between partners of the opposite sex only,[17] his conclusion that this was a 'politically opportune' method, chimes in this respect with Richardson-Self et al.'s analysis of the Australian postal vote.[18]

Part 3: rainbow families

Children from same-sex couple relationships (referred to as 'rainbow families') often face multiple legal challenges. Tryfonidou's chapter illustrates the possibilities of the EU system still further by analysing the current status of EU citizens and rainbow families to move freely between EU Member States. In particular, she focuses on the parent-child relationship and examines whether the refusal of the host Member State to legally recognise the relationship between a child and one or both of his/her same-sex parents amounts to a breach of EU law, when the family moves between territories. Schuster considers both the role of the ECtHR and the EU in shaping future EU law regarding a hypothetical EU family law code. Burton examines social change in rainbow families by referring to examples from contemporary culture to illustrate the points made. She considers the social acceptance of same-sex relationships and their use of human-assisted reproduction methods to provide same-sex parents with genetically related children. These challenges have affected the crucial role of surrogacy in assisting male same-sex couples to father genetically related progeny.

Part 4: the importance of civil partnership in an era of same-sex marriage

When civil partnership was the only formal status available to same-sex couples, this was criticised as reducing LGBTQ+ people and same-sex couples to second-class status.[19] Civil partnership did not suit those who saw marriage as the 'privileged and preferred status.'[20] Comparisons were made with the former treatment of African-American people in the USA and the apartheid regime in South Africa.[21] In an era of same-sex marriage, debate continues around whether civil partnership is a valuable institution in its own right, or whether its only value is that of a 'stepping-stone' on route to same-sex marriage, allowing time for public opinion to adjust.[22] The ECtHR recognises that civil partnerships has intrinsic value.[23] In the United Kingdom, opposite-sex couples have also successfully campaigned to have access to civil partnership opened to them.[24] Hayward's chapter considers whether civil partnership can now have a symbolic value of its own. Maine's chapter considers where civil partnership sits on a hierarchy of recognised relationships.

Part 5: the heteronormative underpinnings of same-sex marriage

Queer theorists question the very need for same-sex marriage, in the view that LGBTQ+ people are 'not the marrying kind.'[25] Lisa Duggan, for instance, argues that same-sex marriage means that the 'dominative heteronormative assumptions' are not questioned.[26] This reflects the fact that many within the LGBTQ+ community remain divided about whether same-sex marriage is a positive goal.[27] Feminists are also reluctant to embrace marriage with the long-running negative associations for women that this includes.[28] Marriage was understood as 'at best problematic for, and at worst deeply oppressive to, women as a class.'[29] Ryan's chapter interrogates the heteronormative underpinnings of marriage, which continues to lead to questions about the reality of marriage equality even following equal marriage legislation in his chosen jurisdictions of study, the ROI and England and Wales.

Part 6: consideration of the necessity of both social and legal change, and the interaction between them

Donovan's chapter uses the case study of domestic violence and abuse in LGBTQ+ relationships to discuss the lived reality for LGBTQ+ persons and same-sex couples following recent legislation. In considering the inter-relationship between public opinion and legal change, incrementalist scholars set out a step-by-step process, otherwise known as the theory of small change. Leading advocate Waaldijk argues this is useful in allowing change over time.[30] This is because it 'permit[s . . .] gradual adjustment of antigay mind-sets, slowly empowers . . . gay right advocates and . . . discredit[s] antigay arguments.'[31] Statistics demonstrate the correlation between favourable public opinion and legal change in order to achieve long-term successful change.[32] Aloni's chapter critiques the incrementalist theory in relation to same-sex marriage legalisation.

Notes

1 Sexual Offences Act 1967.
2 28 countries worldwide now recognise same-sex marriage. These include Argentina, Australia, Austria, Belgium, Brazil, Canada, Colombia, Denmark, Ecuador, Finland, France, Germany, Iceland, Ireland, Luxembourg, Malta, Mexico, the

Netherlands, New Zealand, Norway, Portugal, South Africa, Spain, Sweden, Taiwan, the United Kingdom, the United States and Uruguay.

3 *Obergefell v Hodges* 576 US, 135 S Ct 2584 (2015).

4 *Obligaciones Estatales en Relacion Con El Cambio De Nombre, La Identidad de Genero, Y Los Derechos Derivados De Un Vinculo Entre Parejas Del Mismo Sexo*, Judgment of the Inter-American Court, 9 January 2018.

5 See '72 Countries Where Homosexuality Is Illegal' *76 Crimes* (11 June 2019) <https://76crimes.com/76-countries-where-homosexuality-is-illegal/> accessed 16 September 2019.

6 *Schalk and Kopf v Austria* App No. 30141/04 (ECtHR, 24 June 2010).

7 See Donovan (chapter 13).

8 *Schalk and Kopf* (n 6).

9 See Hamilton (chapter 1).

10 *Obergefell* (n 3).

11 Ian Loveland, 'A Right to Engage in Same-Sex Marriage in the United States' (2014) 1 *European Human Rights Law Review* 10, 17.

12 See for comment Ibid., 18–19.

13 David Richards, 'Book Review: Governing Sexuality: The Changing Politics of Citizenship and Law Reform' (2004) 2 *International Journal of Constitutional Law* 727, 733.

14 See Chapter 6 in this collection.

15 Ibid.

16 This Chapter is a reprint of Brian Tobin, 'Marriage Equality in Ireland: The Politico-Legal Context' (2016) 30 *International Journal of Law, Policy and the Family* 115, and is reprinted with the kind permission of Oxford University Press.

17 See Ibid.

18 See Richardson-Self et al.

19 See for example, Jonah Crane, 'Legislative and Constitutional Responses to *Goodridge v Department of Public Health*' (2003–2004) 7 *New York University Journal of Legislation and Public Policy* 465, 471; and, Michael Dorf, 'Same-Sex Marriage, Second-Class Citizenship, and Law's Social Meanings (2011) 97 *Virginia Law Review* 1267.

20 See also, Erez Aloni, 'Incrementalism, Civil Unions and the Possibility of Predicting Legal Recognition of Same-Sex Marriage'(2010–2011) 18 *Duke Journal of Gender Law & Policy* 105, 110, which describes marriage as the 'privileged and preferred legal status in Europe and the United States,' referring to Yuval Merin, *Equality for Same-Sex Couples* (University of Chicago Press 2002) 55–56.

21 Kathryn Marshall, 'Strategic Pragmatism or Radical Idealism? The Same-Sex Marriage and Civil Rights Movements Juxtaposed' (2012) 2 *William & Mary Policy Review* 194.

22 Frances Hamilton, 'Strategies to Achieve Same-Sex Marriage and the Method of Incrementalist Change' (2015–2016) 25 *Journal of Transnational Law & Policy* 121.

23 *Oliari and Others v Italy* App Nos. 18766/11 and 36030/11 (ECtHR, 21 July 2015).

24 *R (Steinfeld and Keidan) v Secretary of State for International Development* (2018) UKSC 32.

25 Nicola Barker, *Not the Marrying Kind: A Feminist Critique of Same-Sex Marriage* (Palgrave Macmillan 2012).

26 Lisa Duggan, 'The New Homonormativity: The Sexual Politics of Neoliberalism' in Dana Nelson and Russ Castronovo (eds), *Materializing Democracy: Toward a Revitalized Cultural Politics* (Duke University Press 2002) 175.

27 See for example *Barker* (n 25) and Rosemary Auchmuty, 'Law and the Power of Feminism: How Marriage Lost Its Power to Oppress Women' (2012) 20 *Feminist Legal Studies* 71.
28 See for example, Yvonne Zylan, *States of Passion, Identity and Social Construction of Desire* (Oxford University Press 2011) 204.
29 Ibid.
30 Kees Waaldijk, 'Small Change: How the Road to Same-Sex Marriage Got Paved in the Netherlands' in Robert Wintermute and Mads Andenæs (eds), *Legal Recognition of Same-Sex Partnerships: A Study of Nation, Europe, and International Law* (Hart Publishing 2001) 437.
31 William Eskridge Jr, *Equality Practice: Civil Unions and the Future of Gay Rights* (Routledge 2002) 119; Marshall (n 21) 199–200; Maggie Gallagher, 'Why Accommodate? Reflections on the Gay Marriage Culture Wars' (2010) 5 *Northwestern Journal of Law & Social Policy* 260; and Nancy Polikoff, 'We Will Get What We Ask for: Why Legalizing Gay and Lesbian Marriage Will Not "Dismantle the Legal Structure of Gender in Every Marriage"' (1993) 79 *Virginia Law Review* 1535.
32 Hamilton (n 22); referring to the David Masci and Drew Desilver, 'A Global Snapshot of Same-Sex Marriage' *Pew Research Center* (21 June 2019) <www.pewresearch.org/fact-tank/2013/06/04/global-snapshot-sex-marriage/> accessed 16 September 2019. The Pew Research Center conducts surveys annually in seventeen nations on this subject.

References

Primary sources

Obergefell v Hodges 576 US, 135 S Ct 2584 (2015).

Obligaciones Estatales en Relacion Con El Cambio De Nombre, La Identidad de Genero, Y Los Derechos Derivados De Un Vinculo Entre Parejas Del Mismo Sexo, Judgment of the Inter-American Court, 9 January 2018.

Oliari and Others v Italy App Nos. 18766/11 and 36030/11 (ECtHR, 21 July 2015).

R (Steinfeld and Keidan) v Secretary of State for International Development (2018) UKSC 32.

Schalk and Kopf v Austria App No. 30141/04 (ECtHR, 24 June 2010).

Sexual Offences Act 1967.

Secondary sources

Aloni E, 'Incrementalism, Civil Unions and the Possibility of Predicting Legal Recognition of Same-Sex Marriage'(2010–2011) 18 *Duke Journal of Gender Law & Policy* 105.

Auchmuty R, 'Law and the Power of Feminism: How Marriage Lost Its Power to Oppress Women' (2012) 20 *Feminist Legal Studies* 71.

Barker N, *Not the Marrying Kind: A Feminist Critique of Same-Sex Marriage* (Palgrave Macmillan 2012).

'72 Countries Where Homosexuality Is Illegal' *76 Crimes* (11 June 2019) <https://76crimes.com/76-countries-where-homosexuality-is-illegal/> accessed 16 September 2019.

Crane J, 'Legislative and Constitutional Responses to Goodridge v Department of Public Health' (2003–2004) 7 *New York University Journal of Legislation and Public Policy* 465.

Dorf M, 'Same-Sex Marriage, Second-Class Citizenship, and Law's Social Meanings' (2011) 97 *Virginia Law Review* 1267.

Duggan L, 'The New Homonormativity: The Sexual Politics of Neoliberalism' in Nelson D and Castronovo R (eds), '*Materializing Democracy: Toward a Revitalized Cultural Politics*' (Duke University Press 2002).

Eskridge Jr W *Equality Practice: Civil Unions and the Future of Gay Rights* (Routledge 2002).

Gallagher M, 'Why Accommodate? Reflections on the Gay Marriage Culture Wars' (2010) 5 *Northwestern Journal of Law & Social Policy* 260.

Hamilton F, 'Strategies to Achieve Same-Sex Marriage and the Method of Incrementalist Change' (2015–2016) 25 *Journal of Transnational Law & Policy* 121.

Loveland I, 'A Right to Engage in Same-Sex Marriage in the United States' (2014) 1 *European Human Rights Law Review* 10.

Marshall K, 'Strategic Pragmatism or Radical Idealism? The Same-Sex Marriage and Civil Rights Movements Juxtaposed' (2012) 2 *William & Mary Policy Review* 194.

Masci D and Desilver D, 'A Global Snapshot of Same-Sex Marriage' *Pew Research Center* (21 June 2019) <www.pewresearch.org/fact-tank/2013/06/04/global-snapshot-sex-marriage/> accessed 16 September 2019.

Merin Y, *Equality for Same-Sex Couples* (University of Chicago Press 2002) 55–56.

Polikoff N, 'We Will Get What We Ask For: Why Legalizing Gay and Lesbian Marriage Will Not "Dismantle the Legal Structure of Gender in Every Marriage"' (1993) 79 *Virginia Law Review* 1535.

Richards D, 'Book Review: Governing Sexuality: The Changing Politics of Citizenship and Law Reform' (2004) 2 *International Journal of Constitutional Law* 727.

Tobin B, 'Marriage Equality in Ireland: The Politico-Legal Context' (2016) 30 *International Journal of Law, Policy and the Family* 115.

Waaldijk K, 'Small Change: How the Road to Same-Sex Marriage Got Paved in the Netherlands' in Wintermute R and Andenæs M (eds), '*Legal Recognition of Same-Sex Partnerships: A Study of Nation, Europe, and International Law*' (Hart Publishing 2001) 437.

Zylan Y, *States of Passion, Identity and Social Construction of Desire* (Oxford University Press 2011).

Part I

The role of the European Court of Human Rights and the European Union in relation to the treatment of same-sex couples' relationships

Chapter 1

The potential of European Union law to further advance LGBTQ+ persons and same-sex couples' rights

Frances Hamilton

Introduction

Traditionally both the Court of Justice of the European Union (CJEU) and the European Court of Human Rights (ECtHR) have been reluctant to recognise LGBTQ+ couples in their varying concepts of 'family life.' The situation is further complicated due to the diversity of responses across Europe to the recognition of same-sex relationships. Whilst 16 European countries (14 within the European Union [EU']) now recognise same-sex marriage, other European countries recognise civil partnership only, with varying degrees of rights given to each same-sex couple.[1] In contrast, seven states within the EU, all in Eastern Europe, continue to constitutionally define marriage as between partners of the opposite sex only.[2] This difference in treatment of same-sex couples forms a complex web, made more difficult by the impact of globalisation.[3] On a practical basis, couples need to know whether their same-sex union will be legally recognised.[4] For proponents of same-sex marriage, there is also the added motivation of considering which court and type of claim may offer the best prospect of succesful recognition of rights.

This chapter argues that in recent years, the CJEU has begun to take a leading approach in furthering rights for LGBTQ+ persons and same-sex couples across Europe. The European Convention on Human Rights (European Convention, ECHR) is not an EU instrument, but the EU Charter of Fundamental Rights (EUCFR) provides that: '[i]n so far as this [EUCFR] contains rights which correspond to rights guaranteed by the [European Convention], the meaning and scope of those rights shall be the same as those laid down by the . . . [European Convention.],[5] and expressly states that '[t]his provision shall not prevent [EU] law providing more extensive protection.'[6] Two cases demonstrating a trend from the CJEU to offer more extensive protection for LGBTQ+ persons and same-sex couples in the context of both free movement and non-discrimination provisions are discussed throughout this chapter.

In *Relu Adrian Coman and Others v Inspectoratul General pentru Imigrări and others:* Case C-673/16 *(Coman)*, the CJEU confirmed the prior opinion of Advocate General Melchior Wathelet that a same-sex marriage conducted in one

EU Member State must be recognised in another for the purposes of free movement and residence rights of the non-EU citizen spouse.[7] This is the case even when the receiving country, as is the case for Romania, does not recognise same-sex marriage. *Coman* represents a 'welcome first step,'[8] in moving away from years of EU stress on subsidiarity and demonstrates the expanding nature of EU citizenship and considerations of who are EU family members. In *MB v Secretary of State for Work and Pensions* (*MB*), the CJEU determined that provisions of the UK Gender Recognition Act 2004 (GRA) which required transpersons to annul existing marriages in order not only be recognised in their new sex but to access state pension benefits at the age ascribed to their acquired gender was discriminatory on the ground of sex.[9] The requirement to annul a pre-existing marriage is no longer necessary to obtain a full gender recognition certificate,[10] but that requirement still applied at the time MB came to claim her pension in 2008.[11] This had a direct impact on MB, as the United Kingdom (UK) state still officially recognised her as male (as she did not wish to annul her pre-existing marriage), she could only claim her pension from the age of 65, as opposed to the age of 60 for women as then stipulated by legislation (prior to state pension reform).[12] The CJEU's judgement demonstrates a willingness to depart from more restictive case law on this particular point,[13] but also to reach further expanding understandings of the widening concept of non-discrimination rights to be given to LGBTQ+ persons who are EU citizens.

After a brief critique of the traditional position of the EU and the ECtHR regarding treatment of LGBTQ+ persons and same-sex couples, the next sections examine further influences widening CJEU opportunities to act in this respect. Factors of EU citizenship resulting in extensive free movement provisions and non-discrimination requirements, coupled with the promince of these points in comparison to subsidiarty considerations before the CJEU, will be discussed, all demonstrating the possibilities of CJEU expansion of rights for LGBTQ+ persons and same-sex couples. If Brexit affects free movement of persons, as it is likely to, UK LGBTQ+ persons and same-sex couples will no longer be able to benefit from expanding EU free movement rights and interventions by the CJEU.

Traditional position of the ECtHR and the EU regarding treatment of LGBTQ+ persons and same-sex couples

The ECtHR has played a major role in the advancement of LGBTQ+ persons' rights. ECtHR cases have resulted in judgements requiring contracting states to decriminalise sodomy laws,[14] to require equality in employment as regards sexual orientation[15] and in tenancy conditions for LGBTQ+ persons.[16] Historically, however, the ECtHR did not consider that same-sex relationships could generate 'family life.'[17] Such unions were considered as being relevant in reference to a right to a private life only.[18] This led to much criticism that the traditional position before the ECtHR overtly favoured heterosexual relationships[19] and restricted the 'evolution' of LGBTQ+ persons' rights in Europe.[20] The ECtHR has continued to incrementally advance the position of same-sex couples. Same-sex couples are now included within the definition of family life,[21] advances have been made to protect LGBTQ+ persons' adoption rights[22] and contracting states are required to recognise some form of legal protection for same-sex couples[23] and to recognise same-sex marriages conducted abroad.[24] Ultimately, due to concerns about the 'deep rooted social and cultural connotations' of marriage,[25] leading case law from the ECtHR confirms that a consensus must develop between contracting states, before it is prepared to move forwards on this issue.[26] Whilst on other areas of family law the ECtHR also prefers to be deferential towards contracting states and allows them a large margin of appreciation (MoA) to determine matters for themselves as informed the national context,[27] when considering the quickly advancing case law for LGBTQ+ persons just set out, in contrast, same-sex marriage can be regarded as being a 'lex specialis' which requires special consideration.[28]

Traditionally the CJEU was even stricter than the ECtHR with regards to its treatment of LGBTQ+ persons and same-sex couples. Former case law rejected inclusion of sexual orientation within the ground of sexual orientation discrimination.[29] Only traditional family formats were included within the scope of family life.[30] Although free movement provisions referred to spouses and registered partners within the definition of family member, prior to the recent *Coman* case,[31] EU law stressed subsidiarity. Member States were free to determine their own policy with regards to recognition of same-sex unions.[32] This ignored not only the apparent gender neutrality of the word spouse,[33] but the imperative of free movement.[34] In one commentator's view, this privileged the heterosexual norm.[35] Cohabitants have never been explicitly included within the EU 'family member' definition, having to prove their relationship 'duly attested.'[36] This latter definition is vague, and does not automatically allow partners to move with their EU citizen partner. Instead, all it requires is for the host Member State to be able to demonstrate thoroughly that they have investigated the personal circumstances concerned.[37]

The restrictive interpretation of 'family member' had real consequences. Prior to the *Coman* case, non-EU national same-sex spouses could not relocate with their EU citizen spouse to an EU country which did not recognise their union. Being denied the status of 'family member' also led to being denied the 'plethora of benefits'[38] which would otherwise have been accorded to EU citizens and their family members. These included rights to residence,[39] recourse to a Member State's social assistance scheme,[40] ensuring equal treatment with host-country nationals,[41] allowing family members to take up employment or self-employment[42] right of continuous legal residence after 5 years,[43] schooling provisions[44] and protections from non-discrimination.[45] It is argued that the cases of *Coman* and *MB* demonstrate the willingness to expand free movement and non-discrimination rights for LGBTQ+ persons. There remains a debate as to whether such examples are limited to their particular facts, or whether they can truly be considered as part of a trend. The next section looks at the normative understanding of the EU concept of citizenship. Further sections then consider how the relationship of this concept to extensive free movement provisions and non-discrimination requirements as further enhanced by strengthening ties between the EU and the Council of Europe provides an opportunity to develop rights for LGBTQ+ persons and same-sex couples. Consequently, following Brexit, UK LGBTQ+ persons and same-sex couples where this affects free movement of persons and the remit of the CJEU would no longer be able to benefit from these expanding EU protections.

How should the concept of EU citizenship be understood?

Citizenship is one of the key concepts utilised by the CJEU to justify expansion of rights for EU citizens. The emergence of new populations such as LGBTQ+ persons poses a challenge to existing concepts of citizenship. It is therefore interesting to consider different theoretical considerations of the meaning of citizenship and reflect on this in the EU context. Historically, theorists concentrated on the deep connection between citizenship and equality rights.[46] Classical theorist T H Marshall considered that citizenship required that 'all who possess the status are equal with respect to the rights and duties with which the status is endowed.'[47] This consideration of citizenship as inherently including equality can also be seen in classic constitutional text associated with the French Revolution[48] and the Irish constitution.[49] Equality arguments have also been prominent in same-sex marriage cases which have been successful worldwide.[50] I have argued elsewhere that the connections between citizenship, equality and marriage all led to strong practical and symbolic arguments for proponents of same-sex marriage.[51]

The connection between citizenship and equality has been heavily critiqued. Queer and feminist authors have questioned the reality of equality for feminist and LGBTQ+ groups. Following *Coman*, the position of the CJEU – determining that free movement and residence rights (essential elements of EU citizenship) should also include non-EU citizen same-sex spouses[52] — could lead to criticism by those who dispute the appropriateness of same-sex marriage as a goal.[53] Many feminists would question the need for marriage for LGBTQ+ persons on the basis that over the course of history, it has been an institution which has raised concerns as being 'deeply oppressive to, women as a class.'[54] On this view if one of the driving forces for change behind LGBTQ+ movements is egalitarianism, same-sex marriage is seen as deeply 'inappropriate.'[55] Some queer theorists would also reject same-sex marriage as a goal due to concerns about 'dominative heteronormative assumptions' not being questioned.[56] This includes concerns that same-sex marriage is trying to incorporate LGBTQ+ persons into the mainstream,[57] and that the advent of same-sex marriage is interrupting LGBTQ+ persons' unique interpretation of family life.[58] Queer theorists consider that same-sex marriage could result in LGBTQ+ persons being de-sexualised[59] and losing their unique LGBTQ+ identity.[60] Ultimately, on this view, the EU requirement in *Coman* of Member State recognition of same-sex marriage for free movement and residency purposes, contributes to the creation of 'sexual hierarchies'[61] and actually prevents the citizenship of LGBTQ+ persons being fully realised.[62] Instead, queer theorists prefer a more 'thoroughgoing resistance to regimes of the normal.'[63] They reject labels and statuses such as same-sex marriage and civil partnership, and argue that the multifarious ways in which LGBTQ+ persons have built their own relationships should be celebrated.[64] The attractiveness of ever advancing models of family life cannot be denied. Such theoretical perspectives continue to be of immense value in questioning what the role of law should be in this area. Beresford also acknowledges the role which queer theory has played in destabilising hetereosexual norms.[65] Yet queer and feminist theorists are often divided amongst themselves, with Beresford arguing that queer theory has become synonymous with white gay men, thus denying its origins and becoming distinctly anti-feminist, failing to fully acknowledge patriarchy and rendering lesbian women invisible, consequently failing to acknowledge and accommodate the lived experience of women.[66] Therefore, any recommendation of a wholesale change in society by queer theorists may be disputed, is academic in nature and does not fit with the EU's inherently practical and rights based approach.

Other authors would look to different interpretations of citizenship. Moving away from contested understandings of equality, this would instead consider wider conceptions of citizenship to include considerations of responsibilities towards the wider community and social processes through which individuals and social groups engage in claiming, expanding or losing rights.[67] This view of citizenship includes the drive to question what it means to be included and to belong.[68] On this view, citizenship would be understood as granting legal, political and social rights, and conferring membership, identity, values and rights of participation and assuming a body of common political knowledge.[69] This has led to a sociologically informed definition of citizenship in which the emphasis is less on legal rules and more on normal practices, meanings and identities.[70] In turn, citizens in a democracy should have membership status and ascribe to an identity and set of values usually involved as practising a degree of participation in political life and understanding relevant laws, documents, structures and processes of governance in the political unit.[71] Werbner and Yuval-Davis argue that citizenship is no longer understood simply in terms of 'the formal relationship between the individual and the state' but as 'a more total relationship inflected by identity, social positioning, cultural assumptions, institutional practices and a sense of belonging.'[72] This accords with the EU's aspiration to engage with citizens in a 'more meaningful and direct way'[73] and for EU citizens to feel a sense of belonging to the EU.[74] This is arguably of essential importance in a Brexit era.

If citizenship is seen as having a 'long history of evolution,'[75] always being an aspirational ideal which is 'less than complete,'[76] one of the driving forces of change is the need to accommodate new populations.[77] This chapter grapples with the question as to how the EU concept of citizenship is gradually being extended to include otherwise 'disenfranchised' LGBTQ+ groups.[78] The *Coman* case would therefore support movement towards those who view marriage as having a constitutional nature and involving 'participation in the public order.'[79] For proponents of same-sex marriage, a right to marriage would on this view be considered as a 'right central to citizenship.'[80] Recognition of same-sex marriage allows a choice for those who view this as a 'gold-standard.'[81] This accords with research from Pew, which demonstrates growing public opinion in favour of same-sex marriage across liberal democracies worldwide,[82] the result of the Republic of Ireland referendum,[83] leading cases[84] and the changing position of gay rights movements to adopt a more positive view towards same-sex marriage.[85] In contrast, authors have commented that denying access to marriage provides LGBTQ+ persons 'partial citizenship' status only.[86] Equally the *MB* case, extending non-discrimination rights to LGBTQ+ persons claiming state pension benefits, would support views of inclusive citizenship, on both 'social and legal' levels.[87] Following Brexit, UK same-sex couples would not be able to benefit from advances in rights connected to EU citizenship. The next section considers the impact of further expansion of non-discrimination rights before the EU.

Expanding non-discrimination rights for LGBTQ+ persons

Although the EU and the Council of Europe were set up for very different purposes, with the ECtHR being a recognised world leading human rights court and the EU primarily concentrating on economic rights, recent years have seen the EU working closely with the Council of Europe.[88] The European Covnention does have a 'significant impact' on the EU.[89] It is part of the agreement, under the Lisbon Treaty, for the EU to accede to the ECHR,[90] and it is part of the accession criteria for applicant EU Member States to comply with human rights.[91] The *Coman* and *MB* cases[92] are just some of many recent instances of 'judicial borrowing' between the institutions.[93] The joint focus of both the EU and the ECHR on non-discrimination provisions[94] has given both organisations a common goal.[95] Previously, the CJEU's approach to LGBTQ+ persons and same-sex couples was undermined by the continued emphasis on subsidiarity.[96] Recent case law as exemplified by *MB* and *Coman*[97] together with recent legislation from the EU,[98] demonstrates that the CJEU is expanding its non-discrimination principles where LGBTQ+ persons and same-sex couples are concerned. Perhaps previous predictions that the CJEU is engaging in a 'rights revolution'[99] are coming to fruition.

The EUCFR has given additional prominence to human rights considerations in an EU context. Sexual orientation is set out as a protected discrimination characteristic,[100] thereby arguably 'creat[ing] a completely new crosscutting fundamental right.'[101] This allows the CJEU an opportunity to provide more 'exensive protection' to human rights than the ECtHR.[102] The European Convention drafted in the 1950s does not specifically refer to sexual orientation as a protected ground of discrimination. Under Article 14 European Convention, non-discrimination is a conditional right only.[103] Litigants have to bring their case under the ambit of another human rights article together with an alleged breach of Article 14. Cases concerning LGBTQ+ rights before the ECtHR have therefore been commonly framed under Article 8 right to a private life,[104] in combination with Article 14. Whilst the ECtHR now recognises LGBTQ+ persons as falling within the family life definition before the ECtHR,[105] and more prominence has been placed on equality arguments,[106] the continued status of article 14 as a conditional right makes claims to the ECtHR more complex. If free standing non-discrimination Protocol 12 of the European Convention were to be ratified, this would greatly improve the position of litigants before the ECtHR. Currently, this is only ratified by 20 out of 47 ECHR contracting states, and the UK is not a signatory.[107]

Both *Coman* and *MB* are examples of cases where the CJEU has been prepared to take a leading role, as compared to the equivalent stance of the ECtHR.[108] In the *Coman* judgement, limited reference to human rights arguments was made by the CJEU.[109] The influential Advocate General Opinion of Melchior Wathelet prior to the CJEU judgement in *Coman* saw more reference to human rights arguments. His conclusion that spouse should be interpreted in a 'gender neutral' manner[110] was made by reference to ECtHR case law.[111] ECtHR case law was used as authority for LGBTQ+ persons' right to family life,[112] prohibition of discrimination against LGBTQ+ persons[113] and a requirement that contracting states should provide 'couples [with] legal recognition and the legal protection of their relationships.'[114] In reality, Melchior Wathelet's interpretation goes further than that actually provided by the ECtHR. First, as stated previously, Article 14 is a conditional right, reliance on which depends upon falling within the ambit of another alleged breach of human rights. It is also debatable as to what concrete result *Oliari and Others v Italy*[115] provide to same-sex couples. Fenwick and Hayward argue, that *Oliari and Others v Italy* should be confined to the facts where same-sex couples were socially accepted on the ground.[116] This claim is now being tested by a Russian same-sex couple.[117] Finally, *Oliari and Others v Italy*[118] did not require any conditions to be attached to the legal framework to be provided to same-sex couples. This may result in minimal legal protection. *Schalk and Kopf v Austria* is still authority for the ECtHR not requiring Council of Europe contracting states to recognise same-sex marriage.[119]

The CJEU ruling in *MB*[120] is also progressive as compared to the comparative position of the ECtHR. The ECtHR has continued to allow contracting states an MoA in relation to the specific challenge around the legal recognition of acquired gender being condition upon annulment of that person's marriage.[121] Whilst more recent case law has seen the ECtHR finding violations of Article 8 in relation to state requirements concerning gender assignment regarding where the applicant is required to be compulsorily sterilised[122] or required to wait lengthy periods,[123] there remains nothing to prevent ECtHR contracting states from putting in place other onerous pre-conditions prior to recognising the gender sex reassignment. If and where Brexit were to affect the remit of the CJEU, this would mean that UK-based LGBTQ+ persons would no longer be able to benefit from such far-reaching judgements of the CJEU.

Subsidiarity concerns at the European Union level

Due to concerns about a lack of consensus, the ECtHR does not require contracting states to legalise same-sex marriage.[124] This leads the ECtHR to provide a wide MoA, otherwise known as a 'latitude of deference or error'[125] to contracting states on this issue. The main purpose of the MoA doctrine is to respect the 'social identity'[126] or moral values[127] of individual countries. Whilst universalists would always consider that human rights should have prominence,[128] regionalists consider that on issues concerning moral and cultural values, contracting states should be free to determine their own policies.[129] The European Convention itself enshrines subsidiarity under Art 1, which places the prime duty to protect human rights on individual contracting states.[130] These concerns are exacerbated at present as the ECtHR is adjudicating in a very nationalistic context. There are many criticisms about relying on consensus as a deciding factor. It is argued that the consensus doctrine ignores the interests of minority groups,[131] and allows contracting states to determine matters without thorough going legal analysis and scrutiny.[132] Despite ECtHR statements observing a movement towards consensus, it remains unclear when this will be reached.[133]

Subsidiarity is, of course, a pressing concern for the EU, as well. Political pressures have increased following Brexit, However, arguably the EU has greater opportunity to act in this area. The Council of Europe has 47 extremely divergent contracting states,[134] including countries such as Russia where gay propaganda laws are still in force.[135] In comparison the EU Member States are more homogeneous, (although divides should not be ignored).[136] The CJEU gives concerns about subsidiarity less prominence than over-riding EU law imperatives such as free movement of persons and non-discrimination provisions. The EU Member States are increasingly bound together through the EU concept of an 'ever closer' union.[137] One of the 'core objectives' of the EU is free movement of persons,[138] enabling all Member State nationals the power to move freely between Member States.[139] *Coman* saw the CJEU stressing the importance of free movement provisions, as opposed to subsidiarity concerns. The Latvian government had submitted a public-interest consideration on the basis of the 'fundamental nature of the institution of marriage'[140] arguing that a restriction of the free movement of EU citizens[141] was justified 'on ground of public policy and national identity.'[142] Although this public concern was treated with respect,[143] ultimately the CJEU determined that it had to give way to the free movement imperative.[144] In *MB*, the UK government referred to ECtHR case law to emphasise the MoA given Member States to 'make recognition of a change of gender conditional on the annulment of the person's marriage.'[145] The CJEU conceded this discretion to Member States, but stated that in so doing, they had to continue to comply with EU principles of non-discrimination.'[146] Once again, the CJEU (in contrast to the position of the ECtHR) was prepared to over-rule subsidiarity concerns in favour of other pressing issues; here, non-discrimination.

The EU also has far more effective enforcement mechanisms than the European Convention system. Whilst Article 46 European Convention gives ECtHR judgements binding force,[147] this primarily depends upon contracting states complying with ECtHR judgements under supervision from the Committee of Ministers. In practice, this means that many ECtHR judgements from the ECtHR remain unenforced.[148] Arguably, this could deter the ECtHR from making far-reaching judgements, due to concerns that judgements may not be observed. In contrast, the CJEU has stronger enforcement methods – not least the principles of EU supremacy[149] and state liability.[150]

Conclusion

Traditionally the CJEU was even stricter than the ECtHR system in refusing to recognise non-conventional family types. This chapter has demonstrated that EU law has much potential to further advance LGBTQ+ persons and same-sex couples' rights. Whilst the normative meaning of citizenship remains contested, with some feminist and queer theorists questioning the reality of equality for their component citizens and disaffection with the recognition of same-sex marriage,[151] the EU concept of citizenship is to offer an ever expanding array of practical rights, to include emerging groups such as LGBTQ+ persons and same-sex couples. EU citizenship has commonly been utilised by the EU to justify expansion of rights to EU citizens, and provide a plethora of benefits.[152] Of prominence here are expanding free movement and non-discrimination rights. The *Coman* and MB case studies demonstrate the potentiality of these concepts to further rights for LGBTQ+ persons and same-sex couples.[153] In *Coman*, subsidiarity concerns were over-ridden in preference for the principle of free movement.[154] Similarly in *MB*, non-discrimination rights were given prominence as opposed to Member States public policy concerns.[155]

All of these factors point towards the CJEU being well placed to bring forwards development of rights for LGBTQ+ persons and same-sex couples. However, both the *Coman* case and the *MB* case were strictly confined to their facts.[156] The CJEU observed clearly in *Coman*, that the case did not result in a requirement of Member States to legalise same-sex marriage, but rather for Member States to allow free movement and residence rights for non-EU citizen spouses of same-sex marriages conducted in other Member States.[157] The *MB* case was strictly confined to the facts of non-discrimination in relation to state retirement pension provisions.[158] In addition, as Noto La Diega's chapter demonstrates that there is a different and varied experience across the EU following *Coman*, with some Eastern European states currently reacting against this judgement.[159] Still it seems that the CJEU has many opportunities to act to further LGBTQ+ persons and same-sex couple's rights. The inherent symbolic value of the *Coman* judgement,[160] which is also present in *MB* cannot be ignored.[161] This contrasts with the position before the ECtHR where concerns about a lack of consensus, among a more divergent group of 47 Council of Europe states, still retains dominance. Ties between the EU and the Council of Europe are increasing in strength and following the EUCFR have become increasingly prominent. The free standing non-discrimination ground in the EUCFR[162] together with the possibility that the EU can give human rights more 'exensive protection'[163] than the equivalent position before the ECtHR, are slowly coming to fruition. If as anticipated, one of the consequences of Brexit is to affect free movement of persons, this means that UK same-sex couples will have to continue to rely on whatever rights their country of destination sees fit to grant them. Further if Brexit impacts on the remit of the CJEU, this will mean that UK same-sex couples will miss out on developments in this regard in relation to expanding non-discrimination law.

Notes

1 Sixteen European nations have recognised same-sex marriage. As of July 2019, this includes Austria, Belgium, Denmark, Finland, France, Germany, Iceland, Ireland, Luxembourg, Malta, Netherlands, Norway, Portugal, Spain, Sweden and the United Kingdom (excluding Northern Ireland, although this will change on 21 October unless a devolved government is re-established) and many more recognise civil partnership (Andorra, Croatia, Cyprus, the Czech Republic, Estonia, Greece, Hungary, Italy, Liechtenstein, Slovenia and Switzerland).

2 Bulgaria, Croatia, Hungary, Latvia, Lithuania, Poland and Slovakia. For further discussion, see Alina Tryfonidou, 'The EU Top Court Rules That Married Same-Sex Couples Can Move Freely Between EU Member States as "Spouses": Case C-673/16, Relu Adrian Coman Robert Clabourn Hamilton, Asociaţia Accept v Inspectoratul General pentru Imigrări, Ministerul Afacerilor Interne' (2019) *Feminist Legal Studies* 1; Case C-673/16 *Relu Adrian Coman, Robert Clabourn Hamilton, Asociaţia Accept v Inspectoratul General pentru Imigrări, Ministerul Afacerilor Interne* ECLI:EU:C:2018:2.

3 The Centre for Social Justice, 'European Family Law: Faster Divorce and Foreign Law' (2009), at 5 explains that there are 350,000 international marriages each year. <www.centreforsocialjustice.org.uk/core/wp-content/uploads/2016/08/CSJEuropeanFamilyLaw.pdf> accessed 31 July 2019.

4 See Robert Jackson J in *Estin v Estin*, 334 US 541, 553 (1948) and Barbara Stark, 'When Globalization Hits Home: International Family Law Comes of Age' (2006) 36 *Vanderbilt Journal of Transnational Law* 1551.

5 EUCFR, art 52(3).

6 Ibid.

7 See *Coman* (n 2).

8 See Tryfonidou (n 2) 1.

9 Case C-451/16 *MB v Secretary of State for Work and Pensions* ECLI:EU:C:2018:492. This was found to violate Article 4 of Directive 79/7 on the Progressive Implementation of the Principle of Equal Treatment for Men and Women in Matters of Social Security.

10 Gender Recognition Act 2004, Sch 5, amended by the Marriage (Same-Sex Couples) Act 2013, providing the spouse consents.
11 Pre-existing Schedule 5, paragraph 7 Gender Recognition Act 2004 (prior to reform by the Marriage (Same-Sex Couples) Act 2013).
12 Section 44 of the Social Security Contributions and Benefits Act 1992 read in conjunction with section 122 of that Act and with Schedule 4 paragraph 1 of the Pensions Act 1995 stated that a woman born before 6 April 1950 becomes eligible for the state retirement pension from the age of 60. In contrast, men born before 6 December 1953 become eligible at the age of 65.
13 Case C-117/*01 K.B. v National Health Service Pensions Agency and Secretary of State for Health* ECLI:EU:C:2004:7 and Case C-243/04 *Sarah Margaret Richards v Secretary of State for Work and Pensions* ECLI:EU:C:2006:256.
14 *Dudgeon v UK* App No. 7525/76 (ECtHR, 22 October 1981).
15 *Smith and Grady v UK* App Nos. 33985/96 and 33986/96 (ECtHR, 27 September 1999); *Lustig-Prean and Beckett v UK* App Nos. 31417/96 and 32377/96 (ECtHR, 27 September 1999).
16 *Karner v Austria* App No. 40016/98 (ECtHR, 24 July 2003); *EB v France* App No. 43546/02 (ECtHR, 22 January 2008).
17 *X and Y v UK* App No. 21830/93 (ECtHR, 22 April 1997); *Simpson v UK* App No. 11716/85, (Commission Decision, 14 May 1986); *Kerkhoven and Hinke v The Netherlands* App No. 15666/89 (Commission Decision, 19 May 1992) and *Mata Estevez v Spain* App No. 56501/00 (ECtHR, 10 May 2001).
18 Susana Cabellero, 'Unmarried Cohabiting Couples Before the European Court of Human Rights: Parity with Marriage?' (2004–2005) 11 *Columbia Journal of European Law* 151, 152.
19 Helen Stalford, 'Concepts of Family Under EU Law – Lessons from the ECHR' (2002) 16 *International Journal of Law, Policy and the Family* 410, 411.
20 Paul Johnson, '"An Essentially Private Manifestation of Human Personality": Constructions of Homosexuality in the European Court of Human Rights' (2010) 10 *Human Rights Law Review* 67, 76.
21 See *Schalk and Kopf v Austria* App No. 30141/04 (ECtHR, 24 June 2010), para 94. Described by Connor O'Mahoney, 'Irreconcilable Differences? Article 8 ECHR and Irish Law on Non-Traditional Families' (2012) 26 *International Journal of Law Policy and the Family* 31 at 38 as a 'landmark judgment' and Elaine Sutherland, 'A Step Closer to Same-Sex Marriage Throughout Europe' (2011) 15 *Edinburgh Law Review* 97.
22 See for example *EB* (n 16) which concerned single parent adoption in France.
23 *Oliari and Others v Italy* App Nos. 18766/11 and 36030/11 (ECtHR, 21 July 2015).
24 *Orlandi and Others v Italy* App Nos. 26431/12, 26742/12, 44057/12 and 60088/12 (ECtHR, 14 December 2017).
25 *Schalk and Kopf* (n 21) para 62.
26 *Schalk and Kopf* (n 21).
27 For example, in relation to abortion, see the European Court of Human Rights' judgments in *Paton v UK* App No. 8416/78 (ECtHR, 13 May 1980); *Vo v France* App No. 53924/00 (ECtHR, 8 July 2004); and *A, B and C v Ireland* App No. 25579/05 (ECtHR, 16 December 2010).
28 See US Legal Dictionary, 'Lex Specialis Law and Legal Definition' *USLegal.com* (n.d.) <http://definitions.uslegal.com/l/lex-specialis/> accessed 31 July 2019. Loveday Hodson, 'A Marriage by Any Other Name? Shalk and Kopf v Austria' (2011) 11 *Human Rights Law Review* 170 at 177 argues that marriage is being

set apart from the other family rights and being treated as an 'untouchable, almost sacred, category.'

29 See for example, Case C-249/96 *Grant v South West Trains* ECLI:EU:C:1998:63. See for discussion Dimitri Kochenov, 'On Options of Citizens and Moral Choices of States: Gays and European Federalism' (2009) 33 *Fordham International Law Review* 156, 175.

30 For example, Case C-59/85 *Netherlands v Reed* ECLI:EU:C:1986:157: The CJEU determined that '"spouse" only included an individual in a marital relationship.'

31 *Coman* (n 2).

32 Parliament and Council Directive 2004/38/EC of 29 April 2004 on the right of citizens of the Union and their family members to move and reside freely within the territory of the Member States (2004) OJ L158 (Citizenship Directive), art 2(2) provides that '(f)amily member' means . . . (b) the partner with whom the Union citizen has contracted a registered partnership on the basis of the legislation of a Member State if the legislation of the host Member State treats registered partnerships as equivalent to marriage and in accordance with the conditions laid down in the relevant legislation of the host Member State.' Commentary on Article 9 of the EUCFR provided that 'There is, however, no explicit requirement that domestic laws should facilitate such marriages. International courts and committees have so far hesitated to extend the application of the right to marry to same-sex couples. . . . The position is now transformed following the high-profile case of *Coman* (n 2).

33 See Kochenov (n 29) 190. Advocate General Melchior Wathelet's recent Advocate General's Opinion in *Coman* (n 2) endorsed the approach that spouse should be interpreted in a gender-neutral manner.

34 See Stalford (n 19) 419 and also Barbara Cox, 'Same-Sex Marriage and Choice of Law: If We Marry in Hawaii, Are We Still Married When We Return Home?' (1994) *Wisconsin Law Review* 1033, 1040 which states that non-recognition of a foreign marriage means that the right to same-sex marriage is a 'meagre right indeed.'

35 See Kochenov (n 29) 201.

36 Citizenship Directive 2004/38/EC, art 3(2).

37 Case C-83/11 *Secretary of State for the Home Department v Muhammad Sazzadur Rahman and Others* ECLI:EU:C:2012:519 and Case C-89/17 *Secretary of State for the Home Department v Rozanne Banger* ECLI:EU:C:2018:570.

38 See Stalford (n 19) 427.

39 Citizenship Directive 2004/38, art 14(1).

40 Ibid., art 14(3).

41 Ibid., art 24.

42 Ibid., art 23.

43 Ibid., art 16.

44 For discussion see John Fairhurst, *Law of the European Union* (9th edn, Pearson Publishing 2012) at 405 who refers to Case C-9/74 *Donato Casagrande v Landeshauptstadt München* ECLI:EU:C:1974:74 and Case C-412/99 *Baumbast and R v Secretary of State for the Home Department* ECLI:EU:C:2002:493.

45 Citizens are protected from discrimination on grounds of nationality under Article 18 TFEU. See also Article 19 TFEU, which allows the European Council together with the European Parliament to adopt measures preventing discrimination non the ground of 'sex, racial or ethnic origin, religion or belief, disability, age or sexual orientation.' The EU has also adopted the provision of the EUCFR which at art 21(1) includes 'same-sex orientation' as ground for discrimination.

46 See for example Nicholas Bamforth, 'Sexuality and Citizenship in Contemporary Constitutional Argument' (2012) 10 *International Journal of Constitutional Law* 477; Michel Rosenfeld, 'Introduction: Gender, Sexual Orientation and Equal Citizenship' (2012) 10 *International Journal of Constitutional Law* 340; and Connor O'Mahoney, 'There Is No Such Thing as a Right to Dignity' (2012) 10 *International Journal of Constitutional Law* 551.
47 Bamforth (n 46) 478 referring to Thomas H Marshall, 'Citizenship and Social Class' in Thomas H Marshall and Tom Bottomore (eds), *Citizenship and Social Class* (Pluto Press 1992) 18.
48 Rosenfeld (n 46) 340, who explains that citizenship acquired its 'its distinct modern meaning as equal citizenship at the time of the French Revolution.'
49 Constitution of Ireland, art 40(1). O'Mahoney (n 46) 554–555 who refers to the Irish constitution which states that '[a]ll citizens shall, as human persons be held equal before the law.' He also refers to *Ghaidan v Godin-Mendoza*(2004) UKHL 30; (2004) 2 AC 557, where Baroness Hale states that "[d]emocracy is founded on the principle that each individual has equal value."
50 See for example *Goodridge v Department of Public Health* 798 NE 2d 941 (Mass 2003); *Loving v Virginia* 388 US 1 (1967); and *Obergefell v Hodges* 576 US, 135 S Ct 2584 (2015).
51 Frances Hamilton, 'The Differing Treatment of Same Sex Couples by European Union Law and the European Convention on Human Rights: The European Union Concept of Citizenship' (2015) 2 *Journal of International and Comparative Law* 87.
52 *Coman* (n 2).
53 For example, see Lisa Duggan, 'Beyond Same-Sex Marriage' (2008) 9 *Studies in Gender and Sexuality* 155.
54 Rosemary Auchmuty, 'Same Sex Marriage Revived: Feminist Critique and Legal Strategy' (2004) 14 *Feminist and Psychology* 101, 104. See also, Yvonne Zylan, *States of Passion, Identity and Social Construction of* Desire (Oxford University Press 2011) 204.
55 Auchmuty (n 54) 104.
56 Lisa Duggan, 'The New Homonormativity: The Sexual Politics of Neoliberalism' in Dana Nelson and Russ Castronovo (eds), *Materializing Democracy: Toward a Revitalized Cultural Politics* (Duke University Press 2002) 175.
57 Diane Richardson, 'Desisting Sameness? The Rise of Neoliberal Politics of Normalisation' (2005) 37 *Antipodes* 519.
58 Jyl Josephson, 'Citizenship, Same-Sex Marriage and Feminist Criitques of Marriage' (2005) 3 *Perspectives on Politics* 269 at 273 referring to Mark Warner, *The Trouble With Normal: Sex, Politics, and the Ethics of Queer Life* (Free Press 1999).
59 Richardson (n 57).
60 Duggan (n 53).
61 Brian Heaphy, Carol Smart and Anna Einarsdottir, *Same Sex Marriages: New Generations, New Relationships* (Palgrave MacMillan 2013) 132.
62 Josephson (n 58).
63 Mark Warner (ed), *Fear of a Queer Planet: Queer Politics and Social Theory* (University of Minnesota Press 1993) 7.
64 Duggan (n 53).
65 Sarah Beresford, 'The Age of Consent and the Ending of Queer Theory' (2014) 3 *Laws* 759.
66 Beresford (n 65).
67 Ruth Lister, 'Why Citizenship: Where, How and Why Children' (2007) 8 *Theoretical Inquiries in Law* 693 and Engin F Isin and Bryan S Turner, 'Citizenship

Studies: An Introduction' in Engin F Isin and Bryan Turner (eds), *Handbook of Citizenship Studies* (Sage 2002).

68 Brenda Cossman, *Sexual Citizens: The Legal and Cultural Regulation of Sex and Belonging* (Stanford University Press 2007).

69 See Kathleen Knight Abowitz and Jason Harnish, 'Contemporary Discourses of Citizenship' (2006) 76 *Review of Educational Research* 653 and Kate Nash, 'Between Citizenship and Human Rights' (2004) 43 *Sociology* 1067 at 1067 referring to Katherine Culliton-Gonzalez, 'Born in the Americas: Birthright Citizenship and Human Rights' (2012) 25 *Harvard Human Rights Journal* 127.

70 Lister (n 67) 699.

71 Penelope Enslin, 'Education and Democratic Citizenship: In Defence of Cosmopoli-tanism' in Mal Leicester, Celia Modgil and Sohan Modgil (eds), *Politics, Education and Citizenship* (Falmer Press 2000).

72 Pnina Werbner and Nira Yuval-Davis, 'Introduction: Women and the New Discourse of Citizenship' in Pnina Werbner and Nira Yuval-Davis (eds), *Women, Citizenship and Difference* (Zed 1999).

73 Stalford (n 19) 413. See Hamilton (n 51).

74 See Nash (n 69) at 1068 referring to Craig Calhoun, *Nations Matter: Culture, History and the Cosmopolitan Dream* (Routledge 2007).

75 Gershon Shafir and Alison Brysk, 'The Globalization of Rights: From Citizenship to Human Rights' (2006) 10 *Citizenship Studies* 275, 279.

76 Lydia Morris, 'Citizenship and Human Rights: Ideals and Actualities' (2012) 63 *British Journal of Sociology* 39 referring to David Lockwood, 'Civil Integration and Class Formation' (1996) 47 *British Journal of Sociology* 531, 536.

77 Shafir and Byrsk (n 75) 279 referring to Will Kymlicka, *Multicultural Citizenship: A Liberal Theory of Minority Rights* (Oxford University Press 1995).

78 Shafir and Byrsk (n 75) 279.

79 Bamforth (n 46) 481 referring to Nancy Cott, *Public Vows: A History of Marriage and the Nation* (Harvard University Press 2002) 1.

80 See Bamforth (n 46); Jeffrey Weeks, 'The Sexual Citizen' (1998) 15 *Theory, Culture and Society* 38; David Bradley, 'Comparative Law, Family Law and Common Law' (2003) 33 *Oxford Journal of Legal Studies* 127; Kochenov (n 29).

81 See Sue Wilkinson in her Witness Statement contained in *Wilkinson v Kitzinger* (2006) EWHC 2022 (Fam), para 6.

82 See Pew Research Center, 'Attitudes on Same-Sex Marriage' (14 May 2019) <www.pewforum.org/fact-sheet/changing-attitudes-on-gay-marriage/> accessed 31 July 2019. Pew Research Center has surveyed public opinion on same-sex marriage since 2001 and documents increasing support for this.

83 In a referendum held on 22 May 2015, with a 60% turnout, 62% voted in favour of same-sex marriage and 38% voted against.

84 See e.g., *Goodridge* (n 50); *Loving* (n 50); and *Obergefell* (n 50).

85 *See* Zylan (n 54) 205 referring to Evan Wolfson, 'Crossing the Threshold: Equal Marriage Rights for Lesbians and Gay Men and the Intra-Community Critique' (1994) 21 *New York University Review of Law and Social Change* 567, 611.

86 Bamforth (n 46) 483 referring to Richardson (n 57) 88. See also Angela Harris, 'Loving Before and After the Law' (2008) 76 *Fordham Law Review* 2821, 2822 and Kochenov (n 29) 163.

87 Cossman (n 68) 27.

88 See the 'Memorandum of Understanding Between the Council of Europe and the European Union' CM(2007)74 (10 May 2007) prepared at the 117th Session of the Committee of Ministers (Strasbourg), <https://wcd.coe.int/ViewDoc.jsp?Ref=CM(2007)74&Language=lanEnglish> accessed 31 July 2019. See also,

for comment, Tony Joris and Jan Vandenberghe, 'The Council of Europe and the European Union: Natural Partners or Uneasy Bedfellows?' (2008–2009) 15 *Columbia Journal of European Law* 1, 3.

89 See Chapter 8 by *Tryfonidou* in this volume.

90 TEU art 6(2) provides that "[t]he Union shall access to the European Convention for the Protection of Human Rights and Fundamental Freedoms." In addition, the fundamental rights of the ECHR are incorporated into the EUCFR, which from 1 December 2009 has the same legal status as the treaties.

91 See European Commission, 'Conditions for Membership' <http://ec.europa.eu/enlargement/policy/conditions-membership/index_en.htm> accessed 31 July 2019.

92 *Coman* (n 2); *MB* (n 9).

93 *See* for discussion Janneke Gerards, 'The Prism of Fundamental Rights' (2012) 8 *European Constitutional Law Review* 173, 192.

94 Andrea Eriksson, 'European Justice: Broadening the Scope of European Non-Discrimination Law' (2009) 7 *International Journal of Constitutional Law* 731 at 733 argues that other recent cases show the CJEU is inclined to extend non-discrimination provisions referring to Case C-267/06 *Tadao Maruko v Versorgungsanstalt der deutschen Bühnen* ECLI:EU:C:2008:179 (2008) 2 CMLR 32 [63]; Case C-147/08 *Jurgen Römer v Freie und Hansestadt Hamburg* ECLI:EU:C:2011:286 and Case C-303/06 *Coleman v Attridge Law and Steve Law* ECLI:EU:C:2008:415.

95 Carmelo Danisis, 'How Far Can the European Court of Human Rights Go in the Fight Against Discrimination? Defining New Standards in Its Non-Discrimination Jurisprudence' (2011) 9 *International Journal of Constitutional Law* 793 and Marta Cartabia, 'The European Court of Human Rights: Judging Non-Discrimination' (2011) 9 *International Journal of Constitutional Law* 808.

96 Jakob Cornides, 'Three Case Studies on "Anti-Discrimination"' (2012) 23 *European Journal of International Law* 517, 522. *See* also Kochenov (n 29).

97 *MB* (n 9) and *Coman* (n 2).

98 This includes, for example, Citizenship Directive 2004/38, the Charter of Fundamental Rights of the European Union 2000/C 364/01 and Council Directive 2000/78/EC of 27 November 2000 establishing a general framework for equal treatment in employment and occupation OJ L303.

99 Mark Dawson, Elise Muir and Monica Claes, 'Enforcing the EU's Rights Revolution; The Case of Equality' (2012) 3 *European Human Rights Law Review* 276.

100 The EUCFR art 21(1) provides that '[a]ny discrimination based on any ground such as sex, race, colour, ethic or social origin, genetic features, language, religion or belief, political or any other opinion, membership of a national minority, property, birth, disability, age or sexual orientation shall be prohibited.'

101 Cornides (n 96) 531.

102 EUCFR, art 52(3).

103 Article 14 European Convention provides that: 'The enjoyment of the rights and freedoms set forth in this Convention shall be secured without discrimination on any ground such as sex, race, colour, language, religion, political or other opinion, national or social origin, association with a national minority, property, birth or other status.'

104 See for example *Dudgeon* (n 14) and *ADT v UK* App No. 35765/97 (ECtHR, 31 July 2000) para 37, where the court emphasised the fact that the 'activities . . . were genuinely private.'

105 *Schalk and Kopf* (n 21) para 94.
106 See eg, *Karner* (n 16); *EB* (n 16); *Schalk and Kopf* (n 21).
107 Treaty Office, 'Chart of Signatures and Ratifications of Treaty 177' Council of Europe ETS No. 177 (15 August 2019) <www.coe.int/en/web/conventions/full-list/-/conventions/treaty/177/signatures> accessed 15 October 2019.
108 *Coman* (n 2); *MB* (n 9).
109 *Coman* (n 2) paras 49 and 50.
110 Ibid., Opinion of AG Melchior Wathelet, para 49.
111 Ibid., paras 59–67.
112 Ibid., paras 62–63 referring to among other cases *Schalk and Kopf* (n 21) para 94.
113 Ibid., paras 64–65 referring to, among other cases, *Taddeucci and McCall v Italy* App No. 51362/09 (ECtHR, 30 June 2016) para 93.
114 Ibid., para 62 referring to *Oliari* (n 23).
115 *Oliari* (n 23).
116 For comment, see Helen Fenwick and Andy Hayward, 'Rejecting Asymmetry of Access to Formal Relationship Statuses for Same and Different-Sex Couples at Strasbourg and Domestically' (2017) 6 *European Human Rights Law Review* 545.
117 See *Irina Borisovna Fedotova and Irina Vladimironova Shipitko v Russia* App No. 40792/10 (ECtHR, Communicated on 2 May 2016).
118 *Oliari* (n 23).
119 *Schalk and Kopf* (n 21).
120 See *MB* (n 9) which found a violation of Article 4 of Directive 79/7 which prohibits all forms of discrimination on the ground of sex in relation to accessing state pension benefits.
121 See *Hamalainen v Finland* App No. 37359/09 (ECtHR, 16 July 2014).
122 *A. P. Garcon and Nicot v France* App Nos. 79885/12, 52471/13 and 52596/13 (ECtHR, 6 April 2017).
123 *S.V. v Italy* App No. 55216/08 (ECtHR, 11 October 2018) (only available in French).
124 See *Schalk and Kopf* (n 21) para 57; *Hamalainen* (n 121) para 39; and *Chapin and Charpentier v France* App No. 40183/07 (ECtHR, 9 June 2016).
125 Petra Butler, 'Margin of Appreciation – A Note Towards a Solution for the Pacific' (2008–2009) 39 *Victoria University of Wellington Law Review* 687 referring to Howard C Yourow, *Margin of Appreciation Doctrine in the Dynamics of European Human Rights Jurisprudence* (Brill 1996) 13.
126 Niamh Nic Shuibhne, 'Margins of Appreciation; National Values, Fundamental Rights and EC Free Movement Law' (2009) 34 *European Law Review* 230.
127 For discussion, see Jeffrey Brauch, 'The Margin of Appreciation and the Jurisprudence of the European Court of Human Rights: Threat to the Rule of Law' (2004–2005) 113 *Columbia Journal of European Law* 119.
128 See Eyal Benvenisti, 'Margin of Appreciation, Consensus and Universal Standards' (1998–1999) 31 *New York University Journal of International Law and Politics* 843 who argues at 843 that human rights bodies have a 'duty to set universal standards.'
129 This was recently re-emphasised in the Council of Europe, 'High Level Conference on the Future of the European Court of Human Rights (Brighton Declaration)' (19–20 April 2012) B12 <www.echr.coe.int/Documents/2012_Brighton_FinalDeclaration_ENG.pdf> accessed 31 July 2019.
130 See European Convention, art 1.

131 See Helen Fenwick, 'Same Sex Unions and the Strasbourg Court in a Divided Europe: Driving Forward Reform or Protecting the Court's Authority Via Consensus Analysis' (2016) 3 *EHRLR* 248, 270.
132 See for discussion Brauch (n 127) 137.
133 *Oliari* (n 23) para 163.
134 *See* the Council of Europe, '47 Member States' www.coe.int/en/web/portal/country-profiles accessed 31 July 2019.
135 See Fenwick (n 131) 270 and Paul Johnson, '"Homosexual Propaganda" in the Russian Federation: Are They in Violation of the European Convention on Human Rights?' (2015) 3 *Russian Law Journal* 37.
136 For instance, with Eastern European countries. See (n 2).
137 The Preamble to the TEU which states that the signatories are 'Resolved to continue the process of creating an ever closer union among the peoples of Europe, in which decisions are taken as closely as possible to the citizen in accordance with the principle of subsidiarity.'
138 See Tryfonidou (n 2) 2.
139 TFEU, art 20.
140 *Coman* (n 2) para 42.
141 TFEU, arts 20 and 21.
142 Article 4(2) TEU states that: '[t]he Union shall respect the equality of Member States before the Treaties as well as their national identities, inherent in their fundamental structures, political and constitutional, inclusive of regional and local self-government as discussed in *Coman* (n 2) para 42.
143 Ibid., para 43.
144 Ibid., para 44: referring to Case C-438/14 *Bogendorff von Wolffersdorff* ECLI:EU:C:2016:401, para 67.
145 See UK government's argument at *MB* (n 9) para 24 referring to *Hamalainen* (n 121).
146 See *MB* (n 9).
147 European Convention, art 46.
148 See for discussion, Ginger Hervey, 'Europe's Human Rights Court Struggles to Lay Down the Law' *Politico* (20 September 2017) <www.politico.eu/article/human-rights-court-ilgar-mammadov-azerbaijan-struggles-to-lay-down-the-law/> accessed 31 July 2019.
149 See Tryfonidou (n 2) for discussion.
150 The state liability principle was established in Case C-6/90 and C-9/90 *Francovich v Italy* ECLI:EU:C:1991:428.
151 Duggan (n 53).
152 Stalford (n 19).
153 *Coman* (n 2); *MB* (n 9).
154 *Coman* (n 2).
155 *MB* (n 9).
156 *Coman* (n 2); *MB* (n 9).
157 *Coman* (n 2).
158 *MB* (n 9).
159 See Chapter 2 by Noto La Diega in this volume.
160 Tryfonidou (n 2) referring to *Coman* (n 2).
161 *MB* (n 9).
162 EUCFR, art 21.
163 Ibid., art 52(3).

References

Primary sources

A, B and C v Ireland App No. 25579/05 (ECtHR, 16 December 2010).
ADT v UK App No. 35765/97 (ECtHR, 31 July 2000).
A P Garcon and Nicot v France App Nos. 79885/12, 52471/13 and 52596/13 (ECtHR, 6 April 2017).
Baumbast and R v Secretary of State for the Home Department (Case C-413/99) ECLI:EU:C:2002:493.
Bogendorff von Wolffersdorff (C-438/14) ECLI:EU:C:2016:401.
Chapin and Charpentier v France App No. 40183/07 (ECtHR, 9 June 2016).
Charter of Fundamental Rights of the European Union (2000) 2000/C 364/01.
Coleman v Attridge Law and Steve Law (C-303/06) ECLI:EU:C:2008:415.
Constitution of Ireland 1937 (as amended).
Council Directive 2000/78/EC of 27 November 2000 establishing a general framework for equal treatment in employment and occupation OJ L303.
Donato Casagrande v Landeshauptstadt München (C-9/74) ECLI:EU:C:1974:74.
Dudgeon v UK App No. 7525/76 (ECtHR, 22 October 1981).
EB v France App No. 43546/02 (ECtHR, 22 January 2008).
Estin v Estin 334 US 541, 553 (1948).
Francovich v Italy (C-6/60 and C-9/90) ECLI:EU:C:1991:428.
Gender Recognition Act 2004 (original and as amended).
Ghaidan v Godin-Mendoza (2004) UKHL 30; (2004) 2 AC 557.
Goodridge v Department of Public Health 798 NE 2d 941 (Mass 2003).
Grant v South West Trains (C-249/96) ECLI:EU:C:1998:63.
Hamalainen v Finland App No. 37359/09 (ECtHR, 16 July 2014).
Irina Borisovna Fedotova and Irina Vladimironova Shipitko v Russia App No. 40792/10 (ECtHR, Communicated on 2 May 2016).
Jurgen Römer v Freie und Hansestadt Hamburg (Case C-147/08) ECLI:EU:C:2011:286.
K B v National Health Service Pensions Agency and Secretary of State for Health (C-117/01) ECLI:EU:C:2004:7.
Karner v Austria App No. 40016/98 (ECtHR, 24 July 2003).
Kerkhoven and Hinke v The Netherlands App No. 15666/89 (Commission Decision, 19 May 1992).
Loving v Virginia 388 US 1 (1967).
Lustig-Prean and Beckett v UK App Nos. 31417/96 and 32377/96 (ECtHR, 27 September 1999).
Mata Estevez v Spain App No. 56501/00 (ECtHR, 10 May 2001).
MB v Secretary of State for Work and Pensions (C-451/16) ECLI:EU:C:2018:492.
Netherlands v Reed (Case C-59/85) ECLI:EU:C:1986:157.
Obergefell v Hodges 576 US, 135 S Ct 2584 (2015).
Oliari and Others v Italy App Nos. 18766/11 and 36030/11 (ECtHR, 21 July 2015).
Orlandi and Others v Italy App Nos. 26431/12, 26742/12, 44057/12 and 60088/12 (ECtHR, 14 December 2017).
Parliament and Council Directive 2004/38/EC of 29 April 2004 on the right of citizens of the Union and their family members to move and reside freely within the territory of the Member States (2004) OJ L158.

Paton v UK App No. 8416/78 (ECtHR, 13 May 1980).
Pensions Act 1995.
Relu Adrian Coman, Robert Clabourn Hamilton, Asociaţia Accept v Inspectoratul General pentru Imigrări, Ministerul Afacerilor Interne (C-673/16) ECLI:EU:C:2018:2.
S.V. v Italy App No. 55216/08 (ECtHR, 11 October 2018).
Sarah Margaret Richards v Secretary of State for Work and Pensions (C-243/04) ECLI:EU:C:2006:256.
Schalk and Kopf v Austria App No. 30141/04 (ECtHR, 24 June 2010).
Secretary of State for the Home Department v Muhammad Sazzadur Rahman and Others (C-83/11) ECLI:EU:C:2012:519.
Secretary of State for the Home Department v Rozanne Banger (C-89/17) ECLI:EU:C:2018:570.
Simpson v UK App No. 11716/85 (Commission Decision, 14 May 1986).
Smith and Grady v UK App Nos. 33985/96 and 33986/96 (ECtHR, 27 September 1999).
Social Security Contributions and Benefits Act 1992.
Tadao Maruko v Versorgungsanstalt der deutschen Bühnen (C-267/06) ECLI:EU:C:2008:179.
Taddeucci and McCall v Italy App No. 51362/09 (ECtHR, 30 June 2016).
Treaty on the European Union (2008) OJ C115/13.
Treaty on the Functioning of the European Union (2016) OJ C202/1.
Vo v France App No. 53924/00 (ECtHR, 8 July 2004).
Wilkinson v Kitzinger (2006) EWHC 2022 (Fam).
X and Y v UK App No. 21830/93 (ECtHR, 22 April 1997).

Secondary sources

Abowitz KK and Harnish J, 'Contemporary Discourses of Citizenship' (2006) 76 *Review of Educational Research* 653.
Auchmuty R, 'Same Sex Marriage Revived: Feminist Critique and Legal Strategy' (2004) 14 *Feminist and Psychology* 101.
Bamforth N, 'Sexuality and Citizenship in Contemporary Constitutional Argument' (2012) 10 *International Journal of Constitutional Law* 477.
Benvenisti E, 'Margin of Appreciation, Consensus and Universal Standards' (1998–1999) 31 *New York University Journal of International Law and Politics* 843.
Beresford S, 'The Age of Consent and the Ending of Queer Theory' (2014) 3 *Laws* 759.
Bradley D, 'Comparative Law, Family Law and Common Law' (2003) 33 *Oxford Journal of Legal Studies* 127.
Brauch J, 'The Margin of Appreciation and the Jurisprudence of the European Court of Human Rights: Threat to the Rule of Law' (2004–2005) 113 *Columbia Journal of European Law* 119.
Butler P, 'Margin of Appreciation – A Note Towards a Solution for the Pacific' (2008–2009) 39 *Victoria University of Wellington Law Review* 687.
Cabellero S, 'Unmarried Cohabiting Couples Before the European Court of Human Rights: Parity with Marriage?' (2004–2005) 11 *Columbia Journal of European Law* 151.

Calhoun C, *Nations Matter: Culture, History and the Cosmopolitan Dream* (Routledge 2007).

Cartabia M, 'The European Court of Human Rights: Judging Non-Discrimination' (2011) 9 *International Journal of Constitutional Law* 808.

Centre for Social Justice, 'European Family Law: Faster Divorce and Foreign Law' (2009) <www.centreforsocialjustice.org.uk/core/wp-content/uploads/2016/08/CSJEuropeanFamilyLaw.pdf> accessed 31 July 2019.

Cornides J, 'Three Case Studies on "Anti-Discrimination"' (2012) 23 *European Journal of International Law* 517.

Cossman B, *Sexual Citizens: The Legal and Cultural Regulation of Sex and Belonging* (Stanford University Press 2007).

Cott N, *Public Vows: A History of Marriage and the Nation* (Harvard University Press 2002).

Council of Europe, 'Memorandum of Understanding Between the Council of Europe and the European Union' CM(2007)74 (10 May 2007).

———, 'High Level Conference on the Future of the European Court of Human Rights (Brighton Declaration)' (19–20 April 2012) <www.echr.coe.int/Documents/2012_Brighton_FinalDeclaration_ENG.pdf> accessed 31 July 2019.

———, '47 Member States' <www.coe.int/en/web/portal/country-profiles> accessed 31 July 2019.

Cox B, 'Same-Sex Marriage and Choice of Law: If We Marry in Hawaii, Are We Still Married When We Return Home?' (1994) *Wisconsin Law Review* 1033.

Culliton-Gonzalez K, 'Born in the Americas: Birthright Citizenship and Human Rights' (2012) 25 *Harvard Human Rights Journal* 127.

Danisis C, 'How Far Can the European Court of Human Rights Go in the Fight Against Discrimination? Defining New Standards in Its Non-Discrimination Jurisprudence' (2011) 9 *International Journal of Constitutional Law* 793.

Dawson M, Muir E and Claes M, 'Enforcing the EU's Rights Revolution; the Case of Equality' (2012) 3 *European Human Rights Law Review* 276.

Duggan L, 'The New Homonormativity: The Sexual Politics of Neoliberalism' in Nelson D and Castronovo R (eds), *Materializing Democracy: Toward a Revitalized Cultural Politics* (Duke University Press 2002).

———, 'Beyond Same-Sex Marriage' (2008) 9 *Studies in Gender and Sexuality* 155.

Enslin P, 'Education and Democratic Citizenship: In Defence of Cosmopoli-tanism' in Leicester M, Modgil C and Modgil S (eds), *Politics, Education and Citizenship* (Falmer Press 2000).

Eriksson A, 'European Justice: Broadening the Scope of European Non-Discrimination Law' (2009) 7 *International Journal of Constitutional Law* 731.

European Commission, 'Conditions for Membership' <http://ec.europa.eu/enlargement/policy/conditions-membership/index_en.htm> accessed 31 July 2019.

Fairhurst J, *Law of the European Union* (9th edn, Pearson Publishing 2012).

Fenwick H, 'Same Sex Unions and the Strasbourg Court in a Divided Europe: Driving Forward Reform or Protecting the Court's Authority Via Consensus Analysis' (2016) 3 *EHRLR* 248.

Fenwick H and Hayward A, 'Rejecting Asymmetry of Access to Formal Relationship Statuses for Same and Different-Sex Couples at Strasbourg and Domestically' (2017) 6 *European Human Rights Law Review* 545.

Gerards J, 'The Prism of Fundamental Rights' (2012) 8 *European Constitutional Law Review* 173.

Hamilton F, 'The Differing Treatment of Same Sex Couples by European Union Law and the European Convention on Human Rights: The European Union Concept of Citizenship' (2015) 2 *Journal of International and Comparative Law* 87.

Harris A, 'Loving Before and After the Law' (2008) 76 *Fordham Law Review* 2821.

Heaphy B, Smart C and Einarsdottir A, *Same Sex Marriages: New Generations, New Relationships* (Palgrave MacMillan 2013).

Hervey G, 'Europe's Human Rights Court Struggles to Lay Down the Law' *Politico* (20 September 2017) <www.politico.eu/article/human-rights-court-ilgar-mammadov-azerbaijan-struggles-to-lay-down-the-law/> accessed 31 July 2019.

Hodson L, 'A Marriage by Any Other Name? Shalk and Kopf v Austria' (2011) 11 *Human Rights Law Review* 170.

Isin EF and Turner BS, 'Citizenship Studies: An Introduction' in Isin EF and Turner BS (eds), *Handbook of Citizenship Studies* (Sage 2002).

Johnson P, '"An Essentially Private Manifestation of Human Personality": Constructions of Homosexuality in the European Court of Human Rights' (2010) 10 *Human Rights Law Review* 67.

———, '"Homosexual Propaganda" in the Russian Federation: Are They in Violation of the European Convention on Human Rights?' (2015) 3 *Russian Law Journal* 37.

Joris T and Vandenberghe J, 'The Council of Europe and the European Union: Natural Partners or Uneasy Bedfellows?' (2008–2009) 15 *Columbia Journal of European Law* 1.

Josephson J, 'Citizenship, Same-Sex Marriage and Feminist Criitques of Marriage' (2005) 3 *Perspectives on Politics* 269.

Kochenov D, 'On Options of Citizens and Moral Choices of States: Gays and European Federalism' (2009) 33 *Fordham International Law Review* 156.

Kymlicka W, *Multicultural Citizenship: A Liberal Theory of Minority Rights* (Oxford University Press 1995).

Lister R, 'Why Citizenship: Where, How and Why Children' (2007) 8 *Theoretical Inquiries in Law* 693.

Lockwood D, 'Civil Integration and Class Formation' (1996) 47 *British Journal of Sociology* 531.

Marshall TH, 'Citizenship and Social Class' in Marshall TH and Bottomore T (eds), *Citizenship and Social Class* (Pluto Press 1992).

Morris L, 'Citizenship and Human Rights: Ideals and Actualities' (2012) 63 *British Journal of Sociology* 39.

Nash K, 'Between Citizenship and Human Rights' (2004) 43 *Sociology* 1067.

O'Mahoney C, 'Irreconcilable Differences? Article 8 ECHR and Irish Law on Non-Traditional Families' (2012a) 26 *International Journal of Law Policy and the Family* 31.

———, 'There Is No Such Thing as a Right to Dignity' (2012b) 10 *International Journal of Constitutional Law* 551.

Pew Research Center, 'Attitudes on Same-Sex Marriage' (14 May 2019) <www.pewforum.org/fact-sheet/changing-attitudes-on-gay-marriage/> accessed 31 July 2019.

Richardson D, 'Desisting Sameness? The Rise of Neoliberal Politics of Normalisation' (2005) 37 *Antipodes* 519.

Rosenfeld M, 'Introduction: Gender, Sexual Orientation and Equal Citizenship' (2012) 10 *International Journal of Constitutional Law* 340.

Shafir G and Brysk A, 'The Globalization of Rights: From Citizenship to Human Rights' (2006) 10 *Citizenship Studies* 275.

Shuibhne NN, 'Margins of Appreciation; National Values, Fundamental Rights and EC Free Movement Law' (2009) 34 *European Law Review* 230.

Stalford H, 'Concepts of Family Under EU Law – Lessons from the ECHR' (2002) 16 *International Journal of Law, Policy and the Family* 410.

Stark B, 'When Globalization Hits Home: International Family Law Comes of Age' (2006) 36 *Vanderbilt Journal of Transnational Law* 1551.

Sutherland E, 'A Step Closer to Same-Sex Marriage Throughout Europe' (2011) 15 *Edinburgh Law Review* 97.

Treaty Office, 'Chart of Signatures and Ratifications of Treaty 177' Council of Europe ETS No. 177 (15 August 2019) <www.coe.int/en/web/conventions/full-list/-/conventions/treaty/177/signatures> accessed 15 October 2019.

Tryfonidou A, 'The EU Top Court Rules That Married Same-Sex Couples Can Move Freely Between EU Member States as "Spouses": Case C-673/16, Relu Adrian Coman Robert Clabourn Hamilton, Asociaţia Accept v Inspectoratul General pentru Imigrări, Ministerul Afacerilor Interne' (2019) *Feminist Legal Studies* 1.

US Legal Dictionary, 'Lex Specialis Law and Legal Definition' *USLegal.com* (n.d.) <http://definitions.uslegal.com/l/lex-specialis/> accessed 31 July 2019.

Warner M (ed), *Fear of a Queer Planet: Queer Politics and Social Theory* (University of Minnesota Press 1993).

———, *The Trouble With Normal: Sex, Politics, and the Ethics of Queer Life* (Free Press 1999).

Weeks J, 'The Sexual Citizen' (1998) 15 *Theory, Culture and Society* 38.

Werbner P and Yuval-Davis N, 'Introduction: Women and the New Discourse of Citizenship' in Werbner P and Yuval-Davis N (eds), *Women, Citizenship and Difference* (Zed 1999).

Wolfson E, 'Crossing the Threshold: Equal Marriage Rights for Lesbians and Gay Men and the Intra-Community Critique' (1994) 21 *New York University Review of Law and Social Change* 567.

Yourow HC, *Margin of Appreciation Doctrine in the Dynamics of European Human Rights Jurisprudence* (Brill 1996).

Zylan Y, *States of Passion, Identity and Social Construction of Desire* (Oxford University Press 2011).

Chapter 2

The European approach to recognising, downgrading, and erasing same-sex marriages celebrated abroad*

Guido Noto La Diega

Introduction

Whereas in Europe the right to enter into a same-sex marriage has not been fully recognised,[1] it is becoming increasingly clear that LGBTQ+ peoples' right to see one's existing marriage recognised abroad is part of 'the very essence of the international right to marry.'[2] In the last two years, there has been an unprecedented move towards a stronger protection of same-sex couples who cross borders.[3] First, in *Orlandi and Others v Italy*,[4] the European Court of Human Rights (ECtHR) stated that same-sex marriages celebrated abroad must be recognised at least as civil partnerships, even when a country decides not to allow such marriages to be celebrated within its territory. In the EU, a step forward was then made by the Court of Justice of the EU (CJEU) in *Coman*,[5] which decided that parties to a same-sex marriage are 'spouses' even in Member States that do not allow this marriage within their territory. The ratio decidendi was that national policies cannot justify a violation of the fundamental EU freedoms, e.g. free movement of people and relevant residence rights.[6] Against this backdrop, this chapter analyses those countries that provide some protection for same-sex couples (e.g. civil partnerships), without allowing them to marry. The author found that the models that countries adopt when dealing with same-sex marriages celebrated abroad are recognition, downgrading, and erasure. Recognition means that these marriages are recognised as marriages, either for all purposes, or for some of them, e.g. for the exercise of EU freedoms. Romania is the case study of this model, because *Coman*[7] – the legal basis of the recognition model – concerned a Romanian case and therefore it is important to see how Member States implement the CJEU's ruling. 'Downgrading' is the second model: the foreign marriage is treated as if it were a national civil partnership. Italy is a good case study for this approach because the relevant model can be seen as based on *Orlandi*.[8] Finally, the third model is 'erasure,' whereby same-sex marriages celebrated abroad are not even recognised as civil partnerships. An example of this is Hungary, where the government justified the choice by saying that all other countries follow the Hungarian approach. This chapter refutes this justification and exposes its untenability.

This author carried out 20 semi-structured interviews by email with lawyers representing parties in prominent relevant cases, lawyers engaged with local LGBTQ+ organisations, and police officers.[9] Email interviews created 'space to think and time to talk.'[10] These allowed the author to understand the relevant European and national laws and policies. Cases such as *Orlandi* and *Coman* show that in order to understand the national effects of same-sex marriages celebrated abroad, one needs to take – as this book does – an approach that integrates private international law, EU law, and human rights law. The focus of this chapter is on the European countries that do not provide same-sex marriage but offer some form of protection to same-sex couples, and in particular on Romania, Italy, and Hungary.[11]

The recognition model and the power of the single market: same-sex marriages celebrated abroad must be recognised as 'marriages'

The 'recognition' model means that foreign same-sex marriages are recognised as marriages, even though domestic law does not allow these marriages to be celebrated in the territory of the relevant country. 'Recognised' encompasses both the recognition of all the effects of marriage, as well as the recognition of the status of 'spouse' for limited purposes, e.g. residence, impediment to marry, citizenship, and adoption.[12] Examples of this are Romania, Estonia,[13] Slovakia,[14] Latvia,[15] and Andorra.[16]

This model is based on the CJEU's seminal decision in *Coman*.[17] Building on *Pajić v Croatia*,[18] where it was decided that excluding same-sex couples from family reunification breaches the ECHR,[19] *Coman* stressed that it is crucial to recognise these foreign spouses as such, and not downgrade them to generic family members,[20] because the spouses' rights to move and reside freely in the EU cannot be limited by national laws, whereas they can when it comes to partners.[21] The Romanian General Inspectorate for Immigration denied a residence permit to a Romanian man's American husband because the Civil Code expressly prohibits both the celebration of same-sex marriages in Romania and their recognition if celebrated abroad.[22] Local authorities interpreted this as meaning that Romania would adopt the erasure model. This is not the case, as convincingly stated by the CJEU. First, previous case law already harmonised the concept of 'spouse' – that is, 'a person joined to another person by the bonds of marriage.'[23] Since 'person' is gender-neutral, it can cover same-sex spouses.[24] Second, in exercising any national competence – including the regulation of personal status – Member States 'must comply with EU law,'[25] which includes the freedom to reside in any Member States, according to secondary EU rules.[26] Third, interferences with the fundamental freedom to reside are allowed only if based on objective public-interest considerations and if they are proportionate to a legitimate national objective.[27] This is where the 'societal objection' comes into play. The Court accepted that the EU must respect national identities, some of which include a heterosexual view of marriage.[28] However, it held that for the objection to be successful, there must be 'a genuine and sufficiently serious threat to a fundamental interest of society,'[29] which was not the case. The conclusion was that 'spouses' must be treated as such, regardless of their sexual orientation and gender. Even though the decision concerned the right to residence, *Coman* is likely to constitute a stepping stone towards full recognition of foreign same-sex marriages. Indeed, its ratio decidendi goes well beyond the right to residence, this being that Member States '*must comply with EU law*, *in particular* the Treaty provisions on the freedom conferred on all Union citizens to move and reside'[30] anywhere in the EU. Therefore, discriminatory marriage policies cannot be an excuse to breach the pillars of EU law; i.e. the four freedoms of movement and the Charter of Fundamental Rights of the EU (hereinafter 'Charter'). Should *Coman* be interpreted narrowly, as merely the basis of a non-discriminatory right to residence, the case would risk producing no practical effects. LGBTQ+ people are unlikely to exercise their free movement rights if equality[31] and non-discrimination[32] are not fully recognised.

Arguably, *Coman* provided a foundation for the principle of continuity of personal status,[33] whereby, in a context of increasingly geographically fluid families, foreign statuses 'will never be open to challenge by applying a different law.'[34] However, it is being implemented very narrowly, as exemplified by Romania. In July 2018, the Constitutional Court applied *Coman* and stated that same-sex spouses of EU citizens have the same residence rights as different-sex ones.[35] The Court observed that same-sex couples have the 'right to private and family life under Article 8 of the ECHR and Article 7 of Charter, and their relationship is recognised by the law.'[36]

Despite these bold general statements, the Court did not go so far as declaring the unconstitutionality of the Civil Code provision preventing the recognition of foreign same-sex marriages.[37] The provision is still valid 'as long as the Romanian authorities provide a framework to implement the EU decision in *Coman*.'[38] It is unclear what this framework will look like, and we can expect two years of litigation before the Romanian *Coman* case is settled,[39] but the framework that will need to be in place will have to ensure freedom of movement rights to all spouses of EU citizens, without discrimination on the grounds of gender or sexuality. Implementing the spirit of the CJEU's ruling should have meant going beyond the mere residence right to recognising the validity of foreign same-sex marriages for all purposes, but this is not surprising since the Constitutional Court 'is hardly a champion of equal rights.'[40] Such interpretation arguably does not comply with EU Law, because if same-sex marriage is not recognised for all purposes, LGBTQ+ people are unlikely to exercise the residence rights, as suggested by the fact that the Coman-Hamilton family still lives in the US.

Considering the unfavourable attitude of the majority of the Romanian population towards LGBTQ+ rights,[41] one could have expected that the recognition of same-sex marriages by means of a judicial decision imposed by the CJEU would prompt a backlash. Instead, in October 2018, a three-year campaign aimed at changing the Constitution to expressly refer to marriage as the union between a man and a woman[42] resulted in a referendum that failed[43] because only 20.4% of the citizens voted and the quorum was not obtained.[44] *Coman* may produce legal[45] and societal changes going beyond mere residence rights.[46] The opportunity may present itself with one of the four civil partnerships bills to the floor of the Romanian parliament and most political leaders declared to be in favour of the recognition of same-sex couples.[47] Interestingly, 'the only non-controversial provision in the bills'[48] is that foreign same-sex marriages should be treated as civil partnerships. However, any such downgrading would be in breach of the ratio decidendi in *Coman*, i.e. ensuring that same-sex couples feel free to circulate in all Member States without their rights and status being in danger.[49]

For some years now, private international law scholars have wondered whether 'a refusal by a [Member] State to acknowledge the marriage or partnership status of a same-sex couple [is or is not] compatible with EU law or human rights.'[50] Now we know, on the one hand, that EU law requires all spouses to be treated in the same way to ensure free movement of people.[51] On the other hand, the ECtHR decided in *Orlandi*[52] and *Oliari*[53] that states must protect same-sex relationships and cannot erase foreign same-sex marriages.

Finally, it is not by chance that the most advanced decision on foreign same-sex marriages is based on the need to preserve the single market. The convergence between LGBTQ+ rights and capitalism has been convincingly argued by sexuality scholars.[54] For example, Mario Mieli noted that 'contemporary gay movements originated in those countries where the capital reached the stage of real subsumption.'[55] The moment at which LGBTQ+ rights are asserted is congruent with capital's dominion, control, and transformation of *all* social relations and modes of production.[56] Economic modernisation is a key factor that motivates the introduction of LGBTQ+ rights in legislation.[57] Where the queer[58] fled the family unit at the turn of the twentieth century; the LGBTQ+ subject, freshly endowed with rights, returns as a productive member at the turn of the millenium.[59] Moreover, Mieli's pages provide further support to the idea that recognising the right to residence of all spouses is enough to achieve the freedoms of movement and the rights to equality, dignity, and non-discrimination as enshrined in the Charter. Indeed, despite the fact that in 'most capitalist countries, the freedom to be homosexual is recognized as a right . . . such legal freedom means freedom to be excluded, oppressed, repressed, ridiculed, become victims of moral and physical violence, and be isolated into ghettos.'[60] This is also linked to Foucault's idea of using freedom, or the illusion thereof, as a device of power. Accordingly, he argued that the 'freedom of circulation, in the broad sense of the term [is] one of the facets, aspects, or dimensions of the deployment of apparatuses of security.'[61] In order for societies to change and avoid ghettos, mere residence rights are not enough, and accordingly, narrow interpretations of *Coman* must be avoided.

A second-best solution: downgrading foreign same-sex marriages to civil partnerships

Most countries that do not recognise same-sex marriages celebrated abroad as marriages follow the 'downgrading' model.[62] They treat these marriages as if they were civil partnerships, regulated either by foreign law or by the domestic law. These countries include Italy, San Marino,[63] Switzerland,[64] Croatia,[65] Greece,[66] Liechtenstein,[67] Cyprus,[68] and Slovenia.[69] The legal foundation of this model is *Orlandi*,[70] where it was decided that when a couple's situation corresponds to family life – and same-sex married couples fall within the scope – Member States that do not put in place legal safeguards for these relationships are in breach of the right to private and family life.[71] Although the divergence between law and society was not the ratio decidendi in *Orlandi*, the Court did note that the contracting country 'failed to take account of the social reality of the situation.'[72] However, the societal argument in this case was presented as a predominantly negative force against LGBTQ+ rights. Indeed, on the one hand, the lack of consensus around same-sex marriage justified the non-adoption of the recognition model.[73] On the other hand, the societal argument seems the main thread in the dissenting opinion. There, it was observed that societal changes, even when occurring in all the parties to the Convention, do not alter the scope of the parties' engagements,[74] and that societal changes and citizens' needs do not entail human rights under the Convention.[75] The underlying political agenda is evident and exemplified by the dissenting opinion culminating with a quote from conservative judge Scalia: 'no social transformation without representation.'[76] From this, one can infer that the societal argument is a dangerous one: it prevents the full protection of LGBTQ+ rights, and it can be distorted to discriminate against minorities.[77]

Italy is a useful case study from this book's perspective, because despite Italian society being largely accepting of a plurality of family forms and of LGBTQ+ rights,[78] Italy has been the last Western European country to recognise same-sex relationships. It did so in 2016 with the Civil Unions Act,[79] which introduced the civil partnerships following the ECtHR's decision against Italy in *Oliari*.[80] The Court stated that in light of the growing European consensus around the recognition of same-sex relationships and because of the conflict between an accepting society and silence of the law, the absence of a legal framework recognising same-sex relationships violated the right to respect for private and family life.[81] A key element of the implementation framework was a decree on private international issues that opted for the downgrading principle, though with the caveats explained ahead.[82] Even though the Italian Parliament asked the government to pass a decree whereby same-sex marriages celebrated abroad were regulated by the Italian rules on civil unions, the government adopted a more nuanced and favourable approach, with different rules applying to Italian couples and couples of Italians and foreigners on the one hand, and couples of foreigners on the other hand.

With couples in which at least one spouse is Italian, the marriage will be downgraded to a civil union and the applicable law will be the Italian Civil Unions Act Italian.[83] The downgrading would already be problematic if it produced the 'mere' loss of the name 'marriage,' without practical effects. In Italy, however, the differences between marriage and civil unions are both symbolic and substantive,[84] the main ones being that civil partners do not have a duty of fidelity[85] and cannot adopt.[86] The main ratio of such downgrading is to 'prevent elusive behaviours of Italian citizens who go abroad to marry with the purpose of circumventing Italian law.'[87] Therefore, same-sex marriages celebrated abroad between foreigners will be recognised in Italy as marriages, as opposed to downgraded to civil unions.[88] Reflecting on the anti-elusive rationale of the downgrading rule, arguably same-sex marriages should be recognised and not downgraded whenever it is not celebrated to circumvent Italian law. One could contend[89] that when couples of different nationalities marry abroad, they are not trying to circumvent the Italian ban on same-sex marriage; accordingly, the anti-elusive rationale of the downgrading rule should not apply and, therefore, their marriage should not be downgraded. Similarly, it could be said that the downgrading provision should apply only to marriages in which both parties are Italian citizens and reside in Italy; should any of these elements vary (e.g. an Italian couple genuinely residing abroad), the application of the Civil Unions Act would be unwarranted.[90] However, the Supreme Court did not follow this reasoning and applied the downgrading provision to all same-sex marriages celebrated abroad, with the sole exception of those couples in which both spouses are foreigners.[91]

Another critique that can be moved to the Supreme Court's 2018 decision on couples of mixed nationality is that it downplays the increasing European consensus around same-sex marriage, thus clearly diverging from the case law of the ECtHR in *Oliari*[92] and *Orlandi*.[93] Third, and more importantly, the Supreme Court stresses that both human rights and constitutional case law state that lawmakers have discretion on the type of protection same-sex couples can access.[94] However, the court inappropriately conflates the (indeed, discretional) decision on whether or not to introduce same-sex marriage (a right) and the simpler taking account of the effect of a marriage that has already happened and is fully effective in another Member State (a status). Under Article 9, the right to marry can be limited only by national laws governing its exercise.[95] In the event of the recognition, or lack thereof, of same-sex marriages celebrated abroad, the couple already exercised the right to marry and, accordingly, national restrictions should not apply. Statuses should be recognised in a non-discriminatory way.[96] The difference between marriage as a right to be exercised and marriage as an already existing act is reflected in the different private international law rules that apply to the formalities of marriage and those that apply to the spouses' capacity. On the one hand, there 'is no rule more firmly established . . . that that which applies the maxim *locus regit actum* to the formalities of marriage,'[97] which means that countries demand to retain full control on the exercise of the right to marry by a monopoly on the law applicable to the formalities of marriage. On the other hand, marriages that could not be celebrated within one's territory (for example, polygamous marriages), if they have been celebrated abroad, will be valid under private international law if contracted between parties of full capacity[98] and pursuant to the foreign rules on formalities.[99]

The argument could be reinforced by noting that the 'downgrading' model breaches other fundamental human rights that do not allow national exemptions, such as discrimination on ground of sexual orientation,[100] equality,[101] and freedom of movement and residence.[102] This latter is likely to be the key to unlocking the recognition model. Despite *Orlandi* legitimising the 'downgrading' option, an argument can be made for the 'recognition' model. On the one hand, as done earlier in this chapter, it can be shown how *Orlandi* and the Italian Supreme Court inadvertently conflated the celebration of marriage and recognition of its effects. On the other hand, the CJEU case law can prevail on that of the ECtHR. Indeed, the Charter expressly recognises that the Charter's rights cannot restrict or adversely affect 'human rights and fundamental freedoms as recognised . . . by Union law.'[103] Therefore, the case law on free movement, and namely *Coman*, could prevail on *Orlandi*. Indeed, a major difference between the ECHR and EU law is that 'where the Convention sets out *minimum* standards, EU law *sets* the standard.'[104] This is also a result of the *Åkerberg*[105] case that decided that the Charter is binding when states act within the scope of EU law, not only when they implement EU law, thus ultimately increasing 'judicial oversight by the CJEU in human rights affairs.'[106] Even though *Coman* mandated the 'recognition' model in a case regarding residence rights, an implementation that aspires to be true to the spirit of *Coman* and of the EU Treaties more generally should lead to the admission that, practically, same-sex married couples will not exercise their EU freedoms (to move, reside, work, etc.), if they know that their status will be in danger and they will be treated as second-class citizens. Therefore, the downgrading model arguably breaches EU Law (*Coman*) and human rights including freedom of movement, equality, and non-discrimination.

The erasure of same-sex marriages celebrated abroad breaches both EU Law and European Human Rights Law

Alongside countries that recognise foreign same-sex marriages and countries that downgrade them to civil unions, a minority of countries adopt the erasure model, whereby perfectly valid same-sex marriages celebrated abroad do not produce any effects despite the virtual availability of civil unions to nationals. In Europe, this is the case of Hungary and Czech Republic,[107] and is in direct breach of both EU Law and European human rights law as enshrined in *Coman* and *Orlandi*.

In Hungary, as in most Eastern European countries,[108] the majority of the population opposes same-sex marriages (64%). This, however, does not per se explain why Hungary adopts the erasure model, given that in other countries, the population is more strongly opposed to equal marriage and yet they recognise foreign same-sex marriages (Armenia) or downgrade them to civil partnerships (Greece).

In 2018, a reform of Hungarian private international law came into force.[109] A provision in the relevant bill provided for the downgrading of foreign same-sex marriages to registered partnerships,[110] but it did not pass because the Government claimed that such a recognition is not common in international private law.[111] As demonstrated in this chapter, such an assertion is plainly not correct. Indeed, in most countries foreign same-sex marriages are effective either as marriages or as civil partnerships.

The Hungarian case study is important also because it shows how *Coman* cannot be interpreted as meaning merely that residence rights must be recognised for same-sex spouses. Indeed, even before *Coman*, Hungarian authorities would grant spouses in same-sex marriages celebrated abroad a residence permit, without any clarification as to whether this was based on the recognition of the relationship as marriage, registered partnership, or cohabitation.[112] Nonetheless, same-sex married couples are still fighting in court to be recognised at least as registered partners. A decision of a first instance court ordered the registration of a same-sex marriage as a registered partnership,[113] and this was upheld on appeal. In January 2019, however, on further appeal by the Government, the Supreme Court quashed those rulings. Even though no provision prevents the recognition of same-sex marriages at least as registered partnerships, the Government referred to the lack of ad-hoc provision on downgrading and to the constitutional definition of marriage 'as the union of a man and a woman.'[114] Such argument is based on the conflation, criticised above, between allowing same-sex marriages to be celebrated within the national territory and the recognition of unions where the right to marry has already been exercised, namely through same-sex marriage celebrated abroad. When it comes to the former, the 'right to marry' applies and this is guaranteed only 'in accordance with the national laws governing'[115] its exercise;[116] conversely, in relation to the latter, freedoms of movement, dignity, and non-discrimination will apply and the exercise of these rights cannot be limited by national provisions. Therefore, national rules – including national constitutional bans on same-sex marriage – do not apply to marriages celebrated abroad, since the right to marry has already been exercised.

To make one hopeful as to a positive outcome of the Hungarian dispute is the fact that the Supreme Court concluded that it was not possible to order the registration of foreign same-sex marriages as civil partnerships for the technical reason that the claimants asked for their relationship to be recognised as marriage, not as civil partnership. The parties have submitted a new request of recognition as civil partnership and, given the 'technical grounds'[117] on which the lower courts' decisions were quashed, one can expect a positive outcome for this dispute and, accordingly, the adoption by Hungary of the downgrading model. Thus, Hungary will avoid claims for state liability (*Coman*) and breach of human rights (*Orlandi*).

Conclusions

Despite a variety of approaches towards same-sex marriages celebrated abroad, there is a clear trend towards the recognition of their effects even in those countries where the society does not seem particularly favourable to LGBTQ+ rights.[118] Nonetheless, there has not been that change in jurisprudence that would have been necessary for the 'realization of universal Convention rights for gay men and lesbians.'[119] The societal objection does not seem to play a great role in the decisions concerning foreign same-sex marriages, probably because the latter are perceived as less of a threat for society, compared to domestic same-sex marriages.

Whilst ideologies and politics are not always explicitly present in the legal developments around cross-border same-sex marriages, they still play an important role. For example, one of the few times that the societal argument has played a prominent role has been the dissenting opinion in *Orlandi*,[120] where society and national identity have been used to serve a conservative legal agenda and to slow down the progress of LGBTQ+ rights. At the same time, where human rights failed (*Orlandi*), the free market succeeded (*Coman*). The fact that the ratio decidendi of the most advanced decision on same-sex marriages celebrated abroad is the unity of the single market is not accidental and speaks volumes about the convergence between LGBTQ+ rights and capitalism and the shift from radical queer to LGBTQ+ citizen and labourer.

After *Orlandi*, the 'erasure' model must be ruled out because it is a direct breach of human rights law. The recognition model should be preferred to the downgrading one, despite the latter being legitimised by *Orlandi*. First, this decision can be criticised for conflating national same-sex marriages and foreign ones. The former falls under the right to marry under Article 8 of the Charter and national laws can limit its exercise. The latter concerns instances where the right to marry has already been exercised and, therefore, falls under rights to equality, non-discrimination, and free movements; for these rights, the Charter does not allow national exemptions. Second, under certain circumstances EU law can prevail on the ECHR law and, for the purposes of this chapter, this means that *Coman* can prevail on *Orlandi*. Member States should not limit themselves to implement *Coman* as a mere obligation to open the right to residence to LGBTQ+ spouses: they should recognise the validity of foreign same-sex marriages for all purposes; otherwise, it is unlikely that a same-sex couple will move to a country where they would be legally free, but still members of a ghetto.

Notes

* A previous version of this chapter was presented at the Journal of Private International Law Conference 2017 (Rio de Janeiro), Conference on the Future of European Private Law (Ricadi), and at Universidad Internacional SEK Ecuador (Quito). Thanks to Adrian Coman, Liis Valk, Tamás Dombos, Dimitra Kamarinou, Eva Gračanin, Thomas Nigg, Reimo Mets, Andrej Havko, Vlad Viski,

Elpida Amoiridou, Giuseppe Zago, Daria Onitiu, and the reviewers for helpful comments to a previous draft.

1 *Schalk and Kopf v Austria* App No. 30141/04 (ECtHR, 24 June 2010).

2 Kees Waaldijk, 'The Gender-Neutrality of the International Right to Marry: Same-Sex Couples May Still Be Excluded from Marriage, but Their Exclusion – And Their Foreign Marriages – Must Be Recognised' in Andreas R Ziegler (ed), *International LGBTI Law – Sexual Orientation and Gender Identity Law from an International-Comparative Perspective* (forthcoming).

3 In this chapter, 'foreign,' 'celebrated abroad,' and 'cross border' are synonyms. A more adequate, albeit cumbersome, expression would be 'same-sex marriages with transnational relevance.' The usual phrases will be preferred for readability purposes.

4 *Orlandi and Others v Italy* App Nos. 26431/12, 26742/12, 44057/12 and 60088/12 (ECtHR, 14 December 2017).

5 Case C-673/16 *Coman and Others v Inspectoratul General pentru Imigrări* ECLI:EU:C:2018:385.

6 The only national measures that can restrict the free movement and residence rights must be based on public policy, public security, or public health (Directive 2004/38/EC of the European Parliament and of the Council of 29 April 2004 on the right of citizens of the Union and their family members to move and reside freely within the territory of the Member States [2004] OJ L158/77, art 27[1]). Public policy is 'a genuine and sufficiently serious threat affecting one of the fundamental interests of society' (Case C-30/77 *Regina v Pierre Bouchereau* ECLI:EU:C:1977:172, para 4). In turn, public security is something 'that might directly threaten the calm and physical security of the population as a whole or a large part of it' (Case C-145/09 *Land Baden-Württemberg v Panagiotis Tsakouridis* ECLI:EU:C:2010:708). Such measures are subject to a 'proportionality' test and must be based 'exclusively' on the 'personal conduct' of the individual (art 27[2]).

7 Ibid.

8 *Orlandi* (n 4).

9 In qualitative research, participant selection should have a clear rationale and purpose. Here I contacted the main LGBTQ+ organisations in the countries that fell within the scope of the research, and they acted as gatekeepers introducing me to experts in the field. I selected twenty interviewees because I analysed 16 countries and some of the interviewees were not able to answer all the questions. The number is not high, but qualitative research does not aim to represent the entire relevant population and offsets the limited quantity with a more intensive study of the sample. See Michelle Cleary, Jan Horsfall and Mark Hayter, 'Data Collection and Sampling in Qualitative Research: Does Size Matter?' (2014) 70 *Journal of Advanced Nursing* 473.

10 Nalita James, 'Using Email Interviews in Qualitative Educational Research: Creating Space to Think and Time to Talk' (2016) 29 *International Journal of Qualitative Studies in Education* 150.

11 The study of individual legal systems in order to shed light on more general issues of LGBTQ+ rights in Europe is similar to the method adopted by Jule Mulder, *EU Non-Discrimination law in the Courts* (Hart Publishing 2017).

12 These are the aspects considered in Kees Waaldijk (ed), 'More and More Together: Legal Family Formats for Same-Sex and Different-Sex Couples in European Countries – Comparative Analysis of Data in the LawsAndFamilies Database' (2017) 75 *Families and Societies Working Paper Series* 1.

13 Private International Law Act (*Rahvusvahelise eraõiguse seadus*), arts 55–56; and Aliens Act 2009 (*Välismaalaste seadus*), arts 118(1) and 137.

14 A visible effect of *Coman* (n 5) has been the change of policy in Slovakia where, right after the publication of the Court of Justice's decision, the government

declared that his country would recognise same-sex marriages celebrated abroad for free movement purposes.

15 Constitutional Court of Latvia (*Latvijas Republikas Satversmes tiesa*), 21 May 2016.
16 Tribunal Superior de Justícia, Sala Administrativa, sentència No. 108-2012.
17 *Coman* (n 5). There are two pending Supreme Court cases on this issue.
18 App No. 47082/12 (ECtHR, 23 February 2016). Cf. Danielle Teutonico, 'Pajic v. Croatia: The European Court of Human Rights Continues the Incremental Trend Towards Equal Legal Recognition of Same-Sex Couples' (2017) 25 *Tulane Journal of International and Comparative Law* 461.
19 ECHR, arts 8 and 14. The CJEU build on *Pajić v. Croatia* but goes beyond it. Freedom of movement is not part of the ratio decidendi in *Pajić v. Croatia*, but, as will be argued below, its importance in the context of *Coman* may bring to the recognition of same-sex marriages for all purposes, and not just for residence purposes.
20 However, according to Andy Hayward in Chapter 10 of this edited collection, civil partnerships have their own symbolic value.
21 Directive 2004/38/EC, art 2(2)(b).
22 Codul civil al României, art 277(2), incorrectly referred to in *Coman* (n 5) [8] as art 227.
23 *Coman* (n 5) [34], that refers to C-127/08 *Metock and Others* ECLI:EU:C:2008:449.
24 *Coman* (n 5) [35].
25 Ibid. [38].
26 C-148/02 *Garcia Avello v The State of Belgium* ECLI:EU:C:2003:539.
27 *Coman* (n 5) [40].
28 EU Treaty, art 4(2).
29 *Coman* (n 5) [44].
30 Ibid. [38], italics added.
31 EU Charter of Fundamental Rights (2000) OJ C-364/01, art 20. (hereinafter "Charter").
32 Ibid., art 21.
33 The principle had already been affirmed in other contexts, see *Wagner and J.M.W.L. v Luxembourg* App No. 76240/01 (ECtHR, 28 June 2007), para 117 ff. and *Paradiso and Campanelli v Italy* App No. 25358/12 (ECtHR, 24 January 2017), para 150 ff. In the context of same-sex relationships, see Frances Hamilton and Lauren Clayton-Helm, 'Same Sex Relationships Choice of Law and the Continued Recognised Relationship Theory' (2016) 3 *Journal of International and Comparative Law* 1; Stuart M Davis, *Conflicts of Law and the Mutual Recognition of Same-Sex Unions in the EU* (PhD Thesis, University of Reading 2015) and, in private international law in general, see Toni Marzal Yetano, 'The Constitutionalisation of Party Autonomy in European Family Law' (2010) 6 *Journal of Private International Law* 158. From an EU law perspective, with a focus on the Charter (n 31) art 9; see Massimo Condinanzi and Chiara Amalfitano, 'La libera circolazione della "coppia" nel diritto comunitario' (2008) 13 *Dir EU* 399. A more nuanced version was proposed by Vincenzo Scalisi, '"Famiglia" e "famiglie" in Europa' (2013) *Riv dir civ* 8.
34 Yetano (n 33) 185. On the compatibility of the portability principle and the recognition method in conflicts of law see Silvia Pfeiff, *La portabilité du statut personnel dans l'espace* européen (Bruylant 2017).
35 Constituţională a României, *decizia* 18 July 2018 No. 534.
36 Ibid.
37 Codul civil al României, art 277(2).
38 Constituţională a României (n 35).

39 After Ibid., the case went back to a first instance court in Bucharest and should the decision be favourable, the government may appeal, thus further delaying the final settlement of the case.
40 Elena Brodeala, 'Paying Lip Service to the CJEU: The Unsurprising Decision of the Constitutional Court of Romania in the Coman Case' *Oxford Human Rights Hub* (26 July 2018) <ohrh.law.ox.ac.uk/paying-lip-service-to-the-cjeu-the-unsurprising-decision-of-the-constitutional-court-of-romania-in-the-coman-case/> accessed 12 March 2019.
41 The last available data from 2017 suggests that 74% of the Romanian population is against same-sex marriage (Pew Research Center, *Eastern and Western Europeans Differ on Importance of Religion, Views of Minorities, and Key Social Issues* [Pew 2018] 12). According to an interviewee, this attitude depends on the importance of the Orthodox Church and on the delay with which Romania decriminalised homosexuality; in 1996, a lesbian woman was imprisoned for three years for her sexuality, and the decriminalisation law was passed only in 2001.
42 The Lege de revizuire a Constituţiei României 2018 amended the Constitution, art 48, in order to include an express reference to marriage as the union between a man and a woman, and called for a referendum to approve the amendment.
43 On the reasons of the failure, see Valerie Hopkins, 'Romanian Voters Ignore Referendum on Same-Sex Marriage Ban' *Financial Times* (7 October 2018) <www.ft.com/content/9bbcf3ce-ca62-11e8-b276-b9069bde0956> accessed 10 March 2019.
44 The referendum campaign started in 2015, well before the *Coman* ruling, but after the national lawsuit that ultimately led to *Coman* was initiated (2013). However, the lawsuit became public on 19 July 2016, one day before the first hearing at the Constitutional Court.
45 So far, there have not been meaningful legal changes, but Hungarian MPs have used *Coman* to justify the introduction of civil partnerships in recently presented bill.
46 According to one of the interviewees, there has already been a positive change in societal attitudes towards LGBTQ+ people, with even conservative Romanian media giving positive visibility to the case.
47 This data emerged from the interviews and suggests that Romanian laws may change more rapidly than Romanian society.
48 Email from Vlad Viski to Author (4 March 2019).
49 Since the next 48 months will see Romanian politicians busy with several electoral campaigns, it seems unlikely that civil unions will be at the top of the public agenda.
50 Davis (n 33) 37.
51 *Coman* (n 5).
52 *Orlandi* (n 4).
53 *Oliari and Others v Italy* App Nos. 18766/11 and 36030/11 (ECtHR, 21 July 2015).
54 See Mario Mieli, *Elementi di critica omosessuale* (Einaudi 1977), translated to English as *Towards a Gay Communism* (tr David Fernbach and Evan Calder Williams, Pluto 2018); and John D'Emilio, 'Capitalism and Gay Identity' in Ann Snitow, Christine Stansell and Sharan Thompson (eds), *Powers of Desire: The Politics of Sexuality* (Monthly Review Press 1983) 100.
55 Mieli (n 54) 9.
56 Mieli refers to Marx's categories of formal and real subsumption. In early capitalism, there is only a formal subsumption of labour by capital, which means that the labour process is not directly affected but the worker's submission is a consequence of the capitalist's control over the means of production. The following stage of 'real subsumption' refers to when the capitalist mode of production changes the nature itself of labour and its conditions. Mieli (n 54) 9 refers to Karl

Marx, *Il capitale: Libro I* (La Nuova Italia 1969) ch 6. For a critical reading of these concepts and their interpretations, see Sandro Mezzadra, 'The Topicality of Prehistory: A New Reading of Marx's Analysis of "So-Called Primitive Accumulation"' (2011) 23 *Rethinking Marxism* 302, 313 ff.

57 Phillip M Ayoub, 'Contested Norms in New-Adopter States: International Determinants of LGBT Rights Legislation' (2015) 21 *EJIR* 293, 297.

58 Queer here is not used as an umbrella term for LGBTQ+ people; it characterises the radical queer who rebels against both the heteronormative and homonormative societies. See e.g. Sandra Jeppesen, 'Queer Anarchist Autonomous Zones and Publics: Direct Action Vomiting Against Homonormative Consumerism' (2010) 13 *Sexualities* 463.

59 This is consistent with D'Emilio (n 54), who suggests that capitalism reorganises the traditional model of family, making men travel in search of external sources for their families' subsistence; thanks to said mobility, new sexual relations could be pursued relatively freely. See also Jeffrey Weeks, *Coming out: Homosexual Politics in Britain from the Nineteenth Century to the Present* (rev edn, Quartet 1990) on parallels between regulation of homosexuality and regulation of the working class. Others have noted that the 'penetration of the market deeper into everyday life has created spaces for commodified forms of lesbian and gay existence' (Alan Sears, 'Queer Anti-Capitalism: What's Left of Lesbian and Gay Liberation?' (2005) 69 *Science & Society* 92).

60 Mario Mieli, 'Per la critical della questione omosessuale' (1972) 3 *Fuori!* 1–2, as cited by Massimo Prearo, 'Introduction', in Mieli (n 54) xvii.

61 Michel Foucault, '18 January 1978' in Michel Senellart, François Ewald and Alessandro Fontana (eds), *Security, Territory, Population* (Palgrave Macmillan 2007) 49.

62 Following Hayward (n 20), the recognition as national civil partnerships could be seen as a change in name but not necessarily a 'downgrade.'

63 Legge 20 November 2018, art 3(4).

64 Federal Law on Private International Law of 18 December 1987, art 45(3).

65 Life Partnership Act, arts 73, 74 and 75. See Teutonico (n 18).

66 Civil Partnership Act No. 4356 of 2015.

67 Registered Partnership Act of 16 March 2011 and the Registered Partnership Decree of 16 August 2011.

68 Civil Union Act 2015 (L. 184(I)/2015), s 43.

69 The Civil Union Act 2016, art 6(4).

70 *Orlandi* (n 4).

71 ECHR (n 19) art 8; *Orlandi* (n 4) paras 209–211.

72 *Orlandi* (n 4) para 209.

73 Ibid.

74 Dissenting Opinion of Judges Pejchal and Wojtyczek: Ibid., para 2.

75 Ibid., para 4.

76 Ibid., para 14.

77 As noted by Mulder (n 11) 271, the various ideologically influenced approaches to equality law explain the difficulties in its harmonisation.

78 According to Pew Research Center (n 41), in 2017, 59% of the Italian population was in favour of same-sex marriage.

79 Legge 20 May 2016 No. 76 '*Regolamentazione delle unioni civili tra persone dello stesso sesso e disciplina delle convivenze.*'

80 *Oliari and Others* (n 53) para 178 and passim.

81 ECHR (n 19) art 8.

82 Decreto legislativo 19 January 2017 No. 7 '*Modifiche e riordino delle norme di diritto internazionale privato per la regolamentazione delle unioni civili.*' (Decreto No. 7/2017).

83 Legge 31 May 1995 No. 218, art 32-bis, inserted by Decreto No. 7/2017.
84 As argued by, Diego Lasio and Francesco Serri, 'The Italian Public Debate on Same-Sex Civil Unions and Gay and Lesbian Parenting' (2019) 22 *Sexualities* 691, the 'differences between heterosexual marriage and same-sex union are the bedrock of the current expression of heteronormativity in Italy.'
85 Legge No. 76/2016, art 1(11). On the point, see L Olivero, 'Unioni civili e presunta licenza d'infedeltà' (2017) *Riv trim dir proc civ* 213.
86 Nonetheless, case law recognises that same-sex couples can access the stepchild adoption. See e.g. Corte di Cassazione 31 May 2018 No. 14007 (2018) 10 *Corr giur* 1204.
87 Explanatory Memorandum to Draft Decreto No. 7/2017, 2. This argument was raised also at the time when the first European countries started introducing same-sex marriage, but it was proved to be untenable: Katharina Boele-Woelki, 'The Legal Recognition of Same-Sex Relationships within the European Union' (2008) 82 *Tulane Law Review* 1949, 1954. See also Carla Garlatti, 'Comma 28' in Cesare Massimo Bianca (ed), *Le unioni civili e le convivenze* (Giappichelli 2017) 432, 442.
88 This is not expressly provided in the Civil Unions Act, but it is inferred by Corte di Cassazione 14 May 2018 No. 11696 (2018) 6(1) Foro it 1948 from the anti-elusive objective of the private international law provisions in said Act and in Decreto No. 7/2017.
89 As done convincingly by Matteo Winkler, '"A case with Peculiarities": Mixed Same-Sex Marriages before the Supreme Court' (2018) 4 *Italian Law Journal* 273, 282.
90 Garlatti (n 88) 442–443.
91 Corte di Cassazione (n 89).
92 *Oliari and Others* (n 53).
93 *Orlandi* (n 4).
94 Corte di Cassazione (n 89) refers to Corte Costituzionale 2014 No. 170; *Oliari and Others* (n 53); *Schalk and Kopf* (n 1).
95 Charter (n 31) arts 9 and 18; ECHR (n 19) art 12.
96 Charter (n 31) art 21; ECHR (n 19) art 14.
97 Paul Torremans (ed), *Cheshire, North & Fawcett Private International Law* (15th edn, Oxford University Press 2017) 893.
98 The prevalent view is that the parties have capacity to marry if they meet the requirements set forth by the laws of both domiciles (dual domicile theory). The alternative theory looks at the intended matrimonial home. In both instances, the Member State does not demand full control over marriages that have already been celebrated abroad: indeed, both the dual domicile theory and the intended matrimonial home doctrine allow the validity of marriages that could not be celebrated in the UK. See Torremans (n 98) 910.
99 Private International Law Act 1995 (Miscellaneous Provisions), s 5; *Baindail v Baindail* (1946) P 122 at 127–128.
100 Charter (n 31) art 21.
101 Ibid., art 20.
102 Ibid., art 45.
103 Ibid., art 53.
104 Martin Kuijer, 'The Challenging Relationship Between the European Convention on Human Rights and the EU Legal Order: Consequences of a Delayed Accession' (2018) *The International Journal of Human Rights* 1, 7, italics in the text, referring to Case C-399/11 *Melloni v Ministerio Fiscal* ECLI:EU:C:2013:107, paras 56–60.

105 Case C-617/10 *Åklagaren v Åkerberg Fransson* ECLI:EU:C:2012:340, paras 20–21. Cf. Emily Hancox, 'The Meaning of "Implementing" EU Law Under Article 51(1) of the Charter: *Åkerberg Fransson*' (2013) 50 *CMLR* 1411.
106 Kuijer (n 105) 6.
107 In Czech Republic, the law regulates only foreign different-sex marriages and foreign civil partnerships, allowing their registration in a special registry. Under Czech public law, the Office for the Registration of Civil Acts has the power to act only when expressly provided by the law and the lacuna has the unfortunate effect of recognising foreign civil partnerships, but erasing foreign same-sex marriages.
108 Czech Republic and Slovakia constitute the only exception, with 'only' 29% and 47%, respectively, opposing same-sex marriage, according to Pew Research Center (n 41) 12.
109 Private International Law Act 2017.
110 Concept of the new International Private Law Act.
111 Email from Tamás Dombos (Háttér Society) to author (4 August 2017).
112 Email from Tamás Dombos (Háttér Society) to author (9 March 2019).
113 'Sajtóközlemény – Bíróság: a magyar államnak is el kell ismernie a külföldi melegházasságokat bejegyzett élettársi kapcsolatként' *Háttér* (27 April 2017) <hatter.hu/hirek/birosag-a-magyar-allamnak-is-el-kell-ismernie-a-kulfoldi-meleghazassagokat-bejegyzett> accessed 11 March 2019.
114 Fundamental Law of Hungary 2011, art L(1).
115 Charter (n 31) art 9.
116 This 'national safeguard' clause explains why *Oliari and Others* (n 53) reiterated *Schalk and Kopf* (n 1) in finding that Member States have a wider margin of appreciation on whether or not to introduce same-sex marriage. This margin of appreciation has become a 'rather empty rhetorical device,' rather than a tool to balance uniform protection of human rights and national traditions, as argued by Janneke Gerards, 'Margin of Appreciation and Incrementalism in the Case Law of the European Court of Human Rights' (2018) 18 *Human Rights Law Review* 495.
117 Email from Tamás Dombos (Háttér Society) to author (28 February 2019).
118 This confirms the data analysed by Waaldijk (n 2). If one compares them to a report the same editor published twelve years before, one gets the sense of significant increase of protection for LGBTQ+ rights. See Kees Waaldijk (ed), *More or Less Together: Levels of Legal Consequences of Marriage, Cohabitation and Registered Partnership for Different-Sex and Same-Sex Partner* (INED 2005).
119 Paul Johnson, *Homosexuality and the European Court of Human Rights* (Routledge 2013) 211.
120 *Orlandi* (n 4).

References

Primary sources

Åklagaren v Åkerberg Fransson (C-617/10) ECLI:EU:C:2012:340.
Aliens Act 2009 (*Välismaalaste seadus*).
Baindail v Baindail (1946) P 122.
Civil Partnership Act No. 4356 of 2015.
Civil Union Act 2015 (L. 184(I)/2015), s 43.
The Civil Union Act 2016, art 6(4).

Codul civil al României, art 277(2).

Coman and Others v Inspectoratul General pentru Imigrări (C-673/16) ECLI:EU:C:2018:385.

Concept of the new International Private Law Act.

Constitutional Court of Latvia, *Latvijas Republikas Satversmes tiesa* 21 May 2016.

Constituţională a României, *decizia* 18 July 2018 No. 534.

Corte Costituzionale 2014 No. 170.

Corte di Cassazione 14 May 2018 No. 11696 (2018) 6(1) *Foro it* 1948.

Corte di Cassazione 31 May 2018 No. 14007 (2018) 10 *Corr giur* 1204.

Decreto legislativo 19 January 2017 No. 7 *Modifiche e riordino delle norme di diritto internazionale privato per la regolamentazione delle unioni civili* (Decreto No. 7/2017).

Directive 2004/38/EC of the European Parliament and of the Council of 29 April 2004 on the right of citizens of the Union and their family members to move and reside freely within the territory of the Member States (2004) OJ L158/77.

EU Charter of Fundamental Rights (2000) OJ C-364/01.

European Convention on Human Rights (ECHR).

Explanatory Memorandum to Draft Decreto o 7/2017.

Federal Law on Private International Law of 18 December 1987, art 45(3).

Fundamental Law of Hungary 2011, art L(1).

Garcia Avello v The State of Belgium (C-148/02) ECLI:EU:C:2003:539.

Land Baden-Württemberg v Panagiotis Tsakouridis (C-145/09) ECLI:EU:C:2010:708.

Lege de revizuire a Constituţiei României 2018.

Legge 20 May 2016 No. 76 *Regolamentazione delle unioni civili tra persone dello stesso sesso e disciplina delle convivenze.*

Legge 20 November 2018, art 3(4).

Legge 31 May 1995 No. 218, art 32-bis, inserted by Decreto No. 7/2017.

Legge No. 76/2016, art 1(11).

Life Partnership Act, arts 73, 74 and 75.

Melloni v Ministerio Fiscal (C-399/11) ECLI:EU:C:2013:107.

Metock and Others (C-127/08) ECLI:EU:C:2008:449.

Oliari and Others v Italy App Nos. 18766/11 and 36030/11 (ECtHR, 21 July 2015).

Orlandi and Others v Italy Apps Nos. 26431/12, 26742/12, 44057/12 and 60088/12 (ECtHR, 14 December 2017).

Pajić v Croatia App No. 47082/12 (ECtHR, 23 February 2016).

Paradiso and Campanelli v Italy App No. 25358/12 (ECtHR, 24 January 2017).

Private International Law Act 1995 (Miscellaneous Provisions).

Private International Law Act (*Rahvusvahelise eraõiguse seadus*).

Private International Law Act 2017.

Regina v Pierre Bouchereau (C-30/77) ECLI:EU:C:1977:172.

Registered Partnership Act of 16 March 2011

Registered Partnership Decree of 16 August 2011.

Schalk and Kopf v Austria App No. 30141/04 (ECtHR, 24 June 2010).

Tribunal Superior de Justícia, Sala Administrativa, sentència No. 108-2012.

Wagner and J.M.W.L. v Luxembourg App No. 76240/01 (ECtHR, 28 June 2007).

Wilkinson v Kitzinger (2006) EWHC 2022 (Fam).

Secondary sources

Ayoub PM, 'Contested Norms in New-Adopter States: International Determinants of LGBT Rights Legislation' (2015) 21 *EJIR* 293.

Boele-Woelki K, 'The Legal Recognition of Same-Sex Relationships Within the European Union' (2008) 82 *Tulane Law Review* 1949.

Brodeala E, 'Paying Lip Service to the CJEU: The Unsurprising Decision of the Constitutional Court of Romania in the Coman Case' *Oxford Human Rights Hub* (26 July 2018) <ohrh.law.ox.ac.uk/paying-lip-service-to-the-cjeu-the-unsurprising-decision-of-the-constitutional-court-of-romania-in-the-coman-case/> accessed 12 March 2019.

Cleary M, Horsfall J and Hayter M, 'Data Collection and Sampling in Qualitative Research: Does Size Matter?' (2014) 70 *Journal of Advanced Nursing* 473.

Condinanzi M and Amalfitano C, 'La libera circolazione della "coppia" nel diritto comunitario' (2008) 13 *Dir EU* 399.

Davis SM, *Conflicts of Law and the Mutual Recognition of Same-Sex Unions in the EU* (PhD Thesis, University of Reading 2015).

D'Emilio J, 'Capitalism and Gay Identity' in Snitow A, Stansell C and Thompson S (eds), *Powers of Desire: The Politics of Sexuality* (Monthly Review Press 1983) 100.

Email from Tamás Dombos (Háttér Society) to author (28 February 2019).

Email from Tamás Dombos (Háttér Society) to author (4 August 2017).

Email from Tamás Dombos (Háttér Society) to author (9 March 2019).

Email from Vlad Viski to Author (4 March 2019).

Foucault M, '18 January 1978' in Senellart M, Ewald F and Fontana A (eds), *Security, Territory, Population* (Palgrave Macmillan 2007) 49.

Garlatti C, 'Comma 28' in Massimo Bianca C (ed) *Le unioni civili e le convivenze* (Giappichelli 2017) 432.

Gerards J, 'Argin of Appreciation and Incrementalism in the Case Law of the European Court of Human Rights' (2018) 18 *Human Rights Law Review* 495.

Hamilton F and Clayton-Helm L, 'Same Sex Relationships Choice of Law and the Continued Recognised Relationship Theory' (2016) 3 *Journal of International and Comparative Law* 1.

Hancox V, 'The Meaning of "Implementing" EU Law Under Article 51(1) of the Charter: *Åkerberg Fransson*' (2013) 50 *CMLR* 1411.

Hopkins V, 'Romanian Voters Ignore Referendum on Same-Sex Marriage Ban' *Financial Times* (7 October 2018) <www.ft.com/content/9bbcf3ce-ca62-11e8-b276-b9069bde0956> accessed 10 March 2019.

James N, 'Using Email Interviews in Qualitative Educational Research: Creating Space to Think and Time to Talk' (2016) 29 *International Journal of Qualitative Studies in Education* 150.

Jeppesen S, 'Queer Anarchist Autonomous Zones and Publics: Direct Action Vomiting Against Homonormative Consumerism' (2010) 13 *Sexualities* 463.

Johnson P, *Homosexuality and the European Court of Human Rights* (Routledge 2013).

Kuijer M, 'The Challenging Relationship Between the European Convention on Human Rights and the EU Legal Order: Consequences of a Delayed Accession' (2018) *The International Journal of Human Rights* 1.

Lasio D and Serri F, 'The Italian Public Debate on Same-Sex Civil Unions and Gay and Lesbian Parenting' (2019) 22 *Sexualities* 691.
Marx K, *Il capitale: Libro I* (La Nuova Italia 1969).
Marzal Yetano T, 'The Constitutionalisation of Party Autonomy in European Family Law' (2010) 6 *Journal of Private International Law* 158.
Mezzadra S, 'The Topicality of Prehistory: A New Reading of Marx's Analysis of "So-Called Primitive Accumulation"' (2011) 23 *Rethinking Marxism* 302.
Mieli M, 'Per la critical della questione omosessuale' (1972) 3 *Fuori!* 1–2, as cited by Prearo M, 'Introduction' in Mario Mieli (ed) *Elementi di critica omosessuale* (Einaudi 1977).
———, *Elementi di critica omosessuale* (Einaudi 1977).
———, *Towards a Gay Communism* (tr David Fernbach and Evan Calder Williams, Pluto 2018).
Mulder J, *EU Non-Discrimination Law in the Courts* (Hart Publishing 2017).
Olivero L, 'Unioni civili e presunta licenza d'infedeltà' (2017) *Riv trim dir proc civ* 213.
Pew Research Center, *Eastern and Western Europeans Differ on Importance of Religion, Views of Minorities, and Key Social Issues* (Pew 2018).
Pfeiff S, *La portabilité du statut personnel dans l'espace européen* (Bruylant 2017).
'Sajtóközlemény – Bíróság: a magyar államnak is el kell ismernie a külföldi melegházasságokat bejegyzett élettársi kapcsolatként' *Háttér* (27 April 2017) <hatter.hu/hirek/birosag-a-magyar-allamnak-is-el-kell-ismernie-a-kulfoldi-meleghazassagokat-bejegyzett> accessed 11 March 2019.
Scalisi V, '"Famiglia" e "famiglie" in Europa' (2013) *Riv dir civ* 8.
Sears A, 'Queer Anti-Capitalism: What's Left of Lesbian and Gay Liberation?' (2005) 69 *Science & Society* 92.
Teutonico D, 'Pajic v. Croatia: The European Court of Human Rights Continues the Incremental Trend Towards Equal Legal Recognition of Same-Sex Couples' (2017) 25 *Tulane Journal of International and Comparative Law* 461.
Torremans P (ed), *Cheshire, North & Fawcett Private International Law* (15th edn, Oxford University Press 2017).
Waaldijk K (ed), *More or Less Together: Levels of Legal Consequences of Marriage, Cohabitation and Registered Partnership for Different-Sex and Same-Sex Partner* (INED 2005).
———, 'More and More Together: Legal Family Formats for Same-Sex and Different-Sex Couples in European Countries – Comparative Analysis of Data in the LawsAndFamilies Database' (2017) 75 *Families and Societies Working Paper Series* 1.
———, 'The Gender-Neutrality of the International Right to Marry: Same-Sex Couples May Still Be Excluded from Marriage, but Their Exclusion – And Their Foreign Marriages – Must Be Recognised' in Ziegler AR (ed) *International LGBTI Law – Sexual Orientation and Gender Identity Law from an International-Comparative Perspective* (forthcoming).
Weeks J, *Coming out: Homosexual Politics in Britain from the Nineteenth Century to the Present* (rev edn, Quartet 1990).
Winkler M, '"A Case with Peculiarities": Mixed Same-Sex Marriages Before the Supreme Court' (2018) 4 *Italian Law Journal* 273.

Chapter 3

Harmonisation of choice of law rules on same-sex marriage

An international perspective

Lauren Clayton-Helm

Introduction

At present, each Member State of the EU controls its own laws on marriage, and, thus, determines what legally recognised relationships same-sex couples can enter. Whilst the decision in *Oliari and Others v Italy*[1] requires all European Convention on Human Rights (ECHR) Contracting States, and thereby all EU Member States, to permit and recognise a form of civil union, this does not extend to same-sex marriage. Similarly, with the exception of matters pertaining to free movement,[2] each Member State is free to determine whether it will recognise a same-sex marriage legitimately entered into in another jurisdiction. In determining essential validity,[3] at present, each Member State is able to do so by reference to a choice of law rule of its choosing. Choice of law rules are used within Private International Law as a way of determining the applicable law when more than one country is involved in a particular legal issue. Consequently, with differing laws on the rights of same-sex couples to marry, and the ability of different choice of law rules to be utilised by Member States, the potential for limping marriages – whereby a marriage is recognised and considered valid in one country, but not in another – is apparent. In an attempt to address this deleterious consequential effect, harmonisation of the choice of law rule used for assessing the validity of same-sex marriages across the EU was propounded in previous research as an adventitious solution.[4] This chapter will now extend such proposals, by showing that such harmonisation is possible. Through analysis of the United States (US) Supreme Court decision in *Obergefell v Hodges*,[5] requiring all US states to permit and recognise same-sex marriages, and the Court of Justice of the European Union (CJEU) ruling in *Coman*,[6] determining that same-sex marriages be recognised as marriages for the purposes of free movement of individuals, this chapter will bring a new and original argument to support Europeanisation within this area.

In proposing a harmonised choice of law rule for same-sex marriage, previous research sought to provide same-sex couples with certainty surrounding the validity of their marriage in any Member State.[7] In order to assess what that rule ought to be, the various choice of law rules used within marriage validity were analysed, before proposing a new and original choice of law rule: the continued recognised relationship theory. This theory applies the law of the country where the couple intend to live, or the country where they have lived if their marriage has subsisted for a reasonable period of time. With a bid to unify the law in this area, it was acknowledged that some Member States may be required to recognise a relationship that they would not normally permit, and so it was anticipated that some criticism may be levelled at the proposal. This was addressed by discussion of an incremental approach by introducing harmonised choice of law rules as opposed to substantive law. An incrementalist approach is, in effect, a step-by-step method of achieving change[8] much like many countries introduced civil partnerships ahead of same-sex marriage. Further to the support from using an incremental approach, this chapter will demonstrate that harmonisation is achievable through analysis of the aforementioned cases. Upon highlighting the similarities between the EU and the US prior to the *Obergefell* ruling, it will be demonstrated how *Obergefell* acts as precedent for Europeanisation, and shows that a unitary approach can be achieved despite opposing laws. Finally, it will be shown that harmonisation has, in fact, already begun within this remit, in the shape of *Coman*, and, thus, the extent to which this case adds further weight to the argument for harmonisation will be propagated.

The validity of same-sex marriages across the EU v the US pre-*Obergefell*

The EU position

When determining the essential validity of any relationship, there is no consensus across the EU on the choice of law rule that ought to be applied. Whilst many Member States often refer to the law of each parties' nationality,[9] this is not guaranteed, and may be avoided if the application of such a rule would be contrary to public policy. Characteristically, the public policy doctrine provides the court with an escape clause in circumstances such that applying the normal choice of law rule would lead to a marriage that is contrary to their countries' public policy; it is a doctrine 'which when all else fails, can be relied on to ensure application of the lex fori.'[10] Furthermore, whilst it has been recognised that it is more usual within the EU to apply the personal law of each of the parties,[11] this is not definitive and jurisdictions may apply alternative choice of law rules. For instance, in England, the dual domicile theory[12] (in place of nationality) is often described as the most 'orthodox view.'[13] This theory applies the law of each parties' pre-nuptial domicile and is the approach which 'commands the most support in English law';[14] it is the only theory that is mentioned in respect of marriage validity in England on the EU database, which supplies information on the choice of law rules in operation in many of the EU Member States.[15] In reality, other choice of law rules, as explored in previous works, are in operation in England,[16] and specifically in relation to civil partnerships it is apparent from s.215(2) of the Civil Partnership

Act 2004, that the essential validity is governed by the *lex loci regsitrationis.*[17] Therefore, it cannot be said with any certainty that other Member States are not also derogating from what appears to be their most orthodox approach.

As a consequence, couples are left in a state of uncertainty surrounding their marital status as they move across the EU. Even when the applicable choice of law rule is apparent, the potential invocation of public policy exceptions makes determining a couple's status difficult, and it may come into question every time a couple crosses state borders. Though this is an area that has been developed through European Court of Human Rights case law such as *Oliari and Others v Italy*,[18] it is still a long way from being problem free. The case of *Oliari* was important in its requirement that all ECHR contracting states permit and recognise a form of civil union, as it means that all same-sex couples in a registered relationship within the European Council, and therefore the EU, should be entitled to some form of recognition. However, such an interpretation of *Oliari* – and thereby, its development of the law – is brought into question by Fenwick and Hayward's interpretation of the case, as they suggest that the requirement only extends to those countries that are socially accepting of same-sex relationships.[19] Regardless, as a result of subsidiarity, this did not extend to the recognition or permission to enter into a same-sex marriage, nor did it dictate the form of civil union or the rights attached to it. Consequently, couples may still face problems in respect of the rights that are attached to their relationship status depending upon the status they are given, and the level of rights that come with it. This may be particularly pertinent if they are married in accordance with their personal law, but move to a country that only offers a form of a civil union with far less rights attached to it than those of a marriage. Although this caused concern for a same-sex couples' right to free movement,[20] this has largely been addressed within the EU context in the recent CJEU case of *Coman*, which will be discussed further later in this chapter. However, other rights attached to marriage – such as financial provision on breakdown, succession and taxation implications – means that the problems caused by non-recognition as a marriage, remain significant and should be addressed. Furthermore, aside from the apparent ramifications of a limping marriage, other general policy concerns when assessing the validity of a marriage must also be considered, such as upholding the validity of marriage, simplicity in assessing validity and certainty.[21] Moreover, it is argued that additional policy concerns of citizenship, symbolism and equality apply when assessing same-sex relationships.[22] Thus, regardless of *Coman*, Europeanisation of the choice of law rules to allow for the continued recognition of a legitimate same-sex marriage remains vitally important.

The US position pre-Obergefell

Prior to the decision in *Obergefell*, inconsistent perspectives on validity of same-sex marriages blighted US state law precepts and, mirrored EU vacillations pre-*Oliari*. As a result of the Tenth Amendment to the Constitution of the United

States, which reserves certain powers to the states, family law is largely dealt with at a state level: '[B]ecause domestic relations belongs primarily to the localities of the states, America is a hotchpot of local and varying rules.'[23] Consequently, each state was able to have its own laws on same-sex relationships and the Defense of Marriage Act (DOMA) prevented states from having to recognise a same-sex marriage validly entered into in an alternative state. S.2 of DOMA provided that no state was required to give effect to any relationship between persons of the same sex that is treated as a marriage under the laws of another state, and therefore need not recognise any rights that may arise from that relationship when they have strong public policies to the contrary. S.3 stated that for the purposes of federal laws and rights, a marriage was a relationship between a man and a woman, and that the term 'spouse' referred only to person of the opposite sex who is a husband or wife. This, like the position under subsidiarity within the EU, meant that each state was able to determine whether it would recognise a same-sex relationship conducted in another state: it was 'within the prerogative of each individual state to determine what status to accord to same-sex couples who want to formalize their relationship and/or what rights should attach to such relationships.'[24] In a bid to ensure that same-sex marriages need not be recognised, many states introduced what were termed mini-DOMAs, declaring that same-sex marriages were not recognised within that state, and that a marriage was a relationship between a husband and a wife.[25] This, in turn, meant that a same-sex marriage could be deemed valid in one state but not in the next, with beguiling 'limping marriage' ramifications.

Similarly to the position in the EU, prior to the *Obergefell* decision, in addition to s.2 of DOMA meaning a same-sex marriage need not be recognised in other states, varying choice of law rules in use across the states made it difficult to ascertain the law that would be applied, and thus whether the marriage would be recognised.[26] The choice of law rules at play included the First Restatement of the Conflict of Laws,[27] interest analysis[28] and the Second Restatement of the Conflict of Laws.[29] Restatements of Law, whilst persuasive, are not binding, and so states were free to apply any of those choice of law rules, or an alternative, when assessing validity; there was no 'dominant view on how to mediate among the interests of the celebrating state, the domiciliary state, and other states.'[30] Though it is not necessary to understand the rules in detail, a brief explanation offers insight into how recognition of same-sex marriages may have altered from state to state.

In accordance with the Restatement First, the applicable law is that of the state where the marriage occurred[31] and is thus not too dissimilar to the *lex loci regsitrationis*, mentioned earlier, that is used within the Civil Partnership Act. Alternatively, interest analysis in its most basic form is the application of the law of the state with the most interest in the marriage, and in instances where there is more than one state with an interest, the *lex fori*[32] was originally held to apply. Finally, the Restatement Second applies the law of the state that has the most significant relationship to the spouses and marriage under s.283(1) or, under s.283(2), considers it valid if the marriage was valid where contracted, unless it violates the strong public policy of another state which has the most significant relationship at the time of the marriage. What is evident here is that validity could be dependent upon which rule was applied. For instance, if the couple married in a state that permitted same-sex marriage and very quickly thereafter moved to a state that did not, the marriage may be valid under the Restatement First, but not for instance under s.283(1) of the Restatement Second if that state has the most significant relationship to the spouses.[33] Moreover, as with the EU, utilisation of public policy as an escape clause is possible under the Restatement Second, adding a further layer of complexity and uncertainty to the recognition of marriages. It is therefore evident that prior to *Obergefell*, the uncertainty surrounding the recognition of same-sex marriages, and the potential for limping marriages in the US mirrored the position of same-sex marriages migrating around EU Member States.

Obergefell: harmony from the US Supreme Court

Under DOMA, and in accordance with federal law, states were free to refuse recognition of same-sex marriages, as federally, the term 'spouse' only applied to a person who was married to a person of the opposite sex.[34] This began to evolve in the 2013 case of *United States v Windsor*.[35] The case involved two female residents of New York who had entered into a valid marriage in Ontario before returning to New York where their marriage was recognised. Regardless of this recognition, as a result of DOMA, upon the death of her wife, Mrs Windsor was required to pay estate tax, as she did not qualify for spousal exemption under the s.3 definition of spouse. The United States District Court and the Court of Appeals ruled that s.3 was unconstitutional as it violated the Due Process Clause of the Fifth Amendment, in failing to provide liberty and equality to all. The court thereby ordered the US government to refund Mrs Windsor, and the decision was later upheld by the US Supreme Court. Although this did not result in the legalisation of same-sex marriage, it was a 'civil rights landmark,'[36] and led federal district courts in other states to invalidate state prohibitions on same-sex marriage.[37] It was, therefore, an important incremental step because whilst s.2 permitted states to determine the validity of same-sex marriages, it was the start of a chain reaction, it caused states to stop and think about their approach.[38]

Obergefell then took these developments much further and required that all states permit same-sex marriage. The Supreme Court case was a consolidation of various cases in which couples had sought the right to marry or have their marriage recognised in a different state. In a majority ruling it was held, first, that the right to marry was a fundamental right inherent in the liberty of the person, and under the Due Process and Equal Protection Clauses of the Fourteenth Amendment, couples of the same sex may not be deprived of that right and that liberty. Second, it was decided that states must recognise lawful same-sex marriages performed in other states. In the leading judgement, Justice Kennedy recognised that: 'Being married in one state but having that valid marriage denied in another is one of "the most perplexing and distressing complication[s]" in the law of domestic relations.'[39] Justice Kennedy also recognised that: 'Leaving the current state of affairs in place would maintain and promote instability and uncertainty.'[40] This demonstrates not only a recognition of the unconstitutional nature of s.2 of DOMA, but also the problems caused to same-sex couples through uncertainty and non-recognition.

In ensuring that same-sex couples could marry and have their marriages recognised in all fifty states, the judgement was monumental, not least for what it achieved, but for doing so amidst controversy. This was a decision that made tremendous strides in US law, and this was partly due to its controversial nature, as the law was 'anything but settled with respect to same-sex marriage.'[41] At the time of the ruling, not all US states permitted same-sex marriage, and indeed, some had continued in that vein despite court rulings within their respective states that the ban was unconstitutional.[42] The decision, due to its federal nature, therefore forced same-sex marriage upon states that were clearly not ready to legalise it, and this juxtaposition is certainly of fundamental significance given the dissonant views on same-sex marriage amongst the Member States of the EU. It demonstrates that harmonisation is possible at a supranational level regardless of opposing states, and will be explored further when discussing the use of *Obergefell* as a 'precedent' for positivist change across the EU.

Finally, it is important to note that in addition to the controversial nature of the decision in *Obergefell*, family law is not usually an aspect of law that is controlled at a federal level. Under the federal legal structure, certain basic rights and laws are dealt with federally, and then a state may expand on these to create a more comprehensive set of rights and laws for its citizens. Furthermore, the Tenth Amendment reserves certain powers to the states, and one such power is the right to control family law legislation. Consequently, when dealing with family law matters, it is generally state law that is of importance, and it is the state Supreme Court that would have final say on the matter; however, this does not wholly prevent federal intervention. This is of particular significance when considering that a potential criticism of harmonisation of choice of law rules in this area across the EU could be that the EU is not competent to legislate on family law, and this will be discussed in greater detail later in this research. Regardless of the norms pertaining to the regulation of family law, *Obergefell* is evidence of what can be achieved by a unified decision. This critique will now analyse the extent to which *Obergefell* supports the promulgation that harmonisation of choice of law rules for same-sex relationships can be achieved across the EU.

A precedent for change?

The drive for harmonisation originates from the uncertainty same-sex couples face when they cross state borders, and in relation to complementary rights attached to their marital status.[43] Arguments around equality, and the emotive impact on the couple as a result of the symbolic nature of marriage, also added to these factorisations. This impact was, as noted in the previous section, recognised by Justice Kennedy in *Obergefell*, as being 'perplexing' and 'distressing.' Importantly, Justice Kennedy recognised that without change, the situation would only worsen across the US, as more same-sex marriages would lead to the potential for more same-sex couples crossing state borders where their marriages would not be recognised: 'In light of the fact that many states already allow same-sex marriage and hundreds of thousands of those marriages already have occurred – the disruption caused by the recognition bans is significant and ever growing.'[44] The same is true within the EU. Whilst many Member States now permit same-sex marriage, thereby increasing the number of marriages, there are still states that do not,[45] and so there is an increased number of married couples who may face problems of non-recognition when entering such jurisdictions. Academicians, including Curry-Sumner, in similar vein to the plan for holistic recognition made by Justice Kennedy in *Obergefell*, have recognised that this further adds to the need for change: '[A]s long as private international law rules remain national, application of these rules could lead to decisional discord and limping relationships.'[46] With the same concerns around uncertainty for couples crossing state borders, and the ever increasing number of couples who have the potential to face such problems, it is apparent that the EU has the same need for harmonisation in this area, and, thus, *Obergefell* could act as a precedent for beneficial recalibration.

One of the primary concerns that could be raised in relation to the proposal of harmonisation of the choice of law rule is that Member States may, on occasion, be required to recognise a marriage it would not permit in its own borders, and thus the proposal could be argued to be going too far, too fast. This is where *Obergefell* as a precedent highlights that harmonisation is achievable. Whilst the EU consists of Member States which are able to determine their own laws on the ability of same-sex couples to marry, and indeed the recognition of existing marriages, the fifty states of the US had the same capability prior to the ruling in *Obergefell*. Furthermore, as already set out, both jurisdictions had states that permitted and recognised same-sex marriage, and states that did not, and regardless of those US states that did not, the judiciary still felt able to come to the decision that they did. It is on this premise that it is suggested that harmonisation can be achieved despite some EU Member States not currently recognising same-sex marriages.[47] When countering the argument of going too far, too fast, it is crucial to note that whilst *Obergefell* required all US states to permit same-sex marriage, and thus provide same-sex couples with a licence to marry, despite the states which had until that time banned such relationships, the iteration herein propounds the less dramatic reformulation of a harmonised choice of law rule as opposed to substantive law. Therefore, whilst a Member State may, in accordance with harmonisation, be required to recognise a same-sex marriage, it would not permit the celebration of in its own borders; this is a less dramatic reform than was accomplished across the fifty states of the US, therefore strengthening the argument that Europeanisation can be achieved.

Finally, when considering *Obergefell* as a precedent for harmonisation, the very fact that family law would not normally be dealt with at a federal level is significant. Historically, 'The lack of competence of the EC to regulate family law has been recognised by the ECJ [CJEU].'[48] This sentiment was also concurred with in the UK House of Lords in its report on the Rome III proposal,[49] in which the EU sought to harmonise the choice of law rules to determine the applicable law in divorce cases.[50] In more recent times, EU involvement within family law has grown due to the likes of Brussels II legislation[51] that provides uniform rules for jurisdiction in divorce proceedings. This legislation has been described as a 'watershed in the evolution of EU family law,'[52] and runs alongside the establishment of the Commission on European Family Law in 2001. However, regardless of the advancement, it may still be suggested that harmonisation within family law is not a matter for the EU. Therefore, the fact that the same argument could have been made in the US, and the Supreme Court made the pronouncement regardless, is significant in the argument for harmonisation. It shows that whilst some may object, this does not, and should not, prevent harmonisation. US state law in this area created a 'hotchpot' of various rules that led to 'instability and uncertainty' that could only be fixed at a federal level; the 'federal legal system create[d] confusion, contentious conflicts of law and unsettling legal outcomes.'[53] Likewise, a combination of Member State substantive law, and individualised choice of law rules, hamper 'the sound operation of the internal market [and] [T]here are accordingly grounds for enacting provisions to unify the rules.'[54] Certainty across the EU is not something which can be achieved at a state level, but instead, requires internationalisation.[55]

Read together, these crucial factors within *Obergefell* convey that harmonisation of the choice of law rules for same-sex marriage is achievable. Although the US and the EU are far from carbon copies of each other's legal systems, they are, in essence, a group of states with differing, and at times controversial, laws within an overarching system. This has been recognised by Weiss in his comparisons of the EU with the US prior to *Obergefell*, and he describes the EU as a federal system, on the understanding that 'federal' means a division of sovereignty between two superimposed levels of government.[56] Similarly, Aballe recognises the likeness between the two unions, describing them as building on an 'interstate private law . . . to ensure legal certainty.'[57] It is therefore argued, that if the laws on the controversial matter of same-sex marriage can be unified across the fifty states of the US, so too can the choice of law rules on the essential validity of same-sex relationships across the current twenty-eight Member States of the EU.[58] Whilst this may appear a dramatic shift, *Obergefell* provides a precedent for more by unifying substantive law in a similarly controversial terrain of states. Though this author recognises that across the EU, there are countries with potentially greater cultural and societal differences,[59] when drawing together the decision in *Obergefell*, Weiss' arguments around similarities in legal structure, and the fact that harmonisation of the choice of law rules alone is sought as opposed to substantive law on same-sex marriage, it is promulgated that the proposal is within the realms of legislative responsiveness.

Obergefell: the dissenters

Obergefell was not a unanimous decision, and thus its use as a precedent for change may be subject to criticism. Such criticism may, however, be refuted upon analysis of the reason behind the dissenting judgements. The disagreement across the bench came not as a result of the arguments in favour of extending marriage to same-sex couples not being compelling, but because the legal requirement for the judiciary to make said extension was not. Chief Justice Roberts was of the opinion that it was not within the court's role to change each state's definition of marriage: 'Under the Constitution, judges have the power to say what the law is, not what it should be.'[60] Thus, rather than acting as a criticism of the assertions made herein, this author propounds that the concerns raised by Chief Justice Roberts and the others who dissented in *Obergefell* act as support for the approach suggested. To date, whilst the European Court of Human Rights has made pronouncements in the arena of same-sex relationships, like the dissenters, it has felt unable to require the respective states to recognise same-sex marriages due to the margin of appreciation and the dissonance between contracting states.[61] The CJEU has had similar reservations until the recent decision in *Coman*, which whilst demonstrating progress, demonstrates it in a limited regard, as recognition applies only in respect of permitting free movement. Thus, with insufficient development within the courtroom, an alternative approach is required. It is propounded that instead, a Regulation is needed within the area, in turn dispelling Chief Justice Roberts' concerns about judicial over-stepping.

The impact of *Coman*

As indicated, the uncertainty faced by same-sex couples when crossing state borders has, until recently, had the potential to affect free movement rights when one of the parties to a same-sex marriage is a third-country national. Though *Coman* appears to have alleviated such concerns, it is important that the case and its effects on the perspective are analysed. The case concerned Mr Coman, who held dual Romanian and US citizenship, and Mr Hamilton, who was a US citizen. After living in the US together for a period of four years, Mr Coman moved to Brussels in order to work at the European Parliament, before seeking to return to live in Romania with Mr Hamilton. During Mr Coman's time living in Brussels, the couple married, and in seeking to return to Romania, Mr Coman requested that Mr Hamilton be permitted to reside there with him for a period of more than three months as his spouse and family member. As Romania did not permit or recognise marriage between parties of the same sex, this was denied, and the couple contested the decision at the Constitutional Court of Romania, which in turn sought a preliminary ruling. In providing the preliminary ruling, the CJEU held that where a union citizen has exercised their right to free movement under Art 21(1) of the Treaty of the Functioning of the European Union (TFEU), and family life has been strengthened or created in that time, such family life should be able to continue upon their return to their country of nationality. In turn, their spouse, as a third-country national, should then be given a derived right of residence, as a refusal to do so would interfere with the union citizen's right to free movement. In essence, it means that where a same-sex couple have genuinely resided in a different Member State and have married in accordance with its laws, their home state will be required to recognise that marriage for the purpose of enabling citizens to exercise their rights to free movement protected under EU law – meaning, in cases like *Coman*, an EU citizen would be able to return to live in their home state with their spouse, regardless of their country's law on same-sex marriage.

In addition to situations like Mr Coman's, it is possible to see how the same rules would apply to an analogous case in which the EU citizen was using their free movement rights to move to an alternative Member State that did not recognise same-sex marriage, and wished for their spouse to reside with them. This analogy is possible because, again, their rights to free movement under Art 21(1) TFEU would be denied if their spouse would not be recognised as such, and they would be unable to move with them under Art 2(2)(a) of Directive 2004/38.[62] In fact, this was the initial question put to the CJEU in *Coman*, but the court held that under those particular set of facts, this was not the question that needed to be answered, as the Directive only applies to citizens who wish to enter and reside in a Member State other than that of which they are a national.[63] On that premise, it would appear that *Coman* prevents previously expressed concerns that without a unified choice of law rule, those in a same-sex marriage may be denied their rights to free movement.[64] However, it is contested that, whilst free movement concerns may have been put to bed in this regard, it does not completely dispel the problems faced within immigration.

In analysing the judgement, it is propounded that a same-sex couple who have lived and married in a non-EU country, and only one of the parties is an EU national, may face difficulties when seeking to return to the EU citizen's state of nationality under current law. In the *Coman* judgement, the Grand Chamber stated that the 2004/38 Directive 'does not confer a derived right of residence on third-country nationals who are family members of the Union citizen in the Member State of which the citizen is a national.'[65] This is because the Directive only applies when a Union citizen is seeking to enter and reside in an alternative state. Whilst in the case of *Coman*, Art 21(1) TFEU could still be relied upon as an analogous situation because Mr Coman was seeking to return to Romania, having exercised his right to free movement, this would not be the case if he had moved to, and married in, a non-EU country. In the event of moving to a non-EU country, EU free movement rights are not invoked; therefore, if the home state does not recognise same-sex spouses as 'spouses,' the third-country national may be unable to accompany them. Without the scope for raising the rights to free movement under Art 21(1) TFEU as guaranteed by *Coman*, problems can still arise in a modern migratory society. The need for change is then yet further emphasised when considering that same hypothetical couple's ability to move to another EU state. The couple, due to national legislation of the citizen's home state, may be prevented from returning from a third country and residing as a family, yet EU law would, as a result of *Coman*, mean their marriage was recognised in an alternative EU Member State; the couple would have more rights to live in a country that they had no real connection to than they would to return to the one of the parties' home states in their chosen relationship.

It is suggested that these advancements in *Coman* add further weight to the argument that harmonisation in this area can be achieved, and that it, and *Obergefell*, are precedents for such change whilst demonstrating the proposition is not guilty of going 'too far, too fast.' Despite the differing approaches to same-sex marriage across the EU, it has previously been argued that the choice of law rule in determining recognition could be harmonised.[66] This research highlights that if *Obergefell* can be decided in the way it was under similar circumstances, such harmonisation is achievable. *Coman* adds weight to this argument as the CJEU has, although only in respect of the right to free movement, required all Member States to recognise same-sex marriages that have been lawfully entered into. Given that the arguments propounded herein only seek to harmonise the choice of law rules as opposed to substantive law, it, like *Coman*, is only about recognition for the purpose of associated rights, and when combining the results achieved in these two cases, there is no reason to believe it is not possible. Taking such an approach could be considered the next step in an incremental approach, as previously iterated by Hamilton, to achieve same-sex marriage across the EU without 'backlash.'[67] Furthermore, whilst *Coman* addresses issues around free movement, a loophole in recognition remains for EU citizens moving outside of the EU before returning to their home state, thereby demonstrating that harmonisation is essential to ensure that those who have emigrated are not prevented from returning. Likewise, with *Coman* only addressing the right to residence, as opposed to recognition for all purposes, the denial of other associated rights is likely to mean that an EU citizen's rights to free movement remain at least indirectly affected. If a couple is allowed to reside, but is for all intents and purposes still not considered married, the loss of marital status in relation to other associated rights, and indeed, the loss of said status within society in of itself, may prevent couples from exercising their rights to free movement: 'same-sex couples are less likely to move to such Member States if, as the U.S. Supreme Court recently stated in *Obergefell v Hodges*, their marriage 'is stripped from them . . . as they travel across state lines.'[68]

Conclusion

This is an area that lacks certainty that can only really begin to be achieved through harmonisation as a consequence of large-scale migration. Regardless of this need for change, it is anticipated that, as a result of some Member States taking a very different view of same-sex marriage than others, such an approach could be criticised for going 'too far, too fast.' The pragmatic reality is rather different; *Obergefell*, combined with the recent decision in *Coman*, demonstrates that harmonisation is achievable in spite of the potential for resistance from some Member States.

In making its judgement in *Obergefell*, the US Supreme Court recognised the uncertainty faced by same-sex couples crossing state borders, and the problems they may face as a consequence of non-recognition of their marital status. They, therefore, sought to rectify this despite the controversy that would surround such a decision. In doing so, they act as a comparator and an example of what can be achieved. With a very similar landscape in respect of differing state laws, the court was able to achieve harmonisation of a higher order than that proposed for the EU, by harmonising substantive law on the area. This, in turn, demonstrates that the proposition is achievable, which is then furthered by the recent judgement in *Coman*, as all Member States are now required to recognise same-sex marriage for at least one purpose. Straddling these cases, it is argued that harmonisation of the choice of law rules for same-sex relationships across the EU is achievable. Whilst some commentators may criticise such an approach,[69] *Obergefell* is a precedent for harmonisation within this area, and provides evidence that this is essential and should be achieved. This is furthered by the *Coman* decision, which requires all Member States to recognise same-sex marriages for the purpose of free movement, and acts as a stepping stone to the further recognition required in terms of all same-sex marriages being recognised that have been lawfully entered into, and have been subsisting for a reasonable period of time. Thus, whilst criticism may be levelled at the recommendation of harmonisation, the combined effect of *Obergefell* and *Coman* is to signify that it is not a step 'too far, too fast,' but is instead the requisite step in achieving certainty for same-sex couples across the EU.

In demonstrating that there is support for the previous postulation for harmonisation, this article provides further backing for the effective and complementary harmonisation of choice of law rules within the essential validity of same-sex marriages. In utilising *Obergefell* and *Coman* as precedents for change, the debate in this area now goes beyond initial suggestions for reform, and evidences why, regardless of criticism or dissonant Member State rules, reform is still absolutely possible: it demonstrates that there is sustenance to the holistic clarion calls for harmonisation.

Notes

1 *Oliari and Others v Italy* App Nos. 18766/11 and 36030/11 (ECtHR, 21 July 2015).

2 The recent decision in Case 673/16 *Relu Adrian Coman, Robert Clabourn Hamilton, Asociaţia Accept v Inspectoratul General pentru Imigrări, Ministerul Afacerilor Interne* ECLI:EU:C:2018:2 introduced the requirement that same-sex marriages must be recognised for the purposes of free movement of EU citizens and their families.

3 Essential validity deals with issues of validity aside from formalities, and though not the only element of essential validity, the main example – and the one discussed in this chapter – is the capacity to marry. For instance, whether at their age parties had capacity, or in this chapter, whether couples of the same sex have capacity to marry.
4 Frances Hamilton and Lauren Clayton-Helm, 'Same-Sex Relationships, Choice of Law and the Continued Recognised Relationship Theory' (2016) 3 *Journal of International and Comparative Law* 1.
5 *Obergefell v Hodges* 576 US, 135 S Ct 2584 (2015).
6 *Coman* (n 2).
7 Hamilton and Clayton-Helm (n 4).
8 Ibid., 27–28.
9 Examples include France in accordance with Art 3 of the French Civil Code, Italy in accordance with Art 27 of Act 218 of 31st May 1995, and Germany under Art 13(1) of the Introductory Act to the Civil Code.
10 CMV Clarkson, 'Marriage in England: Favouring the Lex Fori' (1990) 10 *Legal Studies* 80, 86.
11 Helen Toner, *Partnership Rights, Free Movement and EU Law* (Hart Publishing 2004) 44.
12 As propounded by Dicey in John Morris, *Dicey and Morris on the Conflict of Laws* (8th edn, Stevens 1967) Rule 31 at 254–255.
13 David McClean and Kisch Beevers, *Morris: The Conflict of Laws* (7th edn, Thomson Reuters (legal) Limited 2009) 211.
14 CMV Clarkson and Jonathan Hill, *Clarkson & Hill's Conflict of Laws* (4th edn, Oxford University Press 2011) 355.
15 European Commission, 'Applicable Law – England and Wales' (6 October 2006) <http://ec.europa.eu/civiljustice/applicable_law/applicable_law_eng_en.htm> accessed 11 January 2019.
16 Hamilton and Clayton-Helm (n 4).
17 The law of the place where the relationship was registered.
18 *Oliari and Others* (n 1).
19 For comment, see Helen Fenwick and Andy Hayward, 'Rejecting Asymmetry of Access to Formal Relationship Statuses for Same and Different-Sex Couples at Strasbourg and Domestically' (2017) 6 *European Human Rights Law Review* 545.
20 Hamilton and Clayton-Helm (n 4) 26.
21 See Michael Davie, 'The Breaking-Up of Essential Validity of Marriage Choice of Law Rules in English Conflict of Laws' (1994) 23 *Anglo-American Law Review* 32 and Alan Reed, 'Essential Validity of Marriage: The Application of Interest Analysis and Dépeçage to Anglo-American Choice of Law Rules' (2000) 20 *New York Law School Journal of International and Comparative Law* 387.
22 Hamilton and Clayton-Helm (n 4) 17–21.
23 Walter Wadlington and Raymond C O'Brien, *Family Law in Perspective* (2nd edn, The Foundation Press 2007) 19.
24 Linda Silberman, 'Same-Sex Marriage Refining the Conflict of Laws Analysis' (2004–2005) 153 *University of Pennsylvania Law Review* 2195.
25 States with mini-DOMAs included Texas, Ohio, Mississippi and Tennessee.
26 Wardle, in her research points to six possible positions across the states in, Lynn D Wardle, 'From Slavery to Same-Sex Marriage: Comity Versus Public Policy in Inter-Jurisdictional Recognition of Controversial Domestic Relations' (2008) *Brigham Young University Law Review* 1855.
27 Restatement (First) of Conflict of Laws (1934), hereafter referred to as the Restatement First.

28 As introduced by Brainerd Currie in Brainerd Currie, *Selected Essays on the Conflict of Laws* (Duke University Press 1963).
29 Restatement (Second) of Conflict of Laws (1971), hereafter referred to as the Restatement Second.
30 William Baude, 'Beyond DOMA: Choice of State Law in Federal Statues' (2012) 64 *Stanford Law Review* 1371, 1387.
31 Restatement (First) of Conflict of Laws (n 27) s121.
32 The law of the forum.
33 Whilst not in relation to same-sex marriage, the potential for such an outcome is evidenced in the differing outcomes of *Wilkins v Zelichowski* 140 A 2d 65, 26 NJ 370 (NJ 1958) and in *Re May's Estate* 144 NE 2d 4 (NY 1963) in which the Restatement First was applied in one case to find the marriage valid, and in the other applied the exception within the Restatement First to invalidate the marriage – contrasting approaches were taken.
34 Defense of Marriage Act (1996) 110 Stat 2419, s3.
35 *United States v Windsor* 133 S Ct 2675 (2013).
36 Adam Liptak, 'Supreme Court Bolsters Gay Marriage with Two Major Rulings' *New York Times* (New York, 26 June 2013) <www.nytimes.com/2013/06/27/us/politics/supreme-court-gay-marriage.htlm?pagewanted=all> accessed 11 August 2017.
37 See, for instance, in Virginia: *Bostic v Rainey* 970 F Supp 2d 456 (US District Court Eastern District VA 2014); in Kentucky: *Bourke v Beshear* 996 F Supp 2d 542 (US District Court Western District KY 2014); and in Michigan; *Deborah v Snyder* 772 F 3d 388 (MI 2014).
38 Liptak (n 36).
39 *Obergefell* (n 5) 2607, referencing to *Williams v North Carolina* 317 US 287, 299, 63 S Ct 207, 87 L Ed 279 (1942).
40 *Obergefell* (n 5) 2607.
41 Sheldon D Pollock, 'Same-Sex Marriage and the Conflict of Law: The "Other" Constitutional Issue' (2015) 13 *Georgetown Journal of Law and Public Policy* 477, 485.
42 Prior to *Obergefell v Hodges* same-sex marriage was banned in North Dakota, Michigan, Ohio, Kentucky, Tennessee, Georgia and Louisiana. The ban had also been ruled unconstitutional, but was still in place in Alabama, Arkansas, Mississippi, Missouri, Nebraska, South Dakota and Texas. See 'Local Government Responses to Obergefell v. Hodges' *Ballotpedia* (1 July 2015) <http://ballotpedia.org/local_government_responses_to_Obergefell_v._Hodges#Background_of_local_control_in_same-sex_marriage> accessed 23 March 2016.
43 Hamilton and Clayton-Helm (n 4).
44 *Obergefell* (n 5) 2607.
45 For example, Italy and Cyprus.
46 Ian Curry-Sumner, 'Interstate Recognition of Same-Sex Relationships in Europe' (2009) 13(1) *The Journal of Gender, Race & Justice* 59, 60.
47 Such harmonisation of 'common conflict rules' was also suggested by Melcher to ensure validly acquired statuses are not changed or lost abroad, in Martina Melcher, '(Mutual) Recognition of Registered Relationships via EU Private International Law' (2013) 9 *Journal of Private International Law* 149, 152.
48 Aude Fiorini, 'Rome III – Choice of Law in Divorce: Is the Europeanization of Family Law Going Too Far?' (2008) 22 *International Journal of Law, Policy and the Family* 178, 192.

49 The Rome III Proposal (Commission, 'Proposal for Council Regulation Amending Regulation [EC] No. 2201/2003 as Regards Jurisdiction and Introducing Rules Concerning Applicable Law in Matrimonial Matters' COM [2006] 399 Final) was proposed with the aim of harmonising the choice of law rule to determine the applicable law in divorce cases.
50 House of Lords European Union Committee, *Rome III – Choice of Law in Divorce* (HL 2005–06 272) Written evidence 34.
51 Council Regulation (EC) 1347/2000 of 29 May 2000 on jurisdiction and the recognition and enforcement of judgments in matrimonial matters and in matters of parental responsibility for children of both spouses (Brussels II) (2000) OJ L160/19.
52 Marie Ni Shuilleabhain, 'Ten Years of European Family Law: Retrospective Reflections from a Common Law Perspective' (2010) 59 *International Comparative Law Quarterly* 1021, 1022.
53 Pollock (n 41) 500.
54 Brussels II (n 51), Recital 4 (while this argument was made in relation to matters of divorce and parental responsibility, it is argued that it equally applies to marriage recognition due to the impact on associated rights).
55 Curry-Sumner (n 46).
56 Adam Weiss, 'Federalism and the Gay Family: Free Movement of Same-Sex Couples in the United States and the European Union' (2007) 41 *Columbia Journal of Law and Social Problems* 81.
57 Vanessa Abballe, 'Comparative Perspectives of the Articulation of Horizontal Interjurisdictional Relations in the United States and the European Union: The Federalization of Civil Justice' (2009) 15 *New England Journal of International and Comparative Law* 1, 1.
58 This chapter is written at a time when the United Kingdom's future as a Member State is unclear. It is however stressed that whether the UK is a Member State or not, harmonisation across the Member States can and should be achieved.
59 Such differences were recognised by Ni Shuilleabhain when discussing the differences in the approach to substantive family law across the EU in (n 52) 1049–1050.
60 *Obergefell* (n 5) 2611.
61 *Schalk and Kopf v Austria* App No. 30141/04 (ECtHR, 24 June 2010), para 105, as was reiterated in *Orlandi and Others v Italy* App Nos. 26431/12, 26742/12, 44057/12 and 60088/12 (ECtHR, 14 December 2017), para 192.
62 Directive 2004/38 EC of the European Parliament and of the Council of 29 April 2004 on the right of citizens of the Union and their family members to move and reside freely within the territory of the Member States (2004) OJ L158/77.
63 *Coman* (n 2) para 20.
64 Hamilton and Clayton-Helm (n 4).
65 *Coman* (n 2) para 20.
66 Hamilton and Clayton-Helm (n 4).
67 Frances Hamilton, 'Strategies to Achieve Same-Sex Marriage and the Method of Incrementalist Change' (2015–2016) 25 *Journal of Transnational Law & Policy* 121.
68 Martijn Van Den Brink, 'What's in a Name Case? Some Lessons for the Debate Over the Free Movement of Same-Sex Couples Within the EU' (2016) 17(3) *German Law Journal* 421, 422, quoting *Obergefell* (n 5) 2595.
69 See Dale Carpenter, 'A Traditionalist Case for Gay Marriage' (2008) 50 *South Texas Law Review* 93 as discussed further by Hamilton and Clayton-Helm (n 4) 27–28.

References

Primary sources

Art 13(1) of the Introductory Act to the Civil Code (Germany).
Art 21(1) of the Treaty of the Functioning of the European Union (TFEU).
Art 27 of Act 218 of 31 May 1995 (Italy).
Art 3 of the French Civil Code.
Bostic v Rainey 970 F Supp 2d 456 (US District Court Eastern District VA 2014).
Bourke v Beshear 996 F Supp 2d 542 (US District Court Western District KY 2014).
Civil Partnership Act 2004.
Constitution of the United States.
Council Regulation (EC) 1347/2000 of 29 May 2000 on jurisdiction and the recognition and enforcement of judgments in matrimonial matters and in matters of parental responsibility for children of both spouses (Brussels II) (2000) OJ L160/19.
Deborah v Snyder 772 F 3d 388 (MI 2014).
Defense of Marriage Act (1996) 110 Stat 2419.
Directive 2004/38 EC of the European Parliament and of the Council of 29 April 2004 on the right of citizens of the Union and their family members to move and reside freely within the territory of the Member States (2004) OJ L158/77.
May's Estate, Re, 144 NE 2d 4 (NY 1963).
Obergefell v Hodges 576 US, 135 S Ct 2584 (2015).
Oliari and Others v Italy App Nos. 18766/11 and 36030/11 (ECtHR, 21 July 2015).
Orlandi and Others v Italy App Nos. 26431/12, 26742/12, 44057/12 and 60088/12 (ECtHR, 14 December 2017).
Relu Adrian Coman, Robert Clabourn Hamilton, Asociaţia Accept v Inspectoratul General pentru Imigrări, Ministerul Afacerilor Interne (C-673/16) ECLI:EU:C:2018:2.
Restatement (First) of Conflict of Laws (1934).
Restatement (Second) of Conflict of Laws (1971).
Schalk and Kopf v Austria App No. 30141/04 (ECtHR, 24 June 2010).
United States v Windsor 133 S Ct 2675 (2013).
Wilkins v Zelichowski 140 A 2d 65, 26 NJ 370 (NJ 1958).
Williams v North Carolina 317 US 287, 299, 63 S Ct 207, 87 L Ed 279 (1942).

Secondary sources

Abballe V, 'Comparative Perspectives of the Articulation of Horizontal Interjurisdictional Relations in the United States and the European Union: The Federalization of Civil Justice' (2009) 15 *New England Journal of International and Comparative Law* 1.
Baude W, 'Beyond DOMA: Choice of State Law in Federal Statues' (2012) 64 *Stanford Law Review* 1371, 1387.
Carpenter D, 'A Traditionalist Case for Gay Marriage' (2008) 50 *South Texas Law Review* 93.
Clarkson CMV, 'Marriage in England: Favouring the Lex Fori' (1990) 10 *Legal Studies* 80.

Clarkson CMV and Hill J, *Clarkson & Hill's Conflict of Laws* (4th edn, Oxford University Press 2011).

Commission, 'Proposal for Council Regulation Amending Regulation (EC) No. 2201/2003 as Regards Jurisdiction and Introducing Rules Concerning Applicable Law in Matrimonial Matters' COM (2006) 399 final.

Currie B, *Selected Essays on the Conflict of Laws* (Duke University Press 1963).

Curry-Sumner I, 'Interstate Recognition of Same-Sex Relationships in Europe' (2009) 13(1) *The Journal of Gender, Race & Justice* 59.

Davie M, 'The Breaking-Up of Essential Validity of Marriage Choice of Law Rules in English Conflict of Laws' (1994) 23 *Anglo-American Law Review* 32.

European Commission, 'Applicable Law – England and Wales' (6 October 2006) <http://ec.europa.eu/civiljustice/applicable_law/applicable_law_eng_en.htm> accessed 11 January 2019.

Fenwick H and Hayward A, 'Rejecting Asymmetry of Access to Formal Relationship Statuses for Same and Different-Sex Couples at Strasbourg and Domestically' (2017) 6 *European Human Rights Law Review* 545.

Fiorini A, 'Rome III – Choice of Law in Divorce: Is the Europeanization of Family Law Going Too Far?' (2008) 22 *International Journal of Law, Policy and the Family* 178.

Hamilton F, 'Strategies to Achieve Same-Sex Marriage and the Method of Incrementalist Change' (2015–2016) 25 *Journal of Transnational Law & Policy* 121.

Hamilton F and Clayton-Helm L, 'Same-Sex Relationships, Choice of Law and the Continued Recognised Relationship Theory' (2016) 3 *Journal of International and Comparative Law* 1.

House of Lords European Union Committee, *Rome III – Choice of Law in Divorce* (HL 2005–06 272) Written evidence 34.

Liptak A, 'Supreme Court Bolsters Gay Marriage with Two Major Rulings' *New York Times* (26 June 2013) <www.nytimes.com/2013/06/27/us/politics/supreme-court-gay-marriage.htlm?pagewanted=all> accessed 11 August 2017.

'Local government responses to Obergefell v. Hodges' *Ballotpedia* (1 July 2015) <http://ballotpedia.org/local_government_responses_to_Obergefell_v._Hodges#Background_of_local_control_in_same-sex_marriage> accessed 23 March 2016.

McClean D and Beevers K, *Morris: The Conflict of Laws* (7th edn, Thomson Reuters (legal) Limited 2009).

Melcher M, '(Mutual) Recognition of Registered Relationships via EU Private International Law' (2013) 9 *Journal of Private International Law* 149.

Morris J, *Dicey and Morris on the Conflict of Laws* (8th edn, Stevens 1967).

Pollock SD, 'Same-Sex Marriage and the Conflict of Law: The "Other" Constitutional Issue' (2015) 13 *Georgetown Journal of Law and Public Policy* 477.

Reed A, 'Essential Validity of Marriage: The Application of Interest Analysis and Dépeçage to Anglo-American Choice of Law Rules' (2000) 20 *New York Law School Journal of International and Comparative Law* 387.

Shuilleabhain MNI, 'Ten Years of European Family Law: Retrospective Reflections from a Common Law Perspective' (2010) 59 *International Comparative Law Quarterly* 1021.

Silberman L, 'Same-Sex Marriage Refining the Conflict of Laws Analysis' (2004–2005) 153 *University of Pennsylvania Law Review* 2195.

Toner H, *Partnership Rights, Free Movement and EU Law* (Hart Publishing 2004).

Van Den Brink M, 'What's in a Name Case? Some Lessons for the Debate Over the Free Movement of Same-Sex Couples Within the EU' (2016) 17(3) *German Law Journal* 421.

Wadlington W and O'Brien RC, *Family Law in Perspective* (2nd edn, The Foundation Press 2007).

Wardle LD, 'From Slavery to Same-Sex Marriage: Comity Versus Public Policy in Inter-Jurisdictional Recognition of Controversial Domestic Relations' (2008) *Brigham Young University Law Review* 1855.

Weiss A, 'Federalism and the Gay Family: Free Movement of Same-Sex Couples in the United States and the European Union' (2007) 41 *Columbia Journal of Law and Social Problems* 81.

Part 2

Differing paths towards legalisation of same-sex marriage

Chapter 4

Marriage equality in Ireland

The politico-legal context*

Brian Tobin

Introduction

On 22 May 2015, the Marriage Equality Referendum was held in the Republic of Ireland. The people of Ireland were asked to vote on whether they wanted to make express provision for same-sex marriage in the Irish Constitution. By noon the following day, it was clear that a significant majority of those who had turned out to vote had voted in favour of the proposed constitutional amendment, Article 41.4, which provides that "marriage may be contracted in accordance with law by two persons without distinction as to their sex."[1] The result of the Marriage Equality Referendum makes Ireland the first country in the world to legalise same-sex marriage via a popular vote. This is nothing short of phenomenal in a country where 84% of the people still identify as Catholic, and where several referenda on controversial social issues have failed in the past.[2]

This chapter examines the move towards marriage equality in Ireland, which culminated in the recent referendum, from both political and legal perspectives. The article will analyse why the referendum was unnecessary from a legal standpoint, and it will demonstrate that holding a referendum on marriage equality was not a laudable move on the part of the present Irish government. This crude, uncertain but ultimately effective method of recognising marriage equality actually resulted from a lack of political determination to tackle the issue in Parliament and governmental recourse to a politically convenient exercise in participative democracy.

The chapter initially examines how liberal international developments may have fuelled the introduction of the first statutory prohibition on same-sex marriage in 2004. The chapter then discusses the significance of the Irish courts' deference to the Irish Parliament (Oireachtas) on complex matters of social policy for any same-sex marriage legislation that might subsequently have been proposed. Consequently, the chapter critiques the reasons why civil partnership legislation was enacted instead of same-sex marriage legislation by the Fianna Fáil/Green Party coalition government. The chapter intimates the existence of on-going circuitousness between Parliament and the courts on the issue of marriage equality; consequently, it explains why the establishment of the Constitutional Convention was a political masterstroke by the current Fine Gael/Labour coalition government. The article concludes by examining why the referendum was a crude and risky undertaking, but ultimately an effective means of making marriage equality a reality in Ireland.

Statutory definition of marriage

The Civil Registration Act 2004

The express prohibition of same-sex marriage in Ireland came about little over a decade ago. The Civil Registration Act 2004 was mainly introduced to modernise the procedures for registering births, deaths and marriages; the law had never expressly outlawed same-sex marriage prior to the enactment of this statute. Nonetheless, section 2(2) (e) reiterated the common law exclusion of same-sex couples from marriage in the following terms: "For the purposes of this Act there is an impediment to a marriage if . . . both parties are of the same sex." The fact that this was the first statutory provision to restrict marriage to parties of the opposite sex is somewhat curious given that subsection (2) (e) was an amendment inserted into the Civil Registration Bill 2003 in early 2004. In 2003, Canadian courts had struck down the limitation of marriage to opposite-sex couples as being in violation of the Canadian Charter of Rights and Freedoms.[3] Consequently, Witzleb observes that in Australia, "the then Liberal/National Government became concerned that Australian courts might follow Canadian decisions" and hence the Marriage Amendment Act 2004 was enacted to amend the Marriage Act 1961 so that section 5(1) now defines marriage as "the union of a man and a woman to the exclusion of all others, voluntarily entered for life."[4] As Witzleb points out in the Australian context, "[t]he amendment gave the common law definition statutory force and thus put it beyond the reach of reform-minded courts."[5] In Ireland, subsection (2)(e) was inserted into section 2 of the Civil Registration Bill 2003 at about the same time as these developments were taking place in Australia, and that alone lends credence to the notion that the then Irish Government *most likely* had similar concerns pertaining to same-sex marriage and judicial activism in the Irish courts.

The legislative history of section 2(2) of the 2004 Act

Subsection (2)(a-e) of section 2 of the 2004 Act was an amendment to the legislation, introduced at Committee Stage[6] to clarify "what is an impediment to a marriage"[7], as explained by the then Minister for Social and Family Affairs, Mary Coughlan. During the Committee Stage, revisions of this amendment based on changes in the law and social perceptions were suggested. Deputy Penrose suggested that subsection 2(a) should be amended to take account of the availability of divorce in Ireland since 1996 so that there would no longer be an impediment to a marriage between a person and the divorced spouse of that person's sibling.[8] Deputy Neville, obviously aware of the contemporary, informed social perception of persons with impaired mental abilities, felt that the wording of subsection 2(d) was not appropriate for a modern piece of legislation because it rendered void the marriage of "lunatics."[9] At no point during the Committee's debate was the impediment to same-sex marriage contained in subsection 2(e) discussed. This is most disappointing because, akin to the earlier amendments that were tabled, socio-legal changes had taken place which arguably necessitated debate as to whether it was justifiable to continue to ban same-sex marriage. Such developments were indicative of an increasing acceptance of the normality of the sexual identity of gay and lesbian persons. In 1973, the American Psychiatric Association dropped homosexuality from classification as a mental illness in its diagnostic and statistical manual. In 1993, in Ireland, private consensual sexual activity between homosexual males had been decriminalised by legislative enactment "and legislative protections for gay and lesbian persons were subsequently imposed in the fields of insurance, employment, and goods and services."[10]

In light of this, one might ask why the Oireachtas did not see fit to debate the ban on same-sex marriage, possibly one of the greatest obstacles to the full assimilation of gay and lesbian citizens into Irish society. It must be remembered that, when section 2(2) was being debated on 3 February 2004, the global recognition of same-sex marriage was little more than embryonic. Merely two countries in the world had come to recognise same-sex marriage, in 2001 and 2003, respectively.[11] Hence, even if the deputies had sought to contest the contemporary meaning of marriage, "it is not the case that the meaning of marriage has unequivocally shifted."[12] In addition, when the 2004 Act was being debated, the deputies did not have the benefit of the judgment in *Zappone v Revenue Commissioners*[13], which – as we shall see – seems to accord the Oireachtas primacy in determining any future amendments to the meaning of marriage. In fact, as I shall now proceed to demonstrate, the deputies had quite the opposite at this time.[14]

Constitutional definition of marriage

In Article 41.3.1 of the Irish Constitution, "The State pledges itself to guard with special care the institution of Marriage, on which the Family is founded, and to protect it against attack." While "Marriage" and "Family" are terms undefined by the Irish Constitution, the latter concept is solely founded on the former institution, as indicated by the insertion of the words "on which" in Article 41.3.1. Hence, as Doyle affirms, marriage is a "necessary condition for a group of persons to constitute a family unit protected by Art 41," and so the right to marry is recognised as being implicit from the terms of that provision.[15] Given the Catholic ethos of the Irish Constitution, the document's conflation of the concepts of "marriage" and "family" is understandable since, as Duncan observes, "Roman Catholic social teaching emphasises the central importance to society of the family based on indissoluble marriage."[16] Further, the constitutional notion of marriage has always been recognised in Irish case law as "the basis of the family and as a . . . union of man and woman."[17]

Therefore, Doyle is correct in his observation that "marriage, as constitutionally defined by the Courts, is the union of a man and a woman."[18] In 2003, shortly before the deputies would have been debating section 2(2) of the 2004 Act, the Supreme Court reiterated in *DT v CT* the understanding that "marriage itself remains a solemn contract of partnership entered into between man and woman with a special status recognised by the Constitution."[19] Thus, as Carolan points out, "the Irish courts' consistent and conventional characterization of marriage evidently deprives homosexuals of access to this important social institution."[20] Hence, the deputies may not have felt the need to address, let alone debate, section 2(2) (e) because they were aware of the role of the Oireachtas in enacting legislation in compliance with the Constitution.[21] Section 2(2) (e) as enacted was in compliance with the constitutional understanding of marriage as delineated by the judiciary.

Zappone v Revenue Commissioners

In 2006, section 2(2) (e) was a crucial deciding factor in a High Court action taken by a lesbian couple to have their Canadian same-sex marriage recognised in Ireland. Dr Katherine Zappone and Dr Ann Louise Gilligan had married in Canada in 2003, following the opening up of the institution of marriage to same-sex couples in that country. Upon their return to Ireland, they wrote to the Office of the Registrar General seeking confirmation that their marriage was legally binding, but they were informed by letter-response that a declaration on the validity of foreign marriages was a matter for the courts by virtue of family law legislation.[22] The plaintiffs also wrote to the Revenue Commissioners seeking the recognition of their marriage in order to obtain the various tax benefits available to married couples in Ireland. However, the Revenue Commissioners replied with an interpretation that confined the provisions of tax law relating to married couples to a "husband" and a "wife" only, citing the Oxford English Dictionary's gender-specific definitions of such terms.

The plaintiffs then sought and were granted leave to apply for judicial review of the Revenue Commissioners' decision. When the matter came on for hearing before the High Court, the plaintiffs argued that the Revenue Commissioners' decision was in breach of their right to marry under the Constitution. They sought to have the impugned provisions of Irish tax law declared unconstitutional for excluding same-sex marriages from their ambit.

In the High Court, Dunne J recognised the question at the heart of the action: does the right to marry inherent in the Constitution encompass a right to marry for same-sex couples? Dunne J acknowledged that "the definition of marriage to date has always been understood as being opposite-sex marriage"[23] and that the plaintiffs wanted the High Court to "redefine marriage to mean something which it has never done to date."[24] In deciding the issue, Dunne J placed great store on section 2(2) (e) of the 2004 Act. Judicial deference to legislative enactments is not unusual because, as O'Mahony observes:

> When invited to re-interpret a provision of the Constitution from its original or established interpretation, deference theory states that the courts should look to the legislative position for guidance.[25]

Dunne J found that "the Act of 2004 is in force, is entitled to a presumption of constitutionality and is to my mind an expression of the prevailing view as to the basis for capacity to marry."[26]

Indeed, Dunne J's deference towards the 2004 Act's traditional notion of marriage was never more apparent than when she posed the following question:

> Is [section 2(2) (e)] not *of itself* an indication of the prevailing idea and concept in relation to what marriage is and how it should be defined? *I think it is.*[27]

Therefore, Dunne J actually viewed section 2(2) (e) as *the* expression of the prevailing view as to the basis for capacity to marry. However, Dunne J's strict adherence to the approach to marriage enshrined in section 2(2) (e) of the 2004 Act is frustrating when one considers the manner in which this provision came about. As discussed, section 2(2) (e) was never debated by the Oireachtas prior to its enactment; hence, Dunne J's assertion that the provision represented the prevailing legislative view on the capacity to marry is not necessarily accurate. As O'Mahony argues, section 2(2) (e) "did not represent a considered legislative judgment on the issue to which the court could defer."[28] Indeed, Foley has cogently emphasised that:

> The essence of deference, however, is deference to a *decision actually made*. If the legislature *does not actually* decide on matters of rights, then it starts to make less sense to 'defer' to its decisions because they *do not exist.*[29]

While all of this is true, it must be remembered that in treating section 2(2) (e) as evidence of a legislative consensus Dunne J could not have made herself aware of the unsatisfactory manner in which this statutory provision came about. This is because in Ireland a judge is precluded from having regard to the parliamentary debates concerning a statutory provision.[30]

A synergy between the constitutional and statutory understandings of marriage

However, Dunne J's deference to the legislature's understanding of marriage was most significant, and because of the synergy between any future legislation altering the capacity to marry and the constitutional right to marry that she envisaged, the recent Marriage Equality Referendum may not have been at all necessary.

Since Dunne J appeared to view section 2(2) (e) of the Civil Registration Act 2004 as cementing "*of itself*"[31] the concept of marriage as a union between two parties of the opposite sex, she appears to be granting the Oireachtas primacy in this contentious matter. Carolan's observation on this aspect of Dunne J's judgement now appears wholly apposite:

> The fact that Dunne J. relied so heavily on the Civil Registration Act 2004 as indicative of the nature of the existing social consensus suggests a preeminent role for the Oireachtas in determining the social (and thus constitutional) appropriateness of any future amendments to the meaning of marriage.[32]

Further, and perhaps unsurprisingly, given her adherence to the legislative concept of marriage contained in section 2(2) (e) of the 2004 Act, Dunne J went on to state that "ultimately, it is for the legislature to determine the extent"[33] of the legal recognition to be accorded to same-sex unions. Thus, it is arguable that Dunne J appeared to be indicating that, if the Oireachtas chose to alter the capacity to marry by legislating for same-sex marriage, then the courts would abide by this and recognise any legislation as being in harmony with the Constitution. As Carolan points out, Dunne J:

> Appears to posit the existence of a more complex and dynamic relationship [between the Oireachtas and the courts] in which statute in some way informs the meaning of the constitutional text.[34]

On this reading, it would appear that same-sex marriage legislation could have been introduced by the Oireachtas, absent a constitutional referendum, and it would not have been rendered unconstitutional by the courts for updating the constitutional notion of marriage. Dunne J was giving "due respect to the superior institutional capacity of the Oireachtas to reflect public opinion, and its democratic primacy on matters of political controversy"[35] Dunne J had good reason to pass the issue to the Oireachtas because, as Kavanagh observes:

> If there is intense social controversy about an issue, suggesting that people may not be ready to accept a particular change in the law (or at least may not be prepared to accept it from an unelected court) considerations about democratic legitimacy and social acceptance may lead the courts to exercise caution before making the decision themselves.[36]

Thus, the Oireachtas could have introduced same-sex marriage through legislation, just as the UK Parliament did in July 2013 when it passed the Marriage

(Same Sex Couples) Act 2013. Since Dunne J left remarkable leeway to the Oireachtas to determine the appropriate legal status for same-sex relationships, I shall now try to deduce why the then Irish government did not seek to take advantage of this judicial deference towards legislative enactments and proceed to legislate for same-sex marriage.

Same-sex relationship recognition post-*Zappone*

In 2007, with the *Zappone* judgement under appeal to the Supreme Court[37], a new Fianna Fáil/Green Party coalition government was formed in the Republic of Ireland. The coalition's Programme for Government contained a commitment to introduce civil partnership legislation for same-sex couples:

> Taking into account the Options Paper prepared by the Colley Group, and the pending Supreme Court case, we will legislate for civil partnerships at the earliest possible date in the lifetime of this Government.[38]

This statement on civil partnership legislation is interesting because the coalition claimed to be committing to its introduction in light of the Working Group on Domestic Partnership's Options Paper and the *Zappone* appeal. Granted, the Options Paper concluded that full civil partnership was the best mode of relationship recognition for same-sex couples because the introduction of same-sex marriage was likely to be vulnerable to constitutional challenge. However, this recommendation was published on 28 November 2006, a few weeks before the High Court decision in *Zappone* which seems to grant the legislature primacy in determining the meaning of marriage.[39] Dunne J's judgement surely abrogates what might otherwise be a sound recommendation because "it certainly implies that a court should exercise considerable constraint in preferring its own perception of society's norms to that evinced in a statutory instrument."[40] Thus, it is unclear why the government committed to civil partnership over marriage when one considers the High Court's judgement. Nonetheless, the "pending Supreme Court case" was another reason why the government claimed to be committing to civil partnerships. Although Dunne J's judgement left the issue of same-sex marriage to the legislature, such a pronunciation indicates that the government was, in turn, waiting for the matter to be decided at the Supreme Court level. Indeed, the upshot of all this circuitousness is that at the time neither branch of government was willing to be responsible for making what would undoubtedly have been a significant social change.

In 2006, prior to entering into government with Fianna Fáil, the Green Party issued a policy on marriage and partnership rights in which it stated that:

> The Green Party sees it as completely legitimate that the Oireachtas, as the body most appropriate to take decisions on social policy, should take the

> lead and seek to have the right of same-sex couples to marry guaranteed in legislation.[41]

Given the tenor of the High Court judgement, why then did this partner in government not rally its Fianna Fáil colleagues and do just this when given the opportunity in 2007? In 2008, when civil partnership legislation was proposed, the then Minister for Justice, Dermot Ahern, claimed that the government was acting on the advice of the then Attorney General, Paul Gallagher, who was of the view that "anything that would provide, or try to replicate 'marriage' in this legislation would not stand constitutional scrutiny."[42] It is respectfully submitted that the Attorney General, and consequently the Government, failed to accord adequate weight to the statute-sensitive approach to marriage evident in *Zappone*. Hence, the non-introduction of same-sex marriage can either be attributed to a (perhaps inadvertent) lack of appreciation as to the ramifications of the High Court judgement Court judgement or a lack of political will on the part of the coalition.

Would the Supreme Court have declared same-sex marriage legislation unconstitutional?

The government may have been apprehensive about introducing same-sex marriage legislation because any bill purporting to do so could have been referred to the Supreme Court by the President of Ireland via the Article 26 reference procedure. Article 26 of the Constitution provides that, before signing it into law, the President may refer a bill to the Supreme Court for a decision as to whether the bill or any specified provision thereof is repugnant to the Constitution. However, the Article 26 reference procedure is rarely invoked; there have been 15 such references in the Constitution's 78-year history. Nonetheless, if such a reference was made in respect of a same-sex marriage bill, it is possible that the bill might have been deemed unconstitutional by the Supreme Court because marriage in Ireland has traditionally been opposite-sex in nature.[43] Thus, the highest court in the land could have slammed the door firmly shut on same-sex marriage, declaring it an "attack" on the age-old institution of marriage which the State "pledges itself to guard with special care" in Article 41.3.1°.

Conversely, if the Supreme Court replicated the High Court's approach to marriage in *Zappone* and "used statute rather than its own experience as evidence of the prevailing social view,"[44] then a same-sex marriage Bill could very well have passed muster. Indeed, in its policy on marriage and partnership rights, the Green Party claimed to anticipate the adoption of this manner of judicial approach to a same-sex marriage bill:

> We believe that the Supreme Court would be unlikely to strike down such an expression of the democratic will of the Oireachtas on the grounds that marriage under Article 41 can only be defined in relation to Christian beliefs.[45]

The Irish superior courts have already affirmed that, as a legal concept, marriage is regulated by the Constitution and statute law; thus, it can be expanded beyond Christian beliefs. In *TF v Ireland*, Murphy J in the High Court held that:

> It may well be that *'marriage'* as referred to in our Constitution derives from the Christian concept of marriage. However, whatever its origin, the obligations of the State and the rights of parties in relation to marriage are now contained in the Constitution and our laws.[46]

This reasoning was subsequently approved by the Supreme Court. Further, the Supreme Court is most deferential to the Oireachtas when it comes to matters of social policy.[47] This is evidenced in the very recent case of *MR and Others v An tArd Chláraitheoir and Others*.[48] There is no legislation regulating surrogacy in Ireland, and in this case the Supreme Court reversed the High Court's decision that the genetic mother of twins born to a gestational surrogate be registered as the mother on the twins' birth certificates. Existing legislation only permits the birth mother, i.e. the gestational surrogate in this instance, to be registered on the twins' birth certificates. Nonetheless, in the Supreme Court, Denham CJ held that:

> Such lacuna should be addressed in legislation and not by this Court . . . [u]nder the current legislative framework it is not possible to address issues arising on surrogacy, including the issue of who is the mother for the purpose of the registration of the birth. *The issues raised in this case are important, complex and social, which are matters of public policy for the Oireachtas.*[49]

Hence, why the Green Party failed to test its previously mentioned belief while part of a coalition government is unclear, though the author of its policy on marriage and partnership rights claims that its coalition partner Fianna Fáil stood opposed to the introduction of same-sex marriage when the Programme for Government was being negotiated.[50] However, the fact that the Green Party failed to remain true to its ideals in this area while in government makes much of what is stated in its policy on marriage and partnership rights read like simple political rhetoric.

Not only is it highly unlikely that the Supreme Court would have struck down same-sex marriage legislation as being unconstitutional but, internationally, constitutional challenges to same-sex marriage laws have foundered. The superior courts of countries like Spain, Mexico and France all upheld the validity of same-sex marriage legislation when constitutional challenges were mounted against it. Thus, as Encarnacion observes, "[i]n sum, it is not unthinkable that a same-sex marriage law in Ireland could have survived constitutional scrutiny, just as similar laws have in other countries."[51]

Constitutional Convention

The Civil Partnership and Certain Rights and Obligations of Cohabitants Act 2010 entered into force on 1 January 2011, and enabled same-sex couples to gain legal recognition of their relationship largely akin to marriage. Despite this positive development (pragmatically, if not symbolically), the struggle for same-sex marriage continued unabated with advocacy groups like Marriage Equality and LGBT Noise continuing to mobilise. Hence, when a Fine Gael/Labour coalition government came to power in February 2011, it established a Constitutional Convention to consider comprehensive constitutional reform. It was agreed between the parties in the Programme for Government that the issue of same-sex marriage would go to the Constitutional Convention.[52] The Convention was a venture in participative democracy tasked with considering certain aspects of the Constitution to ensure that it was fully equipped for the twenty-first century. Once it debated an aspect of the Constitution, the Convention prepared a report containing recommendations for consideration by Parliament. The Convention was required to report back to Parliament on each aspect of the Constitution under its consideration within a 12-month period. The Convention was comprised of a chairman, 33 Members of Parliament and 66 citizens who were randomly selected by a polling company using the electoral register. The citizen members were broadly representative of Irish society and generally balanced in terms of gender, age, region, social class and occupational status.

The Convention was slow to begin its work, which led to the body being dubbed as the "'garden shed', a dumping ground for any issue likely to cause Coalition grief until it's safe to resurrect it – ideally, sometime in the next term."[53] Despite these initial misgivings, by now it has completed its work on the specific issues assigned to it. In 2013, the Constitutional Convention voted by an overwhelming majority for express constitutional provision to be made for same-sex marriage. Indeed, in the Third Report of the Convention on the Constitution, it was reported that:

> A strong majority favoured amendment of the Constitution to provide for same-sex marriage. A similarly strong majority favoured ***directive or mandatory wording*** in the event of such amendment going ahead.[54]

Thus, rather than vote in favour of a permissive amendment providing that the State *may* enact laws providing for same-sex marriage, the vast majority of the Convention's members (78 out of 100) voted in favour of a directive amendment providing that the State *shall* enact laws providing for same-sex marriage.[55] The Third Report of the Convention on the Constitution, which contains this recommendation, was deposited in the library of the Houses of the Oireachtas in June 2013. Shortly thereafter the Fine Gael/Labour coalition government committed itself to holding a same-sex marriage referendum in 2015.[56] The coalition government should not be lauded for its willingness to hold a referendum on the issue when one acknowledges that it only agreed to do so because the Constitutional Convention, a body comprised largely of ordinary Irish citizens, voted in favour of making provision for same-sex marriage in the Constitution. Indeed, sending the matter to the Constitutional Convention for deliberation was a political masterstroke. If the Fine Gael/Labour coalition had simply announced that it was holding a referendum on the issue without any intervention from the Convention, it might have lost much public support from those opposed to such a move. Instead, the government made it look as though it was giving the people the chance to 'have their say' through a constitutional referendum, because this is what the people, as represented by the members of the Constitutional Convention, had indicated that they were in favour of.

The potential pitfalls associated with referenda in Ireland

Although allowing the people to ultimately decide in a referendum as to whether same-sex marriage should be granted constitutional protection was transparent (and politically convenient), it was a somewhat risky venture. In 2006, the All-Party Oireachtas Committee reported that in the submissions made to it as to whether the constitutional definition of the family should be expanded there was "a sharp division" and that many wished Articles 41 and 42 to remain unchanged as:

> They fear that any change would threaten the position of the family based on marriage. It would undermine the stability of the traditional family and all the enhancement of the common good that flows from it.[57]

This led the All-Party Oireachtas Committee to conclude that a proposed constitutional amendment to extend the definition of the family would cause deep and long-lasting division in Irish society and would not necessarily be passed by a majority of voters in a referendum. In addition, the Gay and Lesbian Equality Network had noted that no referendum anywhere in the world had passed same-sex marriage.[58] Further, the All-Party Oireachtas Committee had observed that the "Irish experience of constitutional amendments shows that they may be extremely divisive and that however well-intentioned they may be they can have unexpected outcomes."[59] This is true because, as Ryan points out, "the removal of the ban on divorce, most notably, took two attempts, in 1986 and 1995, the ban eventually being discarded in 1995 by the tiniest of margins." Instead of inviting "such anguish and uncertainty," the All-Party Oireachtas Committee recommended that the "principal developments" in the area of same-sex relationship recognition should be made at a legislative level and that this could take the form of civil partnership legislation.[60] Notably, this recommendation was made prior to the High Court's judgement in *Zappone*, which would appear to countenance same-sex marriage legislation. However, Keane was critical of the

Committee for recommending civil partnership legislation over a constitutional referendum on Article 41 because:

> Virtually every proposal to amend the Constitution provokes opposition from some quarters . . . [t]hat is an inevitable consequence of the democratic process: it is not a justification for leaving untouched the framework of [Article 41].[61]

Nonetheless, a referendum may have proved rather divisive, because the Committee's conclusions suggested that traditional views on the marital family remained dominant in a society where, as recently as 2011, 84% of the population still identified as Catholic.[62]

Conversely, in the years following the All-Party Oireachtas Committee's report many opinion polls leaned heavily in favour of marriage equality. In 2010, an opinion poll in the *Irish Times* indicated that just over two-thirds (67%) of the Irish people believed that same-sex couples should be allowed to marry.[63] In 2011, Red C, a research and marketing group based in Dublin, conducted another opinion poll on same-sex marriage, which found that 73% of the population was in favour.[64] In 2014, an *Irish Times* opinion poll indicated that 76% of the electorate supported the introduction of same-sex marriage.[65] The last opinion poll published by Red C just prior to the Marriage Equality Referendum indicated that support for a 'yes' vote had dropped slightly, to 69%.[66] All of these polls indicated that the Irish people had adopted a more tolerant, liberal attitude towards LGBT relationships. However, favourable opinion polls were no guarantee of a positive outcome for same-sex couples in the recent Marriage Equality Referendum since:

> The idea that opinion polls amount to indicators of the "will of the people" is itself repugnant to democracy: they are cybernetic indicators based on scientific sampling techniques and devoid of democratic content or status.[67]

The Children and Family Relationships Act 2015

Having committed itself to a referendum in 2013, the Fine Gael/Labour coalition then moved to try and ensure that issues relating to same-sex parenting would not be brought to the fore of the referendum campaign by the 'No' side. In 2014, the government unveiled the Children and Family Relationships Bill. The bill was designed, *inter alia*, to enable civil partners and cohabiting same-sex couples to apply to adopt a child for the first time, and it also enabled a biological parent's same-sex partner to apply to become a guardian of the child that they were raising together. Most significantly, the Bill regulated donor-assisted human reproduction (but not any form of surrogacy) for the first time. The members of a same-sex or opposite-sex couple who conceived a child in a clinical setting via sperm or egg donation, or both, could both be registered as the parents of that child once certain criteria were fulfilled.[68] The Bill had a lengthy gestation period before bring passed by the Oireachtas and signed into law by the President of Ireland on 6 April 2015.

The enactment of this Bill a mere six weeks prior to the holding of the Marriage Equality Referendum was a bold last-minute move by the government. However, throughout the referendum campaign, the 'No' campaigners played on the electorate's fears concerning surrogacy, something that was not regulated under the bill. It was claimed that the constitutionalisation of same-sex marriage would later lead to a corresponding constitutional right of access to surrogacy for same-sex couples, and that this would be detrimental to child welfare.[69] However, this claim was quite sensationalist. First, the constitutional right to procreate of married couples is subject to limitations (indeed, such right and its non-absolute nature were established in a case in which a husband and wife were serving life sentences for capital murder in separate prisons and wanted the state to facilitate their right to conjugal relations[70]), and it has never been extended in the case law beyond a right to procreate naturally. Second, *MR v An tArd Chláraitheoir*[71] was decided as recently as November 2014, and in that case the Supreme Court was deferential to the legislature in the complex area of surrogacy. Thus, even if the courts did expand the right of married couples to procreate to include a right to procreate via assisted reproduction, it is highly unlikely that the courts would stipulate that the Oireachtas must legalise surrogacy to assist same-sex couples in achieving that goal. Nonetheless, if – and this is quite a leap – the courts did require that *altruistic* surrogacy had to be legalised in order to vindicate the constitutional right of same-sex married couples to procreate via assistance, there is nothing to suggest that the resulting child of such an arrangement would suffer detriment. There is a plethora of evidence indicating that same-sex couples are equally as capable as their opposite-sex counterparts when it comes to responsible childrearing.[72]

Marriage Equality Referendum: crude, but effective

The Marriage Equality Referendum was held on 22 May 2015, and there was concern that those who had indicated that they would vote 'yes' in the polls may not turn out to vote. The previous referendum, the Children's Referendum in November 2012,[73] saw a mere 33.49% of the Irish electorate cast their votes.[74] Any concern as to voter turnout proved unfounded, as more than 60% of the people cast votes.[75] Voter turnout was among the highest since the Constitution was enacted in 1937, with young and working class voters coming out in force to show solidarity with the LGB community.[76] By noon on 23 May, it was abundantly clear that the Irish people had voted in favour of allowing constitutional recognition of, and protection for, same-sex marriage. The national electorate comprises some 3,222,681 people, and 1,949,725 of them turned out to vote. There were 13,818 spoiled votes.[77] The final result saw 1,201,607 votes to allow same-sex marriage, with 734,300 votes against, giving the 'yes' campaign a victory with a very comfortable margin of 62.07% to 37.93%.[78] Ireland had made history by becoming the first country in the world to legalise same-sex marriage by means of a popular vote.

The Marriage Equality Referendum can best be described as a crude but effective method of legalising same-sex marriage. The referendum process was crude because placing the rights of a minority group in the hands of the majority seems almost ludicrous, as a sizeable number of the electorate could have simply voted against the issue without being properly informed in the way that elected politicians would usually be when legislating. Indeed, the 'No' campaign was attempting to misinform citizens and conflate issues.[79] In addition, if the majority had voted against the measure, gay and lesbian citizens would undoubtedly have felt a profound sense of rejection.

Nonetheless, the referendum was successful, and the result is perhaps timely and beneficial not only for Ireland's LGB community, but for the government of a country where a general election is on the horizon for early 2016. For the current coalition government, the positive referendum result is surely pristine. One envisages that, in the months ahead, government politicians will scramble to take the credit for holding a successful referendum on the civil rights issue that is marriage equality. Given that the referendum was held so close to a general election, the positive result is likely to be fresh in the minds of the electorate.

Conclusion

In Ireland, same-sex marriage was a veritable political "hot potato" that was passed between the courts and the legislature because neither branch of government was really that keen to champion its introduction for fear of a backlash. Although the political will to hold a referendum on marriage equality eventually surfaced, the Fine Gael/Labour coalition government should not be lauded for this development; it really only resulted from the recommendations of the Constitutional Convention, a reform-oriented forum comprised primarily of ordinary members of the electorate. However, once it had committed itself to a referendum, the coalition government did attempt to secure a successful outcome by enacting the Children and Family Relationships Act 2015 in order to quash arguments pertaining to same-sex parenting during the referendum campaign.

A far less crude and uncertain means of legalising same-sex marriage would have been for the Irish Parliament to legislate in that regard, an option available to it for almost a decade, since the *Zappone* judgement in December 2006.[80] In any event, it is indubitable that the great experiment that was the Marriage Equality Referendum was a resounding success. Encarnacion properly declares it to be 'a milestone in Irish history, a monumental achievement in the country's social and political development, and a repudiation of the Catholic Church's outmoded views on homosexuality.'[81]

Notes

* This Chapter is a reprint of Brian Tobin, 'Marriage Equality in Ireland: The Politico-Legal Context' (2016) 30 *International Journal of Law, Policy and the Family* 115, and is reprinted with the kind permission of Oxford University Press.

1 The legislation giving effect to the constitutional amendment, the Marriage Bill 2015, is currently being debated by the Irish Parliament and is expected to be passed into law by the end of October 2015.

2 Census 2011, *This Is Ireland: Part 1* (CSO 2012).

3 See *Halpern v Canada (Attorney General)* (2003) 65 OR (3d) 161 (CA); *EGALE Canada Inc v Canada (Attorney General)* (2003) 225 DLR (4th) 472 (BC CA).

4 Normann Witzleb, 'Marriage as the "Last Frontier"? Same-Sex Relationship Recognition in Australia' (2011) 25 *International Journal of Law, Policy and the Family* 135, 153.

5 Ibid., 154. Unlike Ireland, Australia does not have a Bill of Rights. Thus, there is no constitutional protection for marriage that the courts could find to be in conflict with section 5 (1) of the Marriage Act 1961, as amended.

6 During the legislative process, a bill is sent to a specialist parliamentary committee that meets outside the parliamentary chamber in adjacent committee rooms. Each specialist committee is comprised of a small number of senators and parliamentary deputies who consider and amend the bill, point by point, before reporting back. Given its subject matter, the Civil Registration Bill 2003 was sent to, considered and reported back on by the Select Committee on Social and Family Affairs in early 2004.

7 Select Committee on Social and Family Affairs Debate (3 February 2004) 4 <http://debates.oireachtas.ie/FAS/2004/02/03/00004.asp> accessed 12 June 2015.

8 Ibid.

9 Ibid.

10 Brian Tobin 'EB v France: Endorsing Un-"Convention"-al Families?' (2008) 11(4) *Irish Journal of Family Law* 78, 79.

11 The Netherlands opened up marriage to same-sex couples in 2001, followed by Belgium in 2003.

12 Oran Doyle, *Constitutional Law: Text, Cases and Materials* (Clarus Press 2008) 234.

13 *Zappone v Revenue Commissioners* (2008) 2 IR 417.

14 The then recent judgement in *DT v CT* (2003) 1 ILRM 321, where the Supreme Court reiterated the understanding that "marriage itself remains a solemn contract of partnership entered into between man and woman with a special status recognised by the Constitution."

15 Doyle (n 12) 225. However, in *Ryan v Attorney General* (1965) IR 294, at 313, Kenny J referred to the right to marry as one of the unenumerated personal rights protected under Article 40.3.1. In *O'Shea v Ireland* (2007) 2 IR 313, Laffoy J confirmed that the right to marry is also protected by Article 40.3.1.

16 WR Duncan, 'Supporting the Institution of Marriage in Ireland' (1978) 13 *Irish Jurist* 215, 221. Marriage in Ireland is no longer indissoluble since the introduction of divorce in 1996, following a referendum to remove the ban on divorce contained in Article 41.3.2 of the Constitution. The provision was replaced by a new Article 41.3.2 which expressly permits divorce in certain circumstances.

17 *Murphy v Attorney General* (1982) IR 241; *B v R* (1995) 1 ILRM 491.

18 Doyle (n 12).

19 *DT* (n 14) 374 (Murray J).

20 Eoin Carolan, 'Committed Non-Marital Couples and the Irish Constitution' in Oran Doyle and William Binchy (eds), *Committed Relationships and the Law* (Four Courts Press 2007) 242.
21 Article 15.4.1 of the Constitution of Ireland provides that "the Oireachtas shall not enact any law which is in any respect repugnant to this Constitution or any provision thereof."
22 Family Law Act 1995, s29.
23 *Zappone* (n 13) 504.
24 Ibid., 505.
25 Conor O'Mahony, 'Societal Change and Constitutional Interpretation' (2010) 1 *Irish Journal of Legal Studies* 71, 78.
26 *Zappone* (n 13) 506.
27 Ibid, Emphasis added.
28 Conor O'Mahony, 'Principled Expediency: How the Irish Courts can Compromise on Same-Sex Marriage' (2012) *Dublin University Law Journal* 198, 213.
29 Brian Foley, *Deference and the Presumption of Constitutionality* (Institute of Public Administration 2008) 230, Emphasis added.
30 See *Crilly v Farrington Ltd* (2001) 3 IR 25.
31 *Zappone* (n 13) 506, Emphasis added.
32 Carolan (n 20) 265–266.
33 *Zappone* (n 13) 513.
34 Carolan (n 20) 266.
35 O'Mahony (n 28) 226.
36 Aileen Kavanagh, 'Strasbourg, the House of Lords or Elected Politicians: Who Decides About Rights After *Re P*?' (2009) 72 *Modern Law Review* 828, 843.
37 The Zappone appeal never made it to the Supreme Court. It was dropped in June 2012, as the parties wished to initiate a new High Court action instead. However, this action was never progressed and is now unnecessary in light of the result of the Marriage Equality Referendum: Charlie Taylor, 'Couple to Issue Renewed Legal Challenge to Civil Registration Act in Bid for Marriage' *Irish Times* (Dublin, 7 June 2012) 8.
38 Programme for Government 2007–2012 (Stationery Office 2007) 87.
39 The High Court handed down judgment in *Zappone* (n 13) on 14 December 2006.
40 Carolan (n 20) 266.
41 Green Party, *Valuing Families: A Policy on Marriage and Partnership Rights* (Green Party 2006) 8.
42 Mark Hennessy and Carl O'Brien, 'Bill to Grant Legal Protection to Same-Sex Couples' *Irish Times* (Dublin, 25 June 2008) 3.
43 See *DT* (n 14) 374 (Murray J).
44 Carolan (n 20) 266.
45 Green Party (n 41) 8.
46 *TF v Ireland* (1995) 1 IR 321, 333.
47 *Sinnott v Minister for Education* (2001) 2 IR 545; *D v Ireland* (2012) IESC 10.
48 (2014) IESC 60.
49 Ibid [116–118]. Emphasis added.
50 'Green Party Decision' *Gay Community News* (Dublin, February 2008) 2.
51 Omar Encarnacion, 'There's Something About Marriage' *Foreign Affairs* (31 May 2015) <www.foreignaffairs.com/articles/ireland/2015-05-31/theres-something-about-marriage> accessed 11 February 2019.
52 'Programme for Government 2011–2016' <www.socialjustice.ie/sites/default/files/attach/policy-issue-article/3292/2011-03-06-programmeforgovernment2011-2016.pdf> accessed 17 September 2019.

53 Kathy Sheridan, 'How Gay Marriage went Mainstream' *Irish Times* (Dublin, 14 July 2012) 2.
54 *Third Report of the Convention on the Constitution: Amending the Constitution to Provide for Same-Sex Marriage* (Convention on the Constitution 2013) <www.constitution.ie/Meetings.aspx> accessed 12 June 2015, Emphasis added.
55 Ibid.
56 Kieran Rose, 'Historic Step in Remarkable Journey to Equal Marriage: Ireland Has Made Huge Progress in Evolving Toward Full Equality for LGBT People' *Irish Times* (Dublin, 8 November 2013) 18.
57 See the All-Party Oireachtas Committee on the Constitution, *Tenth Progress Report: The Family* (Stationery Office 2006) 122. The committee received 7,989 submissions on Article 41 and the family from members of the public and interested bodies.
58 Sheridan (n 53) 2.
59 See the All-Party Oireachtas Committee on the Constitution (n 57) 122.
60 Fergus Ryan, '21st Century Families, 19th Century Values: Modern Family Law in the Shadow of the Constitution' in Oran Doyle and Eoin Carolan (eds), *The Irish Constitution: Governance and Values* (Thomson Round Hall 2008) 374–375.
61 Ronan Keane, 'The Constitution and the Family: The Case for a New Approach' in Oran Doyle and Eoin Carolan (eds), *The Irish Constitution: Governance and Values* (Thomson Round Hall 2008) 355.
62 Census 2011 (n 2).
63 Carl O'Brien, 'Two-Thirds Support Gay Marriage, Poll Finds' *Irish Times* (Dublin, 15 September 2010) 1.
64 Michael Marsh, Jane Suiter and Theresa Reidy, 'Report on Reasons Behind Voter Behaviour in the Oireachtas Inquiry Referendum 2011' Department of Public Expenditure and Reform (2012).
65 Stephen Collins, 'Support for Same-Sex Marriage Increasing, Poll Finds' *Irish Times* (Dublin, 7 April 2014) 1.
66 Alberto Nardelli, 'Could Polls Be Wrong About Outcome of Ireland's Gay Marriage Referendum?' *The Guardian* (London, 18 May 2015) <www.theguardian.com/society/2015/may/18/could-polls-be-wrong-irelands-gay-marriage-referendum-vote-same-sex> accessed 14 June 2015.
67 John Waters, 'Let Norris Enter Race – And Be Treated Like Anyone Else' *Irish Times* (Dublin, 16 September 2011) 16.
68 Children and Family Relationships Act 2015, Pt 2.
69 Sarah Bardon, 'Surrogacy and Adoption Rights Will Not Be Affected: Minister Accuses No Side of Trying to Confuse Voters with Irrelevant Issues' *Irish Times* (Dublin, 13 May 2015) 4.
70 *Murray v Ireland* (1985) IR 532.
71 (2014) IESC 60.
72 Brian Tobin, '"First Comes Love, Then Comes Marriage . . . ": Allaying Reservations Surrounding Marriage Equality and Same-Sex Parenting in Ireland' (2015) 18 *Irish Journal of Family Law* 9.
73 This was a referendum which proposed the insertion of a new article into the Constitution, Article 42A, to provide express constitutional protection for the rights of the child. The referendum was successful and Article 42A now forms part of the Constitution of Ireland.
74 Marie O'Halloran, 'Young Voter Surge Pushes Turnout into Top Five Highest' *Irish Times* (Dublin, 25 May 2015) 2.
75 Ibid.

76 Over 100,000 new voters were registered in the months prior to the referendum, most of whom were young first-time voters and students. Further, the percentage of 'yes' votes in some of the most socially deprived areas of the capital, Dublin, was quite remarkable. 87% of voters in Dublin's Jobstown voted 'yes,' with 88% of voters in Coolock and The Liberties voting the same way, while 85% of voters in Ballyfermot also voted 'yes.'
77 Fiach Kelly, 'Kenny Hails Vote as Pioneering: 62% of Voters Support Constitutional Amendment with 38% Against' *Irish Times* (Dublin, 25 May 2015) 2.
78 Ibid.
79 Bardon (n 69) 4.
80 See *Zappone* (n 13).
81 Encarnacion (n 51).

References

Primary sources

B v R (1995) 1 ILRM 491.
Children and Family Relationships Act 2015, Pt 2.
Civil Partnership and Certain Rights and Obligations of Cohabitants Act 2010
Civil Registration Act 2004.
The Constitution of Ireland.
Crilly v Farrington Ltd (2001) 3 IR 25.
D v Ireland (2012) IESC 10
DT v CT (2003) 1 ILRM 321.
EGALE Canada Inc v Canada (Attorney General) (2003) 225 DLR (4th) 472 (BC CA).
Family Law Act 1995, s 29.
Halpern v Canada (Attorney General) (2003) 65 OR (3d) 161 (CA).
MR v An tArd Chláraitheoir (2014) IESC 60.
MR and Others v An tArd Chláraitheoir and Others (2014) IESC 60.
Murphy v Attorney General (1982) IR 241.
Murray v Ireland (1985) IR 532.
O'Shea v Ireland (2007) 2 IR 313.
Ryan v Attorney General (1965) IR 294.
Sinnott v Minister for Education (2001) 2 IR 545
TF v Ireland (1995) 1 IR 321.
Zappone v Revenue Commissioners (2008) 2 IR 417.

Secondary sources

All-Party Oireachtas Committee on the Constitution, *Tenth Progress Report: The Family* (Stationery Office 2006).
Bardon S, 'Surrogacy and Adoption Rights Will Not Be Affected: Minister Accuses No Side of Trying to Confuse Voters with Irrelevant Issues' *Irish Times* (Dublin, 13 May 2015) 4.
Carolan E, 'Committed Non-Marital Couples and the Irish Constitution' in Doyle O and Binchy W (eds), *Committed Relationships and the Law* (Four Courts Press 2007).

Census 2011, *This Is Ireland: Part 1* (Dublin: CSO 2012).

Collins S, 'Support for Gay Marriage Increasing, Poll Finds' *Irish Times* (Dublin, 7 April 2014) 1.

Doyle O, *Constitutional Law: Text, Cases and Materials* (Clarus Press 2008).

Duncan WR, 'Supporting the Institution of Marriage in Ireland' (1978) 13 *Irish Jurist* 215.

Encarnacion O, 'There's Something About Marriage' *Foreign Affairs* (31 May 2015) <www.foreignaffairs.com/articles/ireland/2015-05-31/theres-something-about-marriage> accessed 11 February 2019.

Foley B, *Deference and the Presumption of Constitutionality* (Institute of Public Administration 2008).

Green Party, *Valuing Families: A Policy on Marriage and Partnership Rights* (Green Party 2006).

'Green Party Decision' *Gay Community News* (Dublin, February 2008) 2.

Hennessy M and O'Brien C, 'Bill to Grant Legal Protection to Same-Sex Couples' *Irish Times* (Dublin, 25 June 2008) 3.

Kavanagh A, 'Strasbourg, the House of Lords or Elected Politicians: Who Decides About Rights After *Re P*?' (2009) 72 *Modern Law Review* 828.

Keane R, 'The Constitution and the Family: The Case for a New Approach' in Doyle O and Carolan E (eds), *The Irish Constitution: Governance and Values* (Thomson Round Hall 2008).

Kelly F, 'Kenny Hails Vote as Pioneering: 62% of Voters Support Constitutional Amendment with 38% Against' *Irish Times* (Dublin, 25 May 2015) 2.

Marsh M, Suiter J and Reidy T, 'Report on Reasons Behind Voter Behaviour in the Oireachtas Inquiry Referendum 2011' Department of Public Expenditure and Reform (2012).

Nardelli A, 'Could Polls Be Wrong About Outcome of Ireland's Gay Marriage Referendum?' *The Guardian* (London, 18 May 2015) <www.theguardian.com/society/2015/may/18/could-polls-be-wrong-irelands-gay-marriage-referendum-vote-same-sex> accessed 14 June 2015.

O'Brien C, 'Two-Thirds Support Same-sex Marriage, Poll Finds' *Irish Times* (Dublin, 15 September 2010) 1.

O'Halloran M, 'Young Voter Surge Pushes Turnout into Top Five Highest' *Irish Times* (Dublin, 25 May 2015).

O'Mahony C, 'Principled Expediency: How the Irish Courts Can Compromise on Same-Sex Marriage' (2012) *Dublin University Law Journal* 198.

———, 'Societal Change and Constitutional Interpretation' (2010) 1 *Irish Journal of Legal Studies* 71.

Programme for Government 2007–2012 (Stationery Office 2007).

'Programme for Government 2011–2016' <www.socialjustice.ie/sites/default/files/attach/policy-issue-article/3292/2011-03-06-programmeforgovernment2011-2016.pdf> accessed 17 September 2019.

Rose K, 'Historic Step in Remarkable Journey to Equal Marriage: Ireland Has Made Huge Progress in Evolving Toward Full Equality for LGBT People' *Irish Times* (Dublin, 8 November 2013) 18.

Ryan F, '21st Century Families, 19th Century Values: Modern Family Law in the Shadow of the Constitution' in Doyle O and Carolan E (eds), *The Irish Constitution: Governance and Values* (Thomson Round Hall 2008).

Select Committee on Social and Family Affairs Debate (3 February 2004).

Sheridan K, 'How Same-sex Marriage Went Mainstream' *Irish Times* (Dublin, 14 July 2012) 2.

Taylor C, 'Couple to Issue Renewed Legal Challenge to Civil Registration Act in Bid for Marriage' *Irish Times* (Dublin, 7 June 2012) 8.

Third Report of the Convention on the Constitution: Amending the Constitution to Provide for Same-Sex Marriage (Convention on the Constitution 2013) <www.constitution.ie/Meetings.aspx> accessed 12 June 2015.

Tobin B, 'EB v France: Endorsing Un-"Convention"-al Families?' (2008) 11 *Irish Journal of Family Law* 78.

———, 'First Comes Love, Then Comes Marriage. . . ': Allaying Reservations Surrounding Marriage Equality and Same-Sex Parenting in Ireland' (2015) 18 *Irish Journal of Family Law* 9.

Waters J, 'Let Norris Enter Race – And Be Treated Like Anyone Else' *Irish Times* (Dublin, 16 September 2011) 16.

Witzleb N, 'Marriage as the 'Last Frontier'? Same-Sex Relationship Recognition in Australia' (2011) 25 *International Journal of Law, Policy and the Family* 135.

Chapter 5

The aftermath of marriage equality in Australia

Religious freedom and LGBTQ+ non-discrimination

Louise Richardson-Self, Bronwyn Fielder, and Douglas Ezzy

Introduction and background

Marriage equality is a recent achievement in Australia, passing the Parliament on 7 December 2017 and receiving royal assent the following day. Australia is the 26th country to recognise same-sex marriages, following what activists called the 'long march toward equality.'[1] Internationally, formal same-sex relationship recognition first started gaining momentum in the late 1980s, following from the gay and lesbian liberation, and, later, LGBTQ+ rights movements.[2] Broadly speaking, the various strands of these movements can be cast into three categories: first, legalising same-sex sexual activity; second, the introduction of anti-discrimination measures, including anti-discrimination law; and third, legislating for the recognition of same-sex relationships, either as marriages or some other state-recognised union.[3] Tasmania was first to formally recognise same-sex relationships in Australia with the introduction of the Relationships Act 2003 (Tas), which came into effect on 1 January 2004. With this, the tacit assumption that marriages in Australia must be comprised of one (cisgender, heterosexual) man and one (cisgender, heterosexual) woman was increasingly challenged. Thus, to eradicate any doubt as to which couples may marry according to Australian *federal* law, the Howard government introduced the Marriage Amendment Bill 2004 (Cth), which restricted the union to one man and one woman, and passed with bipartisan support from both major parties (the Australian Labor Party and the Liberal Party of Australia). This bill came into effect as the Marriage Amendment Act 2004 (Cth) on 16 August that same year.

At that time, public support for same-sex marriage was only at 38%.[4] Yet, thanks to the ongoing efforts of grassroots activists and the influence of a transnational "soft law" norm of relationship recognition, social attitudes towards same-sex relationships gradually started to shift among the general public.[5] Polling from 2007 onward consistently showed majority support for marriage equality in Australia,[6] and, over the next decade, Australia continued to formally recognise same-sex *relationships* in small stages in a variety of ways. Same-sex *marriage* remained elusive, however. Since the 2004 amendment to the Marriage Act 1961

(Cth), 23 bills were tabled at the federal level to deal with marriage equality and the recognition of overseas same-sex marriages.[7] By 2013, the Australian Capital Territory and Tasmania both attempted to legislate for marriage equality at the local level. However, the proposal to legislate for same-sex marriage was rejected by Tasmania's Upper House,[8] and though the Marriage Equality (Same-Sex) Act 2013 (ACT) came into force for a brief period, this was challenged in the High Court and the legislation was overturned.[9]

Factions between conservatives and progressives in both major parties effectively stalled progress at the federal level. Whilst the centre-left Labor party supported a conscience (or "free") vote on the matter since 2011, they determined at their 2015 national conference that if same-sex marriage was not legislated by 2020, a conscience vote would no longer be permitted and that Labor federal Members of Parliament (MPs) would be bound to support it.[10] The centre-right Liberal National Party (Coalition) alternatively required that members adhere to the party position opposing same-sex marriage.[11] But intense debate seeking a conscience vote continued among the Coalition and, by way of compromise, a plebiscite or constitutional referendum was pledged to follow the 2016 election.[12] Ultimately, the proposal to hold a compulsory plebiscite was twice blocked by Labor and the Greens, and a non-compulsory Marriage Law Postal Survey was held in its place in 2017. The Coalition also announced 'it would give MPs a free vote in Parliament if a majority of the public voted in favour of change but would not proceed with the vote if a majority voted against.'[13] Every Australian enrolled to vote was posted one copy of the survey. Although this survey was non-compulsory, 79.5% of the population voluntarily voted. It consisted of only one question: should the law be changed to allow same-sex couples to marry? Ultimately, the survey found that 61.6% of those who voted believed that the law should be changed.[14]

However, this survey was also preceded by a campaign period for both "Yes" and "No" positions, lasting approximately three months. It is important to note that the reason the Labor opposition, LGBTQ+ activists, and many allies strongly opposed a national vote on the issue of same-sex marriage was due to the potentially harmful impact such campaigning could have on the LGBTQ+ community.[15] There were concerns, for example, that the medium (postal service) was outdated, and that this would skew results to older Australians who are more likely to oppose same-sex marriage.[16] A further, more pressing concern was that the campaign 'was not subject to the stringent advertising restrictions which apply to federal elections,' which could enable the spread of misinformation about the LGBTQ+ community.[17] This latter concern was indeed founded, as anti-equality campaigners were caught advertising claims that were 'deliberately misleading.'[18] Several first-hand accounts, including those of some interviewees in the present study, also reflected pain and suffering caused by the prejudicial public scrutiny over LGBTQ+ lives during this period.[19]

The Yes campaign, whose most visible organisation was Australian Marriage Equality (AME), retained the argumentative strategy they had employed during the preceding period of activism. The predominant rhetoric of this advocacy emphasised sameness: that same-sex attraction does not preclude a couple from upholding the core values of marriage, that LGBTQ+ people are *just like you*, and that all love is the same, no matter the gender of whom that love originates and to whom it is directed. (This "same love" rhetorical strategy has had a high degree of resonance across the Western world).[20] Marriage equality was figured by AME as a change which would not negatively impact the majority of Australians in any way, but would enable same-sex couples to participate in an inherently valuable public good. By representing same gender relationships as overwhelmingly heteronormative, and by personalising the battle for marriage equality – so that a heterosexual ally could be seen to be supporting *their* son or daughter, *their* brother or sister, *their* aunt, uncle, mother, or father, *their* friends – many heterosexual Australians came to see this 'second order issue' as one that was nonetheless important to take a stand on, which can explain the high voter turnout.[21]

However, the No campaign was more successful in converting undecided voters than the Yes campaign, seeing a rise from 25% to 38.4% opposition.[22] The No campaign's most visible organisation was the Coalition for Marriage (CfM), which used a strikingly different argumentative strategy as compared to previous anti-equality campaigns.[23] No campaigners warned of dire social consequences that did *not* pertain to the institution of marriage itself.[24] They offered three main lines of argument. First, they argued that if same-sex marriage were legalised, parents would lose control over their children's sex education in schools. This arm of CfM's campaign primarily targeted trans and non-binary identity, and some criticised AME for its failure to respond to this misinformation and fearmongering. Witness: 'Rather than defend trans people, Safe Schools, and queer families, these groups have rolled out doctors and heterosexual families to provide reassurance that marriage equality does not involve a gay agenda of radical "gender theory." '[25] Second, CfM argued that the right to free speech would be undermined by marriage equality, as it would become a form of "hate speech" to oppose same-sex unions, piggy-backing on recent public debate about racist hate speech in Australia.[26] Finally, they argued that same-sex marriage posed a threat to the right to religious freedom.

Interestingly, CfM's Neighbour Visitation Campaign training materials focused overwhelmingly on the first two arguments, even going so far as to remind its campaigners that 'This is a *political* not a *religious* exercise.'[27] However, religious freedom became the main focal point in the days preceding the announcement of the survey results and continues to have prominence today. To this end, amendments were proposed to the marriage equality bill in order to "protect" this freedom.[28] The proposed amendments were ultimately defeated, but not before then-Prime Minister Malcolm Turnbull established an Expert Panel led by Philip Ruddock whose objective was to investigate and report to the Prime Minister on 'whether Australian law (Commonwealth, State and Territory) adequately protects the human right to freedom of religion.'[29]

The review was set up in response to pressure from conservatives within the Coalition government immediately prior to the passing of the amended Marriage Act legalising same-sex marriage.[30] Central to the desire of the conservatives was the legalisation of religious exemptions on a federal level, enabling religious organisations to be exempt from anti-discrimination laws on the basis of their faith. In Australia, laws and practices between the states vary widely in this regard, with some states allowing broad exemptions and others very few. This applies, for example, to religious schools, which, in some states, may discriminate against teachers and even students on the basis of their sexuality.[31] The Panel received well over 16,000 submissions from interested parties on this issue. Its report was delivered on 18 May 2018 and was released by the government on 13 December 2018 (alongside the government's response).

It is in this climate that our present study into the experiences of LGBTQ+ individuals is situated. As reported by the Ruddock Panel, many Australians believe that 'religious adherence in Australia is at a critical juncture,' with marriage equality the catalyst which brought this issue to the surface.[32] 'Changing patterns of religious adherence, a loss of trust in mainstream institutions, and changing social mores,' the Panel said, 'are challenging the traditional role that religion has played in Australian society.'[33] Yet, whilst the current discussion of freedom of religion ostensibly includes all religions (as well as one's right not to ascribe to any religion), it is clear that Christian views are those which conservatives are most concerned to protect. Indeed, Christians comprise the largest faith group in Australia, with 52.1% of the population identifying as such in the 2016 census.[34] (However, the number of Australians who identify as having "no religion" is increasing, especially among young Australians, and the number of Australians who identify as Christian is decreasing. Many Christians feel apprehensive in this new climate – even fearful.[35])

Ultimately, the Panel did not accept the claim that religious freedom is in 'immediate peril,' but did agree that such a freedom 'requires constant vigilance.'[36] It made 20 recommendations to ensure that freedom of religion is adequately protected *and* balanced with other human rights. They explain that 'there is no hierarchy of rights: one right does not take precedence over another,' and 'Australia does not get to choose . . . between protecting religious freedom and providing for equality before the law. It must do both under its international obligations.'[37] For this reason, the Panel was openly 'circumspect in recommending changes to Australia's existing laws . . . unless there was clear evidence that they are inadequate.'[38] It is also important to note that any changes recommended by the Panel relate mostly to federal law, and as such are intended to sit parallel to state and territory laws. But, as mentioned previously, these laws vary widely; exemptions for religion are not uniform across the board.[39] For example, Tasmania – the region where this study occurred – currently has 'no special exemptions for religious bodies, including schools,' whereas New South Wales is currently considering the Anti-Discrimination

Amendment (Religious Freedoms) Bill 2018 (NSW), 'which would allow broad ranging discrimination on the basis of religious belief.'[40] Further comparative research will therefore be necessary to gain a holistic understanding of LGBTQ+ equality.

In summing up, we do not want to overstate the division between "the religious" on the one hand, and "the LGBTQ+ community" on the other. According to the 2016 census, 49.7% of Tasmanians identify as Christian, with a further 2.3% identifying with another religion.[41] Tasmania is also estimated to have one of the smallest adult LGBTQ+ populations at 2.7%.[42] And yet, 63.6% of Tasmanians voted in favour of marriage equality, and every voting electorate had a majority Yes vote.[43] The statistical data alone tells us that at least some Christian people view marriage equality as consistent with their religious beliefs (and, indeed, some Christians are also LGBTQ+).[44] Likewise, it would be an oversimplification to assert that only religious believers voted No; after all, as previously noted, CfM's very own neighbourhood campaign strategy purposefully framed marriage equality as a *political* issue. With this in mind, we now explore the impact of this recent history on LGBTQ+ Tasmanians who work in religious organisations.

Method

We conducted nine qualitative interviews with LGBTQ+ Tasmanians who work in government-funded religious organisations and schools in order to better understand their experiences of discrimination and/or inclusion in the workplace, in a region where LGBTQ+ non-discrimination is well-protected, at a time when there is great fear for the protection of freedom of religion (as a consequence of marriage equality). The recruitment of employees from faith-based organisations was driven by the possibility that changes to *federal* legislation could mean that LGBTQ+ employees in Tasmanian religious organisations may be discriminated against in the future. (This would not be the case in secular organisations.) It is also of interest to understand whether legislation – in this case, strong anti-discrimination law – has any effect on the culture of an organisation, in particular a religious organisation. Data was collected using one-on-one semi-structured interviews with individual volunteers. Qualitative data obtained through interviews has allowed us to attend to the nuances and ambiguity of these people's individual experiences.[45] The data, however, is limited and cannot be generalised. In the case of this pilot study the small number of interviewees (n = 9) means that the data can only be indicative of meanings and patterns. (See Table 5.1 for demographic detail of the participants and employers.) Participants were mostly recruited through social media flyers distributed through LGBTQ+ advocate organisations in Tasmania, as well as secondary sources or 'snowball' sampling. Several interviewees informed others of the study, who subsequently contacted the researchers. Snowball sampling is

Table 5.1 Participant details

Pseudonym	*Age*	*Sexuality*	*Gender*	*Out at work?*	*Out at home*	*Employment*
Damien	20s	G	Cis-M	Partly	Yes	Welfare
Angela	60s	G	Cis-W	Yes	Yes	Welfare
Melissa	20s	L	Cis-W	Yes/No	Yes	Welfare
Andy	30s	Q	Trans (non-binary)	Yes	Yes	Welfare
Peta	40s	B	Cis-W	Partly	Yes	Welfare
Tony	50s	G	Cis-M	Yes	Yes	Education
Emma	20s	L	Cis-W	No	Yes	Education
Tamara	30s	Not straight	Cis-W	Partly	Yes	Education
Jac	40s	L	Cis-W	Yes	Yes	Education

useful when individuals or groups of individuals are vulnerable.[46] In this case, there are risks associated with being identified, as not all organisations are supportive of sexuality and gender diversity within their workforce. Those who were interested contacted the researchers by email, and were subsequently sent an information sheet. At the time of the interview, interviewees signed a consent form.

In line with the qualitative and explorative nature of the research, sampling was purposive; that is, participants were recruited to provide information-rich cases relating to the aim of the research. In addition, when possible, the researchers aimed to represent maximum variation of characteristics within the criteria informed by the research questions.[47] Five interviewees were from welfare organisations, and four from schools. The employee organisations were all Christian faith-based, predominantly Catholic and Anglican. Participants were of diverse sexualities and gender, with two cis-men and one cis-woman identifying as gay, three cis-women as lesbian, one cis-woman as bisexual, one cis-woman as 'not straight' and one as queer and trans (non-binary).

Each interview lasted between 45 and 80 minutes, and although semi-structured, they were conversational. This was an intentional method, allowing the participants to relax and share more detail. The interview schedule was in alignment with the interdisciplinary nature of the study, with questions being posed relating to legal, philosophical, and relational aspects of the workplace experience for the interviewees. Analysis was also based upon these categories. In the interest of confidentiality and anonymity, pseudonyms are used throughout this chapter. Similarly, potentially identifying information has been either deleted or generalised. Quotations taken from the interviews have occasionally been edited for clarity. Some repeated words have been deleted and the insertion of clarificatory words are indicated by square brackets.

Discussion

In our discussion we consider the following questions:

- *The marriage equality debate* – How has the rhetoric employed in the Postal Survey campaign period affected LGBTQ+ Tasmanians, in general and at work?
- *Ruddock review and anti-discrimination law* – To what extent are our interviewees aware of their legal rights, and to what extent did they follow the Ruddock review?
- *Religious freedom and non-discrimination* – Do they see religious freedom and LGBTQ+ non-discrimination as compatible, or fundamentally opposed (as was the impression given by much mainstream media)?
- *Anxiety and vigilance* – Has the predominant "sameness" framing of same-sex marriage been useful for reducing stigma toward different members of the LGBTQ+ community, in their experience?
- *Cis-hetero-norms* – What difficulties, if any, do these members of the LGBTQ+ community continue to face?

The marriage equality debate

The period of the Postal Survey was difficult for many of the interviewees. Emma expressed how generally exhausted she'd felt throughout the campaign, saying 'I'm just still so exhausted from the plebiscite.' Tony felt hurt and disgusted at the negative advertising campaign, expressing that 'there was just too much agitation being stirred up . . . the religious side of it is what really disgusted me, because of the way they went about it . . . when they bring the word paedophilia into it, I just find that sick.' Those working in Catholic organisations were also aware of the ongoing stance of the Church against marriage equality which preceded the Survey. Jac explains,

> The marriage debate . . . that's gone on for years really. It wasn't just that several months last year; and there was that time with the *Don't Mess with Marriage* booklet that was released by the Catholic Archbishop's Council . . . I probably found that more difficult than the stuff during last year [*crying*].

Some witnessed homophobic comments in the wider community *and* the workplace. Peta, who passes as straight, said 'it was really upsetting me . . . driving to work, big billboards, and I get to work and I'm hearing these [negative] conversations . . . I'd never actually felt it encroach on me so personally in my life.' Tamara felt that discrimination from a direct supervisor was magnified during the Postal Survey. Damien said most people were 'not disrespectful enough to bring up anything negative,' although he did overhear negative conversations at work.

But negative conversations were not so common in the workplace. For Melissa, the same-sex marriage campaign did not have any impact on her workplace; she said, 'it was kind of the same before and after. Not really acknowledged or – yeah, it didn't really impact it at all.' Emma, similarly, found 'no one really talked about it.' There were also more subtle issues to deal with. Damien describes having generally supportive managers, but also noted that his workplace was unwilling to actively advocate for LGBTQ+ persons and marriage equality – they made 'the decision to not act on that and create safe spaces.' Damien also felt stuck in 'a no-win situation where if you don't speak then you are accused of not supporting or not trying hard enough, and if you do speak you are told you are speaking too much, or "shoving it in our faces."' However, for some, there was considerable support. A few workplaces greeted the successful Yes campaign with congratulations and warmth. Angela explains: 'all of our colleagues were so happy for us. And they congratulated us and hugged us . . . . on the day that it all happened, and it went through, it was just beautiful for us.' Support for Tony came both from fellow workers and from parents of clients and students: 'they'd be like, "why do they have all this shit going on about marriage equality? Why don't the government just allow it?"' Finally, though Andy expressed that they've 'never been interested in marriage,' they felt they would 'definitely' be accepted in a queer marriage in their workplace, saying 'all of my co-workers are very accepting . . . I would have no worries or fears.' Overall, the workplace response from those who were open about their sexuality/gender was positive from direct management and co-workers. The opposition to marriage equality promoted by the Catholic Archbishop did not directly affect the workers in the Catholic organisations. However, the campaign itself was not necessarily easy or harmless for the participants.

Ruddock review and anti-discrimination law

The interviewees expressed a general feeling that their identity would not jeopardise their employment within their respective organisations. In many cases, this was based upon a general assumption that Tasmanian law would protect them, rather than a detailed knowledge of anti-discrimination laws. Only Jac was explicit in her understanding of workplace policies, as well as state law. She said, 'my understanding is that religious schools are protected under the anti-discrimination act – all employees . . . you can't sack someone because of the protected attributes.' More typical were comments such as Melissa's: 'I mean, I just assumed that I'm not allowed to be discriminated against, but I've never actually looked it up.' Similarly, Peta thought that workplace discrimination could occur, 'but *officially*, they're not allowed to discriminate' (emphasis added). Damien was optimistic about the possibility of redress for any potential discrimination, even though the details of Tasmania's anti-discrimination laws, as distinct from the laws of other states, were unclear to him. He said, 'I do know a bit about other states having it worse. [But] I haven't seen it enacted in Tasmania or the effects . . . again, it's a bit of a bubble for me.' Angela similarly lacked detailed legal awareness, but had enough confidence to 'go straight to my line manager if I felt discriminated against in any way. And then . . . the current CEO.' If that was not successful, she was also willing to take the matter further. Only two of the participants would not have felt free to go to management if met with discrimination. Both were not established in the workplace and did not have confidence they would be supported. Emma said she believed that 'they are allowed to discriminate against you because of your sexuality or your gender identity. Because that's their religion.' Emma also said she believes that federal law can override state law, asking: 'you could [fire people for being LGBTQ+] because of section 109, couldn't you?' Whether this is the case is a matter of legal debate.

Interestingly, whilst there were also concerns for some interviewees that greater exemptions for religion in anti-discrimination law may come about, several interviewees had little to no awareness of the Expert Panel and the final report. For example, Andy did not know about the Review but expressed a general concern about religious exemptions, saying 'it's hard not to be concerned about things like that because discrimination still exists.' Melissa had heard of the Review and worried that young LGBTQ+ people might have to 'deny who they are and live in secret, which is really terrible for mental health.' Tony also reflected on the possible ramifications for young people, saying, 'it's very sad for youth. Imagine being in a religious school now. You'd be quite frightened that you can't work here anymore, because you're gay.' Again, only Jac had good knowledge of the Ruddock Review. When asked how she felt about it, she replied: 'Frustrated! I mean the impression you get is that the panel was only created to appease the people who didn't want marriage equality.' Overall, the participants did not have a lot of detailed knowledge of current anti-discrimination law, nor of how the Review would impact them or young people in the future. However, the majority felt confident they could not be discriminated against in Tasmania. Those who were more confident in their rights were also typically the employees who already felt comfortable being out in their workplace.

Religious freedom and non-discrimination

An interesting finding of this study is that there was a range of attitudes taken towards the compatibility of "religious freedom" and LGBTQ+ non-discrimination, particularly as it pertains to the workplace. Emma suggested that the two were thoroughly incompatible, and had a firm understanding of what "religious freedom" entails in the minds of those advocating for it: 'That you have the freedom to do whatever you want, whatever you believe, even if it hurts other people . . . Even if that means you might discriminate against the people.' She went so far as to say that she would not work in a Catholic school if she could not 'pass' as heterosexual. Moreover, whilst Tony did not outright declare that the two are incompatible, he does believe that strong religiosity is generational and declining, using negative language to describe conservative anti-LGBTQ+ religious attitudes ('we've realised how ridiculously heavy that crap was relied upon'). This statement seems to betray a belief that religious freedom and LGBTQ+ non-discrimination cannot easily co-exist.

Alternatively, some believe that this is *not* a zero-sum game. Australians saw this during the campaign period when one group of cross-denominational Christians came together to advocate marriage equality under the title Australian Christians For Marriage Equality.[48] Such attitudes are also reflected by some of our participants, especially with regard to their own workplace. Witness Tamara, who said, 'it's a manageable balance,' or Andy, who explains that this is 'the first time I've been working in a religiously based organisation, and you know it actually hasn't been too different from any other organisation.' Melissa said that working in a religious organisation has 'opened my mind a bit. . . . Because I definitely think it can work both ways.' And Jac, who is Catholic, believes that 'God created us as we are meant to be. . . . And, therefore there must be something in God's plan about making me feel the way that I do.' Her employee experiences also led her to believe that in Catholic schools, 'the general values don't exclude LGBTQI people.'

Other interviewees seemed to hold inconsistent views about the compatibility of religious freedom and LGBTQ+ non-discrimination. Consider Damien, who at one point said that the Christian response to LGBTQ+ people has been "hijacked" by extremists, and that this 'throws under the bus the majority who are living their life and want to be supportive or be neutral.' However, he also said that 'trying to re-enforce religious values on what is supposed to be a secular nation – that's scary.' Similarly, whilst Peta genuinely endorses the values of her employer organisation, she does not agree that her workplace should aim to 'turn people into disciples,' which is suggestive of apprehension towards religion. In addition, whilst Angela poses the rhetorical question, 'If you're going to have marriage equality, why does that mean all of a sudden that you don't have religious freedom? I mean, it's such bullshit,' she also asked, 'how can you trust priests these days? How can you trust anybody in a cloth?' Additionally, she believes that her workplace is selective about the religious values it emphasises – 'you can take it as a part of that Christian ethic, but we adopt that into the social work ethic' – which is at least suggestive of an attitude which sees a discordance between the two positions. In short, positive experiences do not necessarily make LGBTQ+ people less sceptical of "religious freedom."

Anxiety and vigilance

All participants exercise a degree of vigilance with regard to their sexual orientation and gender status, both within and beyond workplace. Participants highlighted the importance of "safe spaces," even those who recognise they are commonly "read" as LGBTQ+. Some would take proactive steps to avoid potentially discriminatory encounters. Others, who were comfortably out, still would not "advertise" their identity to certain people. Consider the following.

On being out(ed) in the workplace, Andy explains, 'I called a meeting . . . with my lead and I said . . . you know that's my discretion to out myself to people – not that I feel there *is* any danger, but you know *potentially* it could be a safety issue' (emphasis added). Similarly, Jac said 'I've not had . . . any negative experiences myself, other than feeling, oh, OK, that wasn't the right place to be out – it wasn't a safe space to be out.' Likewise, Damien gives the impression that his immediate work context is supportive of his sexual identity, yet he also said, 'there's still a vigilance that's in other spaces,' further explaining that 'I tend to use "they" before coming out very deliberately . . . yeah, so "they" is a very useful tool, like the word "partner."' This is one strategy employed by LGBTQ+ people to test the safety of their surroundings. Emma, however, worries that it may not be safe to out herself even to allies, saying 'if you tell someone [who's supportive], then everyone finds out. And people who you think wouldn't be so supportive find out. So, I feel like I can't tell anyone.' Emma also tries to rationalise her anxiety, explaining 'I've heard [homophobic stereotypes] so often, from many different people, I've probably just internalised that and now that's how I act.' Different strategies were employed by Tamara. When asked how her workplace would respond if she entered a same-sex marriage, Tamara said she would 'decline to share that information.' Similarly, Tamara 'ignored' the No campaign, and tries to keep things 'neutral' at work. This echoes one of Tony's general strategies: 'like if you're in a pub and someone's [saying] . . . "I bash poofters," you don't go up and say, "Hey, I'm a poofter."'

Demonstrating that positive experiences do not necessarily rectify this latent anxiety, consider Melissa's case. When asked what effect entering a same-sex marriage could have on her working environment, Melissa said 'I'm not sure, to be honest . . . everyone sort of has to be friendly on the surface. So, I guess I have that underlying sort of anxiety that . . . they're not really being genuine. . . . You're *always* going to wonder' (emphasis added). Tony described this same anxiety in relation to the same-sex marriage vote, explaining, 'I kind of had in my gut that it was going to be a Yes, but then I was like: I wonder if Australia is ready for this shift?' Looking forward, Peta worries that if religious freedom is too heavily protected, then 'people who fit into that category of being gay could become more vulnerable.' And, although Angela feels very accepted in her workplace, she also said 'I'm probably not ever going to say outwardly to the Archbishop, you know, "I'm gay."' The legacy of LGBTQ+ discrimination lives on in Australia, even after same-sex marriage. It has tangible effects on how LGBTQ+ people inhabit social spaces. They exhibit a particular form of socially based anxiety that undermines a basic public good: the assurance that they can count on being treated as an equally respected member of society.[49] This is not exclusive to religious workplaces, but, for some, religion does heighten their anxiety.

Cis-hetero-norms

A final factor framing our interest in LGBTQ+ experiences of discrimination stems from feminist, leftist, and queer criticisms of the marriage equality movement (including those of this lead author).[50] In the words of Daniel Thompson, 'the problem with framing gender and sexual diversity in [cis]heteronormative terms is that it ultimately . . . positions gender and sexually diverse people within a hierarchically inferior position to [cis]heterosexuals.'[51] Some have suggested that the marriage equality movement privileges the most 'central' members of the LGBTQ+ community – namely cisgender, white, middle- and upper-class gays and, to an extent, lesbians – and leaves its most vulnerable members' concerns on the sidelines.[52] Thus, we are particularly interested in the experiences of Peta (bisexual), Emma (lesbian, but who openly discusses her 'passing' as straight), and Andy (trans).

Peta is a mother and in a different-gender relationship. Because of this, she is presumed heterosexual in her workplace. And whilst there are policies which require non-discrimination towards clients, Peta has witnessed workplace discussions which were hostile towards the LGBTQ+ community, hearing comments like 'I just think it's fucking disgusting.' She believes these would not have occurred in her presence but for the assumption she is heterosexual. She said, 'I found myself . . . kind of angry – hurt and angry – and feeling like: "Oh, so that's what they [believe] – if they knew [I'm bisexual], what would they be saying?"' Here, bi-erasure causes Peta to witness bigotry first-hand. And whilst Peta believes she is 'pretty lucky' to pass, having 'that sense of being an undercover agent,' she was harmed by such workplace debates. She recounts another occasion when a pro-equality colleague was engaging in debate with an anti-equality colleague, and that the ally 'was kind of making a joke of it and jollying along, and I found it really offensive . . . and I didn't think she would have done that if she would have been in the presence of someone who she knew was in the community.' Peta ended up outing herself to this colleague, who subsequently apologised, but she also spoke to her supervisor about the incident 'because I was actually really, really upset.'

Like Peta, Emma passes for heterosexual at her workplace. She said, 'I'm so feminine and no one's going to look at me and think [otherwise].' This allows her to remain closeted, which she sees as a virtue, saying, 'I do sometimes think if I – if I were trans, or if I was masculine presenting, I wouldn't ever have been able to get a job at that school.' This is not an exaggerated fear. Emma explains that recently her colleagues were discussing a proposal to make "sex" an opt-in marker on birth certificates in Tasmania. One of her colleagues stated, 'either you're male or you're female! That's it! True or false.' When asked if anyone else made a comment, Emma replied 'Oh, they were all agreeing. They were saying, "Oh no, that's ridiculous. I can't believe they want to do that. Either you're male or you're female."' Emma did not attempt to correct her colleagues, though. Despite knowing 'that is actually, scientifically, false,' Emma 'held [her] tongue.'

Emma shows a keen awareness that gender and orientation non-conformity remain traits for which people are stigmatised, and this stokes her desire to remain closeted ('I don't want drama. I just want some hush, you know?'). Indeed, it is by ascribing to cisgender norms of femininity that she is able to pass.

Now consider Andy, who is visibly "Other." Andy explains that, at work, they 'feel pretty comfortable. . . . With the exception of being . . . mis-gendered.' Whilst Andy tries 'to keep an open mind because I do know it's really new concept for a lot of people, especially here in Tasmania,' unfortunately not all of their colleagues are willing to change their patterns of behaviour. Whilst Andy's overall work experience is positive and accommodating, their experiences reveal a certain level of ignorance regarding gender status and identity. Andy said,

> We have a self-service system and for gender . . . it just had an X; I thought 'Okay that's alright!' . . . And then a few months later I went in[to my profile] to put some leave in and it had my gender as intersex. Someone had just changed it. . . . So, there was male, female, and intersex. Obviously, intersex is not a gender.

Furthermore, being out and highly visible (which Andy believes is important) means that Andy gets saddled with educating cisgender heterosexuals about gender in their organisation. They say, 'I'm happy to do that labour, but at the same time, I don't think it should be my job.' Instead of being proactive in better understanding marginalised collectives' issues, this workplace unfairly burdened Andy with an educative role – this is a form of what Jean Harvey calls "civilised oppression."[53] It is clear that the mainstream Yes movement, which 'bolstered claims to authenticity by the validation of (presumably) heterosexual kin,'[54] has not done a great deal to increase awareness of intersecting issues faced by the community's most marginal members.[55]

Conclusion

This chapter has considered the content of nine qualitative interviews with LGBTQ+ identifying Tasmanians who work in government funded religious organisations and schools in order to better understand their experiences of discrimination *and* inclusion in the workplace in this time of anxiety about religious freedom. We found that the legacy of LGBTQ+ discrimination lives on in Australia, and that this has tangible effects on how LGBTQ+ people inhabit social spaces. This socially based anxiety is not necessarily caused by or exacerbated in the religious workplace, but for some, religion does heighten their anxiety. Indeed, we found that in many cases, the workplace and organisational response toward those who were open about their sexuality/gender was quite positive. But, interestingly, attitudes towards the compatibility of religious freedom and LGBTQ+ non-discrimination were mixed. Some believed that these were incompatible, others disagreed, and some seemed to unconsciously sway between both positions. Thus, positive workplace experiences do not necessarily make LGBTQ+ people less sceptical of religious freedom, though this did occur for some employees. Finally, it seems that the mainstream marriage movement – which purposefully positioned marriage equality as a small target[56] – has not led to changes in other areas of more marginal LGBTQ+ peoples' lives. Bi-erasure, compulsory heterosexuality, and ignorance surrounding gender identity still seem to be problems in Tasmania. Thus, we must carry on in our long march toward equality, for bigotry and discrimination do not simply disappear with legislative change, and neither do the tangible harmful effects on the LGBTQ+ community.

Notes

1 Mia Sanders, 'Marriage Equality: A History of Struggle' *Green Left Weekly* (2017) 1164 <www.greenleft.org.au/content/marriage-equality-history-struggle> accessed 2 January 2019.
2 Louise Richardson-Self, *Justifying Same-Sex Marriage: A Philosophical Investigation* (Rowman and Littlefield International 2015).
3 Kees Waaldijk, 'Small Change: How the Road to Same-Sex Marriage Got Paved in the Netherlands' in Robert Wintemute and Mads Andenæs (eds), *Legal Recognition of Same-Sex Partnership: A Study of National, European, and International Law* (Hart Publishing 2001).
4 Louise Richardson-Self, 'Same-Sex Marriage and the "No" Campaign' (2018) 9 *Humanities Australia* 32.
5 Richardson-Self (n 2).
6 Andrea Carson, Shaun Ratcliff and Yannick Dufresne, 'Public Opinion and Policy Responsiveness: The Case of Same-Sex Marriage in Australia' (2018) 53 *Australian Journal of Political Science* 3.
7 Deirdre McKeown, 'Chronology of Same-Sex Marriage Bills Introduced into the Federal Parliament: A Quick Guide' *Parliament of Australia* (15 February 2018). <www.aph.gov.au/About_Parliament/Parliamentary_Departments/Parliamentary_Library/pubs/rp/rp1718/Quick_Guides/SSMarriageBills> accessed 2 January 2019.
8 Stephen Smiley, 'Tasmanian Upper House MPs Reject Bid to Revive Debate on Same-Sex Marriage' *ABC News* (26 November 2013) <www.abc.net.au/news/2013-10-29/tasmanian-upper-house-rejects-bid-to-revive-marriage-debate/5056032> accessed 3 January 2019.
9 McKeown (n 7); Ian McAllister and Feodor Snagovsky, 'Explaining Voting in the 2017 Australian Same-Sex Marriage Plebiscite' (2018) 53 *Australian Journal of Political Science* 409.
10 Carson et al. (n 6).
11 Ibid.; Odette Mazel, 'The Politics of Difference: Posting My "Vote" on Marriage Equality' (2018) 43 *Alternative Law Journal* 4; McAllister and Snagovsky (n 9).
12 McAllister and Snagovsky (n 9).
13 Ibid., 412.
14 Richardson-Self (n 4).
15 Mazel (n 11).
16 McAllister and Snagovsky (n 9).
17 Ibid., 413.
18 Matt Connellan, '"Deliberately Misleading": First "Vote No" to Same-Sex Marriage Advertisement Airs' *SBS News* (30 August 2017) <www.sbs.com.au/news/

deliberately-misleading-first-vote-no-to-same-sex-marriage-advertisement-airs> accessed 4 January 2018.

19 Quinn Eades and Son Vivienne (eds), *Going Postal: More than 'Yes' or 'No'. One Year On: Writings from the Marriage Equality Survey* (Brow Books 2018); Mazel (n 11).

20 Richardson-Self (n 2).

21 McAllister and Snagovsky (n 9) 414.

22 Ibid.

23 Richardson-Self (n 4).

24 CfM, 'Neighbour Visitation Campaign: Training Material' *Coalition for Marriage* (2017). <https://d3n8a8pro7vhmx.cloudfront.net/coalitionformarriage/pages/361/attachments/original/1505535929/C4M_Field_-_NVC_Training_Script.pdf?1505535929> accessed 6 January 2019.

25 Amy Thomas and Hannah McCann, 'Marriage Equality: Yes, It's About Gender' (2017) *Overland Literary Journal* <https://overland.org.au/2017/09/marriage-equality-yes-its-about-gender/> accessed 4 January 2019. Note that prolific Tasmanian LGBTQ+ activist Rodney Croome (AM), who stepped down from the role of AME Director in 2016, recently revealed that AME's media and campaign managers 'were uncomfortable engaging with the full breadth of issues marriage equality raised' and that this influenced his decision to leave: Rodney Croome, 'Why It Was a Mistake to Make Marriage Equality a Small Target' *QNews Magazine* (2018) <www.qnews.com.au/mistake-make-marriage-equality-small-target/> accessed 4 January 2019.

26 Richardson-Self (n 4).

27 CfM (n 24) 5, original emphasis.

28 Mazel (n 11) 8.

29 Philip Ruddock (Chair), 'Religious Freedom Review: Report of the Expert Panel' *Australian Government* (2018) iii <www.ag.gov.au/RightsAndProtections/HumanRights/Documents/religious-freedom-review-expert-panel-report-2018.pdf> accessed 6 January 2019.

30 James Elton-Pym, 'Ruddock's Religious Freedom Review Kicks off in Sydney' *SBS News* (10 January 2018) <www.sbs.com.au/news/ruddock-s-religious-freedom-review-kicks-off-in-sydney> accessed 27 March 2019.

31 Carolyn Evans and Leilani Ujvari, 'Non-Discrimination Laws and Religious Schools in Australia' (2009) 30 *Adelaide Law Review* 31.

32 Ruddock (n 29) 8.

33 Ibid.

34 Ibid., 11–12.

35 Ibid., 10.

36 Ibid., 8.

37 Ibid., 13.

38 Ibid., 9.

39 Liam Elphick, Amy Maguire and Anja Hilkemeijer, 'Ruddock Report Constrains, Not Expands, Federal Religious Exemptions' *The Conversation* (10 October 2018) <https://theconversation.com/ruddock-report-constrains-not-expands-federal-religious-exemptions-96347> accessed 6 January 2019.

40 Anja Hilkemeijer, 'In Long-Awaited Response to Ruddock Review, the Government Pushes Hard on Religious Freedom' *The Conversation* (13 December 2018) <https://theconversation.com/in-long-awaited-response-to-ruddock-review-the-government-pushes-hard-on-religious-freedom-108750> accessed 4 January 2019.

41 ABS, '2071.0 – Census of Population and Housing: Reflecting Australia – Stories from the Census' *Australian Bureau of Statistics* (28 June 2016) <www.abs.gov.au/ausstats/abs@.nsf/Lookup/by%20Subject/2071.0~2016~Main%20Features~Religion%20Data%20Summary~70> accessed 6 January 2019.

42 Tom Wilson and Fiona Shalley, 'Estimates of Australia's Non-Heterosexual Population' (2018) 2 *Australian Population Studies* 26.
43 ABS, '1800.0 – Australian Marriage Law Postal Survey' *Australian Bureau of Statistics* (15 November 2017) <www.abs.gov.au/ausstats/abs@.nsf/Lookup/by%20Subject/1800.0~2017~Main%20Features~Tasmania~14> accessed 6 January 2019.
44 Bronwyn Fielder and Douglas Ezzy, *Lesbian, Gay, Bisexual and Transgender Christians* (Bloomsbury 2018).
45 Jennifer Mason, *Qualitative Researching* (2nd edn, Sage Publications 2002); Alan Peshkin, 'In Search of Subjectivity – One's Own' (1988) 17 *Educational Researcher* 17.
46 Earl Babbie, *The Basics of Social Research* (5th edn, Wadsworth 2011).
47 Michael Q Patton, *Qualitative Research and Evaluation Methods: Integrating Theory and Practice* (4th edn, Sage 2014).
48 See Francisco Perales, Gary Bouma and Alice Campbell, 'Religion, Support of Equal Rights for Same-Sex Couples and the Australian National Vote on Marriage Equality' (2018) 80 *Sociology of Religion* 107.
49 Jeremy Waldron, *The Harm in Hate Speech* (Harvard University Press 2012).
50 Louise Richardson-Self, 'Questioning the Goal of Same-Sex Marriage' (2012) 27 *Australian Feminist Studies* 205; Richardson-Self (n 2).
51 Daniel Jay Thompson, 'Your Parents Will Read This: Reading (as) Parents in Journalistic Coverage of the Safe Schools Coalition Australia Controversy' (2018) *Journalism* <https://journals.sagepub.com/doi/pdf/10.1177/1464884918755638> accessed 30 June 2019.
52 For example, Gorrie and Ison's contributions in Eades and Vivienne (n 19).
53 Jean Harvey, 'Victims, Resistance, and Civilized Oppression' (2010) 41 *Journal of Social Philosophy* 13.
54 Benjamin Hegarty, Daniel Marshall, Mary Lou Rasmussen, Peter Aggleton and Robert Ian Cover, 'Heterosexuality and Race in the Australian Same-Sex Marriage Postal Survey' (2018) 33 *Australian Feminist Studies* 400.
55 But note that Damien said his current 'thoughts tend to be around . . . the need for transgender people who were married before the plebiscite to divorce' more so than religious freedom.
56 Croome (n 25).

References

ABS, '2071.0 – Census of Population and Housing: Reflecting Australia – Stories from the Census' *Australian Bureau of Statistics* (28 June 2016) <www.abs.gov.au/ausstats/abs@.nsf/Lookup/by%20Subject/2071.0~2016~Main%20Features~Religion%20Data%20Summary~70> accessed 6 January 2019.

———, '1800.0 – Australian Marriage Law Postal Survey' *Australian Bureau of Statistics* (15 November 2017) <www.abs.gov.au/ausstats/abs@.nsf/Lookup/by%20Subject/1800.0~2017~Main%20Features~Tasmania~14> accessed 6 January 2019.

Babbie E, *The Basics of Social Research* (5th edn, Wadsworth 2011).

Carson A, Ratcliff S and Dufresne Y, 'Public Opinion and Policy Responsiveness: The Case of Same-Sex Marriage in Australia' (2018) 53 *Australian Journal of Political Science* 3.

CfM, 'Neighbour Visitation Campaign: Training Material' *Coalition for Marriage* (2017). <https://d3n8a8pro7vhmx.cloudfront.net/coalitionformarriage/

pages/361/attachments/original/1505535929/C4M_Field_-_NVC_Training_Script.pdf?1505535929> accessed 6 January 2019.

Connellan M, '"Deliberately Misleading": First "Vote No" to Same-Sex Marriage Advertisement Airs' *SBS News* (30 August 2017) <www.sbs.com.au/news/deliberately-misleading-first-vote-no-to-same-sex-marriage-advertisement-airs> accessed 4 January 2018.

Croome R, 'Why It Was a Mistake to Make Marriage Equality a Small Target' *QNews Magazine* (2018) <www.qnews.com.au/mistake-make-marriage-equality-small-target/> accessed 4 January 2019.

Eades Q and Vivienne S (eds), *Going Postal: More than 'Yes' or 'No'. One Year On: Writings from the Marriage Equality Survey* (Brow Books 2018).

Elphick L, Maguire A and Hilkemeijer A, 'Ruddock Report Constrains, Not Expands, Federal Religious Exemptions' *The Conversation* (10 October 2018) <https://theconversation.com/ruddock-report-constrains-not-expands-federal-religious-exemptions-96347> accessed 6 January 2019.

Elton-Pym J, 'Ruddock's Religious Freedom Review Kicks Off in Sydney' *SBS News* (10 January 2018) <www.sbs.com.au/news/ruddock-s-religious-freedom-review-kicks-off-in-sydney> accessed 27 March 2019.

Evans C and Ujvari L, 'Non-Discrimination Laws and Religious Schools in Australia' (2009) 30 *Adelaide Law Review* 31.

Fielder B and Ezzy D, *Lesbian, Gay, Bisexual and Transgender Christians* (Bloomsbury 2018).

Harvey J, 'Victims, Resistance, and Civilized Oppression' (2010) 41 *Journal of Social Philosophy* 13.

Hegarty B, Marshall D, Rasmussen ML, Aggleton P and Cover RI, 'Heterosexuality and Race in the Australian Same-Sex Marriage Postal Survey' (2018) 33 *Australian Feminist Studies* 400.

Hilkemeijer A, 'In Long-Awaited Response to Ruddock Review, the Government Pushes Hard on Religious Freedom' *The Conversation* (13 December 2018) <https://theconversation.com/in-long-awaited-response-to-ruddock-review-the-government-pushes-hard-on-religious-freedom-108750> accessed 4 January 2019.

Mason J, *Qualitative Researching* (2nd edn, Sage Publications 2002).

Mazel O, 'The Politics of Difference: Posting My "Vote" on Marriage Equality' (2018) 43 *Alternative Law Journal* 4.

McAllister I and Snagovsky F, 'Explaining Voting in the 2017 Australian Same-Sex Marriage Plebiscite' (2018) 53 *Australian Journal of Political Science* 409.

McKeown D, 'Chronology of Same-Sex Marriage Bills Introduced into the Federal Parliament: A Quick Guide' *Parliament of Australia* (15 February 2018). <www.aph.gov.au/About_Parliament/Parliamentary_Departments/Parliamentary_Library/pubs/rp/rp1718/Quick_Guides/SSMarriageBills> accessed 2 January 2019.

Patton MQ, *Qualitative Research and Evaluation Methods: Integrating Theory and Practice* (4th edn, Sage 2014).

Perales F, Bouma G and Campbell A, 'Religion, Support of Equal Rights for Same-Sex Couples and the Australian National Vote on Marriage Equality' (2018) 80 *Sociology of Religion* 107.

Peshkin A, 'In Search of Subjectivity – One's Own' (1988) 17 *Educational Researcher* 17.

Richardson-Self L, 'Questioning the Goal of Same-Sex Marriage' (2012) 27 *Australian Feminist Studies* 205.

———, *Justifying Same-Sex Marriage: A Philosophical Investigation* (Rowman and Littlefield International 2015).

———, 'Same-Sex Marriage and the 'No' Campaign' (2018) 9 *Humanities Australia* 32.

Ruddock P (Chair), 'Religious Freedom Review: Report of the Expert Panel' *Australian Government* (2018) iii <www.ag.gov.au/RightsAndProtections/HumanRights/Documents/religious-freedom-review-expert-panel-report-2018.pdf> accessed 6 January 2019.

Sanders M, 'Marriage Equality: A History of Struggle' *Green Left Weekly* (2017) 1164 <www.greenleft.org.au/content/marriage-equality-history-struggle> accessed 2 January 2019.

Smiley S, 'Tasmanian Upper House MPs Reject Bid to Revive Debate on Same-Sex Marriage' *ABC News* (26 November 2013) <www.abc.net.au/news/2013-10-29/tasmanian-upper-house-rejects-bid-to-revive-marriage-debate/5056032> accessed 3 January 2019.

Thomas A and McCann H, 'Marriage Equality: Yes, It's About Gender' (2017) *Overland Literary Journal* <https://overland.org.au/2017/09/marriage-equality-yes-its-about-gender/> accessed 4 January 2019.

Thompson DJ, 'Your Parents Will Read This: Reading (as) Parents in Journalistic Coverage of the Safe Schools Coalition Australia Controversy' (2018) *Journalism* <https://journals.sagepub.com/doi/pdf/10.1177/1464884918755638> accessed 30 June 2019.

Waaldijk K, 'Small Change: How the Road to Same-Sex Marriage Got Paved in the Netherlands' in Wintemute R and Andenæs M (eds), *Legal Recognition of Same-Sex Partnership: A Study of National, European, and International Law* (Hart Publishing 2001).

Waldron J, *The Harm in Hate Speech* (Harvard University Press 2012).

Wilson T and Shalley F, 'Estimates of Australia's Non-Heterosexual Population' (2018) 2 *Australian Population Studies* 26.

Chapter 6

The role of constitutional courts in promoting marriage equality and their relationships with movements and legislators

Angioletta Sperti

Introduction

In continental Europe, same-sex marriage has been mainly introduced through legislative reforms.

Spain, for instance, was the first Southern European country to open marriage to same-sex couples. Despite the Spanish Constitution of 1978 explicitly conferring the right to marry to a 'man' and a 'woman' (art 32, s 1),[1] law no 13 of 2005[2] amended the Spanish Civil Code (art 44, s 2)[3] in order to extend the right to marry to same-sex couples with the same rights and obligations as opposite-sex couples.

In Portugal, homosexuality was decriminalised in 1982 and same-sex *de facto* unions (*união de facto*) were legalised in 2001.[4] In 2010, Parliament adopted law no 9/2010,[5] a five-article statute amending the traditional definition of marriage in the civil code.

In France, the debate on legal recognition of same-sex relationships began at the end of the 1980s, when progressive political parties and LGBTQ+ movements inspired the first parliamentary bills for the regulation of same-sex civil unions.[6] In 1999, the National Assembly introduced the *pacte civil de solidarieté* (PaCS, civil solidarity pact),[7] a 'contract concluded by two adult persons of the same or different sex in order to organise their joint life.'[8] In the following years, the idea of equal marriage began to take shape in French political debate, and in 2012, after the Socialist Party's victory in general elections, government introduced a bill for *mariage pour tous* in the National Assembly. The bill was voted into law in 2013 (*loi* No. 2013–404),[9] following a heated debate at political level and the largest demonstrations in decades.

In Germany, where marriage and the family enjoy a special constitutional protection,[10] the Bundestag in 2001 passed the Civil Partnerships Act legalising same-sex civil unions (*eingetragene Lebenspartnerschaft*, literally life partnership). In order to maintain a proper distinction from the institution of marriage, the Act did not allow civil partners to adopt children and treated them as single persons as far as inheritance and tax law were concerned. In 2004, the Civil Partnerships Act of 2001 was amended in order to include stepchild adoption and divorce rules, and in 2017, the Bundestag opened marriage to same-sex couples (*Ehe für alle*).[11]

At a first glance, the continental European path to same-sex marriage could appear quite different from the approach followed in North America, where marriage equality – at the federal level – was mainly the result of landmark constitutional cases. It is worth remembering that in the United States, Congress adopted in 1996 a federal law (Defense of Marriage Act, DOMA) which provided a definition of 'marriage' and 'spouse' as referred to the opposite-sex couple (s 3).[12] In 2013, the United States Supreme Court held the definition to be an unconstitutional deprivation of liberty and equal protection under the Fifth Amendment to the US Constitution.[13] In 2015, in *Obergefell v Hodges*,[14] the Supreme Court reiterated that denial of the status of marriage to same-sex couples amounted to a violation of their human dignity and autonomy and declared unconstitutional the operative section of DOMA (s 2) that still allowed states to refuse to recognise same-sex marriages performed under the laws of other states. At the same time, the Supreme Court emphasised that the right to marry is a fundamental right and that it should be guaranteed to all individuals, regardless of their sexual orientation. As a consequence, the Supreme Court required all states to issue marriage licences to same-sex couples, recognising same-sex marriage throughout the entire nation.

Canada followed a similar path: as early as in 1995, in *Egan v. Canada*,[15] a narrow majority of the federal Supreme Court dismissed Mr Egan's claim, arguing that the definition of 'spouse' could not be interpreted as including the partner in a same-sex relationship. Nonetheless, the Supreme Court of Canada unanimously considered 'sexual orientation' an illegitimate ground of discrimination under Article 15 of the Canadian Charter of Rights and Freedoms. *Egan* has been a pivotal case: it led to a sequence of relevant judicial decisions through the late 1990s in which same-sex couples were made equal to common law spouses.[16] In 1999, in particular, in *M v H*,[17] the Supreme Court held that the failure to provide stable lesbian and gay couples with the same legal rights and duties accorded to unmarried cohabiting opposite-sex couples, in case of breakdown of the relationships, amounted to an illegitimate discrimination under the Canadian Charter of Rights and Freedoms.

M v H has been, in turn, a powerful stimulus for further achievements for same-sex couples' rights: although this case affected only the province of Ontario, it stimulated the adoption of new legislation at provincial and federal level extending to same-sex partners the rights and obligation afforded to common law opposite-sex couples. At the same time, it inspired new marriage equality lawsuits that resulted in further rulings by the Provincial Courts of Ontario, Quebec and British Columbia recognising the right to marriage to same-sex couples under the Charter.[18] In 2005, these judicial developments led to the adoption of a federal regulation extending the right to marriage to same-sex couples.[19]

My purpose in this chapter is to demonstrate that differences in the path toward same-sex marriage should not be overstated. Although in the United States and in Canada, Supreme Court rulings asserted in clear terms that excluding same-sex couples from marriage amounted to an unconstitutional violation of equality, whereas in Europe constitutional courts have usually been more deferent to national legislators, I aim to clarify that Europe and North America share many similarities in the synergy between national legislators and constitutional courts on the recognition of marriage equality.

In my analysis, I do not aim to provide an exhaustive account of same-sex marriage case law. As far as North America is concerned, in this chapter, I will refer to the rulings of the US Supreme Court and of the Supreme Court of Canada. I will also provide sketches of the most important rulings of continental European constitutional courts on equal marriage, focusing in particular on the constitutional and supreme courts of Spain, Portugal, Germany and France, whose cases have exerted great influence on other constitutional and supreme courts. I will also address the Italian constitutional courts' rulings on marriage equality and same-sex civil partnerships. Although Italian legislation does not allow same-sex couples to marry, I argue that the same arguments concerning the relationship between legislators and constitutional courts in other countries can also shed light on the cautious approach to marriage equality that the Italian constitutional court has followed in its cases.

Nonetheless, I do not intend to deny the differences between legislatures and courts in promoting and protecting the human rights of gays and lesbians: as I argued in previous works,[20] legislatures tend to address equality issues in smaller steps depending on the prevailing trends of public opinion, whereas constitutional or supreme courts exercise more caution due to the concern to preserve their legitimacy and avoid backlash.

In my account, in the first place, I will focus on the synergy between constitutional courts and legislators towards same-sex marriage. In the following section, I will instead emphasise the many differences between constitutional and lower ordinary courts. I argue that the outcome of constitutional litigation also depends on the peculiar procedural and institutional arrangements governing the judicial review of legislation in each jurisdiction and that – especially on issues so deeply entrenched in culture and tradition as those concerning family and marriage – courts of ordinary jurisdiction should not be assimilated to supreme courts.

The contribution of constitutional courts and their synergy with national legislators on marriage equality

Both in Europe and North America courts, especially constitutional or supreme courts, have provided a significant contribution to elevating marriage equality to the public agenda.[21]

In the first place, European constitutional courts have been bringing sexual orientation equality issues to public attention.

In 2010, in France, the Conseil constitutionnel addressed the constitutionality of the provisions of the French civil code that limited marriage to opposite-sex couples.[22] The Conseil moved its reasoning from the established definition of marriage, reiterating that the institution traditionally referred to opposite-sex couples. Nonetheless, the Conseil argued that the National Assembly had the power to amend the civil code in order to open marriage to same-sex couples. In other words, the Conseil seemed to suggest that the Constitution did not prohibit same-sex marriage and that the reform fell within the discretionary powers of the legislature.[23]

Soon after that ruling, the French Socialist Party submitted a first legislative proposal on same-sex marriage to the National Assembly[24] and the Socialist Party candidate, François Hollande, included equal marriage among his commitments during the campaign for the 2012 general elections.

In Germany, in 1993, a three-justice chamber of the First Senate of the Constitutional Tribunal took into consideration the first complaint of a same-sex couple[25] who claimed that denial of the right to marriage to same-sex couples violated the Basic Law. Although the First Senate dismissed the appeal, the judgement seemed to suggest that the legislature might grant an equal treatment to 'forms of social life similar to marriage' in certain specific situations. At the same time, the First Senate emphasised 'the hindrances these couples faced relative to persons united in marriage.' In the early 2000s, this acknowledgement, along with growing demands by the LGBTQ+ community, led the left-wing government to support the introduction of civil partnerships, despite the fierce opposition of large segments of the population and religious groups.[26] Same-sex civil unions (*eingetragene Lebenspartnerschaft*, literally life partnership) were legalised in 2001.[27]

In Italy, in 2010, the Constitutional Court denied that the civil code definition of marriage amounted to a violation of the Constitution,[28] but it recognised the right of same-sex couples to 'live freely as a couple,' pressing the legislature to regulate same-sex unions.[29]

These examples demonstrate that in Europe, as well as in the United States and Canada, courts have been playing a key role in challenging stereotypes against homosexuality and same-sex couples. By describing with greater detail the normalcy of same-sex couples' family life and the difficulties they face daily, courts contributed to de-emphasising many prejudices against homosexuality, and, in Eskridge's words, to the passage from 'backlash politics' to 'identity politics'; i.e. to a rhetoric motivated by identity-based concerns.[30]

It should be noted that European courts' roles in promoting public debate on sexual orientation equality issues have not been limited to judgements resulting in victory for gays and lesbians. Most of the early European constitutional cases actually rejected same-sex couples' claims.

In Spain, the Constitutional Tribunal refused in 1994 to extend to same-sex relationships the constitutional protection of marriage.[31] Nonetheless, the Constitutional Tribunal emphasised that 'this interpretation does not prevent he legislative power from establishing a system of equalisation so that same-sex relationships can enjoy the full rights and benefits of marriage.' The Tribunal's ruling paved the way for the adoption of the first regulations of same-sex unions at the local level.[32] In 2005, Parliament amended the civil code, opening marriage to same-sex couples.[33]

In Portugal, in 2009, a lesbian couple lodged an appeal arguing that the civil code's definition of marriage was unconstitutional and referred the issue of constitutional legitimacy to the Constitutional Tribunal. In particular, the Tribunal was asked to clarify whether the legislature had a constitutional obligation to open marriage to same-sex couples. The Tribunal dismissed the case,[34] arguing that equal marriage could not be introduced through judicial review of legislation but emphasising that marriage is not a 'frozen institution' and the Portuguese Constitution provides a broad definition of marriage. Following the guiding principles of the Constitutional Tribunal, only seven months later, the Parliament voted law no 9/2010,[35] a five- article statute amending the definition of 'marriage' in the civil code (but reserving joint adoption to the opposite-sex married couple).

In France, in an early judgement on the constitutional legitimacy of PaCS[36], the Conseil constitutionnel clearly stated that a PaCS is different from marriage and refused to qualify same-sex couples as families. Nonetheless, the Conseil recognised the importance of same-sex relationships and their constitutional value. The court's ruling forged the further debate on same-sex marriage. As mentioned previously, in a following case, the Conseil constitutionnel suggested that marriage was an institution traditionally reserved to opposite-sex couples, but argued that the legislature had the power to amend the legislation in order to open the institution of marriage to same-sex couples.[37]

These examples demonstrate that although unsatisfactory in their outcome, in the long term, European constitutional courts' arguments were crucial for future achievements. They helped to define the boundaries between the judicial and the legislative powers, and provided guidelines for the proper interpretation of broad (constitutional or statutory) clauses on 'marriage' and 'family.' Courts engaged in a dialogue with national legislators, paving the way for the adoption of legislative reforms.

The European path toward same-sex marriage I summarily sketched demonstrates that what mattered most was not the outcome of the judgements, but the subtle instructions that courts – especially constitutional courts – provided to legislators, social movements and even public opinion. At the same time, as their American counterparts, European courts helped to dismantle prejudice and bias against gays and lesbians, but they also forged the constitutional arguments for the recognition of equal rights for same-sex couples. Since their first rulings courts also channelled the debate into new forms. Accordingly, those opposing same-sex marriage have progressively dismissed traditional arguments of 'nature' or tradition, or – as far as parental rights are concerned – rejected the idea of a 'procreative nature' of marriage.[38]

I do not deny that in this process, courts (especially constitutional courts) *are also influenced* by the prevailing sentiments of public opinion and politics.

For instance, when in 2013 the Conseil constitutionnel released its final ruling on the constitutionality of equal marriage (*mariage pour tous*),[39] the National Assembly had already voted law no. 404 of 2013 that amended article 143 of the French civil code stating that 'marriage is contracted by two persons of different sex or of the same sex.'[40] Although the bill was voted into law only after more than 140 hours of heated debate, with massive rallies and violence across the country, polls revealed that more than 63% of the French population supported equal marriage. In its ruling, the Conseil confirmed the constitutionality of the reform and took a more explicit stance on the nature marriage; at the same time, it argued that the National Assembly had the power to regulate marriage according to constitutional principles, and in particular to regulate sensitive social issues.[41]

In Spain, the Constitutional Tribunal delivered its judgement on same-sex marriage only in 2012,[42] seven years after the Socialist-led government had introduced same-sex marriage and when more than 20,000 same-sex couples were already married. Furthermore, at that time, almost 77 per cent of Spaniards supported same-sex marriage. The Tribunal's long wait for a decision on the constitutionality of same-sex marriage was probably due to its intention to minimise backlash.[43] Choosing not to step into the political and social debate about same-sex marriage, the Constitutional Tribunal favoured political intervention, leaving it to the political branches of government to respond to the claims coming from the open and tolerant Spanish society.[44]

However, at the same time, courts also *influence* social and political change. For instance, the 1999 ruling of the Conseil constitutionnel (on the constitutionality of PaCS) was unsatisfactory in its outcome; nonetheless, as Renyniers emphasises, 'as narrow as the grounds of the judgement are, the decision remain[ed] a form of acceptation of same-sex relationships and sexuality at the apex of the French judicial hierarchy.'[45] Analogously, the 1994 ruling of the Constitutional Tribunal revealed an openness towards the rights of LGBTQ+ people at that time uncommon among constitutional and supreme courts. The rationale of the case paved the way for the adoption of regulations of same-sex unions at local level in Spain and helped to penetrate the idea of the 'normalcy' of same-sex relationships. In Portugal, the Parliament introduced same-sex marriage just a few months after the Constitutional Tribunal's judgement in case no 359 of 2009,[46] which rejected the claims of a lesbian couples, but at the same time suggested to the legislature and to LGBT movements that constitutional clauses did not prohibit same-sex marriage.

My thesis is that these examples demonstrate that what mattered most in the European countries was not the outcome of the judgements, but the subtle instructions that courts, in particular constitutional courts, provided to legislators, social movements and public opinion. Being influenced and at the same time influencing the debate over same-sex marriage, courts paved the way to legislative reforms and helped to forge the constitutional arguments that successfully supported future claims of same-sex couples.

In this respect, I see many similarities with the process that in the United States led to recognition of equal marriage at federal level. American scholarship has focused on the role of social movements in shaping constitutional meaning and the contribution of the courts to this process.[47] This body of work has demonstrated how civil rights movements have shaped constitutional norms and, in turn, have been shaped by those norms. As Reva Siegel emphasises, the Supreme Court ruling in *Obergefell v Hodges*[48] – holding that the right to marry is a fundamental right, regardless of sexual orientation of the spouses, and that states cannot refuse to recognise marriages concluded in other states – was possible not simply because public opinion changed, but also because struggle over the courts created relationships among movements, government officials and citizens that helped change public opinion and forge new constitutional understandings.[49]

The different role of lower ordinary courts

In the previous pages, I focused in particular on the role of constitutional courts in the introduction of equal marriage. Whereas European legislatures, which are politically accountable, have been taking steps in the advancement of same-sex couples rights that are consistent with public opinion,[50] constitutional courts are usually placed in a more difficult position.

For the minorities that resort to them, courts – especially supreme and constitutional courts – are the most important forums where to assert and ask for the protection of their fundamental rights. At the same time, it should be remembered that in the civil law tradition, principles regulating the burden of proof imply that courts cannot refuse to adjudicate: they have a *duty* to release a judgement that supports, totally or partially, the case of one of the parties (prohibition of *non liquet*).[51]

In the United States, the Supreme Court in 2013 delivered its judgement in *Hollingsworth v Perry*,[52] a case concerning the constitutionality of Proposition 8, a ballot measure that amended the California constitution in order to prohibit same-sex marriage and withdrew equal marriage rights six months after the California Supreme Court had recognised them. The US Supreme Court concluded that Prop. 8's proponents did not have standing to appeal the US District Court ruling of 2010,[53] holding that Prop. 8 violated the equal protection and due process rights of same-sex couples under the Fourteenth Amendment to the US Constitution. With its ruling, the Supreme Court made the District Court decision as the final and controlling decision on the merits, leaving same-sex couples in California free to marry. As Yoshino has clearly demonstrated,[54] this victory would have never been achieved without the long legal battle before federal courts and, in particular, the insightful and rigorous argument that District Judge Walker expounded in his 2010 ruling.

The Italian experience is also illustrative of the essential contribution that litigation before lower courts has given to the advancement of the rights of the LGBTQ+ community: against a hard-line position of the Constitutional Court – that in 2010 endorsed an originalist definition of 'marriage' as the union between a man and a woman[55] – in the last few years, Italian lower courts have instead been promoting constitutional change through constitutionally conforming interpretation of statutes and progressive readings of constitutional clauses on marriage and family. Lower courts have also frequently stressed the importance of reading constitutional principles of marriage and family in the light of Articles 8 and 12 ECHR, an argument that the Constitutional Court rejected in 2010, refusing to engage in a dialogue with international case law. The lower courts' progressive approach has been in particular crucial in the recognition of same-sex couples' parental rights.[56] At the same time, lower courts and Corte di Cassazione openings about the rights of same-sex couples were crucial for the adoption of the legislative reform of 2016 introducing same-sex civil unions.[57]

However, the European path makes clear that constitutional and supreme courts should not be assimilated to lower ordinary courts. In my opinion,[58] most of the differences between Europe and the United States in the timing and the path to same-sex marriage are the consequence of the specific features of the *centralised* judicial review of legislation, the prevailing judicial review model in Europe.[59]

It is worth remembering that in a centralised model of judicial review of legislation, the constitutional court is not a court of last resort (and it is distinguished from a supreme court that is the highest court in the judiciary), and it holds the exclusive power to declare parliamentary laws unconstitutional. At the same time, in countries like Italy and Portugal, citizens cannot submit their cases directly to the constitutional court, but constitutional issues are referred to the constitutional court by ordinary (civil, criminal and administrative) courts within a case pending before them.

Instead, in the United States, where judicial review is decentralised (in that it is exercised pursuant to ordinary litigation) and concrete (in that it is exercised pursuant to ordinary litigation), the Supreme Court is a court of general jurisdiction – courts address claims originating from civil society and stimulated by LGBTQ+ movements.

For these reasons, in a centralised judicial review system, constitutional courts are more reluctant to determine radical constitutional changes through their judgements, especially when the issue at stake involves an institution so entrenched in culture, history and tradition as marriage. Conversely, lower courts are more responsive to changing social claims, first of all because they are closer to the public, and second, in comparison with constitutional courts, are less concerned with the prospect of backlash that could undermine their own legitimacy.

Due to these differences, in the beginning, European constitutional courts have been mostly reluctant to anticipate legislative reforms. As mentioned earlier, the French Conseil constitutionnel in 2010 dismissed the first *question prioritaire de constitutionnalité* of the civil code affirming that the institution of marriage had been traditionally referred to opposite-sex couples. In Portugal, in 2009, when asked to decide on same-sex marriage for the first time, the Constitutional Tribunal concluded that there was no constitutional obligation to open marriage to same-sex couples.[60] In Spain, the Constitutional Tribunal held in 1994 that constitutional protection of marriage was reserved to opposite-sex couples and denied that, in the absence of a statutory regulation of same-sex relationships, same-sex couples could be treated the same way as married couples for the purposes of survivor benefits.[61] Nevertheless, the same courts ruled in favour of same-sex marriage when Parliaments had passed legislative reforms extending this right to same-sex couples.

In my opinion, the peculiar relationship between courts and legislatures in a centralised system of judicial review can also provide an explanation of the Italian Constitutional Court's choice not to interfere with the exercise of discretionary powers of the Parliament. In 2010, the Court dismissed the first case on the constitutional legitimacy of the definition of marriage in the civil code,[62] endorsing – as mentioned earlier – an originalist interpretation of the constitutional clause on marriage and family (sec 29). Although, in my opinion, the arguments the Italian constitutional court expounded are weak and objectionable,[63] I argue that the main difference with the other European constitutional courts does not lay in the court's reluctance to introduce same-sex marriage through a declaration of unconstitutionality of the civil code definition of marriage. In my opinion, what is more objectionable is the courts' reliance on an originalist interpretation of marriage in order to reject an evolutionary interpretation of 'marriage' and suggest to the legislature the adoption of a 'double track' solution – a model, based on the first German approach, that reserves special constitutional protection to opposite-sex marriage and regulates same-sex civil unions with rights and obligations similar to marriage. In conclusion, the outcome of the case – i.e. the constitutional court's decision not to introduce same-sex marriage by the means of a declaration of unconstitutionality of the civil code – can be explained in structural terms, and in particular, it is due to the peculiar role of the Italian Constitutional Court in the system of government.

Furthermore, it should be remembered that in centralised systems of judicial review, lower courts are also required to interpret the law in conformity with the country's constitution. This means that before referring a question to the constitutional court, which only has the power to set aside an unconstitutional statute, lower courts are expected to look for an interpretation that will preserve its validity. Especially in countries like Italy that do not have a direct constitutional complaint procedure, and whose citizens are not even allowed to lodge complaints to the constitutional court, constitutional courts can make use of the technique of constitutionally conforming interpretation to avoid direct confrontation with the political branches of government. Some courts – such as the Spanish, Italian and German constitutional courts – are very rigorous in this regard. They explicitly require that the referring court explains in its reference the reasons why it has not been possible to construe legislation in conformity with the constitution; otherwise, the preliminary reference will be dismissed as inadmissible.[64] As the Italian Constitutional Court has repeatedly emphasised since 1996, 'laws are not declared unconstitutional illegitimate because it is possible to give them an unconstitutional interpretation, but because it is not possible to give them a constitutional interpretation.'[65]

A detailed examination of the reasons explaining this trend falls outside the purpose of this chapter, but it suffices to say that the requirement of a preliminary interpretation of statutes in conformity with the constitution is subverting the alleged monopoly of constitutional courts on constitutional interpretation and 'enhancing the importance of the ordinary law courts as lawmakers in their own right.'[66]

In countries like Italy that do not have a direct constitutional complaint procedure and where citizens cannot lodge a complaint to the constitutional court, constitutional courts often make use of the technique of constitutionally conforming interpretation to avoid direct confrontation with the political branches of government. Furthermore, compared to the United States, it should be remembered that constitutional courts cannot make a selection of the cases.

In conclusion, all the features of the judicial review of legislation in centralised systems help to explain why, when same-sex marriage cases reached them for the first time, European constitutional courts preferred to engage in a dialogue with the legislatures, suggesting constitutionally possible solutions or setting a deadline for their intervention. Instead, in countries adopting a decentralised model of judicial review, like the United States, the path to the Supreme Court started from state and lower federal courts. When same-sex marriage reached the Supreme Court, the issue was ripe for decision. *Obergefell v Hodges*,[67] the Supreme Court case on same-sex marriage, has been the culmination of a long fight for equality that LGBTQ+ movements started in the early 1990s before state courts.

However, despite the differences between the two models of judicial review, both in Europe and in the United States, lower courts have been a crucial forum for LGBTQ+ movements' claims. As Martha Nussbaum suggests, none of the achievements would have happened had at least some lower courts had the daring to read their constitutions with an unbiased eye.[68]

Conclusion

In this chapter, I aimed to explain that, both in Europe and North America, courts – in particular, the highest courts – both influence and are influenced by the prevailing sentiments in public opinion and politics. In my opinion, this process results in a 'virtuous cycle' in which each single achievement laid the foundation for further advancement towards sexual equality.

I would like to emphasise that I do not aim at suggesting a normative argument based on a step-by-step approach towards equal marriage. In the last few years, each country has addressed same-sex marriage at a different pace and in different ways, depending on the intensity of disgust-based backlash, but also – as, for instance, the experiences of Portugal and Italy make clear – on the distinctive features of its political landscape and its receptiveness to civil rights reforms.

The history of same-sex marriage in California provides another interesting example. In his insightful analysis of the struggle for same-sex marriage in California, Yoshino emphasises that in the beginning the leaders of the major gay-rights organisations passionately opposed the lawsuit against Proposition 8, 'worried that the suit could rush this case to a defeat at the Supreme Court.'[69] The only same-sex marriage case that had gone to trial before, *Baehr v Lewin*,[70] had raised a strong backlash at political level leading to the introduction of the Defense of Marriage Act (DOMA) at the federal level. However, federal District Judge Walker's decision to strike down the California state ban on same-sex marriage proved the strategic effectiveness of making marriage equality the primary goal.

My purpose in this chapter has been basically to emphasise that experience shows that in civil law countries with centralised systems of judicial review, it is difficult to resort directly to constitutional courts in the hope of bringing about a radical change in the regulation of institutions deeply entrenched in historical and cultural traditions like marriage and family. In conclusion, the general pattern confirms the validity of American scholarship's theories suggesting that courts' intervention is more effective after politics and social movements themselves have created a substantially favourable environment for their intervention.

Of course, *Obergefell*[71] in the United States has not ended the debate about marriage, as well as legislation and constitutional courts cases in Europe have not put an end to marriage equality issues. But both in Europe and in the United States we see that courts, especially constitutional courts, have stimulated social and legal change in the same way.

Notes

1 Spanish Constitution of 1978, art 32 sec 1 ('Men and women have the right to marry with full legal equality').

2 *Ley* 13/2005, de 1 de julio, por la que se modifica el Código Civil en materia de derecho a contraer matrimonio (Act No. 13/2005, of 1 July, amending the Civil Code on the regulation of the right to marry).

3 Art 1 of *Ley* 13/2005 adding a s 2 to art 44 of the Spanish Civil Code of 1889 (stating that 'marriage will have the same requisites and effects, whether both spouses are of the same or different sex').

4 *Lei* 7/2001 de 11 de Maio, Adopta medidas de protecção das uniões de facto (Law No. 7/2001 of 11 May, adopting protection measures on de facto unions), in part art 1, sec 1 (stating that the purpose of the law is to regulate de facto unions, regardless of the sex of the partners).

5 *Lei* 9/2010 de 31 de Maio, Permite o casamento civil entre pessoas do mesmo sexo (Law No. 9/2010 of 31 May permitting the civil marriage between persons of the same sex).

6 For a detailed account of the proposals that preceded the introduction of PaCS in 1999, see generally Daniel Borrillo, 'The "Pacte Civil de Solidarieté" in France: Midway Between Marriage and Cohabitation' in Robert Wintemute and Mark

Andenæs (eds), *Legal Recognition of Same-Sex Partnerships* (Hart Publishing 2001) 475, 476 ff.

7 *Loi* No. 99-944 du 15 novembre 1999 relative au pacte civil de solidarieté.

8 Art 1 amending art 515(1) *Code Civil.*

9 *Loi* No. 2013-404 du 17 mai 2013 ouvrant le mariage aux couples de personnes de même sexe.

10 German Basic Law 1949 (*Grundgesetz*), art 6(1).

11 *Gesetz zur Einführung des Rechts auf Eheschließung für Personen gleichen Geschlechts* (20 July 2017).

12 See Defense of Marriage Act (DOMA), 110 Stat 2419, sec 3, 1 US Code § 7 – definition of 'marriage' and 'spouse' ('In determining the meaning of any Act of Congress, or of any ruling, regulation, or interpretation of the various administrative bureaus and agencies of the United States, the word "marriage" means only a legal union between one man and one woman as husband and wife, and the word "spouse" refers only to a person of the opposite sex who is a husband or a wife').

13 *United States v Windsor* 133 SCt 2675 (2013).

14 *Obergefell v Hodges* 576 US, 135 S Ct 2584 (2015).

15 *Egan v Canada* (1995) 2 SCR 513.

16 *Rosenberg v Canada* (1998) 158 DLR (4th) 664; *M v H* (1999) 2 SCR 3.

17 *M* (n 16).

18 *Hendricks v Quebec* (2004) 238 DLR 4th 577 (Can Que CA); *EGALE Canada, Inc v Canada* (2003) 13 BCLR 4th 1 (Can BC CA); *Halpern v Canada (Attorney General)* (2003) 65 OR 3d 161 (Can Ont CA). See Nicholas Bala and Rebecca Jaremko Bromwich, 'Context and Inclusivity in Canada's Evolving Definition of the Family' (2000) 16 *International Journal of Law, Policy and the Family* 145, 161; William N Eskridge Jr, 'Backlash Politics: How Constitutional Litigation Has Advanced Marriage Equality in the United States' (2003) 93 *Boston University Law Review* 275, 288–289.

19 Civil Marriage Act 2005, ch 33 (Can). For an interesting account of these developments, see also Robert Wintemute, 'Sexual Orientation and the Charter: The Achievement of Formal Legal Equality (1985–2005) and Its Limits' (2004) 49 *McGill Law Journal* 1143.

20 See Angioletta Sperti, *Constitutional Courts, Gay Rights and Sexual Orientation Equality* (Oxford: Hart Publishing 2017) 7 and 103 ff.

21 Eskridge (n 18) 310.

22 Case No. 2010-92 QPC, 28 January 2011 (France).

23 See Case No. 92 of 2010 (n 22) at *considérant* No. 9.

24 Bill No. 586, introduced by P Bloche MP. For a more detailed account of the French political debate about same-sex marriage, see Sperti (n 20) 92 ff. See also Anne Sanders, 'Marriage, Same-Sex Relationship, and the German Constitution' (2012) 13 *German Law Journal* 911.

25 Case No. 1 BvR 640/93, 4 October 1993, 1993 NJW 3058.

26 On the German case law before the introduction of equal marriage, see Sperti (n 20) 97 ff.

27 Act on the Termination of the Discrimination of Same-Sex Couples: Civil Partnerships (*Gesetz zur Beendigung der Diskriminierung gleichgeschlechtlicher Gemeinschaften: Lebenspartnerschaften*) of 16 February 2001 (Federal Law Gazette, *Bundesgesetzblatt*, BGBl I, 266).

28 Constitutional Court Case No. 138 of 15 April 2010.

29 See *Legge* No. 76 of 20 May 2016 (Unioni civili tra persone dello stesso sesso).

30 Eskridge (n 18) 300.

31 Tribunal Constitucional, Sección 1a, Auto No. 222/1994, 11 July 1994.

32 See Sperti (n 20) 86 ff. See also Tiago Fidalgo de Freitas and Diletta Tega, 'Judicial Restraint and Political Responsibility: A Review of the Jurisprudence of the Italian, Spanish and Portuguese High Courts on Same-Sex Couples' in Daniele Gallo, Luca Paladini and Pietro Pustorino (eds), *Same-Sex Couples Before National, Supranational and International Jurisdictions* (Springer 2015) 287, 299 ff.
33 *Ley* 13/2005 (n 2).
34 Tribunal Constitucional, Case No. 359/2009, 9 July 2009, para 9.
35 *Lei* No. 9/2010 (n 5).
36 Case No. 99-419 DC, 9 November 1999.
37 Case No. 2010-92 (n 22) *considérant* No. 9.
38 I have addressed in detail the contribution of courts in dismantling arguments based on nature and tradition in Sperti (n 20) 132 ff.
39 Decision No. 2013-669 DC of 17 May 2013.
40 *Loi* No. 2013-404 (n 9), in particular art 13 adding art 6–1 *Code civil* ('Marriage and Filiation Through Adoption Produce the Same Effects, Rights, and Obligations Provided by Legislation, with the Exception of Those Provided for in Book I, Title VII, of this Code, regardless whether the spouses or parents are of different sex or same sex').
41 Decision No. 2013-669 DC (n 39) *considérant* No. 21-22.
42 Case No. 198/2012 SCT, 6 November 2012.
43 See de Freitas and Tega (n 32) 304, stressing that 'the decision was not taken by one or two votes: there was a clear majority outvoting the dissenters which shows that the cause of the delay was not an internal impasse.'
44 See for further details, Sperti (n 20) 88.
45 Philippe Reyniers, 'Same-Sex Couples in France and Belgium: The Resilient Practise of Judicial Deference' in Daniele Gallo, Luca Paladini and Pietro Pustorino (eds), *Same-Sex Couples Before National, Supranational and International Jurisdictions* (Springer 2015) 249, 252.
46 Tribunal Constitucional, Case No. 359/2009 (n 34).
47 See Jack M Balkin, *Constitutional Redemption: Political Faith in an Unjust World* (Harvard University Press 2011); Douglas NeJaime, 'Constitutional Change, Courts and Social Movements' (2013) 111 *Michigan Law Review* 877; Robert Post and Reva B Siegel, 'Originalism as a Political Practice: The Right's Living Constitution' (2006) 75 *Fordham Law Review* 545; Reva B Siegel, 'Community in Conflict: Same-Sex Marriage and Backlash' (2017) 64 *UCLA Law Review* 1728; but see also Frances Hamilton, 'Strategies to Achieve Same-Sex Marriage and the Method of Incrementalist Change' (2015–2016) 25 *Journal of Transnational Law & Policy* 121.
48 *Obergefell* (n 14).
49 Siegel (n 47) 1731.
50 In this respect, Portugal is an exception: as mentioned earlier, same-sex marriage was introduced at legislative level, *Lei* No. 9/2010 (n 5), just a few months after the Constitutional Tribunal released its judgement No. 359 of 2009 (n 34). The Tribunal held that marriage was not a 'frozen' concept and that it was up to the legislature to decide whether or not open marriage to same-sex couples. As I clarified (Sperti [n 20] 91 ff), the close coordination between the judiciary and the legislature in the advancement of same-sex couples' rights in Portugal did not reflect a widespread support for equal marriage on the part of the general public. In Portugal, the Parliament ruled in favour of same-sex marriage because a strong backlash was unlikely to occur due to the distinctive features of the political national landscape.

51 See Sperti (n 20) 103.
52 *Hollingsworth v Perry* 133 S Ct 2652 (2015).
53 *Perry v Schwarzenegger* 704 F Supp 2d 921 (ND Cal 2010).
54 Kenji Yoshino, *Speak Now. Marriage Equality on Trial* (Broadway Books 2015).
55 Case No. 138 of 2010 (n 28).
56 Same-sex couples' parental rights, in particular step-child adoption, have been recognised by the Italian lower courts and the Corte di Cassazione through progressive readings of the narrow Italian legislation on adoption. A detailed account of these developments is available at www.articolo29.it and in *Genius. Rivista di studi giuridici sull'orientamento sessuale e l'identità di genere* (www.articolo29.it/genius/). Among the cases, see in particular, Tribunale per i Minorenni di Roma, 23 December 2015 and Cass civ (1) Case No. 12962 of 2016.
57 *Legge* No. 76 of 2016 (n 29).
58 See Sperti (n 20) 102 ff.
59 See Mauro Cappelletti, *Judicial Review in the Contemporary World* (Bobbs-Merrill 1971); Martije de Visser, *Constitutional Review in Europe. A comparative Analysis* (Hart Publishing 2014).
60 *Conseil constitutionnel*, Case No. 99-419 DC (n 36); Case No. 92-2010 QPC (n 22); Tribunal Constitucional, Case No. 359/2009 (n 34).
61 Tribunal Constitucional, Sección 1a, Auto No. 222/1994 (n 31).
62 See Case No. 138 of 2010 (n 28).
63 I have expressed my criticism of the arguments the Italian Constitutional court expounded in Case No. 138 of 2010 (n 28) in *Omosessualità e diritti* (Pisa University Press 2013).
64 I addressed this feature of the centralized system of judicial review in Spain and Italy in Sperti (n 20) 104 ff. See also de Visser (n 59) 377; Elisabetta Lamarque, 'Interpreting Statutes in Conformity with the Constitution: The Role of the Italian Constitutional Court and Ordinary Judges' (2010) 1 *Italian Journal of Public Law* 91. See also Vittoria Barsotti, Paolo G Carozza, Marta Cartabia and Andrea Simoncini, *Italian Constitutional Justice in Global Context* (Oxford University Press 2015) 219 ff.
65 Case No. 356 of 14 October 1996.
66 Alex Stone Sweet, 'The Politics of Constitutional Review in France and Europe' (2007) 5 *Icon* 69, 91.
67 *Obergefell* (n 14).
68 Martha Nussbaum, *From Disgust to Humanity. Sexual Orientation and Constitutional Law* (Oxford University Press 2009) 161–162.
69 Yoshino (n 54) 6.
70 *Baehr v Lewin* 74 Haw 530, 852 P2d 44 (1993), a State Supreme Court case concerning same-sex marriage in the state of Hawaii.
71 *Obergefell* (n 14).

References

Primary sources

Act on the Termination of the Discrimination of Same-Sex Couples: Civil Partnerships (*Gesetz zur Beendigung der Diskriminierung gleichgeschlechtlicher Gemeinschaften: Lebenspartnerschaften*) of 16 February 2001 (Federal Law Gazette, *Bundesgesetzblatt*, BGBl I, 266).

Art 1 amending art 515(1) *Code Civil.*

Art 1 of *Ley* 13/2005 adding a s 2 to art 44 of the Spanish Civil code of 1889 (stating that 'marriage will have the same requisites and effects whether both spouses are of the same or different sex').

Baehr v Lewin 74 Haw 530, 852 P2d 44 (1993).

Bill No. 586, introduced by MP P Bloche.

Case No. 1 BvR 640/93, 4 October 1993, 1993 NJW 3058 (Germany).

Case No. 356, 14 October 1996 (Italy).

Case No. 99-419 DC, 9 November 1999 (France).

Case No. 198/2012 SCT, 6 November 2012 (Spain).

Case No. 2010-92 QPC, 28 January 2011 (France).

Cass civ (1) Case No. 12962 of 2016.

Civil Marriage Act 2005, ch 33 (Can).

Constitutional Court Case No. 138, 15 April 2010 (Italy).

Decision No. 2013-669 DC, 17 May 2013 (France).

Defense of Marriage Act (DOMA), 110 Stat 2419, sec 3, 1 US Code § 7.

EGALE Canada, Inc v Canada (2003) 13 BCLR 4th 1 (Can BC CA).

Egan v Canada (1995) 2 SCR 513.

German Basic Law 1949 (*Grundgesetz*), art 6(1).

Gesetz zur Einführung des Rechts auf Eheschließung für Personen gleichen Geschlechts (20 July 2017).

Halpern v Canada (Attorney General) (2003) 65 OR 3d 161 (Can Ont CA).

Hendricks v Quebec (2004) 238 DLR 4th 577 (Can Que CA).

Hollingsworth v Perry 133 S Ct 2652 (2015).

Legge No. 76 of 20 May 2016 (Unioni civili tra persone dello stesso sesso).

Lei 7/2001 de 11 de Maio, Adopta medidas de protecção das uniões de facto (Law No. 7/2001 of 11 May, adopting protection measures on de facto unions), in part art 1, sec 1 (stating that the purpose of the law is to regulate de facto unions, regardless of the sex of the partners).

Lei 9/2010 de 31 de Maio, Permite o casamento civil entre pessoas do mesmo sexo (Law No. 9/2010 of 31 May permitting the civil marriage between persons of the same sex).

Ley 13/2005, de 1 de julio, por la que se modifica el Código Civil en materia de derecho a contraer matrimonio (Act No. 13/2005, of 1 July, amending the Civil Code on the regulation of the right to marry).

Loi No. 2013-404 du 17 mai 2013 ouvrant le mariage aux couples de personnes de même sexe.

Loi No. 99-944 du 15 novembre 1999 relative au pacte civil de solidarieté.

M v H (1999) 2 SCR 3.

Obergefell v Hodges 576 US, 135 S Ct 2584 (2015).

Perry v Schwarzenegger 704 F Supp 2d 921 (ND Cal 2010).

Rosenberg v Canada (1998) 158 DLR (4th) 664.

Spanish Constitution of 1978, art 32 sec 1 ('Men and Women Have the Right to Marry with Full Legal Equality').

Tribunal Constitucional, Case No. 359/2009 (9 July 2009).

Tribunal Constitucional, Sección 1a, Auto No. 222/1994 (11 July 1994).

Tribunale per i Minorenni di Roma (23 December 2015).

United States v Windsor 133 SCt 2675 (2013).

Secondary sources

Bala N and Bromwich RJ, 'Context and Inclusivity in Canada's Evolving Definition of the Family' (2000) 16 *International Journal of Law, Policy and the Family* 145.

Balkin JM, *Constitutional Redemption: Political Faith in an Unjust World* (Harvard University Press 2011).

Barsotti V, Carozza PG, Cartabia M and Simoncini A, *Italian Constitutional Justice in Global Context* (Oxford University Press 2015).

Borrillo D, 'The "Pacte Civil de Solidarieté" in France: Midway Between Marriage and Cohabitation' in Wintemute R and Andenæs M (eds), *Legal Recognition of Same-Sex Partnerships* (Hart Publishing 2001).

Cappelletti M, *Judicial Review in the Contemporary World* (Bobbs-Merrill 1971).

de Visser M, *Constitutional Review in Europe. A Comparative Analysis* (Hart Publishing 2014).

Eskridge Jr WN, 'Backlash Politics: How Constitutional Litigation Has Advanced Marriage Equality in the United States' (2003) 93 *Boston University Law Review* 275.

Fidalgo de Freitas T and Tega D, 'Judicial Restraint and Political Responsibility: A Review of the Jurisprudence of the Italian, Spanish and Portuguese High Courts on Same-Sex Couples' in Gallo D, Paladini L and Pustorino P (eds), *Same-Sex Couples Before National, Supranational and International Jurisdictions* (Springer 2015).

Hamilton F, 'Strategies to Achieve Same-Sex Marriage and the Method of Incrementalist Change' (2015–2016) 25 *Journal of Transnational Law and Policy* 121.

Lamarque E, 'Interpreting Statutes in Conformity with the Constitution: The Role of the Italian Constitutional Court and Ordinary Judges' (2010) 1 *Italian Journal of Public Law* 91.

NeJaime D, 'Constitutional Change, Courts and Social Movements' (2013) 111 *Michigan Law Review* 877.

Nussbaum M, *From Disgust to Humanity. Sexual Orientation and Constitutional Law* (Oxford University Press 2009).

Post R and Siegel RB, 'Originalism as a Political Practice: The Right's Living Constitution' (2006) 75 *Fordham Law Review* 545.

Reyniers P, 'Same-Sex Couples in France and Belgium: The Resilient Practice of Judicial Deference' in Gallo D, Paladini L and Pustorino P (eds), *Same-Sex Couples Before National, Supranational and International Jurisdictions* (Springer 2015).

Sanders A, 'Marriage, Same-Sex Relationship, and the German Constitution' (2012) 13 *German Law Journal* 911.

Siegel RB, 'Community in Conflict: Same-Sex Marriage and Backlash' (2017) 64 *UCLA Law Review* 1728.

Sperti A, *Omosessualità e diritti* (Pisa University Press 2013).

———, *Constitutional Courts, Gay Rights and Sexual Orientation Equality* (Oxford: Hart Publishing 2017).

Sweet AS, 'The Politics of Constitutional Review in France and Europe' (2007) 5 *Icon* 69.

Wintemute R, 'Sexual Orientation and the Charter: The Achievement of Formal Legal Equality (1985–2005) and Its Limits' (2004) 49 *McGill Law Journal* 1143.

Yoshino K, *Speak Now. Marriage Equality on Trial* (Broadway Books 2015).

Part 3

Rainbow families

Chapter 7

The European Court of Human Rights and the notion of family life

A common European standard for the EU framework

Alexander Schuster

Delineating a notion of family life under EU law

The European Union does not have competence to harmonise family law. Only in cross-border situations may the EU, following a special legislative procedure, enact provisions.[1] There is also the possibility of adoption of the ordinary legislative procedure, if the European Council so decides unanimously, and eventually to revert to enhanced cooperation among those Member States that wish to push harmonisation further.

However, outside of the aforementioned realm of judicial cooperation in civil matters, several regulations and directives non-strictly regulating family law and person's statuses refer and rely on concepts such as spouse and child. EU law can self-define the notion of family life under Article 7 of the Charter of Fundamental Rights of the European Union (hereinafter CFREU), as well as the right to marry and the right to found a family under Article 9 of the Charter. However, 'the meaning and scope of those rights shall be the same as those laid down by the [European Convention of Human Rights]. This provision shall not prevent Union law providing more extensive protection.'[2]

Two pillars: de facto and de jure families

The first question that must be addressed is how EU law looks at the family dimension of people's lives. It is worth using the expression "family dimension" in its non-technical and broadest meaning. This dimension encompasses two main pillars.

Traditionally, the law looked at family matters as revolving around a person's status and status was – and still is – widely dependent on the existence of legal acts constituting and proving it. This is, at least, very true in those systems that are built around the notion of a civil status certified by public registries. A spouse is a status conferred by the act of marriage. A parent/child status required in the past a marital union between their parents. This formal approach leads to widespread discrimination against children born out of wedlock. A person's status is formal in that it is certified in public registries. It is founded on a legal act that marks the time when that status was acquired or conferred. The first chapter in family law handbooks was historically devoted to marriage, the central institution that defined parentage, kindred relationship and succession rights.

However, loving and caring relationships, and close personal ties, cannot be confined to legal acts. Family is no longer conceived as necessarily based on marriage; hence the idea of a family life, such as the one protected under Article 8 ECHR, whose existence is essentially a question of fact[3] and regardless of any formal legal attribution or de jure recognition of status.[4] As the ECtHR put it in the landmark case *Marckx v Belgium*, Article 8 'makes no distinction between the "legitimate" and the "illegitimate" family.'[5] Foster parents who care for a child also enjoy protection under the Convention.[6]

It is therefore clear that de facto and de jure family members do not necessarily overlap, and that Article 8 protects both.[7] A formal parent-child relationship may exist notwithstanding the absence of a minimum contact or factual relationship before or after birth (e.g. parentage based on genetics).[8] Under some national laws, written consent to donor insemination given anywhere in the world suffices to establish parentage upon birth based on intent. Marital presumptions may trigger the same outcome. De jure relationships are limited by the juridical formalisations granted by national laws – e.g. marriage – whereas de facto family life knows only the boundaries of love.

It is submitted that the legal evolutions of those two pillars caused marriage to lose its central role and parliaments to relinquish their monopoly. It is for this reason that the notion of what makes a family becomes contentious. By stressing the relevance of formal status or legal recognition, one confers to the law – and ultimately to the legislature – the power to define family and family life. The 'legitimate' family might be the only one that the legislature acknowledges as such, potentially to the exclusion of every other. When the law acknowledges and protects de facto family life, it is not the state, but reality, that legitimises loving relationships. It comes as no surprise that those who support a heteronormative definition of marriage and family also object to the interpretation of Article 8 given by the ECtHR.[9]

EU law: form and substance of family life

In order to understand how EU law defines the notion of family, the analysis must consider whether both pillars – de jure and de facto family life – matter, and whether they enjoy specific and autonomous legal relevance. Then, the question arises as to the existence of a common core with harmonised concepts and terms all across Union legislation. Finally, it is worth investigating how independent EU law can be in shaping its concepts vis-à-vis ECHR case law and vis-à-vis those given under Member State law.

Family status, relationships and dependence

Despite EU law not having competence in regulating domestic family law or status of persons,[10] its legislation relies on terms such as 'spouse' and 'descendants.' It is therefore clear that the formal recognition of a family status is relevant. This is not only true in regard to cooperation in civil matters such as divorce[11] or proprietary regimes.[12] Such terms are also crucial to provisions regulating freedom of movement of citizens[13] and workers,[14] and in many other fields. A family status is potentially relevant in a limitless variety of situations that fall within the application of Union law. As shown by cases such as *K B*[15] and *Maruko*,[16] recognition of legal gender and family status is relevant in assessing employment discrimination. Article 2(1)(b) of the Victims' Rights Directive includes stable cohabiting intimate partners within the notion of 'family members.'[17]

Alongside de jure family statuses, Union law respects also de facto family life in every action or legislative measure enacted within its competence. Family reunification is seen as part of family life, and the latter as a set of relations that exist regardless of formal legal recognition. By exercising its competences, the Union cannot neglect unformalised family patterns in society.

It is therefore clear that both pillars bear a meaning and have relevance under EU law. As there is no European Family Code, notions of formal statuses or de facto relationships may not bear the same meaning across Union legislation. More precisely, in regard to de facto family ties, their appreciation being a question of fact, criteria for the assessment of their existence and their intensity vary considerably.

The Court of Justice has repeatedly stressed the idea of notion autonome: in the absence of an 'express reference to the law of the Member States for the purpose of determining its meaning and scope,' terms in EU provisions 'must normally be given an independent and uniform interpretation throughout the European Union.'[18]

The doctrine of notion autonome applies to de facto family ties, so that the Court may provide those criteria which must be followed in assessing unformalised stable relationships. Their description and qualifying requirements vary across instruments.[19] Free movement directives explicitly mention dependence.[20] In regard to children, dependency is legal and financial, and related to parental responsibility.[21] The impact of separation may violate the child's best interests and the family unity, which becomes relevant under Article 3(2) of Directive 2004/38 and the Member State's obligation to facilitating.[22]

Whereas lawful residence, facilitation duties and de facto family roles are concepts suitable to autonomous definition, this cannot be said for a person's family status. EU law does not bestow the status of spouse or parent; hence, it should not be entitled to define them. The Court refuses to define a 'parent-child relationship' according to a functionalist rather than formalistic approach, although a closer scrutiny of the reasoning in *SM* shows that there is no reference nor deference to national laws. The Court found that 'direct descendant' is not a given status, but a 'concept' that requires an 'independent and uniform interpretation throughout the European Union.'[23] Could there be room in the near future to acknowledge under Union law that parenthood, besides biological ties and adoption,[24] also flows from the intent expressed by a person to proceed to medically assisted reproduction regardless of any genetic connection? The Court of Justice eventually preferred to protect the genuine reality of a child-parent relationship under the Algerian kafala system by virtually erasing the Member State's discretion in denying entry and residence under Article 3.[25]

Moreover, the notion autonome doctrine explicitly excludes those concepts for which legislation explicitly refers to the notion according to Member State law, such as 'registered partner' under Article 2(2)(b), Directive 2004/38. However, as will be discussed later in this chapter, once a formal status is acquired in a legal system, the Union may have competence to compel the Member State not to ignore it whenever this is relevant for the application of EU law.

Interpretation of family concepts should in any event be harmonious across legislative instruments. In the *Depesme*[26] judgement, the Court confirmed that there is a convergence of meaning of family members among the instruments that develop free movement rights of citizens and workers.[27] The Court's reasoning first envisaged continuity with the jurisprudential acquis of the now repealed Regulation No 1612/68, and second established a triangulation among Regulation No 492/2011, Directive No 2004/38 and Directive No 2014/54,[28] and recalled Recital 1 of Directive 2014/54. Homogeneity should apply to both formal and de facto family members.

Convergence of meaning should be sought among instruments that regulate the same area. However, it is unclear in how far convergence can also be advocated across all EU measures. For instance, could the *Coman*[29] reasoning of a gender-neutral recognition of marriage for the sole purpose of entry and residence of the spouse of a Union citizen under Directive 2004/38 also apply equally to employment discrimination cases? This could be the question if an employee who entered a same-gender marriage abroad claims the same benefits of a colleague married to an opposite-gender spouse. What if the Member State of the employer does not grant equal marriage opportunities? The answer may vary depending on whether the employee enjoyed previous family life as a married couple while genuinely residing in another Member State that recognises same-gender marriage or on where marriage was entered into, as the CJEU was of the view in *Coman* that the venue of celebration matters.[30]

It is not possible to transpose the freedom of movement rationale to employment cases, as spousal status matters in view of avoiding discrimination on the ground of sexual orientation, not of protecting family reunification. At the very least, this is true if the situation is purely internal, i.e. without any circulation across Member States.[31] Perhaps, if the employee were a Union citizen working in a host state or a returning migrant, there could be room to sum both arguments: non-discrimination and freedom of movement.

The doctrine of notion autonome does not impose any horizontal homogeneity. The Court of Justice has never indulged in systemic interpretation of terms and notions related to family. Concepts are tailored according to their legislative context and purpose of the law. Freedom of movement, non-discrimination, staff regulations, cooperation in criminal[32] and civil matters: these are all fields where family roles may be construed differently.

The roles of the Charter and of the ECHR

Union law has overcome the piecemeal approach in dealing with family reunification under the freedom of movement legislation, but the picture of what makes a family is still patchy. This does not, however, mean that there is no common core and that the Union is doomed to face fragmented approaches.

The Charter of Fundamental Rights of the European Union canvasses a common standard applicable notwithstanding the material scope of the legislation. Article 52(3) establishes that the minimum standard of protection is provided by the European Convention of Human Rights: 'the meaning and scope of [rights which correspond to rights guaranteed by the Convention] shall be the same as those laid down by the said Convention.' ECHR case law therefore dictates the bottom-line of safeguards under Article 7 ("Respect for private and family life") and Article 9 ("Right to marry and right to found a family").

The last period of Article 52, paragraph 3, by stating that '[t]his provision shall not prevent Union law providing more extensive protection,' may grant EU rainbow families a greater degree of recognition and protection. After all, it is already clear from the explanations[33] referred to in Article 52(7) that Article 9 of the Charter is wider in scope than Article 12 ECHR in respect to the right to marry 'when national legislation so provides.' By the time the Bureau of the Convention drafted the first explanatory notes, the Netherlands was about to reform marriage legislation.[34] In view of the steps forwards taken by the ECtHR in Schalk and Kopf,[35] Articles 12 ECHR and 9 Charter do no longer differ to the extent attested by the Explanations.

A major difference remains, though. It should be noted that Article 12 ECHR is traditionally construed by the ECtHR as not establishing two autonomous fundamental rights. The right to found a family is part and parcel of the right to marry. Under the Convention, a non-married couple would need to rely, to smaller or greater avail, on Article 8 in order to protect their efforts to build a family, e.g. by means of reproductive medicine.

Whereas Article 12 grants protection to found a family only to a married couple, this is not the case with Article 9 of the Charter, whose 'wording . . . has been modernised to cover cases in which national legislation recognises arrangements other than marriage for founding a family.'[36] Unmarried and registered partners enjoy the very same fundamental right to found a family.

The Explanations considerably stress the reference to what is allowed under Member State substantive family law. The Charter is per se silent and without any renvoi. There might be situations when the Charter right to found a family intersects EU freedoms, such as access to reproductive services.[37] Moreover, Article 33 is devoted to family and professional life and mandates that '[t]he family shall enjoy legal, economic and social protection.' This protection seems to stem from de facto family life rather than de jure family statuses.

Whenever the CJEU is required to provide an interpretation of Charter provisions that define or protect the family dimension, the object is never the Charter on its own, but the Charter as a source among others[38] that binds the Union and the Member States when specifically applying and in conjunction with Union law. The Charter does not confer any new competence to the Union, but whenever Union law is at stake, no violation of the Charter is admissible. The same principle applies to the ECHR, as the Union does not have any competence to monitor and oblige Member States to respect the Convention as an international treaty.[39]

The human rights cascade effect

The play of the national, EU and ECHR legal orders represent an excellent example of a multilevel system of protection. The case *K B* ideally shows how they all interact to guarantee fundamental rights and why it is not mere speculation to wonder what the scope of Article 7 or 9 of the Charter is, despite the lack of competence in civil status matters.

The Union has no competence to codify and enforce rules on legal gender recognition, or on marriage. However, the Convention – and thereby the Charter – dictate for those issues minimum standards. In its ground-breaking judgement *Goodwin v UK*,[40] the ECtHR held that the United Kingdom (UK) violated Article 8 by refusing to recognise the perceived gender of a transsexual individual and that by denying as a consequence the right to marry a person of the opposite (legal) gender, there was also a violation of Article 12. Since then,[41] the European human rights standard imposes upon all 47 Council of Europe Member States to grant legal gender recognition and to interpret the right to marry with exclusive regard to the legal and not the biological gender.[42]

R., K.B.'s partner, was denied legal gender recognition and access to marry while UK legislation was still in violation of the Convention. As often is the case with public registries and legal statuses, the victim can hardly escape far-reaching consequences. By denying the couple marriage, R. would not qualify as a spouse and not benefit from bereavement rights. A survivor's pension is part of the broad notion of pay. Transpersons are protected on the ground of sex.[43] Hence, allowing the refusal of an element of pay because of the fact that the worker is unmarried, when the legal obstacle to marry constitutes a violation of the ECHR, means that EU law would tolerate a situation that flows from a violation of human rights. In the Court's words, 'there is inequality of treatment which, although it does not directly undermine enjoyment of a right protected by Community law, affects one of the conditions for the grant of that right.'[44]

K.B. exemplifies how the international and European multilevel system of rights protection affects the Union legal system, which is based on the principle of conferral.[45] This can be called the 'human rights cascade effect.' The Union does not have competence to enforce human rights within the national legal orders, yet must respect them. As such, whenever a violation spreads its effects on the 'enjoyment of a right' protected by EU law, i.e. a right falling within its competences, then the Union cannot accept that its law, even if in the remit of a competence shared with the Member States, becomes a gear of a mechanism reiterating a violation of fundamental rights.

Maruko, *Römer*[46] and *Hay*[47] show how civil status affects employment benefits and may lead to discrimination. *Coman* represents a case of how de jure family ties affect freedom of movement. In all those cases, given the limited competence in the field of family law, the Union can only oblige the Member States to remove any effect that in view of the causality principle reinforces a violation of fundamental rights in the field of family life. The Union cannot impose a rewriting of the national family code. It can only ensure the protection of the right guaranteed by EU law. The obligation on the Member State is to grant that limited right as if the violation of the Convention never occurred. Under *Coman*, Romania would have to treat the applicants for the purpose of the right to entry and reside as if they were married. In *K B*, the UK would merely need similarly to embrace a sort of fiction for the purpose of granting the survivor's pension. This fictitious approach, so long as it prevents each and every effect that redounds in a field of EU competence, complies with Union law.

A hypothetical scenario may explain how far-reaching the cascade effect is. Medically assisted reproductive services are services within the meaning of Article 57 TFEU. Lesbian couples are denied access to those services in several Member States. The need for those services is specific to the female body and according to the reasoning in *Mayr*,[48] regulations on access could be found to depend on the ground of gender and not sexual orientation. Directive 2004/113[49] proscribes any discrimination in the access to goods and services on the ground of sex.[50] It could be argued that allowing an unmarried cohabiting different-sex couple access to those techniques with the use of donor sperm, but denying the same to a same-sex registered or cohabiting couple in need of sperm donation, is discriminatory on the ground of sex. Such a litigation is based on purely non-discrimination arguments, as was the case in *Maruko*. But what if these arguments were reinforced by an obligation to construe the Directive so to respect the fundamental and standalone right to found a family guaranteed under Article 9 of the Charter? The latter, contrary to the ECHR, ensures such fundamental right not just to married couples, but also to 'other arrangements' such as a registered partnership.

Developments in the case law on acquisition and loss of Union citizenship may one day lead the Court to question as discriminatory national provisions that grant parentage when consent to donor insemination is given by the male partner of the gestational mother, but not when the same consent is given by the female partner.[51] If, as a consequence, the child does not become a Union citizen by descent from the intended parent, the *Rottman*[52] doctrine might lead the Court to find a violation of Article 20 read in conjunction with Article 21 of the Charter.[53]

So far, the Court of Justice has been rather reluctant to heighten the standards of protection already set by the Strasbourg case law. In *McB*,[54] the Court extensively relied on the case law of the ECtHR, according to which national legislation conferring custody rights on only one of the unmarried parents was legitimate, provided that the other had the right to seek a court order reversing this initial allocation. As a consequence, the international removal of the child by the mother was not unlawful under the terms of Article 2(11) of Regulation 2201/2003. It remains to be seen if, whenever the ECtHR finds no violation thanks to a wide margin of appreciation or the lack of consensus among the 47 Member States, the Court of Justice is willing to reassess consensus on the basis of the Union's 28 Member States or disregard the sometimes overly generous discretion awarded to the Member States.[55]

A brief overview of the current state

The CJEU is reluctant to quote and interpret the Charter if its provisions are unnecessary to provide the interpretative guidance that is asked in a preliminary ruling. In *Coman*, the Court recalled the right to respect for private and family life,[56] but then added that 'the rights guaranteed by Article 7 [of the Charter] have the same meaning and the same scope as those guaranteed by Article 8' ECHR. In fact, Article 7 could provide greater protection than the corresponding conventional article, as allowed by Article 52(3), last period. The Court then cited two judgements by the ECtHR, *Vallianatos*[57] and *Orlandi*,[58] which confirmed that also same-gender couples enjoy the protection of family life and Member States cannot discriminate on the ground of sexual orientation when introducing legal instruments, such as registered partnerships, as alternative forms to marriage.

'Penumbras' of marriage

If we factor in, among others, the *Oliari*[59] and the *Pajić*[60] judgements and bear in mind the interpretation given by the Court in *Schalk and Kopf* and *Hämäläinen*[61], we can condense the protection awarded to gay couples as follows.

The ECHR defines a human rights standard by which Member States are free to introduce equal marriage, but without any obligation to do so under Article 12. Yet, Article 12 was declared applicable to same-gender couples: 'the Court would no longer consider that the right to marry enshrined in Article 12 must in all circumstances be limited to marriage between two persons of the opposite sex.'[62]

Same-sex marriage falls, therefore, within the ambit of Article 12. Consequently, there might be situations when Article 14 is read in conjunction with the right to marry and found a family. It becomes thus possible to invoke arguments against any difference in treatment between married heterosexual and married homosexual couples. It is hard to sketch out scenarios for this intertwined application of both Articles 14 and 12 under the Convention or under EU law. When it comes to horizontal rights and duties, i.e. involving spouses, differences are hardly found in national legislations. They do, however, exist in regard to parenthood, e.g. access to reproductive techniques, spousal presumptions and adoption.

Litigation around the denial of access to reproductive services has already come up in European fora[63], yet the ECtHR may dismiss a claim by employing the margin of appreciation or by justifying difference in treatment on grounds of biology or pathology.

More solid arguments could be raised against any discrimination in access to joint or second-parent adoption as a married couple. The line of reasoning in *EB v France*[64], a case of discrimination based on sexual orientation against a single woman, and *X v. Austria*[65], a discrimination in regard to second-parent adoption, hardly justifies difference in treatment between married couples on the basis of this protected characteristic.

These hypothetical scenarios prove that *Schalk and Kopf*'s reasoning around Article 12 was not cosmetic, but planted a seed that allows to extend its scope to same-gender married couples. The impact on EU law of this evolution of the Strasbourg case law might be limited, as the Explanations to Article 9 of the Charter already took this view. Broadening the scope of marriage entails consequences in terms of legal protection for rainbow couples.

Let us think of a same-sex couple who got married in a Member State but reside in Latvia, where no recognition at all is given to their union. At some point, they wish to divorce, but the Member State of celebration denies jurisdiction (e.g. for lack of residence). A Latvian court may refuse to apply the law of the Member State of celebration for the limited purpose of divorcing the couple under Article 5 of Regulation 1259/2010 on the law applicable to divorce and legal separation,[66] arguing that it is 'manifestly incompatible with the public policy of the forum' under Article 12 of the aforementioned Regulation.

The ECtHR still considers that Article 12 does not grant a right to divorce,[67] but was willing to find violations of the same articles in cases of limitations to the right to re-marry after divorce[68] or in relation to divorce proceedings.[69] The Latvian couple could argue that once a country recognises the right to divorce, it cannot refuse to limit its scope to opposite-gender couples only, for otherwise there would be a breach of Article 14 taken together with Article 12.

More significantly, EU law might serve the Latvian couple even better. They could rely on Recital 25 of Regulation 1259/2010: the public policy exception cannot run afoul of Charter rights. More specifically, reference therein to the non-discrimination paradigm[70] paralyses the public policy exception even if the regulation explicitly refers to the forum's public policy, i.e. an *ordre public* that varies from Member State to Member State.

It is submitted that the affirmation of applicability of the right to marry to same-gender couples creates favourable 'multilevel penumbras,' i.e. rights derived, by implication or interaction, from other rights explicitly protected in the same or in other legal sources.[71]

Obligations under Oliari as European standards

The European Court of Human Rights found in the *Oliari* judgement that Italy violated Article 8 of the Convention by not providing any legal recognition, alternative to marriage, to same-gender couples. In line with this precedent, the Court held that the refusal by Italy to recognise a same-gender marriage entered into abroad was again an infringement of family life under Article 8.[72]

These precedents seem more relevant than the Grand Chamber decision in *Vallianatos*. The latter was narrowly tailored in terms of non-discrimination of same-gender vis-à-vis opposite-gender couples. Greece provided no justification for protecting by means of registered partnership only one category and not the other. Article 14 ECHR was taken in conjunction with Article 8. *Oliari* did not depend on such a comparison: same-gender couples enjoy protection and legal recognition whenever marriage is not accessible to them.

The ECHR Court's reasoning dwells upon characteristics of the Italian context, such as the Constitutional Court judgement n° 138/2010, identifying a constitutional obligation upon the Parliament to enact a civil union bill, and surveys showing that the population was by a large majority in favour of civil unions. This does not mean, however, that the impact of that decision is limited to Italy. This would be contrary to the idea of a truly European standard of protection of private and family life. If the scope of Convention rights were to be substantiated according to conditions specific to every Member State, the whole system would be severely undermined. The more recent reasoning in the *Pajić v. Croatia*[73] judgement lends support to the emergence of a European standard establishing a right to legal recognition as a couple.

There are solid arguments showing that *Oliari* and the subsequent Strasbourg case law is perceived by the Court of Justice as not limited to the Italian context. In his opinion, AG Wathelet refers to *Oliari* and talks of a 'positive obligation flowing from Article 8 of the ECHR – and therefore from Article 7 of the Charter – to offer homosexual couples the possibility of obtaining legal recognition of their union' and identifies the six EU Member States that do not respect this obligation.[74]

Already in 2013 with the *Hay* judgement, the Court seemed willing to depart from the comparative approach between marriage and the national alternative form of recognition when interpreting Directive 2000/78, if no alternative forms were given. At paragraph 44, the Court held that[75] the difference in treatment based on the employees' marital status and not expressly on their sexual orientation is still direct discrimination because only persons of different sexes may marry, and homosexual employees are therefore unable to meet the condition required for obtaining the benefit claimed.

Quite astonishingly, the First Chamber stated in *Parris*[76] that Member States 'are free to provide or not provide for marriage for persons of the same sex, or an alternative form of legal recognition of their relationship,' as if *Oliari* was never pronounced. The Grand Chamber in *Coman* did refer to *Parris* only in respect to the freedom to introduce equal marriage.[77] More significantly, they cited *Orlandi*, which is based on the findings in *Oliari*, thus conveying the view that protection for same-gender couples as upheld in the case law against Italy relies on a robust European standard of protection of their family life.[78] And this standard binds the Union.

Rainbow children in EU law

Domestic and cross-border non-recognition affects parents in particular, given the vulnerability of children and the need to have adults represent them in many everyday needs (e.g. school, medical care, travels). As the Court has repeatedly stated, citizens moving within the Union territory with their families enjoy under Article 21(1) TFEU the 'right to lead a normal family life.'[79]

The obligation to protect the best interests of children strengthens arguments in support of the recognition of parent-child relationships across Member States whenever freedom of movement is involved. Given the heterogenous protection enjoyed by non-biological parents across national borders, in many cases the issue at play is circulation of their status when acquired elsewhere in the absence of similar recognition – or any recognition at all – in the host state.

Directives on free movement award protection also to de facto family members. For instance, children under the age of 21 years or who are dependants are protected as core family members under Article 2(2)(c) of Directive 2004/38. If the Union citizen is not the legal parent, his or her spouse or registered partner is likely to be the parent. Children derive under the same provision their rights from the rights enjoyed by their legal parent, who in turn derives her or his rights from the EU citizen.

However, the 'registered partner' must comply with the definition given in point (b), which makes recognition conditional on the 'relevant legislation of the host Member State.'[80] As a consequence, a same-gender couple moving from Bulgaria to Lithuania with their child might face obstacles, if the legal parent and the child are third-country nationals and do not enjoy autonomous entry and residence rights. In such a case, the Court of Justice might have two options.

The most appropriate solution would target the renvoi to the host legislation in point (b) and address under the cascade effect the non-recognition of same-gender couples by the Member State. The validity of this provision has already been questioned by Advocate General Wathelet in his view in *Coman* on the basis of the *Oliari* precedent. If all Member States have an obligation 'to afford homosexual couples the possibility to obtain legal recognition and legal protection of their union,' EU law cannot accept to exclude from the category of core family members registered partners because no alternative form to marriage is granted under national law.[81] The invalidity of point (b) would extend to point (c) and thereby protect also common children.

A second solution could apply the reasoning in *SM*, a case dealing with children under the Algerian kafala system, a sort of consensual guardianship under Islamic law that is not equal to adoption, as it does not sever family ties. If the only legal parent is not a same-gender spouse or a registered partner for the purpose of Article 2, and hence the child does not enjoy a derived right as a core family member of the Union citizen, similarly to children in a kafala context, fundamental rights should 'demand, in principle, that that child be granted a right of entry.' The duty to facilitate under Article 3 of Directive 2004/38 is reinterpreted – or perhaps 'rephrased' – in such situations by the Court as ultimately granting a derived right to entry and residence with no discretion left to the States.

Circulation of statuses and documents

Regulation 2016/1191 on the circulation of public documents[82] may suggest a more daring influence of the Charter and of human rights standards on Union law. Since the very initial proposal for facilitating the circulation of public documents on civil status among Member States,[83] the purpose was to promote freedom of movement by avoiding issues of legalisation, apostille and translations. The Regulation excludes any automatic recognition of legal effects of those documents or as a source bearing any impact on the recognition of legal effects to the content of the document.[84] However, there are a few elements that show that this Regulation is not sterile and may contribute to the circulation not merely of the documents, but also of the statuses they certify.

The legal basis of the Regulation is not cooperation in civil matters: it is freedom of movement under Article 21(2) TFUE. This declared objective matters under the principle of speciality.[85] This piece of legislation, therefore, now attracts even more strongly the circulation of civil status documents to the freedom of movement and must be interpreted in view of its objective.

The close connection between civil status and freedom of movement is shown in clear terms by the case law on names, such as *Garcia Avello*[86] and *Grunkin and Paul*.[87] Member States may be required to respect names as attributed by other Member States or apply foreign law as lex personae[88] in matter of names.

Recital 56 of Regulation 2016/1191 recalls that the act must respect the Charter and be applied in accordance with those rights that most matter for family life. The Regulation extends and codifies the reasoning in *Dafeki*,[89] a decision in relation to movement of workers. It also becomes an additional evidence to the need within the Union to ensure the smoothest and widest circulation not just of documents, but more importantly of the person's status itself. As the CJEU already pointed out in *Dafeki*, 'exercise of the rights arising from freedom of movement for workers is not possible without production of documents relative to personal status.'[90] In its 2010 Green Paper[91] on adopting Regulation 2016/1191, the Commission held that 'the legal status acquired by the citizen in the first Member State . . . should not be questioned by the authorities of the second Member State' and added that otherwise 'this would constitute a hindrance and source of objective problems hampering the exercise of citizens' rights.'[92]

Despite there being no room for harmonising substantive family law in cases of free movement within the Union territory, there is a strong need to recognise one's status acquired in another Member State. In line with what was called the 'cascade effect,' the obligation might be limited and confined to specific issues. Yet, other situations may impose full recognition. The latter scenario, theoretically outside the reach of EU law and proper to every State's international private law rules, can nevertheless become, as made clear with respect to the case law on names, an obligation under Article 21(1) TFEU.[93] There is little doubt that refusing to accept the status of parent, spouse or registered partner is a 'serious inconvenience' 'at administrative, professional and private levels'[94] and questionable if freedom of movement is to be 'exercised under objective conditions of dignity.'[95]

Conclusions

Fundamental rights set the standard of protection of family life within EU law. The ECHR, but also the other international law treaties and the constitutional traditions common to the Member States, shape under Article 6(3) TEU the general principles of EU law. These all would be the major components of the main chapter in a hypothetical EU Family Law Code.

The ECHR takes a paramount role, as the case law of the ECHR court – rather than the Convention per se – was receptive to the evolution of family patterns in Europe and ensured that the Convention remains a 'living instrument.'[96] This protection now flows into the Union legal order directly through the Charter, which may provide more extensive protection. This potential is, however, widely untriggered.

The idea of a common core of protection for family life does not mean that the Union is bound to guarantee only what is common to all Member States' legal orders. The obligation to respect the fundamental rights proper to the Union takes precedence over any national system that does not comply with them, with substantial implications under the 'cascade effect' described previously. As the *Kreil*[97] judgement reminded us, the primacy principle applies also in regard to constitutional provisions. Moreover, the Union is based on principles of pluralism and of mutual recognition, not on definitions that aim at excluding national approaches geared towards inclusivity.

Despite this legal framework, one must still acknowledge efforts to restore discrimination in favour of the 'legitimate' family. 'Mum, Dad & Kids,' a failed European Citizens' Initiative,[98] aimed to impose a horizontal and strictly de jure definition of family member. According to the ECI proponents, '[t]his definition would imply that . . . [m]arriage is understood solely as the permanent and life-long union between one man and one woman' and that '"[f]amily members" are the spouses themselves, their common progeny, and the direct ascendants of each of them.'[99] This definition excludes inter alia divorce, same-gender unions, children born out of wedlock and cohabiting couples.

Such a definition is in its face contrary to Article 8 ECHR and Articles 7 and 9 of the Charter, and one may only wonder how the Commission could accept to register it.[100] Recognition across borders of legally formalised relationships does not require or allow for an EU-wide definition of what makes a de jure family.[101]

Pluralism and respect for the diversity of Europe's family patterns is the only viable common standard to ensure free movement, embrace national laboratories that try to adapt family law to the evolution of society and eventually remove discrimination. Moreover, the aforementioned European Citizens' Initiative would have obliterated de facto family life.

In fact, the dimension of family life as a mere question of fact might in the near future lead the Union to question its legal system in relation to polyamorous relations and to multiple parenthood. Non-dualistic family relationships suffer today of exclusion, regardless of the reason for such a way of life.[102]

EU regulations, in line with the tradition that formalised ties should take centre stage in family law definitions, do not prevent non-dualistic de facto relationships from enjoying some kind of recognition, for instance under Article 3(2)(a) of Directive 2004/38. Multiple parenthood already is a reality in some national legal systems. Polyamorous relationships do not – at least not yet – have access to forms of legal formalization, but may reach the threshold of a 'durable relationship, duly attested' for immigration/residence purposes, especially if the other two partners already enjoy Union citizenship. In this perspective, we might one day say that polyamorous families are part of a common European standard of family life potentially relevant under EU law.

Notes

1 Treaty on the Functioning of the European Union (2016) OJ C202/1, art 81.

2 Charter of Fundamental Rights of the European Union (2000) 2000/C 364/01, art 52(3). At the same time, the Court of Justice reiterates that 'the ECHR . . . does not constitute, as long as the European Union has not acceded to it, a legal instrument which has been formally incorporated into EU law': see Case C-524/15 *Luca Menci* ECLI:EU:C:2018:197, para 22.

3 *Paradiso and Campanelli v Italy* App No. 25358/12 (ECtHR, 24 January 2017).

4 *Johnston and Others v Ireland* Series A No. 122 (1986).

5 *Marckx v Belgium* Series A No. 31 (1979).

6 e.g. *Moretti and Benedetti v Italy* App No. 16318/07 (ECtHR, 27 April 2010).

7 A status conferred ipso jure, e.g. in favour of the husband, also qualifies per se as family life. See *Berrehab v the Netherlands* (1988) Series A No. 138: 'from the moment of the child's birth and by the very fact of it, there exists between him and his [married] parents a bond amounting to "family life," even if the parents are not then living together.'

8 Even in case of post-mortem insemination with the sperm of the late husband or partner on the basis of a specific consent to such posthumous use, as decided by the Italian Supreme Court of Cassation in its judgment No. 13000 of 15 May 2019.

9 *Orlandi and Others v Italy* App Nos. 26431/12, 26742/12, 44057/12 and 60088/12 (ECtHR, 14 December 2017), dissenting opinion of Judges Pejchal and Wojtyczek, para 4: 'It transpires from [Article 8 § 1 and Article 12 of the Convention] that the family unit is founded primarily by a man and a woman through marriage.'

10 In regard of staff matters the Court found in Case C-122/99 P and C-125/99 P *D and Kingdom of Sweden v Council* ECLI:EU:C:2001:304, that the 'Community judicature cannot disregard the views prevailing within the Community as a whole' (para 49) and noted 'the great diversity of laws and the absence of any general assimilation of marriage and other forms of statutory union' (para 50). International administrative tribunals generally respect the status as established in the home country by means of the so-called 'renvoi' to the lex patriae of the staff member; see Daniele Gallo, 'International Administrative Tribunals and Their Non-Originalist Jurisprudence on Same-Sex Couples: "Spouse" and "Marriage" in Context, Between Social Changes and the Doctrine of Renvoi' in Daniele Gallo, Luca Paladini and Pietro Pustorino (eds), *Same-Sex Couples Before National, Supranational and International Jurisdictions* (Springer 2014) 511.

11 Council Regulation (EU) No. 1259/2010 of 20 December 2010 implementing enhanced cooperation in the area of the law applicable to divorce and legal separation (2010) OJ L343/10.

12 Council Regulation (EU) 2016/1103 of 24 June 2016 implementing enhanced cooperation in the area of jurisdiction, applicable law and the recognition and enforcement of decisions in matters of matrimonial property regimes (2016) OJ L183/1; and Council Regulation (EU) 2016/1104 of 24 June 2016 implementing enhanced cooperation in the areas of jurisdiction, applicable law and the recognition and enforcement of decisions in matters of the property consequences of registered partnerships (2016) OJ L183/30.

13 Parliament and Council Directive 2004/38/EC of 29 April 2004 on the right of citizens of the Union and their family members to move and reside freely within the territory of the Member States (2004) OJ L158 (Directive 2004/38, also Citizens' Free Movement Directive).

14 Council Directive 2003/86/EC of 22 September 2003 on the right to family reunification (2003) OJ L251/12.

15 Case C-117/*01 K B v National Health Service Pensions Agency and Secretary of State for Health* ECLI:EU:C:2004:7.

16 Case C-267/06 *Tadao Maruko v Versorgungsanstalt der deutschen Bühnen* ECLI:EU:C:2008:179.

17 Directive 2012/29/EU of the European Parliament and of the Council of 25 October 2012 establishing minimum standards on the rights, support and protection of victims of crime, and replacing Council Framework Decision 2001/220/JHA (2001) OJ L315/57 (Victims' Rights Directive).

18 Cases C-424/10 and C-425/10 *Ziolkowski and Szeja v Land Berlin* ECLI:EU:C:2011:866, para 32, with regard to the expression 'legal residence' used in Article 16(1) of Directive 2004/38.

19 Compare, art 2(1)(a), Victims' Rights Directive, and Article 3(2)(b), Citizens' Free Movement Directive.

20 Directive 2004/38, art 2(2)(c) and art 3(2)(a). Dependence is usually construed in financial or material terms. See the Opinion of AG Tizzano in Case C-200/02

Zhu and Chen ECLI:EU:C:2004:307, para 84, who points out at paragraph 85 that the legislation then at play, now repealed, in language versions other than English 'relates unambiguously to material dependency.' Such strict interpretation still obtains today and draws arguments on the non-English language versions of Directive 2004/38, whose Article 2 does indeed recall the idea of material support (French *à la charge*, German *Unterhalt*). However, see Recital 6 and Article 3(2)(a) of this Directive in relation to dependency of extended family members. Dependency as a cause for leaving the territory of a Union is in contrast described by the Court as legal, financial or emotional, see Cases C-356/11 and C-357/11 *O and S v Maahanmuuttovirasto and Maahanmuuttovirasto v L* ECLI:EU:C:2012:776, para 54.

21 Case C-129/18 *SM v Entry Clearance Officer, UK Visa Section (Enfant placé sous kafala algérienne)* ECLI:EU:C:2019:248, para 69.

22 Similarly, see Case C-83/11 *Secretary of State for the Home Department v Muhammad Sazzadur Rahman and Others* ECLI:EU:C:2012:519, para 39; and, in regard to returning migrants, Case C-89/17 *Secretary of State for the Home Department v Rozanne Banger* ECLI:EU:C:2018:570.

23 *SM* (n 21) para 50.

24 Two criteria mentioned by the Court in Ibid., para 54.

25 Ibid., para 71.

26 Cases C-401/15 to C-403/1 *Depesme and Others v Ministre de l'Enseignement supérieur et de la Recherche* EU:C:2016:955.

27 Ibid., para 51 ff. The Court already drew analogies between freedom of movement and family reunification legislation, see e.g. Case C-127/09 *Blaise Baheten Metock and Others v Minister for Justice, Equality and Law Reform* ECLI:EU:C:2008:449, para 64.

28 Directive 2014/54/EU of the European Parliament and of the Council of 16 April 2014 on measures facilitating the exercise of rights conferred on workers in the context of freedom of movement for workers (2014) OJ L128/8.

29 Case C-673/16 *Coman and Others v Inspectoratul General pentru Imigrări* ECLI:EU:C:2018:385.

30 Contrary to the position expressed by the Court in *Metock* (n 27) para 98.

31 On purely internal situation, see Iglesias Sánchez Sara, *Purely Internal Situations and the Limits of Eu Law: A Consolidated Case Law or a Notion to Be Abandoned?* (Cambridge University Press 2018).

32 In criminal matters, see e.g. Cases C-483/09 and C-1/10 *Magatte Gueye and Valentin Salmerón Sánchez* ECLI:EU:C:2011:583, interpreting Council Framework Decision of 15 March 2001 on the standing of victims in criminal proceedings (2001) OJ L82/1. On family life in EU criminal matters, see further Iglesias Sánchez Sara and Keiva Carr, 'The Right to Family Life in the EU Charter of Fundamental Rights' in Maribel González Pascual and Aida Torres Pérez (eds), *The Right to Family Life in the European Union* (Routledge 2018) 62 ff.

33 Explanations relating to the Charter of Fundamental Rights (2007) OJ C303/17.

34 The Act Opening Marriage to Same-Sex Couples of 21 December 2000 entered into force on 1 April 2001. On the political discussions and preparatory works for the Act, see Caroline Forder, 'To Marry or Not to Marry: That Is the Question' in Andrew Bainham (ed), *The International Survey of Family Law* (Jordan Publishing 2001) 301.

35 *Schalk and Kopf v Austria* App No. 30141/04 (ECtHR, 24 June 2010). The ECtHR may consider Article 12 not applicable in the sense that it does not oblige Member States to open up marriage, but may well be applicable to the extent that it awards protection to couple already married.

36 Explanation to Article 9 in (n 33).
37 See the hypothetical scenario discussed later.
38 Among the international treaties ratified by all Member States, see the UN Convention on the Rights of the Child. For its impact in protecting minor EU citizens and their third-country national family members, see Ellen Nissen, *The Rights of Minor EU Member State Nationals Wishing to Enjoy Family Life with a Non-EU Parent in Their Country of Nationality: A Study in the Light of the UN Convention on the Rights of the Child* (Wolf Legal Publishers 2013).
39 See also, Case C-617/10 *Åklagaren v Hans Åkerberg Fransson* ECLI:EU:C:2013:105, para 44.
40 *Goodwin v UK* App No. 28759/95 (ECtHR, 11 July 2002).
41 But see earlier the judgment targeting the French civil status system *B v France* (1992) Series A No. 232-C.
42 Whereas the Court's wording in *Goodwin* referred to 'post-operative transsexuals' – see e.g. *Goodwin* (n 40) para 101, – following *A P Garcon and Nicot v France* App Nos. 79885/12, 52471/13 and 52596/13 (ECtHR, 6 April 2017), the ECtHR holding should now apply regardless of any surgeries undertaken.
43 Case C-13/94 *P v S and Cornwall County Council* ECLI:EU:C:1996:170.
44 *K B* (n 15) para 30.
45 Articles 4 and 5 TFEU.
46 Case C-147/08 *Jurgen Römer v Freie und Hansestadt Hamburg* ECLI:EU:C:2011:286.
47 Case C-267/12 *Frédéric Hay v Crédit agricole mutuel de Charente-Maritime et des Deux-Sèvres* ECLI:EU:C:2013:823.
48 Case C-506/06 *Sabine Mayr v Bäckerei und Konditorei Gerhard Flöckner OHG* ECLI:EU:C:2008:119, para 50.
49 Council Directive 2004/113/EC of 13 December 2004, implementing the principle of equal treatment between men and women in the access to and supply of goods and services (2004) OJ L373/37.
50 Ibid., art 1.
51 A matter that came close to a judgment on the merits in ECtHR, *Charron and Merle-Montet v France* App No. 22612/15 (ECtHR, 16 January 2018).
52 Case C-135/08 *Janko Rottmann v Freistaat Bayern* ECLI:EU:C:2010:104.
53 For a more detailed discussion of such a case and the linkage to relevant ECtHR case law, see Alexander Schuster, 'La tutela multilivello delle persone LGBTI e delle loro famiglie' in Alexander Schuster and Maria Gigliola Toniollo (eds), *La famiglia omogenitoriale in Europa. Diritti di cittadinanza e libera circolazione* (Ediesse 2015).
54 Case C-400/10 PPU *J McB v L E* ECLI:EU:C:2010:582, paras 53–54.
55 The CJEU could reject for its reasonings the margin of appreciation doctrine and consider itself bound to ensure full respect of human rights obligation and adopt a different approach. Compare the following reasoning per Lady Hale in *R (on the application of Steinfeld and Keidan) v Secretary of State for International Development* (2018) UKSC 32 [29]: 'It follows that a national court must confront the interference with a Convention right and decide whether the justification claimed for it has been made out. It cannot avoid that obligation by reference to a margin of appreciation to be allowed the government or Parliament, (at least not in the sense that the expression has been used by ECtHR).'
56 *Coman* (n 29) para 48.
57 *Vallianatos v Greece* App Nos. 29381/09 and 32684/09 (ECtHR, 7 November 2013).
58 *Orlandi and Others* (n 9).

59 *Oliari and Others v Italy* App Nos. 18766/11 and 36030/11 (ECtHR, 21 July 2015).
60 *Pajić v Croatia* App No. 68453/13 (ECtHR, 23 February 2016).
61 *Hämäläinen v Finland* App No. 37359/09 (ECtHR, 2014).
62 *Schalk and Kopf* (n 35) para 61.
63 E.g. *Charron and Merle-Montet* (n 51).
64 *EB v France* App No. 43546/02 (ECtHR, 22 January 2008).
65 *X and Others v Austria* App No. 19010/07 (ECtHR, 19 February 2013).
66 Council Regulation (EU) No. 1259/2010 (n 11).
67 *Johnston and Others* (n 4).
68 See *F v Switzerland* (1987) Series A No. 128.
69 E.g. *Aresti Charalambous v Cyprus* App No. 43151/04 (ECtHR, 19 July 2007).
70 See also the general reference to Article 21 of the Charter in Recital 30 of the Regulation.
71 The concept of penumbras is drawn from US constitutional law. See Burr Henly, '"Penumbra": The Roots of a Legal Metaphor' (1987) 15 *Hastings Constitutional Law Quarterly* 81.
72 See *Orlandi and Others* (n 9).
73 *Pajić* (n 60).
74 *Coman* (n 29), Opinion of AG Wathelet ECLI:EU:C:2018:2, footnote 42.
75 *Hay* (n 47) para 44.
76 Case C-443/15 *David L Parris v Trinity College Dublin and Others* ECLI:EU:C:2016:897, para 59.
77 *Coman* (n 29) para 37.
78 *Vallaniatos* and *Orlandi* are cited in paragraph 50 in support of the view that a 'relationship of a homosexual couple may fall within the notion of . . . "family life,"' whose protection has not been ensured in both cases.
79 *Coman* (n 29) para 32; Case C-165/16 *Toufik Lounes v Secretary of State for the Home Department* ECLI:EU:C:2017:862, para 52; *Metock* (n 27) para 62.
80 For an overview of the stance of Member States in regard to the right of entry and residence of same-gender couples, see Commission, 'Report from the Commission to the European Parliament and the Council on the Implementation of Directive 2003/86/EC on the Right to Family Reunification' COM (2019) 162 Final, 4.
81 Opinion of AG Wathelet (n 74) footnote 25. Under *Oliari* rather than under *Orlandi*, questions of validity arise also if the couple is moving from a home state to a host state and neither offers the possibility to enter into any formalised legal partnership. The lawfulness shifts from non-recognition of a status acquired elsewhere to the use of criteria – the status of spouse or registered partner – that same-gender couples cannot satisfy in either Member State because of they both violate their fundamental right to family life.
82 Regulation (EU) 2016/1191 of the European Parliament and of the Council of 6 July 2016 on promoting the free movement of citizens by simplifying the requirements for presenting certain public documents in the European Union and amending Regulation (EU) No. 1024/2012 (2016) OJ L200/1.
83 Commission, 'Proposal for a Regulation of the European Parliament and of the Council on Promoting the Free Movement of Citizens and Businesses by Simplifying the Acceptance of Certain Public Documents in the European Union and Amending Regulation (EU) No. 1024/2012' COM (2019) 0228 Final.
84 See Article 2(4).
85 Christian Kohler and Jean-Charles Engel, 'Le choix approprié de la base juridique pour la législation communautaire: enjeux constitutionnels et principes directeurs' (2007) 1 *Europe* 5.
86 Case C-148/02 *Garcia Avello v The State of Belgium* ECLI:EU:C:2003:539.
87 Case C-353/06 *Stefan Grunkin and Dorothee Regina Paul* ECLI:EU:C:2008:559.

88 In this context 'lex personae' should be understood as referring to the law of the country of citizenship. On the facts of these cases Member States were required to also apply the law of another Member State where a citizen of that Member State was resident in their jurisdiction.
89 Case C-336/94 *Eftalia Dafeki v Landesversicherungsanstalt Württemberg* ECLI:EU:C:1997:579, para 19.
90 Ibid.
91 Commission, 'Green Paper: Less Bureaucracy for Citizens: Promoting Free Movement of Public Documents and Recognition of the Effects of Civil Status Records' COM (2010) 0474 Final.
92 Ibid., para 4.1.
93 Inconveniences need to be assessed in each individual case, see Case C-391/09 *Malgožata Runevič-Vardyn and Łukasz Paweł Wardyn v Vilniaus miesto savivaldybės administracija and Others* ECLI:EU:C:2011:291, para 82. See also, Christian Kohler, 'La reconnaissance de situations juridiques dans l'Union européenne: le cas du nom patronymique' in Paul Lagarde (ed), *La reconnaissance des situations en droit international privé* (Parution 2013) 75.
94 *Avello* (n 86) para 36; *Grunkin and Paul* (n 87) paras 23–28; and Case C-208/09 *Ilonka Sayn-Wittgenstein v Landeshauptmann von Wien* ECLI:EU:C:2010:806, paras 67, 69 and 70.
95 *Metock* (n 27) para 98.
96 George Letsas, 'The ECHR as a Living Instrument: Its Meaning and Legitimacy' in Andreas Føllesdal, Birgit Peters and Geir Ulfstein (eds), *Constituting Europe: The European Court of Human Rights in a National, European and Global Context* (Cambridge University Press 2013).
97 Case C-285/98 *Tanja Kreil v Bundesrepublik Deutschland* ECLI:EU:C:2000:2.
98 Commission, 'Mum, Dad & Kids – European Citizens' Initiative to Protect Marriage and Family' European Citizens' Initiative, Registration (2015)000006 (11 December 2015).
99 See page 10 of the official ECI submission document, <https://ec.europa.eu/citizens-initiative/public/documents/3168/Submission%20ECI%20Mum%20Dad%20and%20Kids.pdf> accessed 15 June 2019.
100 See the requirements set out in Regulation (EU) No. 211/2011 of the European Parliament and of the Council of 16 February 2011 on the citizens' initiative (2011) L65/1, art 4(2), points (c) and notably (d), according to which the 'initiative [must not be] manifestly contrary to the values of the Union as set out in Article 2 TEU.'
101 The impossibility of defining certain formal statuses to the exclusion of all others would have probably implied that the initiative also run against point (b) of Article 4(2) of the ECI regulation.
102 In the case of polygamous marriage, the reunification of only one spouse is permitted and the entry of children of other spouses to join the sponsor may be refused, see Article 4(4) of Directive 2003/86. The rationale behind this provision is clearly related to the religious law of Islam.

References

Primary sources

Åklagaren v Hans Åkerberg Fransson (C-617/10) ECLI:EU:C:2013:105.

A P Garcon and Nicot v France App Nos. 79885/12, 52471/13 and 52596/13 (ECtHR, 6 April 2017).

Aresti Charalambous v Cyprus App No. 43151/04 (ECtHR, 19 July 2007).
B v France (1992) Series A No. 232-C.
Berrehab v the Netherlands (1988) Series A No. 138.
Blaise Baheten Metock and Others v Minister for Justice, Equality and Law Reform (C-127/09) ECLI:EU:C:2008:449.
Charron and Merle-Montet v France App No. 22612/15 (ECtHR, 16 January 2018).
Charter of Fundamental Rights of the European Union (2000) 2000/C 364/01.
Coman and Others v Inspectoratul General pentru Imigrări (C-673/16) ECLI:EU:C:2018:385.
Constitutional Court Judgement n° 138/2010.
Council Directive 2003/86/EC of 22 September 2003 on the right to family reunification (2003) OJ L251/12.
Council Directive 2004/113/EC of 13 December 2004 implementing the principle of equal treatment between men and women in the access to and supply of goods and services (2004) OJ L373/37.
Council Framework Decision of 15 March 2001 on the standing of victims in criminal proceedings (2001) OJ L82/1.
Council Regulation (EU) No. 2016/1103 of 24 June 2016 implementing enhanced cooperation in the area of jurisdiction, applicable law and the recognition and enforcement of decisions in matters of matrimonial property regimes (2016) OJ L183/1.
Council Regulation (EU) No. 2016/1104 of 24 June 2016 implementing enhanced cooperation in the area of jurisdiction, applicable law and the recognition and enforcement of decisions in matters of the property consequences of registered partnerships (2016) OJ L183/30.
Council Regulation (EU) No. 1259/2010 of 20 December 2010 implementing enhanced cooperation in the area of the law applicable to divorce and legal separation (2010) OJ L343/10.
D and Kingdom of Sweden v Council (C-122/99 P and C-125/99 P) ECLI:EU:C:2001:304.
David L Parris v Trinity College Dublin and Others (C-443/15) ECLI:EU:C:2016:897.
Depesme and Others v Ministre de l'Enseignement supérieur et de la Recherche (C-401/15 to C-403/1) EU:C:2016:955.
Directive 2012/29/EU of the European Parliament and of the Council of 25 October 2012 establishing minimum standards on the rights, support and protection of victims of crime, and replacing Council Framework Decision 2001/220/JHA (2001) OJ L315/57.
Directive 2014/54/EU of the European Parliament and of the Council of 16 April 2014 on measures facilitating the exercise of rights conferred on workers in the context of freedom of movement for workers (2014) OJ L128/8.
EB v France App No. 43546/02 (ECtHR, 22 January 2008).
Eftalia Dafeki v Landesversicherungsanstalt Württemberg (C-336/94) ECLI:EU:C:1997:579.
Explanations relating to the Charter of Fundamental Rights (2007) OJ C303/17.
F v Switzerland (1987) Series A No. 128.
Frédéric Hay v Crédit agricole mutuel de Charente-Maritime et des Deux-Sèvres (C-267/12) ECLI:EU:C:2013:823.

Garcia Avello v The State of Belgium (C-148/02) ECLI:EU:C:2003:539.
Goodwin v UK App No. 28759/95 (ECtHR, 11 July 2002).
Hämäläinen v Finland App No. 37359/09 (ECtHR, 2014).
Ilonka Sayn-Wittgenstein v Landeshauptmann von Wien (C-208/09) ECLI:EU:C:2010:806.
Italian Supreme Court of Cassation Judgment No. 13000 of 15 May 2019.
J McB v L E (C-400/10 PPU) ECLI:EU:C:2010:582.
Janko Rottmann v Freistaat Bayern (C-135/08) ECLI:EU:C:2010:104.
Johnston and Others v Ireland (1986) Series A No. 122.
Jurgen Römer v Freie und Hansestadt Hamburg (C-147/08) ECLI:EU:C:2011:286.
K B v National Health Service Pensions Agency and Secretary of State for Health (C-117/01) ECLI:EU:C:2004:7.
Luca Menci (C-524/15) ECLI:EU:C:2018:197.
Magatte Gueye and Valentin Salmerón Sánchez (C-483/09 and C-1/10) ECLI:EU:C:2011:583.
Malgožata Runevič-Vardyn and Łukasz Paweł Wardyn v Vilniaus miesto savivaldybės administracija and Others (C-391/09) ECLI:EU:C:2011:291.
Marckx v Belgium (1979) Series A No. 31.
Moretti and Benedetti v Italy App No. 16318/07 (ECtHR, 27 April 2010).
O and S v Maahanmuuttovirasto and Maahanmuuttovirasto v L (C-356/11 and C-357/11) ECLI:EU:C:2012:776.
Oliari and Others v Italy App Nos. 18766/11 and 36030/11 (ECtHR, 21 July 2015).
Orlandi and Others v Italy App Nos. 26431/12, 26742/12, 44057/12 and 60088/12 (ECtHR, 14 December 2017),
P v S and Cornwall County Council (C-13/94) ECLI:EU:C:1996:170.
Pajić v Croatia App No. 68453/13 (ECtHR, 23 February 2016).
Paradiso and Campanelli v Italy App No. 25358/12 (ECtHR, 24 January 2017).
Parliament and Council Directive 2004/38/EC of 29 April 2004 on the right of citizens of the Union and their family members to move and reside freely within the territory of the Member States (2004) OJ L158.
R (on the application of Steinfeld and Keidan) v Secretary of State for International Development (2018) UKSC 32.
Regulation (EU) No. 2016/1191 of the European Parliament and of the Council of 6 July 2016 on promoting the free movement of citizens by simplifying the requirements for presenting certain public documents in the European Union and amending Regulation (EU) No. 1024/2012 (2016) OJ L200/1.
Regulation (EU) No. 211/2011 of the European Parliament and of the Council of 16 February 2011 on the citizens' initiative (2011) L65/1.
Sabine Mayr v Bäckerei und Konditorei Gerhard Flöckner OHG (C-506/06) ECLI:EU:C:2008:119.
Schalk and Kopf v Austria App No. 30141/04 (ECtHR, 24 June 2010).
Secretary of State for the Home Department v Muhammad Sazzadur Rahman and Others (C-83/11) ECLI:EU:C:2012:519.
Secretary of State for the Home Department v Rozanne Banger (C-89/17) ECLI:EU:C:2018:570.
SM (Enfant placé sous kafala algérienne) (C-129/18) ECLI:EU:C:2019:248, para 69.
Stefan Grunkin and Dorothee Regina Paul (C-353/06) ECLI:EU:C:2008:559.

Tadao Maruko v Versorgungsanstalt der deutschen Bühnen (C-267/06) ECLI:EU:C:2008:179.
Tanja Kreil v Bundesrepublik Deutschland (C-285/98) ECLI:EU:C:2000:2.
Toufik Lounes v Secretary of State for the Home Department (C-165/16) ECLI:EU:C:2017:862.
Treaty on the Functioning of the European Union (2016) OJ C202/1.
Vallianatos v Greece App Nos. 29381/09 and 32684/09 (ECtHR, 7 November 2013).
X and Others v Austria App No. 19010/07 (ECtHR, 19 February 2013).
Zhu and Chen (C-200/02) ECLI:EU:C:2004:307.
Ziolkowski and Szeja v Land Berlin (C-424/10 and C-425/10) ECLI:EU:C:2011:866.

Secondary sources

Commission, 'Green Paper: Less Bureaucracy for Citizens: Promoting Free Movement of Public Documents and Recognition of the Effects of Civil Status Records' COM (2010) 0474 Final.

Commission, 'Mum, Dad & Kids – European Citizens' Initiative to Protect Marriage and Family' European Citizens' Initiative, Registration (2015)000006 (11 December 2015).

Commission, 'Proposal for a Regulation of the European Parliament and of the Council on Promoting the Free Movement of Citizens and Businesses by Simplifying the Acceptance of Certain Public Documents in the European Union and Amending Regulation (EU) No. 1024/2012' COM (2019) 0228 Final.

Commission, 'Report from the Commission to the European Parliament and the Council on the Implementation of Directive 2003/86/EC on the Right to Family Reunification' COM (2019) 162 Final, 4.

Forder C, 'To Marry or Not to Marry: That Is the Question' in Bainham A (ed), *The International Survey of Family Law* (Jordan Publishing 2001).

Gallo D, 'International Administrative Tribunals and Their Non-Originalist Jurisprudence on Same-Sex Couples: "Spouse" and "Marriage" in Context, Between Social Changes and the Doctrine of Renvoi' in Gallo D, Paladini L and Pustorino P (eds), *Same-Sex Couples Before National, Supranational and International Jurisdictions* (Springer 2014).

Henly B, '"Penumbra": The Roots of a Legal Metaphor' (1987) 15 *Hastings Constitutional Law Quarterly* 81.

Kohler C, 'La reconnaissance de situations juridiques dans l'Union européenne: le cas du nom patronymique' in Lagarde P (ed), *La reconnaissance des situations en droit international privé* (Parution 2013).

Kohler C and Engel J, 'Le choix approprié de la base juridique pour la législation communautaire: enjeux constitutionnels et principes directeurs' (2007) 1 *Europe* 5.

Letsas G, 'The ECHR as a Living Instrument: Its Meaning and Legitimacy' in Føllesdal A, Peters B and Ulfstein G (eds), *Constituting Europe: The European Court of Human Rights in a National, European and Global Context* (Cambridge University Press 2013).

Nissen E, *The Rights of Minor EU Member State Nationals Wishing to Enjoy Family Life with a Non-EU Parent in Their Country of Nationality: A Study in the Light of the UN Convention on the Rights of the Child* (Wolf Legal Publishers 2013).

Sánchez Sara I, *Purely Internal Situations and the Limits of Eu Law: A Consolidated Case Law or a Notion to Be Abandoned?* (Cambridge University Press 2018).
Sánchez Sara I and Carr K, 'The Right to Family Life in the EU Charter of Fundamental Rights' in González Pascual M and Pérez AT (eds), *The Right to Family Life in the European Union* (Routledge 2018).
Schuster A, 'La tutela multilivello delle persone LGBTI e delle loro famiglie' in Schuster A and Toniollo MG (eds), *La famiglia omogenitoriale in Europa. Diritti di cittadinanza e libera circolazione* (Ediesse 2015).

Chapter 8

EU law and the rights of rainbow families to move freely between EU Member States

Alina Tryfonidou

Introduction

European Union (EU) citizens,[1] and – through them – (certain of) their family members, derive from EU law the right to move between EU Member States and reside in the Member State of their choice. This right is enjoyed by all Union citizens regardless of their sexual orientation.[2] However, when rainbow families (i.e. families comprised of a same-sex couple and their child[ren]) move to a Member State which does not provide legal recognition to same-sex couples and/or their families in its territory, they are faced with the possibility that that Member State will refuse to legally recognise the familial ties among all or some members of the family, as these have been legally established elsewhere. This means that such families are not treated in the same way as the typical nuclear family which has as its basis an opposite-sex married couple with its biologically linked children: the familial links among the members of the nuclear family are only very rarely – if ever – legally contested.

This chapter will consider whether the refusal of some Member States to legally recognise – as this has been legally established elsewhere – the relationship between a child and one or both of her same-sex parents when the family moves to its territory, amounts to a breach of EU law.

EU law and the right of families to move between EU Member States

European Union citizens derive from the EU free movement of persons provisions the right to move and reside freely in the territory of another Member State.[3] They also derive a number of secondary rights, the grant of which has been considered necessary for enabling them to exercise the previously stated primary right.[4] One such secondary right is the so-called right to family reunification, which means, simply, that Union citizens who exercise free movement rights can be accompanied or joined by their close family members in the Member State to which they move.[5] This right has been laid down in secondary EU legislation since the 1960s, and is currently found in Directive 2004/38,[6] which applies to Union citizens who have exercised their right to move to, and reside in, a Member State *other than that of their nationality*.[7] Union citizens who have exercised free movement rights but seek to claim family reunification rights *in their Member State of nationality* upon their return, are, therefore, not covered by this Directive,[8] but derive family reunification rights from the free movement of persons provisions, whilst the provisions in the 2004 Directive which concern family reunification rights apply in such instances only 'by analogy.'[9] In order for family reunification rights to be meaningful, they are supplemented by a number of additional rights which have as their aim to ensure that the family can become integrated into the society of the host Member State, after it is admitted. Examples of such rights are the right of the family members to work in the host Member State,[10] and the right of the Union citizen and the family members to enjoy equal treatment with the nationals of the host Member State in situations which fall within the scope of the Treaty.[11]

The important question, of course, is: who is a 'family member' for the purposes of EU free movement law?

Art 2(2) of Directive 2004/38 provides that 'family member' are the Union citizen's (a) spouse; (b) the registered partner (subject to certain conditions); (c) the direct descendants who are under the age of 21 or are dependants and those of the spouse or registered partner; and (d) the dependant direct relatives in the ascending line and those of the spouse or registered partner. It should be noted that anyone who qualifies as a 'family member' because they fall within one of these categories derives – through the Union citizen 'sponsor' – the automatic[12] right to move and reside in the territory of the host Member State. This is so regardless of whether the family member is a Union citizen or not.[13]

If certain family members do not fall within any of these categories, art 3(2) of the same Directive can assist them. It provides that the host Member State shall 'facilitate entry and residence' for the following persons: (a) any other family members who, in the country from which they have come, are dependants or members of the household of the Union citizen, or where serious health grounds strictly require the personal care of the family member by the Union citizen; and (b) the partner with whom the Union citizen has a durable relationship, duly attested. It should be underlined, however, that under this provision, no *automatic* right to join or accompany the Union citizen is granted to the persons who can fall within these categories – the host Member State can merely be required to justify its decision in case it chooses not to admit them and, to do so, it will need to demonstrate that it has undertaken an extensive examination of their personal circumstances.[14]

Free movement of same-sex couples and their children within the EU

Having provided a summary of the legal provisions that govern the free movement rights of Union citizens and their family, the chapter will now focus on the position of same-sex couples with children. In particular, the question that will be explored in the remainder of this chapter is whether when the family moves, the host EU Member State is required – by EU law – to legally recognise the parent-child relationship between a child and both of his/her same-sex parents, as this has been established in another country. Unlike the issue of the cross-border legal recognition of same-sex couples which has been explored by academics[15] and, recently, by the CJEU,[16] this issue has, to date, never been explored.[17] It is a multifaceted issue which requires a consideration not, merely, of the rights of the parents but, also, of the rights and best interests of the child.

Co-parenting by same-sex couples in EU Member States: the current position

As is the case with the legal recognition of same-sex relationships,[18] it is left to EU Member States to decide whether they will allow same-sex couples in their territory to become *de facto* parents and to establish (*ab initio*) a family under the law. This means that the parental rights that same-sex couples enjoy at national level vary considerably throughout the EU.

As the most recent edition of the ILGA Rainbow Europe Index demonstrates,[19] at the moment, only a minority of EU Member States provide full parental rights to same-sex couples. Joint adoption by same-sex couples is only allowed in half of the EU Member States,[20] whilst second-parent adoption by such couples is allowed in fifteen EU Member States.[21] Surrogacy is largely prohibited across EU Member States,[22] and most Member States even refuse to recognise children born of surrogacy arrangements made in other countries.[23] The law allows medically assisted procreation by (female) same-sex couples (*as a couple*) in only twelve EU Member States,[24] whilst it is only in nine EU Member States that same-sex couples enjoy automatic recognition as co-parents.[25]

All in all, in a little less than half of the EU Member States (namely, eleven Member States) same-sex couples are unable to be recognised (legally) as co-parents.[26] In many EU Member States, therefore, a child born to a same-sex couple has only one legal parent, which means that the other parent of the child is not afforded any *legal* recognition as a parent.

The cross-border recognition of the parent-child relationship in situations where rainbow families move between EU Member States: the current (uncertain) position

In the previous sub-section, it was examined whether a same-sex couple can be legally established *ab initio* as the parents of their child in individual Member States. The important question for the purposes of this chapter, nonetheless, is whether EU law can require Member States, *in situations when there is an exercise of free movement rights by rainbow families*, to legally *recognise* the familial links between the children and both of their parents, *as these have already* been legally *established elsewhere* (i.e. in countries which have legislation which permits rainbow families to legally *establish* such links): can the children of same-sex couples move together with their parents in the host Member State and, once there, can they continue to be legally recognised as the children of both of their parents?

There are four ways in which children and their parents can benefit from family reunification rights under EU free movement law.

First, a child can fall under the art 2(2)(c) category of Directive 2004/38, when (s)he is the 'direct descendant' of a Union citizen who exercises free movement rights or of the spouse or registered partner of that Union citizen.[27] The child can fall within this category regardless of whether (s)he is a Union citizen, but (s)he can only be covered if under the age of 21 or a dependant of his/her parent(s). Second, under the art 2(2)(d) category of the Directive, if the child is a Union citizen and is not dependent on his/her parent(s), (s)he can act as the 'sponsor' of family reunification (and related) rights for his/her parent(s), if the latter are not EU citizens and thus do not enjoy free movement rights themselves.

Third, in *Zhu and Chen*,[28] the Court held that minors who are Union citizens, and wish to exercise their right to move and reside in the territory of another Member State in their own right, can claim the right to be joined or accompanied by their primary carer in the host State, provided that the family is economically self-sufficient. This right is derived directly from art 21 TFEU.

Finally, if a child does not fall within any of these categories, (s)he can rely on art 3(2)(a) of Directive 2004/38, as a dependant or member of the household of their parent who is a Union citizen. Alternatively, if the child is a Union citizen, (s)he can be the sponsor of (non-automatic) family reunification rights, if the parents can prove that they are members of the child's household in the home Member State or are dependent on the child.[29] But, as seen earlier, in both these cases, the decision whether to admit the family members falls entirely within the discretion of the host Member State and a decision to admit them under this category does not presuppose recognition of their familial ties.

The applicable EU legislation – Directive 2004/38 – simply speaks about 'direct descendants' and 'relatives in the ascending line,' without interpreting these terms in more detail. Moreover, there is no established EU definition for the words 'parent,' 'primary carer,' or 'child,'[30] which means that it is not clear if, for the purposes of EU law, the relationship between a child and *both* of his/her same-sex parents is recognised and, in particular, whether EU law legally recognises the non-biological parent as a 'parent.' From CJEU case law to date, it is clear that no biological link is required between a child and the Union citizen from whom the family reunification rights are derived.[31] The Court, in particular, has made clear that the step-children of the Union citizen who exercises free movement can join or accompany him or her in the host Member State.[32] Moreover, children who are Union citizens can 'sponsor' the right of residence of a third-country national primary carer *who is not genetically linked to them.*[33] More recently, the Court noted that the concept of a 'parent-child relationship' for the purposes of interpreting the term 'direct descendant' must be construed broadly 'so that it covers any parent-child relationship, whether biological or legal.'[34] In none of these cases, however, did the Court have to deal with a situation which involved the parent-child relationship between a child and his/her non-biological parent *where the parent was in a same-sex relationship with the other parent*. Accordingly, it is unclear if the same approach would have been followed in this latter scenario.

As seen in the previous sub-section of the chapter, currently, only a handful of EU Member States fully recognise rainbow families in their legal systems. Accordingly, when exercising free movement rights deriving from EU law, rainbow families may end up in legal limbo. The lack of clarity in the terms used in the 2004 Directive and the judge-made category of 'primary carer,'[35] and the absence of any clarification offered by the CJEU as regards the children of rainbow families in particular, has given cause to Member States which do not make provision for such families within their own legal system to believe that they are free to refuse to recognise the familial links (as already legally established elsewhere) between the members of such families when they move to their territory.

In some cases, the legal ties between a child and *both* of his/her parents will dissolve when the family moves to another Member State.[36] In other cases, it is only the legal links between the child and *one* of their parents (the non-birth mother or the non-biological parent) that are not recognised when the family moves to another Member State. This is demonstrated by a petition made to the Committee of Petitions (PETI) of the European Parliament, by Eleni Maravelia, a Greek national who is married to a British woman.[37] Ms Maravelia gave birth to a daughter in Spain in 2014. The Spanish birth certificate of the daughter of the couple indicates both Ms Maravelia and her spouse as parents of the child. Yet, in Greece – which does not legally recognise same-sex couples as co-parents – they were told that only the birth mother is recognised as the parent of the child, this making Ms Maravelia the sole parent of the child for the purposes of Greek law.

The important question, therefore, from the point of view of EU law is whether the EU has the competence and the tools to require its Member States to legally recognise the familial links – as legally established elsewhere – between the members of rainbow families in situations where such families move between Member States.

Is the refusal of the host Member State to recognise the familial ties among the members of a rainbow family a breach of the EU free movement provisions?

Where a child is a Union citizen and (s)he is not allowed to be accompanied or joined by both of her parents in the host Member State – because the legal links between the members of the family, as legally established elsewhere, are not recognised in the host Member State – the child's right to move and reside in the territory of another Member State will be breached.[38] Similarly, in situations when, for the same reason, a Union citizen cannot be accompanied or joined by his/her children, (s)he will be deterred from exercising free movement rights.[39] Accordingly, and since Directive 2004/38 – a piece of secondary legislation – needs to be read in a way which complies with primary EU law provisions, and, in particular, with the free movement provisions, the terms 'descendants' and 'relatives in the ascending line' must be read in a way which includes children and parents which constitute a rainbow family. The same approach should, obviously, be followed when interpreting the judge-made term 'primary carer.'

Now, assuming that a rainbow family *is* actually admitted to the host Member State, this is not the end of the story. If that State does not legally recognise the family ties between the members of the family for other legal purposes (e.g. tax law, property law, inheritance law, nationality law, pensions, hospital and school visits, and so on), this will cause great inconvenience to the members of the family which, in its turn, will impede the exercise of their free movement rights.[40]

Accordingly, the failure of the host Member State to legally recognise the familial ties already enjoyed by the members of a rainbow family moving to its territory from another Member State can amount to a breach of the free movement of persons provisions and Directive 2004/38. This is the case when this failure leads to the refusal of family reunification rights or of other entitlements which the family seeks to claim once it has been admitted into the territory of the host Member State. Such an obstacle to free movement is unlikely to be justified (on the grounds of public policy or the need to preserve their national identity), as the measure is not based on the *personal conduct* of the individual(s) concerned, as required by art 27(2) of Directive 2004/38.

Is the refusal of the host Member State to recognise the familial ties among the members of a rainbow family a breach of fundamental human rights protected under EU law?

Fundamental human rights have been protected as part of the general principles of EU law since the late 1960s.[41] With the coming into force of the Treaty of Lisbon in 2009, the Treaty on European Union (TEU) has been amended and its art 6 now provides that the EU Charter of Fundamental Rights (EUCFR) has the same legal value as the Treaties. Hence, in the EU, there are currently two parallel sources of fundamental human rights protection: the EUCFR and the general principles of EU law.

Although the European Convention on Human Rights (ECHR) is *not* an EU instrument, it has, nonetheless, always had a significant impact on the development of EU fundamental human rights protection, being recognised as a source of 'guidelines' for the CJEU when determining which fundamental human rights form part of the general principles of EU law and how these must be interpreted.[42]

In addition, it plays a crucial role in the interpretation of the EUCFR, as art 52(3) of the latter provides that:

> In so far as this Charter contains rights which correspond to rights guaranteed by the Convention for the Protection of Human Rights and Fundamental Freedoms, the meaning and scope of those rights shall be the same as those laid down by the said Convention. This provision shall not prevent Union law providing more extensive protection.

Given that there have been no CJEU rulings which can contribute to the development of an argument in cases involving rainbow families, the analysis that will follow will consist of an examination of the jurisprudence of the European Court of Human Rights (ECtHR) on the parent-child relationship, as this can, clearly, inform the argument that EU law requires the cross-border legal recognition of the parent-child relationship (also) in cases involving rainbow families.

Breach of the right to private and family life

The ECtHR held in *Gas and Dubois v. France* that a same-sex couple and their child(ren) can together enjoy 'family life' within the meaning of art 8 ECHR.[43] Taking into account art 52(3) EUCFR as previously discussed, the same interpretation must be followed for the purposes of art 7 EUCFR. Hence, in situations where the child in a rainbow family has established de facto 'family ties' with both of his/her parents, it is undisputed that family life exists between the members of the family; and, *a fortiori*, this is the case when those family ties have, already, been legally recognised somewhere.

In *Wagner v Luxembourg*,[44] at issue was the refusal of the Luxembourg authorities to recognise the Peruvian court decision pronouncing the full adoption by Ms Wagner – a Luxembourg national – of her child, JMWL, of Peruvian nationality. The refusal was the result of the absence in the Luxembourg legislation of provisions allowing an unmarried person to obtain full adoption of a child. The ECtHR held that this refusal amounted to an unjustified interference with the right to respect for Ms Wagner's and her child's family life and, thus, amounted to an infringement of art 8 ECHR. The Court, in particular, noted that '[b]earing in mind that the best interests of the child are paramount in such a case . . . the Court considers that the Luxembourg court could not reasonably disregard the legal status validly created abroad and corresponding to a family life within the meaning of art 8 of the Convention.'[45]

The case, therefore, demonstrates that art 8 ECHR requires the contracting Member States to pursue the cross-border continuity of family ties and, thus, '"limping" situations – i.e. situations where a personal status is recognized under the law of State X but not under the law of State Y – should be avoided to the largest possible extent.'[46]

More recently, the ECtHR was called to rule in a case which involved the cross-border recognition of a parent-child relationship lawfully established abroad, albeit in the more controversial context of a surrogacy arrangement (*Mennesson v France*).[47] The ECtHR, following the principles established in *Wagner v Luxembourg*, found that the contested refusal of France to recognise a surrogacy agreement entered into abroad, and the resultant refusal to legally recognise the parent-child relationship as established by this agreement, amounted to a breach of art 8 ECHR. However, unlike in *Wagner*, in this case, the ECtHR found that there was a breach of art 8 ECHR as regards the children's right to private life only. In particular, the Court found that, on the facts of the case, the lack of recognition of the parent-child relationship did not disproportionally affect the applicants' ability to enjoy their family life in a practical sense, and, thus, did not amount to a breach of their right to family life. There was, nonetheless, a breach of the right to private life of the children, since 'respect for private life requires that everyone should be able to establish details of their identity as individual human beings, which includes the legal parent-child relationship';[48] the 'legal uncertainty' caused as a result of the non-recognition in the host Member State is liable to have negative repercussions on the children's definition of their personal identity. More recently, the ECtHR made it clear[49] that in such cases, the right to respect for private life requires that domestic law provides a possibility of recognition of a legal parent-child relationship not only between the children and the intended parent who is biologically linked to them, but also with the intended (non-biologically related) mother designated in the birth certificate legally established abroad as the 'legal mother.' Nonetheless, it is not required that such recognition takes place automatically but, rather, another means, such as adoption of the child by the intended mother, may be used, provided that the procedure laid down by domestic law ensures that it can be implemented promptly and effectively, in accordance with the child's best interests.

Accordingly, relying on the above authorities, rainbow families can claim that the host Member State is in breach of their right to private and family life (as is protected under art 7 EUCFR and as a general principle of EU law) as a result of refusing to pursue the cross-border continuity of the family ties. What is more, such a reading of the right to family life seems to be in line with CJEU pronouncements wherein the Court emphasised the importance of ensuring that Union citizens who move can *continue* to lead a normal family life in the host Member State.[50]

The right to private and family life is, nonetheless, not an absolute right, and Member States are allowed to justify their measures which interfere with its exercise. And – as clarified by the Explanations attached to the Charter which were given interpretative effect by art 6(1) TEU and art 52(7) EUCFR[51] – the limitations that can legitimately be imposed on this right by art 7 EUCFR are the same as those allowed under art 8 ECHR. This means that the interference must have been conducted 'in accordance with the law,' must further a legitimate aim of those mentioned in art 8(2) ECHR, and must be necessary in a democratic society.

Given that it is fairly clear and foreseeable that Member States which do not recognise rainbow families will fail to recognise them also in situations which involve a cross-border element, the interference can be considered to be in accordance with the law.

However, can the contested refusal be justified by the 'legitimate aims' laid down in art 8 ECHR? Member States would most likely argue that their refusal to legally recognise the family ties among the members of rainbow families coming from other Member States has two aims: the 'protection of morals' – with the specific aim of supporting and encouraging the family in the traditional sense which 'is, in principle, a weighty and legitimate reason'[52] – as well as 'the protection of the rights of others,' in this case, 'others' being read as referring to children.

The aim of supporting and encouraging the traditional family has been recognised as a valid objective by the ECtHR,[53] and, thus, can, also, form a possible justification, when examining the issue from the point of view of EU law. However, such a justification would most likely fail, because – to use the reasoning employed in *Marckx v Belgium* – 'in the achievement of this end recourse must not be had to measures whose object or result is . . . to prejudice the' rainbow family, given that the members of the rainbow family can – as established in *Gas and Dubois v France* – enjoy family life. Accordingly, the members of rainbow families who enjoy family life must 'enjoy the guarantees of art 8 on an equal footing with the members of the traditional family.'[54] Moreover, as another commentator has rightly argued:

> The standard 'traditional family' defence would suggest that, by reducing non-heterosexual family rights to the greatest extent possible, national laws disincentivize non-traditional family structures, prioritize heterosexual marriage relationships, and encourage individuals into a socially optimal family model. However . . . such an argument would be intellectually weak (not to mention wholly removed from social reality). Severing the legal connection between gay, lesbian, and bisexual parents and their non-biological children does not persuade such individuals to enter an opposite-gender heterosexual marriage.[55]

In any event, even if the aim described by Dunne could, prima facie, justify the interference with the rights to private and family life in this context, it is unlikely to be found proportionate. The ECtHR has noted that 'the fact that an essential aspect of the identity of individuals is at stake where the legal parent-child relationship is concerned' means that the margin of appreciation afforded to Member States needs to be reduced.[56] And, as the same Court (ECtHR) has stressed,[57] in cases when the margin of appreciation afforded to States is narrow, 'the principle of proportionality does not merely require that the measure chosen is in principle suited for realising the aim sought. It must also be shown that it was necessary in order to achieve that aim to exclude certain categories of people' from a certain entitlement. For the reasons explained earlier, it cannot be shown that it is necessary, in order to protect the family in the traditional sense, to deprive the children of rainbow families and their parents of the entitlement to have their relationship – as established elsewhere – legally recognised in the Member State to which they move.

For similar reasons, a justification based on the need to protect the rights of others, namely the rights of the children of rainbow families, would also be bound to fail. There has been considerable social, scientific, and psychological research which argues that the successful raising of a child is not dependent upon the sexual orientation of his or her parents.[58] Moreover, the ECtHR has pointed out in its case law that 'there is currently a broad consensus – including in international law – in support of the idea that in all decisions concerning children, their best interests must be paramount' and has made a reference to art 24 EUCFR and to the importance of the right of the child to maintain a personal relationship and direct contact with both of his/her parents.[59] The same court has also noted that 'family ties may only be severed in very exceptional circumstances and that everything must be done to preserve personal relations.'[60] Accordingly, the best interests of the child seem to require that the familial ties (s)he has legally established with his/her parents in another country should be maintained when the family moves to another Member State. Same-sex couples should, therefore, continue to be legally recognised as the joint parents of their children in the host Member State, not *despite* the children's best interests, but exactly *because* this is required, if the children's best interests are taken into account.[61]

Accordingly, it can be argued that the failure of the host EU Member State to recognise the legal links between the child in a rainbow family and both of his parents – as these have been legally established elsewhere – can clearly amount to an unjustified breach of the right to private and family life of the child and the parents, as this is laid down under art 7 EUCFR and the general principles of EU law.

Breach of the right to non-discrimination on the ground of sexual orientation

In situations when the host Member State refuses to recognise the parental ties between a child of a same-sex couple and both of his/her parents, as these have been legally established elsewhere, this is clearly done because the parents of the child are of the same sex. In other words, Member States which do not allow a same-sex couple to legally establish a family in their territory, and which do not allow a rainbow family lawfully established elsewhere to be recognised as such, do so for the simple reason that the couple that is founding the family is comprised of two persons of the same sex. If the parents of the child were an opposite-sex couple, in the vast majority of cases, they would both be legally recognised as the parents of the child, even if the child had been adopted or conceived via assisted procreation methods.

Discrimination against rainbow families is discrimination based on the fact that the LGB parents in a rainbow family have acted on their sexual orientation by entering into a long-term couple relationship with a partner of the same sex and is, thus, a form of discrimination on the ground of sexual orientation. In addition, the children of same-sex couples face discrimination because of the sexual orientation of their parents, and in particular, they face discrimination on the ground of sexual orientation *by association* with their LGB parents. As established by the CJEU in *Coleman*,[62] the prohibition of discrimination under Directive 2000/78 also includes discrimination by association. There is no reason why this should not, also, be the case for art 21 EUCFR.

The next question, of course, is whether the host Member State may, nonetheless, be justified in drawing a distinction between rainbow families and families built by opposite-sex couples, in situations where there has been an exercise of EU free movement rights.

The ECtHR has made it clear that it considers discrimination based on sexual orientation to be as serious as discrimination on the grounds of 'race, origin or colour,'[63] and it has also repeatedly held that 'differences based on sexual orientation require particularly serious reasons by way of justification.'[64] This means that where a difference in treatment is based on sexual orientation, the Member State's margin of appreciation is narrow and this strict test will rarely – if ever – be satisfied.

The Member States would – most probably – rely on the same arguments as they would, when justifying an interference with the rights to private and family life: the need to protect and encourage the traditional family and the need to protect the rights of the child. The arguments made earlier for rejecting these aims as sufficient justifications are, naturally, applicable in this context, as well, and therefore will not be repeated here. When examining this discrimination argument, the injustice suffered by the children of rainbow families becomes even more obvious, as they are directly compared with the children of parents who are not in a same-sex relationship. As Judge Villiger noted in his dissenting opinion in *Gas and Dubois v France*, 'how can children help it that they were born of a parent of a same-sex couple rather than of a parent of a heterosexual couple? Why should the child have to suffer for the parents' situation?'[65]

It can, therefore, be argued that the failure of the host EU Member State to recognise the legal links between the child in a rainbow family and both of his/her parents – as these have been legally established elsewhere – can clearly amount to an unjustified breach of the prohibition of discrimination on the ground of sexual orientation, as this is laid down under art 21 EUCFR.

Conclusion

Despite the fact that same-sex couples have often succeeded in creating and sustaining meaningful family relationships, in some EU Member States, the law does not protect relationships between same-sex couples and their children. EU law cannot require those Member States to make provision in their laws for rainbow families *to be legally established* as families in their territory, as this is a matter that falls squarely within the regulatory purview of the Member States. Nonetheless, families which are recognised as families under one legal system cannot have their status as a family, and the rights attached to that status, challenged or ignored in the EU Member State to which they move. This creates gross inconsistencies across Member State lines and great uncertainties for rainbow families. In addition, as shown in this chapter, it gives rise to a breach of the EU free movement rights to which Union citizens are entitled, as well as to fundamental human rights which are protected under EU law.

A court or legislature cannot stop gays or lesbians from forming families. The law's unwillingness to legally recognise and preserve same-sex relationships, and/or the parent-child relationship in rainbow families that move across borders, comes contrary to the best interests of the children of such families and breaches a number of fundamental rights that the members of such families enjoy under EU law. It is, therefore, necessary for EU judges and/or the EU legislature to fashion rules and principles that reflect the reality of the lives of rainbow families when such families move between EU Member States. In particular, the EU institutions should clarify that *all* EU Member States are required by EU law to recognise – in situations involving the exercise of EU free movement rights – the exact legal ties among the members of a rainbow family, as these have been established in another legal system.

Notes

1 Art 20 TFEU provides that every person holding the nationality of an EU Member State is an EU citizen.
2 Hans Ulrich Jessurun d'Oliveira, 'Lesbians and Gays and the Freedom of Movement of Persons' in Kees Waaldijk and Andrew Clapham (eds), *Homosexuality: A European Community Issue* (Martinus Nijhoff 1993) 294.
3 The free movement of persons provisions are, currently, art 45 TFEU (workers), art 49 TFEU (the self-employed), art 56 TFEU (service providers/recipients), and art 21 TFEU, which is the catch-all, *lex generalis*, provision which applies to all Union citizens.
4 For an explanation of the distinction between primary and secondary rights in EU free movement law see Alina Tryfonidou, *The Impact of Union Citizenship on the EU's Market Freedoms* (Hart Publishing 2016) 21–22.
5 For an analysis of the family reunification rights that Union citizens derive from EU law see Chiara Berneri, *Family Reunification in the EU: The Movement and Residence of Third Country National Family Members of EU Citizens* (Hart Publishing 2017).
6 Council and Parliament Directive 2004/38 on the right of citizens of the Union and their family members to move and reside freely within the territory of the Member States (2004) OJ L 158/77 (Citizens' Rights Directive).
7 Ibid., art 3(1).

8 *O v Minister voor Immigratie, Integratie en Asiel and Minister voor Immigratie, Integratie en Asiel v B* (Case C-456/12) ECLI:EU:C:2014:135, paras 37–43.
9 Ibid., paras 46–50.
10 Citizens' Rights Directive (n 6), art 23.
11 Ibid., art 24.
12 Citizens' Rights Directive (n 6), recital 6.
13 Ibid., recital 5. Practically speaking, family reunification rights are more important for Union citizens whose family members are third-country nationals, as family members who are Union citizens can on their own right enjoy free movement rights.
14 Case C-83/11 *Rahman* ECLI:EU:C:2012:519; Case C-89/17 *Banger* ECLI:EU:C:2018:570.
15 See inter alia, Alina Tryfonidou, 'EU Free Movement Law and the Legal Recognition of Same-Sex Relationships: The Case for Mutual Recognition' (2015) 21 *Columbia Journal of European Law* 195; Uladzislau Belavusau and Dimitry Kochenov, 'Federalizing Legal Opportunities for LGBT Movements in the Growing EU' in Koen Slootmaeckers, Heleen Touquet and Peter Vermeersch (eds), *The EU Enlargement and Gay Politics: The Impact of Eastern Enlargement on Rights, Activism and Prejudice* (Palgrave Macmillan 2016).
16 Case C-673/16 *Coman and Others v Inspectoratul General pentru Imigrări* ECLI:EU:C:2018:385.
17 For a forthcoming piece exploring this issue in detail see Alina Tryfonidou, 'EU Free Movement Law and the Children of Rainbow Families: Children of a Lesser God?' (2019) 38 *Yearbook of European Law*.
18 Case C-267/06 *Maruko* ECLI:EU:C:2008:179, para 59; Case C-443/15 *Parris* ECLI:EU:C:2016:897, para 59.
19 ILGA, 'Europe Rainbow Europe Package: Annual Review and Rainbow Europe Map 2019' <https://rainbow-europe.org> accessed 13 May 2019.
20 Austria, Belgium, Denmark, Finland, France, Germany, Ireland, Luxembourg, Malta, Netherlands, Portugal, Spain, Sweden, and the UK.
21 Ibid.
22 For a comparative study of EU Member States' approach to surrogacy see Laurence Brunet and others, *A Comparative Study on the Regime of Surrogacy in EU Member States* (2013) <www.europarl.europa.eu/RegData/etudes/STUD/2013/474403/IPOL-JURI_ET(2013)474403_EN.pdf> accessed 16 April 2019.
23 Matteo M Winkler, 'Same-Sex Families Across Borders' in Daniele Gallo, Luca Paladini and Pietro Pustorino (eds), *Same-Sex Couples Before National, Supranational and International Jurisdictions* (Springer 2014) 390–393.
24 Austria, Belgium, Denmark, Finland, Ireland, Luxembourg, Malta, Netherlands, Portugal, Spain, Sweden, and the UK.
25 Austria, Belgium, Denmark, Ireland, Malta, Netherlands, Portugal, Spain, and the UK.
26 Bulgaria, Cyprus, Czech Republic, Greece, Hungary, Italy, Latvia, Lithuania, Poland, Romania, and Slovakia.
27 In the recent *Coman* case (n 16), the ECJ interpreted the term 'spouse' for the purposes of art 2 of Directive 2004/38, to include the same-sex spouse of a Union citizen who moves and resides in the territory of another Member State. Accordingly, when the parents of a child in a rainbow family are married, the host Member State should recognise them as such, and hence, even if the host Member State refuses to legally recognise the child as the child of one of his/her parents, if the parent who is not legally recognised as such is the Union citizen, the child can still derive family reunification rights from that parent, as it is considered as the child of the Union citizen's spouse.

28 Case C-200/02 *Zhu and Chen* ECLI:EU:C:2004:639, paras 26–34.
29 If the child is a minor it is unlikely that a relationship of dependency satisfying the requirements of this provision (i.e. the parent being (materially) dependent on the child) will be found – see Ibid., paras 43–44; Case C-40/11 *Iida* ECLI:EU:C:2012:691, paras 54–56.
30 See C-7/94 *Gaal* ECLI:EU:C:1995:29, Opinion of AG Tesauro, para 7. See also, Helen Stalford, *Children and the European Union: Rights, Welfare and Accountability* (Hart Publishing 2012) 21.
31 See Ibid., 23–24; Frank Emmert, 'The Family Policy of the European Community' in Kees Waaldijk and Andrew Clapham (eds), *Homosexuality: A European Community Issue* (Martinus Nijhoff 1993) 370.
32 Case C-413/99 *Baumbast and R* ECLI:EU:C:2002:493, para 57.
33 Joined Cases C-356/11 and C-357/11 *O, S and L* (2012) EU:C:2012:776, para 55.
34 Case C-129/18 *SM v Entry Clearance Officer, UK Visa Section* ECLI:EU:C:2019:248, para 54.
35 *Baumbast* (n 32); *Zhu and Chen* (n 28).
36 For examples see Winkler (n 23) 388–389.
37 'Petition No 0513/2016 by Eleni Maravelia (Greek) on the Non-Recognition of LGBT Families in the European Union' (European Parliament, 2016) <https://petiport.secure.europarl.europa.eu/petitions/en/petition/content/0513%252F2016/html/Petition-No-0513%252F2016-by-Eleni-Maravelia-%2528Greek%2529-on-the-non-recognition-of-LGBT-families-in-the-European-Union> accessed 16 April 2019. For additional examples see NELFA Public Petition to EU Commissioner Viviane Reding: NEFLA, 'Same-Sex Parents and their Children Demand True Freedom of Movement in the European Union' (24 September 2013) <http://lgbt-families.eu/wp-content/uploads/2013/05/NELFAPetitiontoCommissionerRedingFINAL.pdf> accessed 17 April 2019.
38 See for instance, *Zhu and Chen* (n 28).
39 See for instance, *Baumbast* (n 32). For a similar argument in the US context, see Andrew Koppelman, *Same Sex Different States: When Same-Sex Marriages Cross State Lines* (Sheridan 2006) 74–76.
40 Here, the argument made by the ECJ in a different context (the cross-border recognition of surnames) is employed: Case C-148/02 *Garcia Avello* ECLI:EU:C:2003:539. For a similar argument see Helen Toner, 'Migration Rights and Same-Sex Couples in EU Law: A Case Study' in Katharina Boele-Woelki and Angelika Fuchs (eds), *Legal Recognition of Same-Sex Relationships in Europe: National, Cross-Border and European Perspectives* (Intersentia 2012) 304–305.
41 Case 29/69 *Stauder* ECLI:EU:C:1969:57.
42 Case 4/73 *Nold* ECLI:EU:C:1974:51.
43 *Gas and Dubois v France* App No. 25952/07 (ECtHR, 15 March 2012), para 37.
44 *Wagner v Luxembourg* App No. 76240/01 (ECtHR, 28 June 2007).
45 Ibid., para 133. See also, *Negrepontis-Giannisis v Greece* App No. 56759/09 (ECtHR, 3 May 2011), which involved the cross-border legal recognition of an adoption lawfully concluded in another country (the US), albeit of an adult.
46 Pietro Franzina, 'Some Remarks on the Relevance of Article 8 of the ECHR to the Recognition of Family Status Judicially Created Abroad' (2011) 3 *Diritti umani e diritto internazionale* 609, 611.
47 *Mennesson v France* App No. 65192/11 (ECtHR, 26 June 2014). See also, *Labassee v France* App No. 65941/11 (ECtHR, 26 June 2014); and *Laborie v France* App No. 44024/13 (ECtHR, 19 January 2017).
48 *Mennesson v France* (n 47), para 96.

49 ECtHR Advisory Opinion Request No P16-2018-001 (10 April 2019).
50 See inter alia, Case C-127/09 *Metock and Others* ECLI:EU:C:2008:449, para 62; *Coman* (n 16) para 32; Case C-165/16 *Lounes* ECLI:EU:C:2017:862, para 52. For a similar argument see Toner (n 40) 307–308.
51 Explanations relating to the Charter of Fundamental Rights (2007) OJ C303/120, Explanation on art 52.
52 *Karner v Austria* App No. 40016/98 (ECtHR, 24 July 2003), para 40.
53 See, for instance, *Vallianatos v Greece* App Nos. 29381/09 and 32684/09 (ECtHR, 7 November 2013), para 83.
54 *Marckx v Belgium* App No. 6833/74 (ECtHR, 13 June 1979), para 40.
55 Peter Dunne, 'Who Is a Parent and Who Is a Child in a Same-Sex Family? Legislative and Judicial Issues for LGBT Families Post-Separation, Part I: The European Perspective' (2017) 30 *Journal of the American Academy of Matrimonial Lawyers* 27, 48–49. See also, Jens M Scherpe, 'The Legal Recognition of Same-Sex Couples in Europe and the Role of the European Court of Human Rights' (2013) 10 *The Equal Rights Review* 83, 92; Nancy Polikoff, 'This Child Does Have Two Mothers: Redefining Parenthood to Meet the Needs of Children in Lesbian-Mother and Other Non-Traditional Families' (1990) 78 *Georgetown Law Journal* 459, 486.
56 See for instance, *Mennesson* (n 48), paras 77, 80; *Orlandi and Others v Italy* App Nos. 26431/12; 26742/12; 44057/12 and 60088/12 (ECtHR, 14 December 2017), para 203.
57 *Karner* (n 52), para 41.
58 See most fundamentally, Susan Golombok, *Modern Families: Parents and Children in New Family Forms* (Cambridge University Press 2015) esp chapters 2 and 7; American Psychological Association, 'Sexual Orientation, Parents, & Children' (2004) <www.apa.org/about/policy/parenting.aspx> accessed 17 April 2019; Nanette Gartrell, Henny Bos and Audrey Koh, 'National Longitudinal Lesbian Family Study – Mental Health of Adult Offspring' (2018) 379 *The New England Journal of Medicine* 297.
59 *Neulinger and Shuruk v Switzerland* App No. 41615/07 (6 July 2010), para 135.
60 Ibid., para 136.
61 Clare McGlynn, *Families and the European Union: Law, Politics and Pluralism* (Cambridge University Press 2006) 108. For a clear statement by the ECJ that when Member States apply and/or implement EU secondary legislation, art 24 EUCFR read together with art 51 requires them in all its decisions to have the child's best interests as their primary consideration; see Case C-648/11 *MA and Others* ECLI:EU:C:2013:367, paras 57–59.
62 S. *Coleman v Attridge Law and Steve Law* Case C-303/06 ECLI:EU:C:2008:415.
63 *Vejdeland and Others v Sweden* App No. 1813/07 (ECtHR, 9 February 2012), para 55.
64 See for instance, *Gas and Dubois* (n 43), para 59; *Smith and Grady v UK* App Nos. 33985/96 and 33986/96 (ECtHR 27 September 1999), para 90; *Kozak v Poland* App No. 13102/02 (ECtHR 2 March 2010), para 92.
65 Dissenting opinion of Judge Villiger in *Gas and Dubois v France* (n 43).

References

Primary sources

Baumbast and R v Secretary of State for the Home Department (C-413/99) ECLI:EU:C:2002:493.

Blaise Baheten Metock and Others v Minister for Justice, Equality and Law Reform (C-127/09) ECLI:EU:C:2008:449.
Carlos Garcia Avello v Belgian State (C148–02) ECLI:EU:C:2003:539.
Coman and Others v Inspectoratul General pentru Imigrări (C-673/16) ECLI:EU:C:2018:385.
Consolidated Version of the Treaty on the Functioning of the European Union (2012) OJ C 326/01.
Council and Parliament Directive 2004/38 on the Right of Citizens of the Union and Their Family Members to Move and Reside Freely Within the Territory of the Member States (2004) OJ L 158/77 (Citizens' Rights Directive).
David L Parris v Trinity College Dublin and Others (C-443/15) ECLI:EU:C:2016:897.
ECtHR Advisory Opinion Request No. P16-2018-001 (10 April 2019).
Erich Stauder v City of Ulm (C-29/69) ECLI:EU:C:1969:57.
Explanations relating to the Charter of Fundamental Rights (2007) OJ C303/120.
Gas and Dubois v France App No. 25952/07 (ECtHR, 15 March 2012).
J. Nold, Kohlen- und Baustoffgroßhandlung v Commission of the European Communities (C-4/73) ECLI:EU:C:1974:51.
Karner v Austria App No. 40016/98 (ECtHR, 24 July 2003).
Kozak v Poland App No. 13102/02 (ECtHR, 2 March 2010).
Kunqian Catherine Zhu and Man Lavette Chen v Secretary of State for the Home Department (C-200/02) ECLI:EU:C:2004:639.
Labassee v France App No. 65941/11 (ECtHR, 26 June 2014).
Laborie v France App No. 44024/13 (ECtHR, 19 January 2017).
Landesamt für Ausbildungsförderung Nordrhein-Westfalen v Lubor Gaal (C-7/94) ECLI:EU:C:1995:29.
Marckx v Belgium App No. 6833/74 (ECtHR, 13 June 1979).
Mennesson v France App No. 65192/11 (ECtHR, 26 June 2014).
Negrepontis-Giannisis v Greece App No. 56759/09 (ECtHR, 3 May 2011).
Neulinger and Shuruk v Switzerland App No. 41615/07 (6 July 2010).
O and S v Maahanmuuttovirasto and Maahanmuuttovirasto v L (C-356/11 and C-357/11) ECLI:EU:C:2012:776.
O v Minister voor Immigratie, Integratie en Asiel and Minister voor Immigratie, Integratie en Asiel v B (C-456/12) ECLI:EU:C:2014:135.
Orlandi and Others v Italy App Nos. 26431/12; 26742/12; 44057/12 and 60088/12 (ECtHR, 14 December 2017).
The Queen, on the Application of MA and Others v Secretary of State for the Home Department (C-648/11) ECLI:EU:C:2013:367.
S. Coleman v Attridge Law and Steve Law (C-303/06) ECLI:EU:C:2008:415.
Secretary of State for the Home Department v Muhammad Sazzadur Rahman and Others (C-83/11) ECLI:EU:C:2012:519.
Secretary of State for the Home Department v Rozanne Banger (C-89/17) ECLI:EU:C:2018:570.
SM v Entry Clearance Officer, UK Visa Section (C-129/18) ECLI:EU:C:2019:248.
Smith and Grady v UK App Nos. 33985/96 and 33986/96 (ECtHR 27 September 1999).
Tadao Maruko v Versorgungsanstalt der deutschen Bühnen (C-267/06) ECLI:EU:C:2008:179.
Toufik Lounes v Secretary of State for the Home Department (C165/16) ECLI:EU:C:2017:862.

Vallianatos v Greece App Nos. 29381/09 and 32684/09 (ECtHR, 7 November 2013).
Vejdeland and Others v Sweden App No. 1813/07 (ECtHR, 9 February 2012).
Wagner v Luxembourg App No. 76240/01 (ECtHR, 28 June 2007).
Yoshikazu Iida v Stadt Ulm (C-40/11) ECLI:EU:C:2012:691.

Secondary sources

American Psychological Association, 'Policy Statement on Sexual Orientation, Parents, & Children' (2004) <www.apa.org/about/policy/parenting.aspx> accessed 17 April 2019.

Belavusau U and Kochenov D, 'Federalizing Legal Opportunities for LGBT Movements in the Growing EU' in Slootmaeckers K, Touquet H and Vermeersch P (eds), *The EU Enlargement and Gay Politics: The Impact of Eastern Enlargement on Rights, Activism and Prejudice* (Palgrave Macmillan 2016).

Berneri C, *Family Reunification in the EU: The Movement and Residence of Third Country National Family Members of EU Citizens* (Hart Publishing 2017).

Brunet L and Others, *A Comparative Study on the Regime of Surrogacy in EU Member States* (2013) <www.europarl.europa.eu/RegData/etudes/STUD/2013/474403/IPOL-JURI_ET(2013)474403_EN.pdf> accessed 16 April 2019.

Dunne P, 'Who Is a Parent and Who Is a Child in a Same-Sex Family? Legislative and Judicial Issues for LGBT Families Post-Separation, Part I: The European Perspective' (2017) 30 *Journal of the American Academy of Matrimonial Lawyers* 27.

Emmert F, 'The Family Policy of the European Community' in Waaldijk K and Clapham A (eds), *Homosexuality: A European Community Issue* (Martinus Nijhoff 1993).

European Parliament, 'Petition No 0513/2016 by Eleni Maravelia (Greek) on the Non-Recognition of LGBT Families in the European Union' (European Parliament, 2016) <https://petiport.secure.europarl.europa.eu/petitions/en/petition/content/0513%252F2016/html/Petition-No-0513%252F2016-by-Eleni-Maravelia-%2528Greek%2529-on-the-non-recognition-of-LGBT-families-in-the-European-Union> accessed 16 April 2019.

Franzina P, 'Some Remarks on the Relevance of Article 8 of the ECHR to the Recognition of Family Status Judicially Created Abroad' (2011) 3 *Diritti umani e diritto internazionale* 609.

Gartrell N, Bos H and Koh A, 'National Longitudinal Lesbian Family Study – Mental Health of Adult Offspring' (2018) 379 *The New England Journal of Medicine* 297.

Golombok S, *Modern Families: Parents and Children in New Family Forms* (Cambridge University Press 2015).

Jessurun d'Oliveira HU, 'Lesbians and Gays and the Freedom of Movement of Persons' in Waaldijk K and Clapham A (eds), *Homosexuality: A European Community Issue* (Martinus Nijhoff 1993).

Koppelman A, *Same Sex Different States: When Same-Sex Marriages Cross State Lines* (Sheridan 2006).

McGlynn C, *Families and the European Union: Law, Politics and Pluralism* (Cambridge University Press 2006).

NELFA, 'Same-Sex Parents and Their Children Demand True Freedom of Movement in the European Union' (24 September 2013) <http://lgbt-families.eu/

wp-content/uploads/2013/05/NELFAPetitiontoCommissionerRedingFINAL.pdf> accessed 17 April 2019.

Polikoff ND, 'This Child Does Have Two Mothers: Redefining Parenthood to Meet the Needs of Children in Lesbian-Mother and Other Non-Traditional Families' (1990) 78 *Georgetown Law Journal* 459.

Scherpe JM, 'The Legal Recognition of Same-Sex Couples in Europe and the Role of the European Court of Human Rights' (2013) 10 *The Equal Rights Review* 83.

Stalford H, *Children and the European Union: Rights, Welfare and Accountability* (Hart Publishing 2012).

Toner H, 'Migration Rights and Same-Sex Couples in EU Law: A Case Study' in Boele-Woelki K and Fuchs A (eds), *Legal Recognition of Same-Sex Relationships in Europe: National, Cross-Border and European Perspectives* (Intersentia 2012).

Tryfonidou A, 'EU Free Movement Law and the Legal Recognition of Same-Sex Relationships: The Case for Mutual Recognition' (2015) 21 *Columbia Journal of European Law* 195.

———, *The Impact of Union Citizenship on the EU's Market Freedoms* (Hart Publishing 2016).

———, 'EU Free Movement Law and the Children of Rainbow Families: Children of a Lesser God?' (2019) 38 *Yearbook of European Law*.

Winkler MM, 'Same-Sex Families Across Borders' in Gallo D, Paladini L and Pustorino P (eds), *Same-Sex Couples Before National, Supranational and International Jurisdictions* (Springer 2014).

Chapter 9

Same-sex relationships and the child law perspectives

Another child protection concern, or simply a new way of creating the modern family?

Frances Burton

Introduction

It is unfortunate that, at the very point when it appears that the lengthy historical background to the normative acceptance of same-sex relationships has taken a positive turn, there should arise an unexpected obstacle to full acceptance of the new family format whereby same sex partners can now found their own families of genetically related children.

The problem seems to have been created by the fluidity of gender created by a new perception of an 'intersex,' or third – 'X' – gender, in cases where individuals claim that they recognise themselves as belonging to neither one established gender nor the other.

In other words, it appears that English law (having finally been proactive in recognising both full conversion in trans cases for all purposes and full recognition of same-sex and opposite-sex relationships in both civil partnerships[1] and marriage) has had to accept that the full equality English law provides has now stalled in cross border contexts; and that English law can do nothing about international impacts on intersex persons of English or Welsh origin (although the United Kingdom [UK] does itself recognise the practical 'X' solution for our own passport purposes). This adverse impact is because some jurisdictions recognise only the traditional binary 'M' and 'F,' although it seems to be accepted in most Western jurisdictiond that the current 'younger' (18–24-year-old) generation 'swings both ways.' Indeed, in a recent YouGov poll, 43% describe themselves as 'sexually fluid' – neither straight nor gay. This group includes Hollywood's 'most prominent bisexual,' film director Desire Akhavan, creator of a new sitcom *The Bisexual*, aired on Channel 4 in late 2018.[2]

Coupled with the lack of an international surrogacy regime, recognising the consequent parent-child relationship which parental orders under current English law[3] bestow, this means that some same-sex partners still do not have true equality if they leave our own jurisdiction despite their status at home. Nevertheless, some other jurisdictions – for example, India – have been proactive in ensuring that surrogacy tourism does not impact adversely on either the resulting child or on the surrogate. The impact of concerns about originally unanticipated and undesirable side effects of surrogacy has not been softened by the fact that positive development for same-sex relationships have arisen concurrently with a major national and international initiative to curb both paedophile child abuse and international trafficking, for which surrogacy is often a perfect pathway for those who are intent on its abuse.

Unfortunately, owing to insufficient surrogates in England and Wales, inter alia no doubt because surrogates can only be paid expenses in our jurisdiction, 'surrogacy tourism' has inevitably afforded such trafficking opportunities, also no doubt as, despite UN efforts, there is no worldwide common law or practice governing surrogacy. Thus, those seeking such facilities in less regulated jurisdictions will inevitably cross borders to a location which permits them the most freedoms.

While there is no essential connection between same-sex relationships and parentage and an escalation in such abuse, nevertheless inevitably child protection concerns arise. This may in turn be because of the relatively new intersex potential which is seen as a likely facilitator for paedophile access to children for such abuse, unlike in previously clearly defined 'M' and 'F' distinctions, which in practice can matter to other M/F segregated users in many contexts, ranging from passports to a wide variety of unisex facilities.

This sadly masks the equally important fact that surrogacy is essential to a relationship, whether same-sex or opposite-sex, in which the partners cannot reproduce naturally so as to create a stable family unit, complete with parental responsibility, gender neutral parenting and welfare paramountcy; which is precisely the sort of stable family unit which governments regularly concede is the backbone of society. Have we thus only made progress that brings an element of retrogression? A look at the past is encouraging, though not entirely conclusive.

Historical and recent past

It is not long since, in the 1990s and the first decade of the 21st century, when families were still apparently formed of two opposite-sex parents with 2.4 children, a dog and a Volvo, which for a short time seemed to be what same-sex parents aspired to in searching for successful mainstreaming of the atypical family formats which are now firmly part of English family law.[4] It would therefore be useful to look first at the historical background, in which to set in context the drivers for change and the subsequent developments which have led to the intersex debate and the challenges faced by same same-sex parents, including in relation to surrogacy.

By 2010, some thirty years after courts doubted the advisability of allowing children to live in lesbian households, such as in the 1991 case of *B v B (Minors) (Custody, Care and Control)*[5] the same sex model was so successful that film director Lisa Chodolenko risked making her (eventually award-winning) family comedy *The Kids Are All Right*, starring Julianne Moore and Annette Bening, whose characters typified the lesbian IVF parents with sperm donor father of their teenage children which was often the model of the time. This was a film which then won both an Oscar nomination and a Golden Globe for Best Film, thus probably constituting a stronger argument for the normativity of atypical families than any other contribution from the arts since the distinguished children's writer, Jeanette Winterson, was first published in 1985.[6] Sadly, though it may have generated some thoughtful acceptance by the broader intelligentsia, it gained little approval from the gay community in general and lesbians in particular, who decided it was far from 'All Right,' despite positive reviews in *The Guardian*,[7] which commended the 'warm and witty' account of 'the post-modern family,' but which did not stop *The Independent's* Arts Writer presenting the counter view that all the prize winning film mainstreamed was straight fantasies about lesbians.[8]

Unfortunately, however, such mainstreaming integration is still not the case in many other jurisdictions, a situation clearly creating problems for contemporary border-crossing families routinely seeking regular employment and established residence – as well as holidays and other short-term stays – outside the UK. Such families are thus finding that English and Welsh child law is one of the most progressively inclusive, while foreign provision may not be nearly as generous as they have at home.

Thus our home jurisdiction's provision compares very favourably with that of only three decades ago, when English and Welsh judiciary used to be wary of even allowing children to live in gay families because of concern that, at that stage, this was so unusual and outside the mainstream that judges worried about embarrassment for such a child. As a result, it was thought that the child was likely, from its atypical gay parented family, to be identified by other children as sufficiently different that bullying at school could be inevitable. For example, the case already mentioned in this context, *B v B (Minors) (Custody, Care and Control)*[9] generated a lengthy courtroom debate about whether it would be 'safe' for a young child to live with his lesbian mother following a divorce, despite the fact that since he was so young, this would otherwise be the obvious place for him. However, owing to the judge's fear that he would be noticeably 'different' at school, coming from a lesbian home, and thus be picked on by children from straight homes, this generated a substantial discussion, fortunately then resolved by the consultant psychiatrist in the case, who thought that in fact this disposal would pose no real risk owing to the continuing influence of the father who had a heterosexual partner whom he hoped to marry. Thus, it was accepted that that would be sufficient to counteract any adverse effects, especially as the judge noted that the mother was 'not a militant lesbian' and could provide continuous child care, while the father would have had to use a childminder. Perhaps this bullying fear was not unreasonable, owing to anecdotal reports of continued contemporary bullying even today of transpeople in some overseas common law jurisdictions[10] where such atypical family members have not yet become sufficiently integrated.

Indeed, it seems that neither Europe in general, nor the EU in particular, has achieved such a high standard of inclusiveness for post-modern family formats as in England and Wales. Despite the fact that in the 2018 *Coman* case,[11] the CJEU required EU states to recognise same-sex marriage from other jurisdictions, even where a state does not recognise same-sex marriage domestically, this has been described as only a 'small step' since it does not extend to registered partners. Moreover, while the decision is naturally welcomed, it seems that its effect on LGBTQ+ relationships is not yet fully assessed, so that border crossing for same-sex relationships is not yet uniform by any means. This is a pity, as these diverse continental legal systems within Europe have between them contributed so much towards the development of English law since Lord Denning's memorable comment on how EU influences would be likely to work after our accession to the then European Economic Community,[12] which he saw as 'an incoming tide' . . . which 'flows into the estuaries and up the rivers. It cannot be held back.'[13]

Considering the role of the European Court of Human Rights (the ECtHR) in developing English family Law, and the Convention on Human Rights and Fundamental Freedoms (ECHR) which its decisions enforce, the fact that English Law is now actually ahead in comparison with such continental resources is surprising, since the obvious initial practical watershed was as recent as the case of *Goodwin v UK* (2002).[14] This case only then finally ended years of argument about the extent of the UK's margin of appreciation in relation to our traditional treatment of the right to marry which, despite EU equality and diversity principles, we had obstinately insisted was reserved only to those opposite sex couples whose biological sex had been irrevocably determined at birth by each individual's chromosomes. This was clearly a tight restriction which had (since *Corbett v Corbett*[15]) prolonged prevention of the marriage of many successfully transpeople in their new gender.

Thus *Goodwin* definitively opened the gates to plurality in family relationships in English law, since the Court famously declared that the margin of appreciation held by individual states is *not* available to reduce Convention rights 'so as to impair the very essence of the right,' though also criticising the UK for not progressing further and sooner on this issue and for failing to take action on the Report of the Interdepartmental Working Group on Transsexual people (2000). It is therefore disappointing that nothing has been done to prevent Member States from placing strict requirements on the conditions for recognition of the new gender. The move across Europe towards the self-declaration model has led to many further challenges before the ECtHR on this issue.

It is also disappointing to find that there are still practical family membership problems in cross border movement in Europe, especially since the UK specifically addressed this perceived problem in relation to English Law, following the case of *Wilkinson v Kitzinger (No 2)*[16] in 2006 by passing the Marriage (Same-Sex Couples) Act 2013. However, persistence of such border problems on the continent has not been for want of effort in Europe.

Following this review of historical progress, it will be convenient to consider drivers for social change and to move on to further currently troubling issues such as transpersons and surrogacy.

Fast forward from the *Goodwin* watershed

Surprising as it is that there has not been a successful initiative to develop a common European standard to create an EU-wide definition of, for example, what makes a *de jure* family – as other state level and federal differences have been harmonised in other large territories with a federal jurisdiction. For example, Australia, which has always had a practical approach to social norms and early exhibited a spirit of leadership in developing the mother country's common law to meet contemporary social demands. Indeed, it was the first of the Commonwealth former colonies to recognise the atypical nature of unmarried families in coining the phrase 'de facto' in relation to cohabiting couples, who are also referred to as 'de factos.'[17]

Nevertheless, it took them time to legislate, and same-sex marriage was not legal until December 2017.[18] It seems there was some opposition and mixed feelings about same-sex relationships which temporarily stood in the way, although this was also anticipated in England and Wales (especially in deeply traditional 'chapel' congregations in Wales) in connection with the Marriage (Same-Sex Couples) Act 2013.

Nevertheless, the eventual disappearance of threatened opposition (rife in the media at the time) to the 2013 Act in England and Wales seems to confirm that such initial opposition evaporated, and the same seems eventually to have happened in Australia.

Curiously, there seems to have been little opposition to same-sex marriage in the Republic of Ireland, which is, of course, not part of the UK (and such legislation is progress indeed in this formerly staunchly Catholic jurisdiction, although the result of the referendum of 22 May 2015, following which a date was set for implementation, showed substantial support for the reform).

Law reform of this sort can be slow. This is because such reform does not stop with its initial legislative action, since it is necessary to examine all the possible consequential amendments required, which may include formerly core principles of the law of marriage, which in turn owed their existence to the formerly 'heteronormative underpinnings of marriage.' For example, in England and Wales, consummation had already had to be taken out of the Civil Partnership Act 2004 and the Marriage (Same-Sex Couples) Act 2013, and neither permits 'adultery' to be a basis, respectively, of dissolution or divorce.

The USA has had a similar experience to Australia, where reform was expected to be quick, but it took a blanket Supreme Court ruling that all states must recognise marriages in other states within the union, *and* that all states must issue marriage licenses permitting same-sex marriages, and thus firmly to retreat from the previous position where permitting such marriages could be decided at state level,[19] but which initially some regional judges were not entirely happy with. However, in practice, this would seem to be the way forward internationally, where young families of spouses, partners and children regularly cross borders in pursuit of work or pleasure, and this consideration was certainly a driver in passing the Marriage (Same-Sex Couples) Act 2013 in England and Wales, following the case of *Wilkinson v Kitzinger*[20] which highlighted the contemporary practical problems.[21] The appellants in this case were two women, married in Canada where same-sex marriage was available, but who then happened to come to England and were surprised to find their marriage was only a civil partnership in England and Wales. However, the point appears immediately to have been grasped at government level that that it would be a different case for a young migratory couple with children following employment or recreation. In that context, the problem would naturally be more practically acute, causing extensive practical problems in contemporary bureaucracy, whether in relation to social welfare benefits or practical parenting, including in such everyday contexts as in giving consents for the various minors' activities and medical care that now require formal permission before a child can do anything much but simply go to school.

The impact of social change more generally in family law

There may be parallels between acceptance of same-sex relationships generally and public opinion's change of view on no-fault divorce (with 2019 legislation in process, following the failed *Owens v Owens*[22] divorce). *Owens* regenerated the no-fault divorce debate, a concept virtually unanimously rejected at the last attempt to introduce it in 1996.[23] At the same time the existing facts on which a divorce is currently still granted under the Matrimonial Causes Act 1973 could be repealed, and adultery also removed from the Act, as well as the other contentious fact of behaviour sufficiently unreasonable for the petitioner to continue to be expected to live with the respondent. Adultery is already thought to be inappropriate in an era of equal marriage[24] and it seems that public responses to surveys and opinion polls have suggested that the ordinary person would probably now not mind if England and Wales had a no-fault divorce system as exists in many other jurisdictions.

Certainly, the original practical justification for the concepts of consummation and adultery, currently retained in the 1973 Act, no longer exists except in a tiny minority of cases since the need for them is rare in modern times.[25] It is no longer necessary even for peers to have doubts about their heirs' legitimacy, as there is now reliable DNA testing which is already often used under the Child Support Acts and is also clearly available for determining parentage in other contexts, such as by trustees of settlements who must pay the correct beneficiaries as set out in the trust deed. Succession to a British peerage or title of honour may still not be achieved by an adopted son or daughter,[26] even though the requirement for male primogeniture is no longer essential in the case of peerages which at the time of grant were bestowed already enabled to descend by special remainder through the female line or to another family member such as a brother, perhaps because it was clear there was already no male heir. There were probably reasons not relevant here for no importation of Roman law's sophisticated adoption system into English law until the first Adoption Act 1926 was amended by the Adoption and Children Act 2002 following the Civil Partnership and Marriage (Same-Sex Couples) Acts. Adoption did not at first really fit the traditions of English life, which subsisted up to the sexual revolution of the 1960s, although the Romans had specifically made such adoptions work when their families were otherwise childless.

Transpersons and other contemporary family formats and identities

Thus, while families are creating their own shapes and functions on the ground, there is now emerging some literature on the subject which suggests that some sort of formal frameworks are desirable to reflect the developments of original terms into less revolutionary and more evolutionary concepts which can now be extracted from what has gone before in preceding periods, but which have since apparently settled well into an contemporary mode capable of embracing post-modern social norms.

Scherpe's contribution to this debate, 'Breaking the Existing Paradigm of Parent and Child Relationships,'[27] emphasises that 'We need a Family Law for families' – addressing reform from a radical starting point as we 'cannot amend law based on a 2 parent paradigm, which depends on individual societal and legal contexts.'

Perhaps, however, not entirely starting with a blank sheet of paper, since sharing family law experience, from both other common law and civil law jurisdictions, can be extremely valuable, including taking relevant experience from all disciplines working in family justice. This is especially so as there already exists a number of contemporary initiatives which bring together such wider experience, rather than just lawyers' resources, so as to enable the worldwide family law community to draw on such sources for mutual benefit.

However, whatever the position in Europe and the EU, there is much in English law that already works to support evolving contemporary family formats, but also inevitably some new and unclear areas which require articulating (for example, intersex identity, which can now apparently blur the same-sex and opposite-sex identity of family members, and also multiple parenthood in human-assisted reproduction), neither of which are arguably yet sufficiently thought out so as to be included in stage 1 of any further likely reforms.

Of these, the intersex debate is arguably the most urgent, but also the most complex. This is because, owing to the *Re Elan Cane* decision in the High Court[28], where the court found that this intensely practical issue – which requires everyone, with rare cultural exceptions, to identify on identity documents used around the world with one of the binary identities, i.e. male or female – did not constitute a breach of the claimant's human rights, regardless of her strongly felt emotional reasons for not wishing to have a gendered identity. Such a clear practical impact is obviously one of the most important drivers of social change in recognising the way in which family formats are themselves changing because of the contemporary changes in the identities of family members. Nevertheless, it was also held that *if* the gender entry required *was* a breach of her human rights, the Passport Office's reasons for not being able at the present time to issue a passport without such identification were a proportionate response to the government's need for gendered identity. However, the decision also noted that this should not continue indefinitely, since the Passport Office staff appear to have told the High Court that their processes will not allow a passport to be issued if the 'M' and 'F' sections on the application form are not completed, and that they are not at present in a position to make changes to address this, but that there is an investigation in process which needs to be completed first.

In fact some jurisdictions – e.g. Australia, New Zealand and Malta – have (it seems quite happily) already agreed to use the non-binary category 'X' on their passports, a solution which could be adopted in the UK (although that would not go far enough for Christie Elan Cane), and it seems that Germany has also already decided that the use of the 'X' category is unconstitutional, since the German constitution requires all German citizens to be described in a positive manner, which it seems the anonymous 'X' category is considered in Germany not to do.

In the meantime, it seems that there is a lobby for a more detailed genetic designation of a child's parentage than is afforded by the present processes under the Births and Deaths Registration Act 1953, and the Human Fertilisation and Embryology Act (HFEA) 2008, even though they currently combine, and have since that 2008 Act, to allow for the contemporary inclusion of two same-sex parents and, where in the case of two women being the child's parents, and both with parental responsibility,[29] the omission of any father on the birth record.[30]

This seems curious because 'the father' was formerly a category of parent historically so revered in English law that courts still will not, pursuant to the Children Act 1989 s 13(1), normally countenance the removal of his family name from that of children whom he has fathered, without very sound benefit supporting the change. Nevertheless, this is often convincingly advocated on the part of (usually) the applicant carer mother, who is, however, usually still routinely suspected of wanting to make this change only to airbrush him out of her post-relationship life, which the courts usually resist.

Similarly, in the case of two men having been enabled to have genetic children – though this was not as common or as publicised before Elton John and David Furnish had their sons, Elijah and Zachary, it seems there is the same lobby for a full genetic record,[31] although it may be queried whether this will now assume the same importance owing to the fact that a man with a womb has since actually given birth, not only once but now three times.[32] This was Thomas Beattie, aged 38 at the time of the first birth, an American female-to-male transperson who became pregnant after living as a man with his male partner in the North of

England for five years, whereupon he gave birth first to a girl in 2011, and then the following year to a boy, after taking female hormones to reverse the effects of his female-to-male sex change treatments. It seems he has since had a third child and is correctly referred to as a 'male mother' in accordance with HFEA 2008, s 33, since he is the person who has given birth to the children.

The impact of the Marriage (Same-Sex Couples) Act 2013

However, it seems that the real catalyst for a settled normative impact on same-sex relationships in English law, and their new family format with genetically related children, has been the 2013 Act which has finally enabled same-sex parents to *marry*. There was actually a lobby for this from the 1980s, when Martin Bowley QC pressed for marriage for gays, *and* for gay men to be on the Bench, for which Lord Hailsham, as Lord Chancellor, was however unwilling at that time. Moreover, although Lord Mackay, as Lord Chancellor in 1991, apparently agreed to gay appointments in the higher courts, the current Master of the Rolls, Sir Terence Etherton, is the first openly gay senior appointment.

This sudden progress from civil partnership to marriage may in fact have been a surprise: when research was conducted into whether the LGBT community really wanted to convert its civil partnerships into full marriage, the results indicated mostly contentment with their existing status. They did not want to upgrade to marriage: there thus appeared a real possibility not only of the threatened disturbances promised by those opposing the statute, but also that there would be no demand for the marriages it would permit. However, clearly these results were no more accurate than election day early returns from polling stations, as shown by the civil partnerships and same-sex marriage statistics in the 18 months following the enactment of the Act: far from there being no demand for same-sex marriages, many new same-sex marriages were conducted once this was possible, but as soon as section 9 was brought into force in March 2014 (enabling conversion of existing civil partnerships marriage), 15,000 more same-sex marriages were contracted and their numbers snowballed dramatically, at the same time giving the marriage statistics a lift.[33]

The likely drivers for this marked degree of social change from civil partnership to same-sex marriage

A first prompt might have been the Elton John-David Furnish conversion of their civil partnership to marriage, actioned as soon as it was possible in March 2014 despite the Birmingham poll: they had to convert, if minded to do so, as they were already in a civil partnership, and would have had to dissolve the earlier civil partnership in order to marry in 2013 before section 9 conversion was possible. It should be remembered that while they live in California, this is a British couple and they have a significant UK following. A second was possibly the lack of pre-supposed adverse reaction to the 2013 Act, expected from the combined religious lobby, but not least from the traditional churches who were vehemently against reform, whereas *nothing* of this expected opposition materialised, still less any disruption. It seems that by 2013, the wider public – as well as the adverse pressure groups – were 'over' the shock of the abandonment of the principles of *Hyde v Hyde* (1866),[34] especially as the 2013 Act was presented as an equality statute. None of the predicted violent opposition therefore happened, and, by 2014 and after, same-sex partners were apparently simply settling into marriage and building families to support their new normative status as married couples.

It would therefore seem that English law had in this instance already managed to place the crucial social and legal change in the right order before the Act reached the statute book, thus recognising the optimum point on the ascending curve of 'social change' as well as on the intersecting graph of 'legal change,' as identified by Maine, one of the forefathers of the modern sociology of law and a leading figure of the English and German schools of historical jurisprudence. While Maine had set out this theory of the relationship between law and social change in his classic text, *Ancient Law*[35] in the mid-19th century, this remains an influential work in more than the academic field of law in society, which had long before 2013 identified changes in *status* and *social custom* in early societies as always *preceding* changes in *the law*, and it seems in modern times (when fundamental changes in our social lifestyles have been recently so radical) that we would be well advised to note such anthropological principles which provide powerful support for the legal reforms introduced.

Thus did the LGBT community achieve statistically unremarkable families, and without any revolutionary or disruptive element.

Was there perhaps a third prompt? If so, was this the simple passage of time from the Civil Partnership Act 2004 to the government's decision to legislate in the 2013 Act? This seems to have been solicitor Duncan Ranton's theory when he examined the likely underlying reason for the comparatively sudden upgrade from civil partnership in 2004 to marriage in 2013,[36] questioning the reason for the government's compromise before 'seizing the nettle' in 2012–2013, followed by the LGBT community's enthusiastic adoption of their newly permitted married status. This theory of the right moment for the impact of social change in family law to find its mature moment[37] is not new and is also identified in mainstream historical jurisprudence, to which 19th-century school, developed in Germany, Maine belonged.

There might also have been a further prompt from the growth of surrogacy following the HFEA 2008, in which new detail emerged in relation to the birth of Elton John's second son, who happened to be born in the year of the 2013 Act – this family inevitably thus focussed attention on LGBT interests, prompting the media to reveal that both boys had the same surrogate mother who was also a good friend, remaining in touch with the family. Whether or not this was truly a happy IVF family as presented, the boys and their parentage clearly generated regular LGBT publicity, drip-feeding that the couple had entered into a civil partnership in 2005 as soon as the 2004 Act came into force, adding children as soon as the 2008 Act provided the obvious normative pathway by updating the original HFEA 1990 to take account of developments in same-sex partnerships afforded by the Civil Partnership Act 2004, and finally marrying when that status was also available.

Since surrogacy is clearly essential for male same-sex genetically related families, some escalation of the numbers of partnerships availing themselves of this pathway to the normative family may be expected. Indeed, further reforms may be expected to reflect changes in circumstances if the escalation continues. This is not least, as there is likely to be a shortage of surrogates leading to cross-border surrogacies with all the problems of competing English and overseas provisions in disparate legal systems. Such problems have already been experienced in adoption, which prior to the 1990 HFEA was the only way forward for couples unable to conceive their children naturally.[38]

Male same-sex families and surrogacy

However, while surrogacy is essential for male same sex genetically related families, unfortunately it also still has some perception problems, not least for the male same-sex partners concerned. It was an unfortunate coincidence that the growth of surrogacy around the HFEA 2008 coincided with both the Yew Tree paedophilia and child pornography investigations which were nationwide in the UK, and with muddled recollections of the historical gay parenting residence order cases when older judges thought lesbian partners needed male influence from somewhere for 'balance.'[39]

Since then, surrogacy appears to be on the cusp of a change of identity following some activity in 2018 under the auspices of Sir James Munby, the outgoing president of the Family Court, who took the opportunity of time available after his retirement to attend the Progress Educational Trust's one day conference on 5 December 2018, which discussed the likely changes that may be needed in surrogacy in the next ten years. This raised questions not only about its regulation – currently a significant concern, as its use is inevitably likely to escalate in step with acceptance of same-sex marriage, but also (in view of its strict regulation in the UK) with the likelihood of escalating links with overseas provision, about the threat to its role in the creation of modern families. This is posed by the potential for links with the obvious adverse publicity attracted by commercial exploitation and human trafficking, which (although entirely valid humanitarian issues of great importance) appear to obscure the equally fundamental issues: (i) surrogacy is an innovative channel through which a new family unit may be created, particularly for same-sex spouses desirous of genetically related children; (ii) if there is to be reform of the law to address the concerns mentioned, this should be approached through the holistic field of family formation.

In fact, while more widespread use of surrogacy may seem worryingly *Brave New World* – as in Aldous Huxley's 1930s novel which anticipated developments in reproductive technology, as well as other developments such as sleep-learning and psychological manipulation, none of which has remained entirely fictional.[40] Even adoption was once seen as a debatable solution to childlessness, since that, too, was once a legislative creation outside the 'natural' norm.

Like adoption in its time, surrogacy now needs to be viewed from the point of view of its role in contributing to family normativity. Thus, its role should perhaps be facilitated by only essential regulation, rather than being heavily regulated from the perspective that it is likely to be only another opportunity for exploitation. Practitioners in India highlighted this earl, since their concerns were both for the risk of exploitation of poor Indian women as surrogates and the future welfare of the child who could originally be taken out of India to an unknown destination where perhaps the welfare of children was not paramount; indeed, its welfare possibly not monitored by the social services provided for the purpose in most Western jurisdictions and the child even being abandoned if the commissioning couple split, or tired of their child. In the context of the Indian government not taking legislation forward with much dispatch to address the international dimension in surrogacy, some Indian lawyers then took the lead in such practical terms as could be effected without waiting for such legislation, by achieving immigration controls so that it is no longer possible to engage in a surrogacy project in India on a tourist visa. Thus, the position in India is that neither the surrogacy agreement nor removal of the resulting child can now take place without control of the entry of the commissioning parents or their exit with the child.[41]

In Australia, Felicity Gerry QC[42] and Hon Anthony Graham QC[43] have been engaged in research on one of the main strands of this topic, which is their specialist interest, namely human trafficking[44] against which responsible states are ever vigilant. This is not the only source of concerns about this downside of the international dimension, since apart from India's early identifying potential problems, the international organisations which regularly meet to confer at conferences also followed this up.

The stage, therefore, now appears to have been reached at which the question must be asked: what, precisely, is the place of surrogacy in the context of Family Law? Is it

- only a species of refined human-assisted reproduction (HAR) requiring close regulation in the paramount interest of the welfare of the resulting child? (welfare being a key principle of child law in most advanced jurisdictions), or
- simply another normative channel through which the modern family is now created, a function which must be acknowledged, alongside same-sex marriage, full gender recognition of transpersons and committed cohabitation?

Child protection issues

English law originally approached surrogacy through child protection and the key core principle of English child law, namely the paramount welfare of the child, which had its origins in the Guardianship of Minors Act 1925, s 1, although that original legislative provision took much longer to have real effect in the 1990s development of a separate corpus of Child Law within family law. At that time, HAR was all about creating genetic families for the historic opposite-sex married couples who, if childless, were not content with adoption, which was still seen as second best, since (outside family adoptions) it usually lacked any link to the adopting couple. Since that date, successive governments have spelled out the importance of the family as the 'fundamental building block of society,'[45] and HAR (which has, meanwhile, developed extensively) means that *all* otherwise childless couples who can afford it, whether same-sex or opposite-sex, can now build a family with genetic children. Indeed, the affordability issue appears already to be being addressed, since it seems that many large corporations are offering fertility and gender reassignment benefits, along with standard medical insurance, as part of their employees' remuneration packages.[46]

The historical background of the legal treatment of HAR technologies in England and Wales is not, in fact, extensive or complex, now depending on the HFEA 2008 as amended. Previously, regulation dated only from around thirty years ago following the Warnock Report,[47] which was itself without much warning, generated by advances in medical science which had made possible the first 'test tube' conceptions, inevitably inaugurating an era of increasing complexity in 'in vitro fertilisation' (IVF).

This was immediately followed by the 'Baby Cotton' case[48], presenting the court with the first actual surrogacy for which the judiciary was completely unprepared, as there was no specific legislation, which then soon followed and has since been refined as time and experience permitted. Following the HFEA 2008, the High Court began ratifying international surrogacy cases, in 2010 same-sex and unmarried couples were added to the statutory scheme, and nationality law was amended to allow surrogate children born overseas to become British automatically on the making of the section 54 parental order granted to the commissioning parents.

In 2016, following the case of *Re Z*,[49] it was decided that the Act must be amended to include single parents, so as to be compatible with Article 8 of the Human Rights Act 1998 (HRA 1998) incorporating the ECHR, although it has taken two drafts of the bill to achieve this, and in 2019 the amending statute was still not complete.

However, judging by the Sir James Munby's continuing interest and comments following his retirement in 2018, further updating can be expected to address potential change still yet to be realised. On the occasion of the Personal Support Unit's seminar at the Law Society on 19 October 2018, he took the opportunity to spell this out, remarking 'every concept of what "family" is, every concept of what a parent-child relationship is, is very much back in the melting pot for change.' He included the now obvious fact that the cutoff point for women to conceive naturally no longer applies, since this now occurs in their 40s and 50s, so that 'the judiciary will endorse a parental order for women of that age,' on which he added that 'age should not stand in the way of having a family, and the menopause does not prevent women from having children by IVF or surrogacy.'

He appeared also not to rule out developments which have previously kept commercial surrogacy out of English law, although permitted in other jurisdictions. Commenting positively on American systems, in particularly in California (suggesting that we may in future have both pre- and post-birth orders), he added that 'once we become more familiar with these changes and developments' we become more accepting, suggesting that we should 'give serious consideration to abolishing the restrictions on commercial surrogacy' to include more than 'reasonable expenses' for the surrogate to carry the child (currently interpreted restrictively in English law to mean expenses alone), but a much wider interpretation was adopted in California over forty years ago. Confirming that he would welcome a move away from 'prohibition regulation,' including opening up of family structures to 'introduce into the law of surrogacy a provision enabling the court to dispense with the need for the surrogate's consent if the child's welfare so requires,' thus mirroring an existing provision in adoption law (and ensuring that no child is left stateless as the result of a surrogacy arrangement).[50]

Interestingly, there was also discussion of a proposed new birth certificate, recognising the surrogate-born child as that of the commissioning intended parents, thus moving towards one of the key US principles to which Sir James Munby refers.[51]

Conclusion

It is obvious why Sir James Munby favours modernising amendment to the HAR legislation. There are several legal philosophical aspects of surrogacy and IVF to be considered, alongside the HFEA 2008 section 54 procedural parental order, which is the mechanism for transferring parental responsibility for the child from the surrogate to the commissioning parents, whether an opposite or same-sex couple, whether related to the child or not, and which in turn depends on whether the surrogacy is 'partial'[52] or 'full.'[53]

The 2008 Act generates most confusion about the legal philosophical infrastructure for surrogacy and IVF. The Act approaches not surrogacy in this respect, but meaningful parenting when a woman receives IVF treatment in a licensed clinic and has no partner or husband treated as the father, by sections 35 or 42. Under sections 36 and 43, she may choose any man – or woman – to become a social father (or in the case of a woman, a second parent), provided the 'agreed parenthood conditions' – sections 37 or 44 – are accepted. This process is used by single women or unmarried female partners to set up their own customised family unit, appearing sentimentally to hark back to the 19th-century social parenting which had neither genetic nor legal basis, save that in 2008 Parliament legislated to permit the concept in the 21st century, regardless of whether the woman receiving treatment had any close relationship, let alone biological tie, with the proposed 'social' parent: this was much criticised in the media.[54]

However, compared to this social parenting provision, surrogacy clearly has much stronger potential for creating stable families for child rearing in a nurturing environment: it can uniquely utilise the genetic link particularly prized in a committed same-sex male relationship. However, surrogacy *is* only one of many contemporary ways of building family units, while stable families are a core requirement of society. Surrogacy reform should thus evidence the same equality and family friendly basis as same-sex marriage, which is clearly the latest driver for existing surrogacy escalation, which motivated India in its visa regulation initiative.

Notes

1 Civil Partnerships, Marriages and Deaths etc Registration Act 2019. s 2.
2 Janice Turner, 'Boys, Girls, Both . . . Desiree Akhavan and the Generation That Swings Both Ways' *The Times* (London, 6 October 2018) <www.thetimes.co.uk/article/boys-girls-both-desiree-akhavan-and-the-generation-that-swings-both-ways-jhv2mnmsk> accessed 1 August 2019.
3 Human Fertilisation and Embryology Act 2008 (HFEA 2008) s 54.
4 Inclusive TV 'sitcoms' did their best to help by showing same-sex relationships as a normative family form but only after the 'child boundary' of 9 p.m.
5 *B v B (Minors) (Custody, Care and Control)* (1991) FLR 402, (1991) Fam Law 174; see further ahead.
6 J Winterson, *Oranges Are Not the Only Fruit* (Pandora Press 1985) – her first, semi-autobiographical, novel about a teenage girl rebelling against the then-conventional values, later adapted for TV. Her later novels continue to explore gender polarities and sexual identities. She was herself adopted.
7 Peter Bradshaw, 'The Kids Are All Right – Review' *The Guardian* (London, 28 October 2010) <www.theguardian.com/film/2010/oct/28/the-kids-are-all-right-review> accessed 5 August 2019.
8 Arifa Akba, 'The Kids Are All Right? Not According to the Lesbian Lobby. Hit Film Accused of Trading on 'Myth that All Gay Women Secretly Desire Men' *The Independent* (London, 23 November 2010) <https://www.independent.co.uk/arts-entertainment/films/news/the-kids-are-all-right-not-according-to-the-lesbian-lobby-2141111.html> accessed 21 November 2019.
9 *B v B* (n 14).
10 Reported by visiting English practitioners in the Caribbean islands.
11 *Coman* (n 9).
12 The precursor of the EU at the time the UK joined the then European market.
13 *Bulmer v Bollinger* (1974) 2 All ER 1226, 1231.
14 *Goodwin* (n 1).
15 *Corbett v Corbett* (1970) 2 WLR 1306 (1970) 2 ALL ER 33.
16 *Wilkinson v Kitzinger (No 2)* (2006) EWHC 2022 (Fam), (2007) 1 FLR 295.

17 Such 'de facto' relationships are defined in s 4AA of the Family Law Act 1975, although this was an amendment to the federal statute which had its origins in the New South Wales De Facto Relationships Act 1984.
18 Marriage (Amendment, Definition and Religious Freedoms) Act 2017.
19 *Obergefell v Hodges* 576 US, 135 S Ct 2584 (2015).
20 *Wilkinson v Kitzinger* (n 24).
21 See the judgment of Sir Mark Potter P in this case.
22 *Owens v Owens* (2018) UKSC 41.
23 Family Law Act 1996 Part II, which received the Royal Assent but the operative part of the Act implementing no-fault divorce was never implemented since it was said that the associated research indicated such hostility on the part of the public to divorce on any basis unless there was fault of some sort that that part of the Act was finally repealed by the last Labour government in 2001 (and it had previously been announced that the no-fault provisions would never be implemented in their original form).
24 And was only retained in the 1969 Divorce Reform Act, and the consolidated legislation in 1973, because some members of the public still thought it wrong to commit adultery, despite the Law Commission having recommended at the time that it was usually considered a symptom, rather than a cause, of marriage breakdown.
25 Only in succession to a peerage, which can still not be succeeded to by an adopted or child born outside lawful wedlock and legitimate succession, must be proved to the satisfaction of the College of Arms which governs all aspects of peerages.
26 Adoption Act 1926; Adoption and Children Act 2002.
27 Jens Scherpe, 'Breaking the Existing Paradigm of Parent and Child Relationships' in Gillian Douglas, Mervyn Murch and Victoria Stephens (eds), *Essays in Honour of Nigel Lowe: International Perspectives on Child and Family Law* (Intersentia 2018).
28 *R (Christie Elan Cane) v Secretary of State for the Home Department* (2018) EWHC 1530 (Admin).
29 HFEA 2008, ss 43–44.
30 Ibid., 'no man is to be treated as the father.'
31 See Maev Kennedy and agencies, 'Elton John Marries His Long-Term Partner David Furnish' *The Guardian* (London, 21 December 2014) <www.theguardian.com/music/2014/dec/21/elton-john-marries-david-furnish> accessed 1 July 2019.
32 See Fiona Roberts, 'He's Definitely Got His Figure Back: World's First Pregnant Man Unveils Muscular Physique After Three Babies in Three Years' *Daily Mail* (London, 28 July 2011) <www.dailymail.co.uk/news/article-2019579/Worlds-pregnant-man-Thomas-Beatie-unveils-muscular-body-3-babies.html>
33 There were 275,000 opposite-sex marriages in 2015, a fall of 3%, +118,000 divorces but 15,000 same-sex marriages in 2014–2015. This is a reference to the Office of National Statistics, 'Marriages in England and Wales 2016' <https://www.ons.gov.uk/peoplepopulationandcommunity/birthsdeathsandmarriages/marriagecohabitationandcivilpartnerships/bulletins/marriagesinenglandandwalesprovisional/2016> last checked 21 November 2019.
34 (1866) 1 LR P&D 130, and Lord Penzance's definition of 'one man and one woman.'
35 Maine (n 2).

36 See Duncan Ranton, 'Beyond the Nuclear: Civil Partnership – Marriage Equality's Missing Link' (*Family Law Newswatch*, 28 June 2012) <www.familylaw.co.uk/articles/DuncanRanton28062012-951> accessed 8 August 2019.
37 See Frances Burton, 'Waiting for Rights-Driven Evolution in Law Reform: The Impact of Social Change in Family Law Reform' (2013) 6 *IBA Family Committee Newsletter* 15–19.
38 See Department for Education, 'A Guide to Inter-Country Adoption for UK Residents, 2011' (DoE 2011); Nigel Cantwell, 'Best Interests of the Child in Intercountry Adoption' *Innocenti Insight* (UNICEF Office of Research 2014).
39 *B v B* (n 14).
40 Aldous Huxley, *Brave New World* (Chatto & Windus 1932).
41 Further information on the Indian immigration law concerned can be obtained from Malhotra & Malhotra, Attorneys, Chandigarh, India, Anglo-Indian local members of the International Academy of Family Lawyers (IAFL).
42 Lecturer in Law, Charles Darwin University, Northern Territory, Australia, also a member of the English Bar, 36 Bedford Row, Grays Inn, WC1.
43 Former Australian family judge.
44 See 'Professor Felicity Gerry QC' <www.felicitygerry.com>.
45 See per Lord Mackay of Clashfern, 'Perceptions of the Children Bill and Beyond' (Joseph Jackson Memorial Lecture, 1989), (1989) 139 NLJ 505.
46 For discussion, see article by Pharmasure, '7 Companies that Offer Fertility Benefits' <https://www.pharmasure.co.uk/news/7-companies-that-offer-fertility-benefits/> last checked 21 November 2019.
47 Department of Health, *Report of the Committee of Inquiry into Human Fertilisation and Embryology* (1988 Reprinted edn, Cmnd 9314, 1984).
48 *Re C (A Minor) (Wardship: Surrogacy)* (1965) FLR 846.
49 *Re Z* (Surrogacy Agreements) (Child Arrangement Orders) (2016) EQFC 34.
50 Sir James Munby, 'The Future of the Family Division' (Personal Support Unit Seminar, Law Society Hall, Chancery Lane, 19 October 2018).
51 Munby (n 58). In addition to facilitating responsible commercial surrogacy, it seems the California experience has inspired English law interest in an enabling rather than prohibiting approach to regulation, and to formally including the commissioning parents on the child's birth certificate, which would radically change our concept of the surrogate's right to be recorded as the mother through having given birth.
52 If the surrogate used her own egg with sperm from one or both of the commissioning male same-sex partners.
53 Sometimes called 'host' surrogacy which involves implantation of an embryo, to which either, both or neither of the commissioning parents has contributed.
54 Sarah-Kate Templeton, 'Who's the IVF Daddy? – Anyone You Care to Name?' *Sunday Times* (London, 1 March 2009) <www.thetimes.co.uk/article/whos-the-ivf-daddy-anyone-you-care-to-name-7rrpm78d3rd>

References

Primary sources

Adoption Act 1926.
Adoption and Children Act 2002.

B v B (Minors) (Custody, Care and Control) (1991) FLR 402 (1991) Fam Law 174.
Births and Deaths Registration Act 1953
Bulmer v Bollinger (1974) 2 All ER 1226.
C (A Minor) (Wardship: Surrogacy), Re (1965) FLR 846.
Civil Partnership Act 2004.
Civil Partnerships, Marriages and Deaths etc Registration Act 2019.
Coman and Others v Inspectoratul General pentru Imigrări (C-673/16) ECLI:EU:C:2018:385.
Corbett v Corbett (1970) 2 WLR 1306, (1970) 2 ALL ER 33.
Family Law Act 1975 (Australia).
Family Law Act 1996.
Gender Recognition Act 2004.
Goodwin v UK App No. 28759/95 (ECtHR, 11 July 2002).
Human Assisted Reproduction Act 2008.
Human Fertilisation and Embryology Act 2008.
Hyde v Hyde (1866) 1 LR P&D 130.
Marriage (Amendment, Definition and Religious Freedoms) Act 2017.
Marriage (Same-Sex Couples) Act 2013.
Obergefell v Hodges 576 US, 135 S Ct 2584 (2015).
Owens v Owens (2018) UKSC 41.
R (Christie Elan Cane) v Secretary of State for the Home Department (2018) EWHC 1530 (Admin).
Wilkinson v Kitzinger (No 2) (2006) EWHC 2022 (Fam), (2007) 1 FLR 295.
Z (Surrogacy Agreements) (Child Arrangement Orders), Re (2016) EQFC 34.

Secondary sources

Akba, A ' The Kids Are All Right? Not According to the Lesbian Lobby. Hit Film Accused of Trading on 'Myth that All Gay Women Secretly Desire Men' *The Independent* (London, 23 November 2010) < https://www.independent.co.uk/arts-entertainment/films/news/the-kids-are-all-right-not-according-to-the-lesbian-lobby-2141111.html> accessed 21 November 2019.

Bradshaw P, 'The Kids Are All Right – Review' *The Guardian* (London, 28 October 2010) <www.theguardian.com/film/2010/oct/28/the-kids-are-all-right-review> accessed 5 August 2019.

Brown A, *What Is the Family of Law? The Influence of the Nuclear Family* (Hart Publishing 2019).

Burton F, 'Waiting for Rights-Driven Evolution in Law Reform: The Impact of Social Change in Family Law Reform' (2013) 6 *IBA Family Committee Newsletter* 15–19.

Cantwell N, *Best Interests of the Child in Intercountry Adoption* (Innocenti Insight, UNICEF Office of Research 2014).

Department for Education, 'A Guide to Inter-Country Adoption for UK Residents, 2011' (DoE 2011).

Department of Health, *Report of the Committee of Inquiry into Human Fertilisation and Embryology* (1988 Reprinted edn, Cmnd 9314, 1984).

Huxley A, *Brave New World* (Chatto & Windus 1932).

Kennedy M and agencies, 'Elton John Marries His Long-Term Partner David Furnish' *The Guardian* (London, 21 December 2014) <www.theguardian.com/music/2014/dec/21/elton-john-marries-david-furnish> accessed 1 July 2019.

Mackay of Clashfern Lord, 'Perceptions of the Children Bill and Beyond' (Joseph Jackson Memorial Lecture, 1989), (1989) 139 NLJ 505.

Maine F, *Ancient Law* (first published 1961, Murray 1906).

Munby J, 'The Future of the Family Division' (Personal Support Unit Seminar, Law Society Hall, Chancery Lane, 19 October 2018).

Office of National Statistics, 'Marriages in England and Wales 2016' < https://www.ons.gov.uk/peoplepopulationandcommunity/birthsdeathsandmarriages/marriagecohabitationandcivilpartnerships/bulletins/marriagesinenglandandwalesprovisional/2016> last checked 21 November 2019.

Pharmasure, '7 Companies that Offer Fertility Benefits' < https://www.pharmasure.co.uk/news/7-companies-that-offer-fertility-benefits/> last checked 21 November 2019.

'Professor Felicity Gerry QC' <www.felicitygerry.com>.

Ranton D, 'Beyond the Nuclear: Civil Partnership – Marriage Equality's Missing Link' (*Family Law Newswatch*, 28 June 2012) <www.familylaw.co.uk/articles/DuncanRanton28062012-951> accessed 8 August 2019.

Roberts F, 'He's Definitely Got His Figure Back: World's First Pregnant Man Unveils Muscular Physique After Three Babies in Three Years' *Daily Mail* (London, 28 July 2011) <www.dailymail.co.uk/news/article-2019579/Worlds-pregnant-man-Thomas-Beatie-unveils-muscular-body-3-babies.html> accessed 1 July 2019.

Scherpe J, 'Breaking the Existing Paradigm of Parent and Child Relationships' in Douglas G, Murch M and Stephens V (eds), *Essays in Honour of Nigel Lowe: International Perspectives on Child and Family Law* (Intersentia 2018).

Templeton S, 'Who's the IVF Daddy? Anyone You Care to Name?' *Sunday Times* (London, 1 March 2009) <www.thetimes.co.uk/article/whos-the-ivf-daddy-anyone-you-care-to-name-7rrpm78d3rd>.

Turner J, 'Boys, Girls, Both . . . Desiree Akhavan and the Generation That Swings Both Ways' *The Times* (London, 6 October 2018) <www.thetimes.co.uk/article/boys-girls-both-desiree-akhavan-and-the-generation-that-swings-both-ways-jhv2mnmsk> accessed 1 August 2019.

Winterson J, *Oranges Are Not the Only Fruit* (Pandora Press 1985).

Part 4

The importance of civil partnership in an era of same-sex marriage

Chapter 10

Relationships with status

Civil partnership in an era of same-sex marriage

Andy Hayward

Introduction

Marriage has long been considered the cornerstone of the law relating to adult interpersonal relationships and a status central to our understanding of what constitutes a family.[1] Such a position in society means that, when asked to define marriage, individuals can readily, albeit perhaps imprecisely, call upon some of its key features such as its historical role, its ceremonial rites and its symbolism. Owing to the glamorisation of marriage in literature and art, often reinforced through its religious origins, a social narrative has developed that for many couples connects marriage with romanticism, almost mysticism.[2] Whilst the popularity of marriage has decreased,[3] and its centrality in our modern definition of family has been questioned,[4] it is patently clear, as Martha Fineman tells us, that society has made marriage much more than just a piece of paper.[5]

But if we accept that marriage is more than just a marriage certificate, can the same be said about civil partnerships? Despite the fact that civil partnerships have been in existence in the United Kingdom (UK) for just over a decade following their introduction in 2005 and therefore are a relative newcomer to the structure of formalised interpersonal relationships, is there a comparable social narrative or emerging ideology for such a relationship status? It is true that the text of the Civil Partnership Act 2004 will reveal its formalities and legal consequences, but if, as with marriage, legal structures form only one part of the societal perception of a relationship form, can it be said that civil partnerships are developing a distinct role, independent of marriage? This questioning of the value of civil partnership forms the central focus of this chapter and is of timely significance in light of the recognition by the European Court of Human Rights that such a status possesses an 'intrinsic value' for couples.[6] Furthermore, the Civil Partnerships, Marriages and Deaths (Registration etc) Act 2019, which now imposes an obligation on the Secretary of State to introduce regulations enabling the registration of different-sex civil partnerships, will undoubtedly generate further debate as to the relationship between civil partnership and marriage.[7]

This chapter critically analyses the relationship between formal statuses alongside the relationships that individuals enjoy with a particular status. The following section sketches the ideology of marriage and reveals that, despite sustained critique of the institution, a marriage-centric approach still dominates modern English family law. More importantly, this trend of eulogising marriage has recently been invigorated by the opening up of marriage to same-sex couples in March 2014. This move, it will be argued, may represent to some a modern redefining of marriage, but ultimately precipitates a retrospective undermining of registration regimes that came before such as civil partnerships or civil unions.[8] After isolating traditionally advanced arguments as to the now superfluous role of civil partnerships, the subsequent section argues that, like marriage, the institution of civil partnership has evolved and that the interaction of civil partners with their status, and the value many ascribe to such relationship form, has had the effect of developing a nascent ideology of civil partnership. Such narrative, shifting same-sex civil partnerships from a mere act of relationship registration to instead a 'status' or an 'institution,' requires much greater acknowledgement when debating their future in England and Wales for both same-sex and different-sex couples.

An ideology of marriage

Marriage has long played a pivotal role in society's understanding of what constitutes a family. The inter-changeability of the terms 'marriage' and 'family' meant that marriage, as an institution, became synonymous with stability, commitment and propriety.[9] Its long period of development and celebration also prompted a societal consciousness or ideology of marriage. As Barker notes, an ideology of marriage is something different from what she terms its 'structures' and 'consequences.'[10] Whereas the latter concepts regulating the entry and exit requirements for marriage and its legal consequences are often easy to discern through consulting the legislation itself or its interpretation in the courts, ideology is open-textured, malleable and much more difficult to define. Despite these challenges, ideology remains highly influential and, as such, its pervasive nature means that individuals can readily call upon 'obvious, even universal (social) understandings of marriage.'[11] These imprecise understandings evolve over time, are refined in response to changing societal attitudes and imbue the status of marriage with qualities, some of which are far removed from what marriage is in a legal sense.

When attempting to trace the source of these ideologies, it is clear that they were undoubtedly fuelled by Lord Penzance's 'definition' of marriage stated in *Hyde v Hyde and Woodmansee* that it was 'the voluntary union for life of one man and one woman to the exclusion of all others.'[12] This starting point, somewhat over-used in academic commentary,[13] proffered a conception of marriage with elements that continue to be emphasised today: indeed, Lord Penzance's definition is regularly cited in marriage ceremonies, showing a connection between social and legal perceptions of this relationship form. Much more recent case law references *Hyde*[14] and the dicta of Lord Nicholls in *Bellinger v Bellinger* echoes the case in his discussion of the meaning of marriage:

> Marriage is an institution, or relationship, deeply embedded in the religious and social culture of this country. It is deeply embedded as a relationship between two persons of the opposite sex.[15]

In addition, it is arguable that an ideology of marriage also develops through discussion of the functions performed, or qualities exhibited, in marriage, and their roles in understanding what constitutes a family. Despite family being a concept that eludes definition, courts have nevertheless deployed techniques, such as the 'reasonable person' definition or functionality analysis, to conceptualise its meaning and articulate its key features. Crucially for this chapter, the methodology deployed by courts and policy-makers in the past, and even today, invariably leads back to marriage. For example, it is likely that under the 'reasonable person' approach, such individual will use the established relationship form of marriage as a reference point when assessing whether a particular unit should be regarded as a family.[16] Similarly, analysis of the functions of a particular unit has often seen family status awarded to groupings that emulate those routinely exhibited within a marriage.[17] Whereas the formal definition of family would readily recognise parties in a civil partnership as capable of constituting a family, marriage has also long been associated as the primary determinant of a family under this particular approach. The aforementioned underlines the overt and implicit influence marriage exerts on the construction of relationship statuses and what it means to be a family. It should, however, be noted that the impact on society of judicial utterances as to the meaning of marriage may be limited. Far more persuasive when delineating the ideologies of marriage has been the participation in marriage of individuals and its support from politicians when promoting policies aimed at supporting the family.[18]

It is argued that at a political level marriage still remains an attractive tool for societal goals and social engineering. In 1998, the Green Paper *Supporting Families* stated that '[m]arriage is the surest foundation for raising children and remains the choice of the majority of people in Britain.'[19] Whilst the strength of that view may have diminished, it is apparent that marriage is viewed by many as capable of fostering stability and commitment between the parties and their children. Underlying this sentiment is the view that marriage creates its own 'social security' system and as such helps the state minimise and avoid the consequential financial liabilities following relationship breakdown. Research by van Acker suggests that, even taking into account negative critiques of marriage, the 'government perceives that marriage lies at the heart of stable families and communities.'[20] However, introducing policies aimed at promoting marriage and strengthening its role in society, is inherently difficult when government aspiration is confronted by the social reality of modern family forms and living patterns. As such, promoting, or even preaching, the virtues of marriage through what she terms the 'conception of the desirable' is a risky strategy that can both strengthen the political base whilst simultaneously alienating voters who view marriage as a private institution.[21] Drawing upon pro-marriage policies such as the marriage tax allowance, couple relationship education and same-sex marriage, van Acker reveals that recent governments have indeed promoted marriage as an ideal but may ultimately fail in their long-term ambition of strengthening marriage as an institution.[22]

Whilst the success of these policies may be limited, it is argued that the prioritisation of marriage has nevertheless continued to the present day. Moreover, as the following section will demonstrate, a key element in the transmission of the message that marriage is the ideal has been the introduction of same-sex marriage. It is the effect of opening up marriage to same-sex couples, and its relationship with civil partnership, to which this chapter now turns.

Eulogising marriage

The introduction of same-sex marriage following the Marriage (Same-Sex Couples) Act 2013 was for many a source of celebration and a significant moment in the historical development of family law.[23] Lauded by politicians and a move unsurprisingly praised by LGBTQ+ organisations, the opening up of marriage to same-sex couples had several consequences.

First, after years of being treated (at best) as strangers in the eyes of the law, same-sex couples were allowed access to what is perceived by many as the premier status for the expression and legal recognition of a relationship. As Barker notes, same-sex marriage is widely viewed as the 'final stop for "full equality" for lesbian and gay men.'[24] Indeed, looking at patterns overseas, access to marriage is often regarded as to ultimate prize that follows on from the earlier stages in a process of acceptance of same-sex relationships such as the decriminalisation of sexual activity, creation of civil law protections and the introduction of domestic partnerships.[25] Whilst it still remains questionable how 'equal' marriage currently is, in light of current prohibitions applicable to the Church of England and Church in Wales when officiating ceremonies, it is indisputable that from a formalisation perspective, access to marriage went some way in expressing state validation of same-sex relationships. Its introduction not only symbolised society's tolerance, but also had an important signalling function by creating kinship links and integrating couples within the wider community. The focus on these particular values in the parliamentary debates in England and Wales was not that dissimilar to the emphasis placed on citizenship and dignity of the individual that was used to challenge same-sex marriage bans in other jurisdictions such as South Africa[26] and the United States of America.[27]

Second, and more important for discerning whether an ideology of civil partnership now exists, the introduction of same-sex marriage evidenced, and was indeed motivated by, functionality analysis of the dynamics of same-sex couples. These sentiments were already present in the earlier law, most notably in the

House of Lords decision in *Ghaidan Godin v Mendoza*, but were equally present when the Marriage (Same-Sex Couples) Bill was going through Parliament.[28] Maria Miller MP remarked that marriage 'is something that should be embraced by more couples' and that the 'depth of feeling, love and commitment between same-sex couples is no different from that depth between opposite-sex couples.'[29] Here, the indicia of what exemplifies a relationship was being transferred onto same-sex couples in the same breath as encouraging couples to embrace marriage. Thus, it was not purely a formalistic equality-based argument that justified extension of marriage to same-sex couples, but one that explored the inherent dynamics or functions of a relationship.[30] Like the description of marriage proffered in *Hyde*, there appeared to be a transferral of the values associated with traditional marriage to same-sex couples wishing to solemnise their relationships.

Third, perhaps the most significant trend, both at a domestic level and in other countries that have recently introduced same-sex marriage, was the eulogising of marriage as the gold standard.[31] Marriage, of course, is an institution of continuity and change, with an individual's perspective invariably placed somewhere on a spectrum between these two points. But for some, same-sex marriage was a game-changing moment as it triggered a revitalisation of a dwindling institution by enabling it to become more egalitarian, modern and inclusive. The fact that marriage had changed over time evidenced both its positive protean nature and a welcome elasticity with its elements subject to re-evaluation and reformulation. Thus, the inclusion of same-sex couples was viewed by some as an opportunity for a beneficial reappraisal of the role of marriage in society. The dicta of Justice Roberts in *Obergefell v Hodges* neatly encapsulated this sentiment in a passage of the judgement now frequently used in same-sex marriage ceremonies:

> No union is more profound than marriage, for it embodies the highest ideals of love, fidelity, devotion, sacrifice, and family. In forming a marital union, two people become something greater than once they were. As some of the petitioners in these cases demonstrate, marriage embodies a love that may endure even past death. . . . Their hope is not to be condemned to live in loneliness, excluded from one of civilization's oldest institutions. They ask for equal dignity in the eyes of the law. The Constitution grants them that right.[32]

As will be further analysed ahead, not only do expressions such as this marginalise the value of civil partnerships and de facto unions, they also help to entrench a monolithic understanding of marriage premised on the listed attributes, some of which same-sex couples may not wish to emulate themselves. These particular concerns have already been explored from feminist and queer perspectives, with scholars often adopting a somewhat ambivalent approach to the campaign towards, and ultimate introduction of, same-sex marriage.[33] Kitzinger and Wilkinson, for example, recognise the progress that same-sex marriage offers as part of an equality project that integrates same-sex couples into established relationship forms. Indeed, such change offered the ability for marriage to eschew its obsession with procreation and heterosexual mores.[34] Conversely, others are far more critical, believing that the differences of same-sex couples are marginalised in this process and as Norrie noted, '[e]quality is granted, but only on heterosexual terms.'[35] Assimilation and emulation represent the key concerns that overlook different visions of interpersonal relationships that are not premised on conjugality, monogamy or even the two-person dyad. Regardless of these positions, it is clear that marriage between different-sex couples has been subject to much more rigorous criticism than same-sex marriage, owing to its long history and the negative effects of coverture especially for women.[36] Of course, same-sex marriage is a much more modern phenomenon and impacts upon a smaller minority of individuals, but the dominance of the equality rationale had the effect of creating a societal fixation on marriage, with advocates and activists viewing it as a prize previously withheld from same-sex couples.

Downgrading civil partnerships

It has been established that even today, and despite negative critiques, marriage remains a highly popular status for both different-sex and same-sex couples. However, more pertinent for this chapter in relation to civil partnerships is the presence of three trends in the academic scholarship and public discourse that, it will be argued, prioritise marriage as the idealised status, which in turn, generates questions as to the value of maintaining civil partnership regimes.

The progression argument

Under this argument, marriage is viewed as the ultimate destination for all couples. Whilst different-sex couples have long had access to all forms of marriage, access to marriage has been a key battle ground for LGBTQ+ activism. The process of reform has been a gradual one, aligning closely with the levels of public acceptance of same-sex relationships at the time in question and exhibiting in the legislative journey political concessions and compromise. Comparative family law analysis clearly evidences this with registered partnership regimes, comparable in legal protection terms to marriage, often initially omitting overly contentious provisions such as same-sex adoption – only for them then to be included within the scheme some years later.[37] Even jurisdictions such as Belgium and France, where the registered partnership regime grants fewer rights than those conferred on married couples, have undergone a gradual process of closer alignment with marriage in terms of the rights accrued.[38] Noting this movement, Kees Waaldijk evidences the influence of the marital model through classifying these types of regimes as marriage, 'quasi marriage' and 'semi-marriage.'[39]

Thus, regardless of the route taken, the opening up of marriage to same-sex couples appears to be the end point. Views to this effect can also be discerned at a domestic level as acknowledged by Baroness Hale in *M v Secretary of State for Work and Pensions*, noting 'the UK following the lead of Council of Europe states.'[40] Evidencing this trend of progression towards marriage, Baroness Hale, writing extra-judicially, stated that eventually:

> The final steps are taken by family law, extending laws applicable to unmarried heterosexual couples to homosexual couples, recognising the parental relationship between homosexual parents and their own, their partners' and even other people's children, providing for registered civil partnerships, and finally providing for civil marriage.[41]

After just under a decade of civil partnership registrations, the parliamentary debates for the Marriage (Same-Sex Couples) Bill reveal that previous developments regarding the legal recognition of same-sex couples helped pave the way but further progress was needed. Indeed, in the debates for the Marriage (Same-Sex Couples) Bill, Yvette Cooper called same-sex marriage 'the next step for equality,' and several Members of Parliament expressed the view that England and Wales should go one step further.[42]

More important for this chapter is the impact that this progression narrative has on existing civil/registered partnership regimes. Drawing upon trends in other countries that introduced same-sex–only registered partnerships, the progression argument would militate towards England and Wales phasing out the regime of civil partnerships following the introduction of same-sex marriage. This so-called Nordic Model is premised on the idea that the availability of marriage for all couples renders pre-existing regimes redundant.[43] Reform in the Nordic countries was not merely motivated by equality arguments, but also premised on a need to avoid the segregation and practical limitations of operating one status for same-sex couples and another identical status for different-sex couples. This belief was canvassed in *Steinfeld and Keidan v Secretary of State for Education*, where Briggs LJ noted that for some civil partnerships had 'an essentially transitional purpose, designed to alleviate the disadvantages which then affected same-sex couples, but do not now.'[44] As the extent of legal protections under the Civil Partnership Act 2004 reflects those of the now repealed Nordic regimes, at face value, England and Wales fall within this model, and a case for abolition can – and has – been made. Ultimately, the progression argument conceptualises civil partnerships as part of a journey, sometimes meandering, towards marriage equality.

However, it is argued that a closer examination of the progression argument reveals that the phasing out of civil partnerships following marriage equality is no longer the predictable outcome, or indeed one that is, in fact, desired by many couples. Developments across Western Europe indicate that the simple alternatives of abolition or retention are no longer the only options for reform and new patterns can be discerned following the introduction of same-sex marriage.[45] Several jurisdictions in Europe have approached civil partnership reform creatively. Austria, for example, introduced marriage equality on 1 January 2019 and simultaneously opened up to different-sex couples their originally same-sex—only civil partnership regime first introduced in 2010.[46] Another example indicating the continued desire for civil partnerships alongside the availability of same-sex marriage is the approach taken to this issue on the Isle of Man.[47] Same-sex civil partnerships were introduced through the Civil Partnerships Act 2011 and during the passage of a bill introducing same-sex marriage, a clause extending the coverage of civil partnerships was discussed in the House of Keys (Lower House of Tynwald, the Parliament of the Isle of Man) in March 2016. The motivation of the clause was, according to Leonard Singer, a Member of the House of Keys, to 'make things equal' and to remove inequalities faced by different-sex couples.[48] The Marriage and Civil Partnerships (Amendment) Act 2016 passed with a significant majority, resulting in the Isle of Man now permitting both marriage and civil partnership for all couples.

More recently, support for the continued relevance of civil partnerships in an era of same-sex marriage can be found in England and Wales. In *R (on the application of Steinfeld and Keidan) v Secretary of State for International Development*, the Supreme Court determined that the ban on different-sex civil partnerships constituted a breach of Articles 8 (right to respect for private and family life) and 14 (prohibition on discrimination) of the European Convention on Human Rights. As a result of that ruling and developments in Parliament, former Prime Minister Theresa May pledged to extend the Civil Partnership Act 2004 to different-sex couples, as opposed to phasing out the regime which would have been a move consistent with the progression narrative.[49] This development has also been supported by LGBTQ+ groups such as Stonewall and the Peter Tatchell Foundation that both believed that the prospect of abolishing same-sex civil partnerships would have been met with considerable resistance.[50] Indeed, activist Peter Tatchell noted it would 'provoke an almighty backlash' and 'do catastrophic damage to relations between the Conservative party and LGBT people.'[51] Moreover, the fact that same-sex couples are continuing to enter civil partnerships despite an availability of marriage and not converting their status to marriage, discussed further ahead, indicates the need for a modern reappraisal of formalised relationship statuses.

Whilst it is clear that the drive towards marriage equality has been a major impetus for reform across Europe, it is argued that the phasing out of civil partnerships as the *inevitable* outcome has been undermined by examples of countries valuing civil partnerships in an era of same-sex marriage. When combined with the drive in some jurisdictions to offer an alternative to marriage for all couples, it is apparent that a trend recognising the intrinsic value of civil partnerships can be identified.

The status argument

Another related argument diminishing the validity of civil partnerships focusses on the societal perception of such a relationship, and like the progression argument, shows hierarchies at play. As noted previously, marriage possesses a lengthy, venerated history and has been, over the centuries, supported both politically and through state incentives.[52] Overlaid on top is a social narrative created through people's engagement with the institution and its depiction in art and literature. As such, marriage influences society's perspective of other non-marital statuses such as civil partnerships. Such relationships, the earliest regimes created in the late 1980s, cannot tap into such a legacy and, as noted by Davies LJ in *R v Bala and Others*, civil partnerships were simply a 'construct of statute.'[53] It is true that for some jurisdictions, this aspect was the precise point behind their inception, as they were originally conceived to offer a more administrative, secular alternative to marriage and often bestowed upon the parties fewer rights than those available through marriage. However, in relation to registered partnership regimes exclusively available to same-sex couples, many regimes have been viewed by some academics as second-rate concessions: a 'painful compromise between genuine equality and no rights at all,'[54] or as 'marriage-lite: same great taste, half the respect of regular marriage.'[55]

The status criticism affects not just the outward expression of a relationship, but also relates to its internal dynamics. Although the extent of legal rights and protections stemming from marriage is frequently misunderstood by society, the relationship is often conceptualised as a sexual union and underpinned by duties of fidelity and mutual support.[56] In contrast, the Civil Partnership Act 2004 is silent on the inherent nature of the relationship and, unlike marriage, the sexual dimension finds no legal expression owing to the inability to dissolve a partnership on the basis of adultery or obtain a decree of nullity relating to non-consummation. Moreover, civil partnerships are concluded through the act of registration and thus possess, for some, a more clinical, administrative dimension.[57] This was clearly encapsulated by Maria Miller MP in the Second Reading of the Marriage (Same-Sex Couples) Bill when she noted that 'a legal partnership is not perceived in the same way and does not have the same promises of responsibility and commitment as marriage.'[58]

Despite these criticisms and just like the progression argument articulated in the previous sub-section, it is arguable that even in an era of same-sex marriage, the value of civil partnership as a status is, in fact, now being recognised. One source of evidence is the changing interpretation of civil partnerships by the courts revealing a shift in attitudes, similar to how Lord Penzance's definition of marriage in *Hyde* has been reimagined, albeit over a much shorter time period. To provide examples, prior to the commencement of the Civil Partnership Act 2004, the judiciary generally acknowledged the change that the forthcoming Act would introduce, without necessarily engaging with the significance for the couples concerned. Referring to the bill before Parliament at the time, Lord Millet in *Ghaidan v Godin-Mendoza* called civil partnership a 'new legal relationship' premised on the parties 'registering themselves.'[59] After the Act came into force, judicial discussion of the regime continued to largely focus on this somewhat administrative registration aspect and that the scheme was very much aligned to marriage in terms of legal consequences. In particular, it was apparent, and not entirely unsurprising, that judges were in a process of acquainting themselves with the scheme. Indeed, as noted by Hedley J, in a case concerning an application for parental responsibility by a father that had assisted a lesbian couple to have a child: 'the speed with which the law responds to social change is not uniform . . . it cannot be assumed, therefore, that the majority of the population necessarily supports the provisions of the Civil Partnerships Act.'[60] This comment was motivated by concerns that the law was advancing at a pace quicker than the pace of change of the views of society, and is echoed in the observation by Black J, as she then was, that language at that time had 'not yet evolved to accommodate them.'[61]

The first wide-ranging discussion of the Act was in *M v SSWP*, the hearing of which began on the date the Act came entered force.[62] Here, there is useful judicial insight into the motivations behind its introduction which offer much greater detail as to the judicial perception of the scheme at that time. Whilst also focussing on the technical implementation of the Act, Baroness Hale reflected on how the Act was passed to give 'equal dignity'[63] to individuals and to change the traditional position of the law that treated same-sex couples as two separate individuals.[64] Importantly, for the development of perceptions relating to civil partnerships, there was a noticeable shift away from focussing on registration to instead discussion of civil partnership as 'a formal status with virtually identical legal consequences to those of marriage.'[65] Indeed, later in *Bull v Hall*, a civil partnership was viewed by Lady Hale as:

> more than a contract. Like marriage, it is a status, in which some of the terms are prescribed by law, and which has consequences for people other than the couple themselves and for the state.[66]

However, caution should be exercised, as the context of the dispute undoubtedly affected the judicial perception of civil partnerships. This is apparent in the earlier case of *Wilkinson v Kitzinger* where Sir Mark Potter P had to determine whether an overseas same-sex marriage could be treated in this jurisdiction as a marriage as opposed to a civil partnership.[67] Through rejecting the couple's application for recognition of their overseas marriage, Potter P, perhaps unsurprisingly, defended the civil partnership regime, calling it an 'institution' that was in no way inferior to marriage or reflected the view that 'same-sex commitment' was any lesser than that exhibited within an different-sex marriage.[68] In particular, he remarked that it was unclear whether the rejection of the civil partnership regime by the petitioners as second class were feelings 'shared by a substantial number of same-sex couples content with the status of same-sex partnership.'[69] Other cases involved a confrontation between marriage and civil partnership where courts were forced to compare entitlements under the regime. What is noticeable in these cases is an emphasis on the fact that the regimes were equivalent, albeit possessing different labels.[70]

More recently, the *Steinfeld* litigation has seen the courts grapple with the value of civil partnership in an era of same-sex marriage. Justifying their decision to seek a civil partnership, the litigants emphasise the more egalitarian, secular and neutral nature of civil partnerships in comparison with what they view as the patriarchal, heteronormative and values-laden concept of marriage.[71] What these observations and their treatment in the numerous government consultations and reports on the future of civil partnerships reveal is that courts and policy-makers are now at a later stage of the process seeking to discern the inherent nature of civil partnerships. This scheme has now been established for over thirteen years, and drawing upon Barker's previously discussed typology, it is apparent that we are now beginning to unpack an ideology of civil partnership, which is an exercise distinct from the earlier evaluation of its structure and legal consequences.[72]

The stasis argument

One final argument used to evidence the superfluous nature of civil partnerships following the introduction of same-sex marriage relates to uptake now that same-sex couples have a choice between two formalised statuses. In many jurisdictions, this issue does not arise, as the introduction of same-sex marriage often simultaneously involves the phasing out of civil partnerships. However, in England and Wales, since the introduction of same-sex marriage in March 2014, there has been a notable decrease in civil partnership registrations, revealing that when faced with a choice, there may exist a preference among couples for marriage. In 2013, there were 5,646 civil partnership registrations, but after the introduction of same-sex marriage, this number decreased to only 1,683.[73] Furthermore, whereas December 2013 saw only 314 civil partnership registrations, one year later, only 58 were formed, constituting a drop of 82 per cent.[74] Similarly, the number of civil partnerships dissolutions has continued to rise since they first became available in 2007. In 2016, there were 1,313 civil partnership dissolutions granted in England and Wales, compared with 1,211 in 2015, representing an increase of 8.4 per cent. Higher numbers of dissolutions have occurred between female couples, despite the fact that historically, more men enter civil partnerships than women.[75] For those critical as to the future of civil partnerships, this data is used to demonstrate that they have become a 'legacy relationship' applicable to a dwindling number of couples.[76] Furthermore, the fact that many registered partnership schemes are very similar in structure to civil marriage means that, once the latter is available, transferring to the latter relationship form presents few difficulties. Thus, whilst it is undoubtable that civil partnerships played an important role in changing societal attitudes, these arguments paint civil partnerships merely as an important milestone on a journey to the greater prize of same-sex marriage. After all, as Scherpe notes, where a partnership scheme is more or less the identical copy of marriage, once the original is made available, it could be argued that there is 'no need to keep the copy.'[77]

It is clear that the appeal of a scheme would naturally feed into its longevity. However, like the progression and status arguments, this argument equally requires careful consideration. It cannot be disputed that same-sex marriage has had a marked impact upon civil partnership registrations in England and Wales, but it should be acknowledged that 2016 saw the first annual increase in registrations; in that year, 890 civil partnerships were formed in England and Wales, which represents an increase of 3.4 per cent compared with 2015.[78] There was a further two per cent increase in civil partnership registrations the following year.[79] Similarly, the initial uptake of same-sex marriage was not as pronounced as that when civil partnerships were first introduced. Thus, in contrast to the relatively large number of civil partnership registrations entered into during the first three days in which registrations could take place in December 2005 (1,227), only 93 same-sex marriages took place during the equivalent period of time. Whilst these statistics are likely to be attributable to a clear demand among couples in 2005 to obtain some form of legal recognition not being replicated in 2014, it does tentatively suggest a more critical engagment with same-sex marriage by couples within the unique context created in England and Wales.

More revealing when rejecting the status arguments are the conversion statistics. Conversion from civil partnership to marriage, but not vice versa, is permitted by section 9 of the Marriage (Same-Sex Couples) Act 2013 and has the effect of back-dating the marriage to the point in which the parties first entered the original civil partnerhsip. At present only 1 in 8 civil partnerships have been converted to marriages.[80] Tim Loughton MP, who has campaigned for the introduction of different-sex civil partnerships, developed this point noting that 'more than 80% of same-sex couples who have committed to a civil partnership do not think that they need to or want to convert that into a marriage.'[81] The reasons why people are not converting are multi-faceted. Without detailed empirical data on this trend, it could be attributable to lack of awareness on the part of couples as to the need to convert or financial reasons with couples waiting so that their marriage can be celebrated. In addition, particularly owing to the high proportion of couples not wishing to convert, it could be attributable to symbolic rather than legal reasons and a desire to retain a particular relationship status. Importantly for this chapter though, these statistics reveal that civil partnerships resonate with some couples and, despite the availability of an alternative status, individuals are actively choosing to express their relationship through this particular relationship form.

Conclusions – a future for civil partnerships in England and Wales

As a jurisdiction England and Wales is clearly at a transitional point in the regulation of adult interpersonal relationships. Unlike other countries where civil partnerships are of largely historical significance, in England and Wales they have a future owing to the Government's recent decision to both retain and extend the regime to different-sex couples. This chapter has challenged some of the assumptions necessitating the phasing of same-sex civil partnerships and sought to argue that their retention was not solely attributable to the Supreme Court's ruling *Steinfeld* noting the exclusion of different-sex couples from the regime constituted a breach of Articles 8 and 14 of the European Convention on Human Rights. After all, the Supreme Court merely required the removal of the discriminatory treatment and that could have been achieved through either extension to different-sex couples or phasing out the same-sex–only regime in its entirety.[82] Instead, this chapter has interrogated the more abstract arguments in favour of retention of the scheme and questioned whether, despite a relatively short existence, civil partnerships are now imbued with a nascent ideology necessitating their future.

As civil partnerships clearly represent a valued status for many same-sex couples, it is important for their viewpoints to feed into the future legislative that extends the regime to different-sex couples through regulations.[83] This is particularly imperative as the public discourse relating to this move has been confused. There has arguably been a palpable silence by the LGBTQ+ community on the introduction of different-sex civil partnerships. Conversely, for different-sex couples, access to civil partnerships has dominated media coverage with, in particular, an emphasis on the discriminatory nature of the current ban and its human rights implications. What is apparent here is that both communities are approaching the rationales behind the introduction and purpose of civil partnerships differently. Whereas groups calling for different-sex civil partnerships such as the Equal Civil Partnership campaign are viewing them as alternatives to marriage, there is evidence in the academic scholarship of resistance by same-sex couples to such a move because historically requiring a civil registration regime is fundamentally different to *desiring* one as an alternative.[84] Without a doubt, these tensions reveal that future reform requires the perspectives and lived experiences of same-sex couples in civil partnerships to underpin the process.

It is true that civil partnerships are a statutory construct created by the state to protect a vulnerable group of citizens at a time when marriage was not available. Owing to their administrative nature and focus on registration, it is perhaps unsurprising that Lord Lester remarked that he doubted Shakespeare would write about civil partnerships in the same way he wrote about marriage.[85] Thus the occurrence of the progression, status and stasis narratives, delineated above, are neither surprising nor without foundation when you compare other jurisdictions and their journey towards same-sex marriage. However, this chapter has argued that even a newly created registration regime can serve an important expressive function for couples, which is a fact that needs full acknowledgement when contemplating its future. Indeed, Eekelaar has cautioned against underestimating the symbolism of both marriage and civil partnership noting that the by permitting relationship formalisation, the state is demonstrating its approval or at least acceptance 'of processes that have symbolic importance for the couple for the growth of love within the relationship.'[86] This observation reveals that just as marriage has changed over time through society's engagement with that institution, so too has civil partnership and long may it continue to do so.

Notes

1 See Sebastian Poulter, 'The Definition of Marriage in English Law' (1979) 42 *Modern Law Review* 409; Rebecca Probert, '*Hyde v Hyde*: Defining or Defending Marriage?' (2007) *Child and Family Law Quarterly* 322.
2 See *S.-T. (Formerly J.) v J.* (1998) Fam 103, 141 where Ward LJ referred to the 'hallowed notion of marriage.'
3 See Office for National Statistics (ONS), 'Marriages in England and Wales: 2016' *Statistical Bulletin* (28 March 2019).
4 See for example, Eric Clive, 'Marriage: An Unnecessary Legal Concept?' in John Eekelaar and Sanford Katz (eds), *Marriage and Cohabitation in Contemporary Societies* (Butterworths 1980); Sheila Jeffreys, 'The Need to Abolish Marriage' (2004) 14 *Feminism & Psychology* 327; Clare Chambers, *Against Marriage: An Egalitarian Defence of the Marriage-Free State* (Oxford University Press 2017).
5 Martha A Fineman, 'Why Marriage?' (2001) 9 *Virginia Journal of Social Policy and the Law* 239.
6 See *Vallianatos v Greece* App Nos. 29381/09 and 32684/09 (ECtHR, 7 November 2013), para 81 and *Oliari and Others v Italy* App Nos. 18766/11 and 36030/11, (ECtHR, 21 July 2015), para 174. See also Andy Hayward, 'Same-Sex Registered Partnerships – A Right to Be Recognised?' (2016) 75 *Cambridge Law Journal* 27.
7 Maya Oppenheim, 'Straight Couples to Be Allowed Civil Partnerships After Law Changed by Government, Theresa May Says' *The Independent* (London, 2 October 2018).
8 The introduction of same-sex marriage has often precipitated the phasing out of same-sex–only registered partnership regimes, as evidenced in the Nordic countries. For analysis, see Jens M Scherpe and Andy Hayward, *The Future of Registered Partnerships – Family Recognition Beyond Marriage?* (Intersentia 2017).
9 See Rebecca Probert, *Marriage Law and Practice in the Long Eighteenth Century: A Reassessment* (Cambridge University Press 2009).
10 See Nicola Barker, *Not the Marrying Kind: A Feminist Critique of Same-Sex Marriage* (Palgrave Macmillan 2012).
11 Ibid., 22.
12 *Hyde v Hyde* (1866) LR 1 P&D 130, 130. See Poulter (n 1).
13 Probert (n 9).
14 *A v A (Attorney General Intervening)* (2012) EWHC 2219 (Fam) [93] where Moylan J noted this 'well-known statement.' See *Sheffield City Council v E and Another* (2004) EWHC 2808 (Fam) [112] where Munby J acknowledged the 'famous definition.'
15 *Bellinger v Bellinger* (2003) UKHL 21 [46].
16 Exemplified in cases such as *Brock v Wollams* (1949) 2 KB 388; cf *Fitzpatrick v Sterling Housing Association Ltd* (1998) 1 FLR 6.
17 See *Fitzpatrick v Sterling Housing Association Ltd* (1999) UKHL 42 and *Ghaidan v Godin-Mendoza* (2004) UKHL 30. See also 'Looking for a Family Resemblance: The Limits of the Functional Approach to the Legal Definition of Family' (1990–1991) 104 *Harvard Law Review* 1640.
18 See Nicola Barker, 'After the Wedding, What Next? Conservatism and Conjugality' in Nicola Barker and Daniel Monk (eds), *From Civil Partnership to Same-Sex Marriage: Interdisciplinary Reflections* (Routledge 2015).
19 Home Office, *Supporting Families: A Consultation Document* (1998).

20 Elizabeth van Acker, 'Disconnected Relationship Values and Marriage Policies in England' (2016) 38 *Journal of Social Welfare and Family Law* 36–37.
21 Ibid., 36.
22 Ibid., 46–47.
23 On the value of marriage over civil partnerships, see the Witness Statements referenced in *Wilkinson v Kitzinger (No 2)* (2006) EWHC 2022 (Fam) [5] (Sir Mark Potter P).
24 Barker (n 10) 2.
25 See Kees Waaldijk, 'Others May Follow: The Introduction of Marriage Quasi-Marriage, and Semi-Marriage for Same-Sex Couples in European Countries' (2003) 38 *New England Law Review* 569, 583.
26 See *Minister of Home Affairs and Another v Fourie and Another* (CCT 60/04) (2005) ZACC 19.
27 *Obergefell v Hodges* 576 US, 135 S Ct 2584 (2015).
28 *Ghaidan* (n 17).
29 HC Deb 5 February 2013, vol 558, col 125.
30 See Helen Fenwick and Andy Hayward, 'From Same-Sex Marriage to Equal Civil Partnerships: On a Path Towards 'Perfecting' Equality?' (2018) 30 *Child and Family Law Quarterly* 97.
31 See *Wilkinson* (n 23) [6] (Sir Mark Potter P).
32 *Obergefell* (n 27) 28.
33 See Rosemary Auchmuty, 'What's So Special About Marriage? The Impact of *Wilkinson v Kitzinger*' (2008) *Child and Family Law Quarterly* 475; Rosie Harding, 'Sir Mark Potter and the Protection of the Traditional Family: Why Same Sex Marriage Is (Still) a Feminist Issue' (2007) 15 *Feminist Legal Studies* 223; Kenneth McK Norrie, 'Marriage Is for Heterosexuals – May the Rest of Us Be Saved from It' (2000) *Child and Family Law Quarterly* 363.
34 Celia Kitzinger and Sue Wilkinson, 'The Re-Branding of Marriage: Why We Got Married Instead of Registering a Civil Partnership' (2004) 14 *Feminism & Psychology* 127.
35 McK Norrie (n 33) 365.
36 See Andy Hayward, 'The Married Women's Property Act 1882' in Erika Rackley and Rosemary Auchmuty (eds), *Women's Legal Landmarks: Celebrating the History of Women and Law in the UK and Ireland* (Hart Publishing 2018).
37 See Ingrid Lund-Andersen, 'Registered Partnerships in Denmark' in Scherpe and Hayward (n 8).
38 See Laurence Francoz Terminal, 'Registered Partnerships in France' in Scherpe and Hayward (n 8).
39 Waaldijk (n 25).
40 *M v SSWP* (2006) UKHL 11 [93].
41 Brenda Hale, 'Homosexual Rights' (2004) 16 *Child and Family Law Quarterly* 125.
42 HC Deb 5 February 2013, vol 558, col 136.
43 See the chapters from the Nordic countries in Scherpe and Hayward (n 8).
44 *Steinfeld and Keidan v Secretary of State for Education* (2017) EWCA Civ 81 [172].
45 See Helen Fenwick and Andy Hayward, 'Rejecting Asymmetry of Access to Formal Relationship Statuses for Same- and Different-Sex Couples at Strasbourg and Domestically' (2017) 6 *European Human Rights Law Review* 544.
46 Austrian Constitutional Court Judgment: G 258/2017, 4 December 2017. Note this was following an earlier unsuccessful challenge in both the Austrian Constitutional Court and before the European Court of Human Rights in *Ratzenböck and Seydl v Austria* (2017) ECHR 947.

47 See Gibraltar, which has permitted same and different-sex civil partnerships from March 2014 and same-sex marriage from December 2016. Note also the Falkland Islands, which in April 2017 introduced same-sex marriage and civil partnerships for both same and different-sex couples.
48 House of Keys Deb 1 March 2016, vol 133, Line 1550.
49 *R (on the application of Steinfeld and Keidan) v Secretary of State for International Development* (2018) UKSC 32. See Andy Hayward, 'Taking the Time to Discriminate – *R (on the Application of Steinfeld and Keidan) v Secretary of State for International Development*' (2019) 41 *Journal of Social Welfare and Family Law* 92; Andy Hayward, 'Equal Civil Partnerships, Discrimination and the Indulgence of Time: *R (on the Application of Steinfeld and Keidan) v Secretary of State for International Development*' (2019) 82(5) *Modern Law Review* 922.
50 Stonewall, 'Abolishing Civil Partnerships Is Not an Option' (27 June 2018) <www.stonewall.org.uk/our-work/blog/abolishing-civil-partnerships-not-option> accessed 15 March 2019.
51 Equal Civil Partnerships Campaign, 'Campaign Responds to Reports of Government U-Turn on Civil Partnerships for Opposite-Sex Couples' (1 February 2018) <http://equalcivilpartnerships.org.uk/2018/02/campaign-responds-reports-government-u-turn-civil-partnerships-opposite-sex-couples/> accessed 15 March 2019.
52 Discussed in van Acker (n 20) 37.
53 *R v Bala and Others* (2016) EWCA Crim 560 [38].
54 Sue Wilkinson and Celia Kitzinger, 'In Support of Equal Marriage: Why Civil Partnership Is Not Enough' (2006) 8 *Psychology of Women Review* 54.
55 Rosie Harding, '"Dogs Are 'Registered', People Shouldn't Be": Legal Consciousness and Lesbian and Gay Rights' (2006) 15 *Social and Legal Studies* 511, 524.
56 This understanding of marriage is sculpted out of the common law duties of consortium, maintenance and unity.
57 See the Civil Partnership Act 2004, s 1(1)(a) noting that such relationship is created through the act of registration.
58 HC Deb 5 February 2013, vol 558, col 127.
59 *Ghaidan* (n 17) [96].
60 *TJ v CV & S & BA* (2007) EWHC 1952 (Fam) [32].
61 *B v A and Others* (2006) EWHC 2 (Fam) [34].
62 *M v SSWP* (n 40).
63 Ibid., 101.
64 See Department of Trade and Industry, *Responses to Civil Partnership: A Framework for the Legal Recognition of Same-Sex Couples* (2003) 17, remarking that same-sex couples were 'treated as two strangers under current law.'
65 *M v SSWP* (n 40) [99] (Baroness Hale).
66 *Bull v Hall* (2013) UKSC 73 [26]. See also *Radmacher v Granatino* (2010) UKSC 42 and *Taiwo v Olaigbe and Another; Onu v Akwiwu and Another* (2016) UKSC 31.
67 *Wilkinson* (n 23).
68 Ibid., 121.
69 Ibid., 116.
70 See *Lawrence v Gallagher* (2012) EWCA Civ 394.
71 See The Equal Civil Partnerships Campaign, 'Why Does It Matter?' <http://equalcivilpartnerships.org.uk/why-does-it-matter/> accessed 28 May 2019.
72 See Barker (n 10) 22.
73 ONS, *Civil Partnerships in England and Wales: 2014* (20 October 2015).

74 Ibid.
75 ONS, *Civil Partnerships in England and Wales: 2017* (16 August 2018).
76 Department for Culture, Media and Sport, *Civil Partnership Review (England and Wales): A Consultation* (2014) para 3.10.
77 Jens M Scherpe, 'The Past, Present and Future of Civil Partnerships' in Scherpe and Hayward (n 8) 577.
78 ONS, *Civil Partnerships in England and Wales: 2016* (26 September 2017).
79 ONS (n 75).
80 See John Haskey, 'Civil Partnerships and Same-Sex Marriages in England and Wales: A Social and Demographic Perspective' (2016) *Family Law* 44.
81 HC Deb 2 February 2018, vol 635, col 1142.
82 Brenda Hale, 'Private Family Law Reform' (2018) *Family Law* 810.
83 As required by the Civil Partnerships, Marriages and Deaths (Registration etc) Act 2019, s 2.
84 See Adam Jowett and Elizabeth Peel, '"A Question of Equality and Choice": Same-Sex Couples' Attitudes Towards Civil Partnership After the Introduction of Same-Sex Marriage' (2017) 8 *Psychology and Sexuality* 69.
85 HL Deb 25 January 2002, vol 630, col 1746.
86 John Eekelaar, 'Family Law and Love' (2016) *Child and Family Law Quarterly* 289, 295–296.

References

Primary sources

A v A (Attorney General Intervening) (2012) EWHC 2219 (Fam).
Austrian Constitutional Court Judgment: G 258/2017, 4 December 2017.
B v A and Others (2006) EWHC 2 (Fam).
Bellinger v Bellinger (2003) UKHL 21.
Brock v Wollams (1949) 2 KB 388.
Bull v Hall (2013) UKSC 73.
Civil Partnership Act 2004.
Civil Partnerships, Marriages and Deaths (Registration etc) Act 2019.
Fitzpatrick v Sterling Housing Association Ltd (1998) 1 FLR 6.
Fitzpatrick v Sterling Housing Association Ltd (1999) UKHL 42.
Ghaidan v Godin-Mendoza (2004) UKHL 30.
Hyde v Hyde (1866) LR 1 P&D 130.
Lawrence v Gallagher (2012) EWCA Civ 394.
M v Secretary of State for Work and Pensions (2006) UKHL 11.
Marriage (Same Sex Couples) Act 2013
Minister of Home Affairs and Another v Fourie and Another (CCT 60/04) (2005) ZACC 19. (South Africa).
Obergefell v Hodges 576 US, 135 S Ct 2584 (2015).
Oliari and Others v Italy App Nos. 18766/11 and 36030/11 (ECtHR, 21 July 2015).
R (on the Application of Steinfeld and Keidan) v Secretary of State for International Development (2018) UKSC 32.
R v Bala and Others (2016) EWCA Crim 560.
Radmacher v Granatino (2010) UKSC 42.
Ratzenböck and Seydl v Austria (2017) ECHR 947.

S.-T. (Formerly J.) v J. (1998) Fam 103.
Sheffield City Council v E and Another (2004) EWHC 2808 (Fam).
Steinfeld and Keidan v Secretary of State for Education (2017) EWCA Civ 81. UKSC 32.
Taiwo v Olaigbe and Another; Onu v Akwiwu and Another (2016) UKSC 31.
TJ v CV & S & BA (2007) EWHC 1952 (Fam).
Vallianatos v Greece App Nos. 29381/09 and 32684/09 (ECtHR, 7 November 2013).
Wilkinson v Kitzinger (No 2) (2006) EWHC 2022 (Fam).

Secondary sources

Auchmuty R, 'What's So Special About Marriage? The Impact of *Wilkinson v Kitzinger*' (2008) *Child and Family Law Quarterly* 475.

Barker N, *Not the Marrying Kind: A Feminist Critique of Same-Sex Marriage* (Palgrave Macmillan 2012).

———, 'After the Wedding, What Next? Conservatism and Conjugality' in Barker N and Monk D (eds), *From Civil Partnership to Same-Sex Marriage: Interdisciplinary Reflections* (Routledge 2015).

Chambers C, *Against Marriage: An Egalitarian Defence of the Marriage-Free State* (Oxford University Press 2017).

Clive E, 'Marriage: An Unnecessary Legal Concept?' in Eekelaar J and Katz S (eds), *Marriage and Cohabitation in Contemporary Societies* (Butterworths 1980).

Department for Culture, Media and Sport, *Civil Partnership Review (England and Wales): A Consultation* (2014).

Department of Trade and Industry, *Responses to Civil Partnership: A Framework for the Legal Recognition of Same-Sex Couples* (2003).

Eekelaar J, 'Family Law and Love' (2016) *Child and Family Law Quarterly* 289.

Equal Civil Partnerships Campaign, 'Campaign Responds to Reports of Government U-Turn on Civil Partnerships for Opposite-Sex Couples' (1 February 2018) <http://equalcivilpartnerships.org.uk/2018/02/campaign-responds-reports-government-u-turn-civil-partnerships-opposite-sex-couples/> accessed 15 March 2019.

The Equal Civil Partnerships Campaign, 'Why Does It Matter?' <http://equalcivilpartnerships.org.uk/why-does-it-matter/> accessed 28 May 2019.

Fenwick H and Hayward A, 'Rejecting Asymmetry of Access to Formal Relationship Statuses for Same- and Different-Sex Couples at Strasbourg and Domestically' (2017) 6 *European Human Rights Law Review* 544.

———, 'From Same-Sex Marriage to Equal Civil Partnerships: On a Path Towards 'Perfecting' Equality?' (2018) 30 *Child and Family Law Quarterly* 97.

Fineman MA, 'Why Marriage?' (2001) 9 *Virginia Journal of Social Policy and the Law* 239.

Francoz Terminal L, 'Registered Partnerships in France' in Scherpe JM and Hayward A (eds), *The Future of Registered Partnerships – Family Recognition Beyond Marriage?* (Intersentia 2017).

Hale B, 'Homosexual Rights' (2004) 16 *Child and Family Law Quarterly* 125.

———, 'Private Family Law Reform' (2018) *Family Law* 810.

Harding R, '"Dogs Are 'Registered', People Shouldn't Be": Legal Consciousness and Lesbian and Gay Rights' (2006) 15 *Social and Legal Studies* 511.

———, 'Sir Mark Potter and the Protection of the Traditional Family: Why Same Sex Marriage Is (Still) a Feminist Issue' (2007) 15 *Feminist Legal Studies* 223.

Haskey J, 'Civil Partnerships and Same-Sex Marriages in England and Wales: A Social and Demographic Perspective' (2016) *Family Law* 44.

Hayward A, 'Same-Sex Registered Partnerships – A Right to Be Recognised?' (2016) 75 *Cambridge Law Journal* 27.

———, 'The Married Women's Property Act 1882' in Rackley E and Auchmuty R (eds), *Women's Legal Landmarks: Celebrating the History of Women and Law in the UK and Ireland* (Hart Publishing 2018).

———, 'Equal Civil Partnerships, Discrimination and the Indulgence of Time: R *(on the Application of Steinfeld and Keidan)* v Secretary of State for International Development' (2019) 82(5) *Modern Law Review* 922.

———, 'Taking the Time to Discriminate – *R (on the Application of Steinfeld and Keidan) v Secretary of State for International Development*' (2019) 41 *Journal of Social Welfare and Family Law* 92.

HC Deb 2 February 2018, vol 635, col 1142.

HC Deb 5 February 2013, vol 558, col 125.

HC Deb 5 February 2013, vol 558, col 127.

HC Deb 5 February 2013, vol 558, col 136.

HL Deb 25 January 2002, vol 630, col 1746.

Home Office, *Supporting Families: A Consultation Document* (1998).

House of Keys Deb 1 March 2016, vol 133, Line 1550.

Jeffreys S, 'The Need to Abolish Marriage' (2004) 14 *Feminism & Psychology* 327.

Jowett A and Peel E, '"A Question of Equality and Choice": Same-Sex Couples' Attitudes Towards Civil Partnership After the Introduction of Same-Sex Marriage' (2017) 8 *Psychology and Sexuality* 69.

Kitzinger C and Wilkinson S, 'The Re-Branding of Marriage: Why We Got Married Instead of Registering a Civil Partnership' (2004) 14 *Feminism & Psychology* 127.

'Looking for a Family Resemblance: The Limits of the Functional Approach to the Legal Definition of Family' (1990–1991) 104 *Harvard Law Review* 1640.

Lund-Andersen I, 'Registered Partnerships in Denmark' in Scherpe JM and Hayward A (eds), *The Future of Registered Partnerships – Family Recognition Beyond Marriage?* (Intersentia 2017).

McK Norrie K, 'Marriage Is for Heterosexuals – May the Rest of Us Be Saved from It' (2000) *Child and Family Law Quarterly* 363.

Office for National Statistics, *Civil Partnerships in England and Wales: 2014* (20 October 2015).

———, *Civil Partnerships in England and Wales: 2016* (26 September 2017).

———, *Civil Partnerships in England and Wales: 2017* (16 August 2018).

———, 'Marriages in England and Wales: 2016' (Statistical Bulletin, 28 March 2019).

Oppenheim M, 'Straight Couples to Be Allowed Civil Partnerships After Law Changed by Government, Theresa May Says' *The Independent* (London, 2 October 2018).

Poulter S, 'The Definition of Marriage in English Law' (1979) 42 *Modern Law Review* 409.

Probert R, '*Hyde v Hyde*: Defining or Defending Marriage?' (2007) *Child and Family Law Quarterly* 322.
———, *Marriage Law and Practice in the Long Eighteenth Century: A Reassessment* (Cambridge University Press 2009).
Scherpe JM, 'The Past, Present and Future of Civil Partnerships' in Scherpe JM and Hayward A (eds), *The Future of Registered Partnerships – Family Recognition Beyond Marriage?* (Intersentia 2017).
Scherpe JM and Hayward A, *The Future of Registered Partnerships – Family Recognition Beyond Marriage?* (Intersentia 2017).
Stonewall, 'Abolishing Civil Partnerships Is Not an Option' (27 June 2018) <www.stonewall.org.uk/our-work/blog/abolishing-civil-partnerships-not-option> accessed 15 March 2019.
van Acker E, 'Disconnected Relationship Values and Marriage Policies in England' (2016) 38 *Journal of Social Welfare and Family Law* 36.
Waaldijk K, 'Others May Follow: The Introduction of Marriage Quasi- Marriage, and Semi-Marriage for Same-Sex Couples in European Countries' (2003) 38 *New England Law Review* 569.
Wilkinson S and Kitzinger C, 'In Support of Equal Marriage: Why Civil Partnership Is Not Enough' (2006) 8 *Psychology of Women Review* 54.

Chapter 11

The hierarchy of marriage and civil partnerships

Diversifying relationship recognition

Alexander Maine

Introduction

With the introduction of same-sex marriage in 2013, same-sex couples in the United Kingdom (UK) who wished to have their relationship legally recognised were able to choose whether to enter into marriage or civil partnership, benefitting from two separate institutions of relationship recognition. This is in contrast to different-sex couples, who could only enter into marriage, as traditionally defined by the Marriage Act 1949 and the Matrimonial Cause Act 1973, having no access to civil partnerships[1] nor any form of recognised cohabitation.[2] Although this situation created *more* opportunities for same-sex couples, the arguably hierarchical nature of such recognition may ensure that marriage retains its privileged status as the 'gold standard'[3] of relationship recognition. Prime Minister Theresa May[4] noted that, following the *Steinfeld* decision,[5] the government would legislate to fully realise equality in relationship recognition. Her statement illustrates the focus on equality of opportunity for different-sex and same-sex couples relationship recognition in the UK.

This chapter will argue that the legal provisions of marriage and civil partnerships in the UK are still subject to a hierarchy of relationship recognition that privileges marriage and presents civil partnerships as a lesser option. This hierarchy will be constructed in this chapter as one that privileges heteronormativity[6] (heteronormativity has been defined as the 'truth regime'[7] in which gender, sexuality, and desire coalesce,[8] and in which heterosexuality is assumed, privileged, and naturalised in society)[9] and relies on homonormativity,[10] promoting coupled, domestic same-sex and different-sex relationships. This chapter will discuss the significance of civil partnerships and their comparisons with same-sex marriage manifested in the hierarchical organisation of relationship recognition. The organisation of relationship recognition framework upholds marriage as the ultimate form of relationship recognition that civil partnerships emulate. I will argue that this reinforces Rubin's sexual hierarchy[11] in the awarding of marital rights to couples and the maintenance of marriage as the ultimate form of recognition that castigates those who do not marry. Empirical evidence will be used to demonstrate the roles of civil partnerships in the lived experiences of LGBTQ+

participants. This will then point to ways in which this hierarchy can be disestablished in the removal of barriers to entering a legally recognised relationship and developing further understandings of the way law may allow for diversified recognition of relationships.

Both marriage and civil partnership establish a form of relationship recognition hierarchy in which differing institutions of relationship recognition offer certain forms of legal and social value to different relationships and their choices of recognition. Same-sex marriage arguably emphasises this hierarchy, adding to the myriad of social, legal, and cultural factors that it consists of, which contribute to the enforcing of social norms regarding sexual behaviour. It will be argued that marriage has retained its place in society as the ultimate form of relationship recognition, bolstered by the introduction of same-sex marriage. Thus, this creates a hierarchy of relationship recognition, stratified by the exclusionary nature of marriage and civil partnerships. This chapter will argue that following *Steinfeld*, it may be possible to alter this hierarchy and instil further equality; however, it will also note that this may not be enough.

This hierarchy will rely on the concepts of heteronormativity and homonormativity.[12] Homonormativity describes a dominant politics of liberal equality, one that upholds and sustains desexualised, depoliticised perspectives of same-sex couples. This chapter will use the homoradical, in opposition to the homonormative, to describe an *anti-assimilationist politic*, one that is actively sexualised and politicised. The homoradical describes a sexualised body of queer identity, one that rejects normative discourse surrounding homosexuality. The homoradical may be excluded from norms surrounding marriage due to the active pursuit of sex outside of the normative realm, including public, group, kink, bareback, and non-monogamous sex. The homoradical will be used to demonstrate the exclusion still felt by those who reject marriage and civil partnership norms that demonstrate the law's focus on dyadic pairings.

Constructing this hierarchy may be significant in developing understanding of the law's role in constructing and regulating choices regarding relationship recognition and the meanings attached to such recognition.[13] This is important in assessing the role of legal recognition of relationships and the specific choices made by same-sex and different-sex couples. This chapter will first assess the legal provisions of civil partnerships and same-sex marriage, and the Supreme Court decision that different-sex couples should have access to civil partnerships. It will then assess empirical evidence demonstrating the socio-legal construction of marriage and civil partnerships, particularly noting the lived experiences of civil partnerships to LGBTQ+ people, in order to construct the symbolism attached to the institution.

Legal hierarchies

Civil partnerships were introduced to be marriage in all but name, offering 'virtually all' of the rights and responsibilities of marriage[14] to same-sex couples.

The Civil Partnership Act 2004, which came at a time when only two jurisdictions in the world had legislated for same-sex marriage,[15] preserved marriage as solely heterosexual while conceding a need, and political will, for some form of recognition of such relationships.[16] The framework introduced was solely for the benefit of same-sex couples, offering similar rights and protections to marriage, while preserving the distinction between the two institutions. This distinction reaffirmed the special status of marriage that arguably maintained its social, legal, and religious privilege. Some have labelled civil partnerships as a 'parody' of marriage[17] that attempts to mimic the functioning and performativity of marriage, while simultaneously being 'not marriage,' lacking in social and legal status[18] that ensures the institutions are separate. Despite this, they do represent a significant institution for same-sex couples, particularly as the first UK recognition of LGBTQ+ relationships, and are still demonstrably popular as a huge tranche of legal rights for same-sex couples.[19]

A civil partnership is a relationship between two people of the same sex, formed via registration[20] and ending only in dissolution, annulment, or death.[21] The registration of a civil partnership differs from the ceremonial process of marriage, as the former is purely a civil and non-religious procedure and does not require any distinct vows to be stated, while containing the same rights and responsibilities as marriage. The dissolution process replicates the divorce process; however, adultery cannot be used as a factor in dissolution proceedings due to the heterosexual definition of adultery,[22] nor is consummation recognised in civil partnerships[23] or same-sex marriage.[24]

However, despite the disparities between marriage and civil partnerships, civil partnerships remain of significance to LGBTQ+ populations as a form of registered partnership free from the patriarchal, paternal requirements of marriage.[25] While for some, marriage represents the ultimate[26] symbol of legally and socially recognised relationship,[27] civil partnerships may present an opportunity to break free from a traditionally religious or patriarchal institution.[28] This gives weight to the importance of retaining, and opening up, civil partnerships to all couples.

The advent of same-sex marriage in the United Kingdom followed a burgeoning international trend in Western Europe and North America, as discussed by other chapters in this volume. The passing of the Marriage (Same-Sex Couples) Act 2013 allowed same-sex couples to finally enter into an institution symbolically similar to traditional marriage, following David Cameron's (small-c) conservative goal[29] of encouraging marriage rates.[30] This equality-based[31] reform follows the incremental familiarisation of LGBTQ+ rights.[32] This development is often critiqued as reliant on normalisation and assimilation,[33] yet is a clear sign of the advancing acceptance and tolerance of LGBTQ+ identity (reliant on recognising certain forms of relationship). However, the 2013 Act, coupled with the 2004 Act, has created a situation in which same-sex marriage and civil partnerships are arguably restrictive institutions, both of which restrict access to certain couples based on sex. The system of relationship recognition, I will argue, constructs a hierarchy that preserves marriage as the best form of recognition, and denies the opportunities to recognise relationships in different ways: marriage is represented as the 'justifiable'[34] location for sex, with civil partnerships replicating marriage. Non-marital relationships, therefore, are still excluded from recognition, meaning that the homoradical form of relationships and other familial relationships are still not recognised.[35]

Consideration of the position post-*Steinfeld*

Following the introduction of same-sex marriage, same-sex couples wishing to have their relationships recognised by the state were presented with a choice to marry or enter into a civil partnership. This 'somewhat absurd'[36] situation meant that different-sex couples could only register their relationship by marriage, and those cohabitating were bereft of any relationship rights.[37] This inequality was the focus of litigation in the Supreme Court, brought by a heterosexual couple and backed by the 'Equal Civil Partnership' campaign,[38] claiming discrimination based on their sexual orientation as to their being unable to register a civil partnership. The Supreme Court in *R (Steinfeld and Keidan) v Secretary of State for International Development*[39] decided that the withholding of civil partnerships from heterosexual couples did indeed engage and constitute a breach of Article 14 (the prohibition of discrimination) of the European Convention of Human Rights when read in conjunction with Article 8 (the right to respect for private and family life). The ruling declared section 1 of the Civil Partnership Act 2004 to be incompatible with the Human Rights Act 1998, constituting an act of discrimination interfering with the couple's right to their private and family life.

Lord Kerr's judgment, with whom the rest of the Supreme Court unanimously agreed, sets out the conditions in which the Declaration of Incompatibility was made. The judgement held that sections 1 and 3 of the Civil Partnerships Act 2004 (which stated that a civil partnership is a relationship between two people of the same sex[40] and those who are of a different sex are not eligible to register as civil partners) was in fact in breach of the right to a private family life.[41] The judgment draws extensively on jurisprudence from the ECtHR, notably set out in *Schalk and Kopf v Austria*,[42] which determined that the ECHR does not oblige contracting states to legislate for same-sex marriage. However, there is a positive obligation to provide legal protection for same-sex couples, following *Oliari and Others v Italy* decision,[43] providing this is socially acceptable on the ground. Lord Kerr notes a contrast between the *Schalk* circumstances to the one presented, in that the Austrian Registered Partnership Act 2009[44] was a 'product of evolving societal acceptance of the need to provide some legal recognition of same sex partnerships'[45]; whereas, the inequality produced by civil partnerships and same-sex marriage in the UK was a deliberate decision, as a 'creature of Parliament.'[46] Such a creation should have been rectified immediately:

> In the case of MSSCA, however, it was Parliament itself that brought about an inequality immediately on the coming into force of the Act, where none

> had previously existed. The redressing by the legislature of an imbalance which it has come to recognise is one thing; the creation of inequality quite another.[47]

Lord Kerr establishes that the introduction of same-sex marriage in England and Wales initiated an inequality that had previously not existed, in the denial of different-sex couples from the right to a civil partner. The creation of this inequality should, according to Lord Kerr, lead to the extension of civil partnerships to different-sex couples. Lord Kerr then notes that this is undeserving of a margin of appreciation for the state, as to how the inequality is 'cured.'[48]

Kerr draws an analogy with *Vallianatos v Greece*. In *Vallianatos*, same-sex couples were excluded from civil unions and Strasbourg ruled that this breached Article 14 in conjunction with Article 8,[49] which is compared to *Steinfeld* as a direct reversal of position.[50] Kerr goes on to point out that the government and Parliament had knowledge of the position created in which an inequality of treatment was bound to arise, one that was not justifiable as a qualification of the Article 14 right.[51] Therefore, Kerr states, the government should have eliminated the inequality of treatment immediately. The five-year-delayed consultation could not have been justified as a legitimate aim for the continuance of discrimination. Kerr suggests that civil partnerships should have been immediately abolished or opened up to different-sex couples in order to rectify the breach of Articles 14 and 8,[52] thus demonstrating the importance and substance of the equality-driven nature of relationship recognition rights, at odds with the hierarchical organisation of relationship recognition. Civil partnerships were not opened to different-sex couples immediately because of concerns from religious institutions, as the government explicitly ruled out its involvement in religious affairs and made efforts to distance civil partnerships from religious groups.[53]

Following the ruling, the government has quickly incorporated the decision and factored this into the legislation for civil partnerships. The Civil Partnerships, Marriages and Deaths (Registration etc) Act 2019 received royal assent on 26 March 2019.[54] This requires the Secretary of State to make regulations to amend the 2004 Act so that different-sex couples are eligible to form civil partnerships.[55] The Act is a welcome step towards eradicating the hierarchy of relationship recognition in the UK by requiring the government to take action over different-sex civil partnerships, however the dyadic form of recognition still excludes certain groups. The Act and the *Steinfeld* case demonstrate the effective use of human rights instruments as methods to enact change, particularly concerning the construction of private family life as incorporating non-marital legal institutions. Doing so will disestablish the separation between heterosexuality and civil partnerships, acting as a conduit to further disestablish marriage's heterosexual underpinnings. In providing an alternative form of recognised relationships for different-sex couples, marriage's presupposed heterosexual nature becomes no longer viable, which, coupled with same-sex marriage, goes further to disestablish the marriage/civil partnership hetero/homosexual binary.[56] The creation of civil partnerships in 2004 was the first step taken towards deconstructing the sexual hierarchy, which had previously only recognised heterosexual sexuality as marital and legitimate. Same-sex marriage, and the creation of different-sex civil partnerships, will further create equality and act to disestablish this hierarchy. However, this still focuses on dyadic pairings, ultimately contributing to a sexual hierarchy in which those outside of the mononormative couplings are not recognised, nor are same-sex couples offered marriage in Northern Ireland.[57] The empirical evidence collected in this research will now be discussed, in order to reveal the socially constructed meanings of civil partnerships.

Empirical significance attached to civil partnerships

The meanings attached to civil partnerships and same-sex marriage will now be discussed, in order to assess the institution's continuing significance to the lives of the LGBTQ+ participants of this study. This section will demonstrate the significance of civil partnerships, but also their maintained 'lesser' status below marriage, recognising a social hierarchy dependent on the legal hierarchy. Investigations into the lived experience of the hierarchy are essential in order to assess the impact of law and to re-evaluate the stratification of relationship recognition that prioritises marital relationships. The institution, however, is one that is facing being subsumed by same-sex marriage as the ultimate form of legal recognition, with more people opting for marriages over civil partnerships.[58] The research utilised semi-structured interviews with 20 self-identified LGBTQ+ people aged 20–67 years old. The interviews were conducted in 2016 in Newcastle-upon-Tyne city centre. These participants were collected through mixed-method sampling including online strategic and snowball sampling, representing a mix of socio-economic backgrounds in the North-East of England. Interviews were used in order to broadcast the voices of the LGBTQ+ people,[59] giving emphasis to their lived experiences and realities.[60]

The significance of civil partnership

Participants often described civil partnerships as a significant institution that, in lieu of marriage provided them with a requisite familial structure. In ascribing significance to civil partnerships, participants often appropriated the language of marriage, denoting the similarity and coinciding of the two that demonstrates its aspirational position:

> I mean, I nearly did get married actually, many years ago – well, would have been civil partnership actually – and, erm, it was really important to my partner at the time, and I did love him.
>
> (Gay man, 28)

This participant discusses a previous relationship that presents an important point to note in terms of the lived experience of civil partnerships as analogous, and representative of aspiring to marriage. This reflects Heaphy et al.'s research,[61] which found that the language of marriage was overwhelmingly appropriated by civil partnered couples as a means of naturalising and emphasising the significance of their relationship. In doing so, this emphasises the similarity and function of civil partnerships to marriage, and confirms the social significance of the terms 'husband' and 'wife,' reaffirming the place of marriage within society. The next participant attributes the improved social and legal standing of LGBTQ+ populations to the impact of civil partnerships as they have become naturalised in the decade of their existence. He states that civil unions, in their long-standing status, have had a greater effect than the more recent same-sex marriage, when asked if society is more accepting of LGBTQ+ people:

> Yeah, they are, but I don't know if marriage has helped that, it was only two year ago anyway. Civil unions definitely have helped.
>
> (Gay man, 32)

In this, the participant posits civil partnerships as a beneficial step forward in equality measures. This may be because of the public status of civil partnerships representing a shift in social understanding of same-sex relationships, that same-sex marriage replicates, rather than transforms, understandings of sexual relationships.[62] Due to the recent passage of the 2013 Act, same-sex marriage falls in line with the incremental development of familial rights[63] – and as a prerequisite for marriage, civil partnerships, in this participant's view, have had a larger effect on society. This the first step taken for same-sex couples who wished for statutorily recognised relationships, and the beginning of the disestablishing of the sexual hierarchy[64] in 2004, in which relationship recognition was exclusive to different-sex relationships. Thus, different-sex civil partnerships will confirm the status and significance of the institution.

A further participant discusses the role civil partnerships had in lieu of marriage:

> I suppose civil partnerships was again about protecting people's rights in property and security, in terms of, I suppose where people, yeah, it provided some financial and legal security, but no, we've never thought about doing anything like that. We wouldn't do it, actually. Civil partnerships was a stepping stone for same-sex marriage, and now people aren't doing it. You don't hear of anyone getting a civil partnership now. It's like 'Oh, that was the weak thing on the way to marriage.'
>
> (Lesbian, 68)

The participant notes the legal protections secured by civil partnerships which may lack the social recognition received by marriage. Though recognising their significance, the participant demonstrates her own reluctance to recognise their relationship, demonstrative of the ways in which resistance to formally recognising a relationship takes on a political meaning. Such resistance may represent polarisation against the norm, and a reluctance to participant in heteronormative structures.[65]

Younger LGBTQ+ people may best represent the impact of the decade-long standing of civil partnerships. The next statement, from a 21-year-old male participant, is demonstrable of Plummer's polarisation theory, in which favourable social attitudes towards LGBTQ+ people are leading younger people to grow less polarised or embittered than those who have grown up when social attitudes were less favourable.[66] The participant, using Plummer's theory, is less likely to have become polarised or embittered by prejudicial or negative social stigma associated with homosexuality, because of the registered partnership:

> so if you look kind of at different generations, there probably is a trend towards there being less stigma and sort of prejudice, I suppose, and having preconceived ideas of gay people, erm, like I've grown up where the age of consent was the same and civil partnerships were introduced and all that, . . . so, same-sex marriage is another step towards that.
>
> (Gay man, 21)

Plummer's theory states that societal hostility towards homosexuality creates the potential for polarisation, and thus less hostile environments may lead to younger LGBTQ+ populations occupying 'simultaneous heterosexual and homosexual roles.'[67] In the preceding quote, the participant notes the improved legal framework established in the early 2000s that has led to improved social acceptance. He posits civil partnerships as a stepping-stone towards same-sex marriage that furthers the equality agenda that relies on assimilationist strategies that benefit LGBTQ+ populations in the constructing of sameness[68] between heterosexual and LGBTQ+ people. These quotes represent the participants' perceptions of civil partnerships as a transformational institution in society that began the recognition of same-sex couples by the law that allowed for calls for same-sex marriage to develop. This demonstrates that in the organisation of relationship recognition, civil partnerships were a necessary stepping-stone, while the introduction of heterosexual civil partnerships will confirm their potential as a transformative institution in relationship recognition.

Civil partnerships as 'lesser' than marriage

Despite the significance of civil partnerships, many LGBTQ+ participants continued to express their opinions that they are lesser than marriage, due to their standing as 'not' marriage and their exclusionary nature. The next participant uses this stepping-stone argument to explicitly spell out the notion that civil partnerships are a 'lesser marriage' due to the politico-legal landscape at the time of their creation:

> Civil partnerships seemed to be the furthest we could go at that point, and it did always feels like it was a, this was a lesser thing than marriage. I know that was how the public presented it, but actually, erm, my friends, no one got civil partnered, I've no intention of getting civil partnered or married, because I've never thought about that personally, . . . I, I think there's always the case that civil partnerships were the best that we can do, I think if the government thought it was possible, or if society had maybe been there at the time.
>
> (Gay man, 25)

Presenting civil partnerships as the best available option in 2004 reinforces the notion that a lesser form of relationship recognition was needed in order to be able to move on to the more equal institution of marriage. Civil partnerships created an institution similar to marriage, but maintained marriage's distinctiveness, framed by Stychin as cultural parochialism.[69] This parochialism is representative of the narrow focus of assimilationist relationship recognition, firmly based within the traditional marriage model. This represents a hierarchy between civil partnerships and marriage, with marriage containing more social and legal value, and in the introduction of same-sex marriage, this hierarchy is maintained and reinforced as these institutions replicate traditional marital structures that normatively presume and privilege[70] domesticity and monogamy. Robinson has stated that this is an inadequate means to enact radical social change in favour of LGBTQ+ populations.[71] If civil partnerships do indeed replicate marriage, they continue to be seen as a 'lesser' institution in their restriction to same-sex couples. This is further reinforced by a participant who, despite having been previously civil partnered, viewed the institution as a lesser form of registered partnership:

> Erm, I actually entered into a civil partnership at the time. It was a cop-out, basically. I did it in Scotland where it came before England, if I remember correctly, but it was a cop-out, but was always going to go in the right direction as people's attitudes change, . . . certainly, that was a watered-down bullshit thing; again, it was better than nothing at the time, but you gotta keep pushing for more.
>
> (Gay man, 46)

For this individual, civil partnerships represented a failure to achieve full equality in registered partnerships with marriage. This failure thus encompasses the view that marriage, as distinct from civil partnerships, is unique as an institution encompassing social and legal privileging.

Further to this, the next participant notes his experiences of a civil partnership as representative of a legal process, distinct from a marriage ceremony:

> it was very unceremonious ceremony, if you think. It was just a signing of a piece of paper, whereas I think a marriage is more the ceremony, the inviting people, the celebration. I think it's to do with that; it's more the celebration of that than the legal side of it, I think.
>
> (Gay man, 36)

This experience of the legal registration of a civil partnership is recounted by the participant as a purely civil event, divorced from the traditional ceremonial minutia and celebrations of a wedding, that Stychin has called an 'empty vessel'[72] in failing to sufficiently replicate the socially recognised components of a marriage celebration. While a marriage may be conducted with very little ceremony, it still requires two witnesses and the reciting of vows; in contrast, civil partnerships may be conducted entirely silently. Both institutions allow for couples to conduct their own ceremonies and celebrations, but there is a socially recognised 'culture' of marriage that has traditionally relied on heteronormative and patriarchal imagery.[73] Civil partnerships may further be viewed as 'empty' in the legislative exclusion of consummation and adultery due to the law's failure to recognise same-sex intercourse.[74] Further qualifying this, the participant went on to state that because of such differences, heteronormative society does not see such registered partnerships in the same way as marriage:

> "and I think, although we did have civil partnerships, erm, there was some elements of heterosexual society said "oh well you're not actually married," and that's eradicated that now, because obviously there's a proper marriage ceremony."
>
> (Gay man, 36)

In doing so, he confirms the notion that same-sex marriage was intended to create equality, going further than that established in 2004, by claiming ownership of the term 'marriage' and including the possibility of legitimate marriage ceremonies. However, the steps taken towards such equality continue to establish a hierarchy, as though same-sex couples may have two opportunities, the fact that marriage is still reserved for different-sex couples, maintains the centrality of heterosexuality to marriage and reaffirms its normative status. This organisation of relationship recognition reinforces hierarchies, in which traditional marriage is maintained as an ideated, undiluted institution, while civil partnerships and same-sex marriage are socially recognised according to their prefixes, marking their distinctiveness from the natural conjugal whole.[75] The empirical evidence presented suggest that while civil partnerships are a significant institution that should be preserved, they are still maintained as 'lesser' than marriage, exacerbated by the introduction of same-sex marriage.

This contributes to a hierarchy of relationship recognition, preserving marriage's privilege.

A further participant's comments may be used to illustrate an apparent disparity between perceptions of civil partnerships and sexual relations outside of such relationships that maintains the ideation of recognised relationships:

> Been a civil partner now for eight years, and it's only something I think about if it's a conscious thing, reinforced by someone else, so if someone points out 'are you in a civil partnership?' or, in the case of us, we have an open relationship, so as soon as you mention your civil partner to someone else, it takes on a whole new meaning to them.
>
> (Gay man, 36)

The participant's sexual partners posit non-monogamy as antithetical to civil partnerships, and may illustrate the mononormative expectations of such relationships. His relationship status is often at the back of his mind while he pursues non-monogamous sex, demonstrative of the compartmentalisation of sex[76] and the freedom to construct sexual relationships outside of normative boundaries.[77] This presumes monogamy in legally recognised relationships that may lead to feelings of exclusion for those described as 'homoradical,' in line with Warner's comments that sex outside of legally recognised relationships becomes stigmatised.[78] While there is no legal bar to non-monogamous relationships in civil partnerships or same-sex marriage (however, different-sex marriages could rely on adultery in divorce proceedings, while same-sex could not),[79] social expectations may heavily influence perceptions of civil partnerships,[80] which contribute to the hierarchical organisation of legally recognised relationships, upholding their mononormative[81] expectations.

Heterosexual civil partnerships breaking down the hierarchy

In analysing the narratives and lived experiences of LGBTQ+ participants, particularly those who have experienced the process of registering their partnership, it becomes possible to conceptualise a hierarchy of relationship recognition with marriage represented as encompassing the natural conjugal whole, and civil partnerships as a lesser institution. The hierarchy which has been argued to exist, through social and legal structures that construct civil partnerships as lesser and uphold marriage as the greater institution, has significant social implications. This hierarchy may lead to pressure to marry due to hegemonic discourse and the exclusion of non-dyadic relationships that upholds and sustains dominant expectations of domesticity, monogamy, and procreation. Reforming relationship recognition, following the *Steinfeld* declaration of incompatibility, will provide a means of establishing more effective, substantive equality that may disturb such a focus and allow the pursuit of different forms of legally recognised relationships.

This comes at a time when the government is currently on course to legislate for heterosexual civil partnerships which goes some way to achieving this goal.

Following the *Steinfeld* decision and the passage of the Civil Partnerships, Marriages and Deaths (Registration, Etc) Bill into an Act, the Parliament at Westminster has the opportunity to disestablish the hierarchy in the creation of equal standards of relationship recognition. By opening up civil partnerships to different-sex couples, the lesser form of relationship recognition, which is currently restricted only to same-sex couples, will no longer be 'lesser.' In allowing different-sex and same-sex couples to enter into such partnerships, the ideation of marriage as the ultimate form of registered partnership will be diminished, in order to establish a more equal and equitable system of recognition. The sexual hierarchy will be diminished, as heterosexual couples are provided with the choice that same-sex couples have had for some time: the ability to choose between marriage and civil partnerships. Such a choice will allow for pluralised forms of relationship recognition that facilities equality in opportunity for couples.

In creating two systems of relationship recognition that are open to all coupled relationships, the centrality of heterosexuality is removed from marriage, and the homosexual nature of civil partnerships would also be removed. By doing so, the maintenance of binary divisions based on sexuality would be disestablished and would therefore diminish the centrality of marriage as a patriarchal, normative institution and allow for the growth of civil partnerships. Following the Equal Civil Partnerships campaign and the publicised *Steinfield* decision, the law has the opportunity to create equal standards of relationship recognition, following society's influence which demonstrates the significance of recognised relationships moving away from the historic reliance on marriage as a social and legal organiser.[82] Giving choice to all those who wish to recognise their coupled relationship creates an opportunity to level the hierarchy; making both marriage and civil partnerships are accessible to all would remove the hierarchical nature of marriage as an exclusive institution. This accessibility will deconstruct the hierarchy, allowing free choice of relationship recognition that is not based on identity or sexual partner, allowing for the further pluralisation of relationship recognition.

While the *Steinfeld* judgment and the future introduction of different-sex civil partnerships would begin to diminish the sexual hierarchy, the hierarchy would continue to exist. This exclusion is predicated on the dyadic focus of relationship recognition, further excluding those from non-normative relationships, such as the exclusion of other familial[83] or polyamorous and non-monogamous relationships that may encompass homoradical sexuality, deviating from normative constructions of sexuality. The hierarchy thus stigmatises those who do not marry,[84] and does little to further the rights of those cohabiting. Further reform should therefore focus on destabilising the sexual hierarchy and aim to improve the status of those who do not conform to normative relationship forms.

Conclusion

Parliament is presented with a chance to develop the ways in which law interacts with and regulates sexuality via relationship recognition, offering a new narrative regarding marriage and civil partnerships that should ultimately lead to greater acceptance and recognition of the diversification of relationship recognition. Equal access to different institutions allows for difference and diversity in terms of recognition, but maintains equal access and opportunity, and further eradicates the superiority of marriage in society. In analysing the narratives provided in the empirical data, it has become possible to conceptualise and establish a hierarchy of relationship recognition. Given the historical, social, and legal value of marriage, and the ideation that stems from same-sex marriage, civil partnerships – as they were – fell to the bottom of the hierarchy. However, the opening of civil partnerships to different-sex couples, and the legislation for same-sex marriage in Northern Ireland,[85] will go further to balance out this hierarchy as relationship recognition becomes diversified, allowing for equality of opportunity to be achieved.

Notes

1 Civil Partnership Act 2004 (CPA 2004), s1.
2 Anne Barlow, Simon Duncan and Grace James, *Cohabitation, Marriage and the Law* (Hart Publishing 2005) 49.
3 *Wilkinson v Kitzinger* (2006) EWHC 2022 (Fam) [6] (Sir Mark Potter P).
4 'This change in the law helps protect the interests of opposite-sex couples who want to commit, want to formalise their relationship but don't necessarily want to get married. As Home Secretary, I was proud to sponsor the legislation that created equal marriage. Now, by extending civil partnerships, we are making sure that all couples, be they same-sex or opposite-sex, are given the same choices in life.': Theresa May in Joe Murphy, 'Straight Couples to Be Allowed to Enter Civil Partnerships, Theresa May Reveals' *Evening Standard* (London, 2 October 2018).
5 *R (Steinfeld and Keidan) v Secretary of State for International Development* (2018) UKSC 32.
6 Judith Butler, *Gender Trouble: Feminism and the Subversion of Identity* (2nd edn, Routledge 1999) 187.
7 Michel Foucault, *The History of Sexuality: An Introduction* (1st edn, Vintage Books 1978).
8 Butler (n 6) 187.
9 Gayle Rubin, 'Thinking Sex: Notes for a Radical Theory of the Politics of Sexuality' in Carole S Vance (ed), *Pleasure and Danger: Exploring Female Sexuality* (Routledge 1984) 151; María Do Mar Castro Varela, Nikita Dhawan and Antke Engel, 'Hegemony and Heteronormativity: Revisiting "The Political" in Queer Politics' in María Do Mar Castro Varela, Nikita Dhawan and Antke Engel (eds), *Hegemony and Heteronormativity: Revisiting 'The Political' in Queer Politics* (Ashgate 2011).
10 Lisa Duggan, 'The New Homonormativity: The Sexual Politics of Neoliberalism' in Dana Nelson and Russ Castronovo (eds), *Materializing Democracy: Toward a Revitalized Cultural Politics* (Duke University Press 2002) 178.
11 Rubin (n 9) 151.

12 Lisa Duggan, *The Twilight of Equality? Neoliberalism, Cultural Politics and the Attack on Democracy* (Beacon Press 2003).
13 See Rubin (n 9).
14 Kenneth McK Norrie, 'The Changing Concept of "Family" and Challenges for Family Law in Scotland' in Jens Scherpe (ed), *European Family Law* (Edward Elgar 2016) 238.
15 The Netherlands and Belgium in 2001 and 2003, respectively.
16 Robert Wintemute, 'Civil Partnership and Discrimination in *R (Steinfeld) v Secretary of State for Education*: Should the Civil Partnership Act 2004 Be Extended to Different-Sex Couples or Repealed?' (2016) *Child and Family Law Quarterly* 265.
17 HL Deb 22 April 2004, vol 660, col 405 (Baroness O'Cathain).
18 Carl Stychin, '"Las Vegas Is Not Where We Are": Queer Readings of the Civil Partnership Act' (2006) 25 *Political Geography* 899, 902.
19 There has been a slight, continual rise in civil partnerships in the last few years, but the rate has still faced a significant decline since 2013 and is marginal compared to marriage. On average, there are around 1,000 civil partnerships a year, and 7,000 same-sex marriages. Office for National Statistics, 'Marriages in England and Wales' (2016).
20 CPA 2004, s1.
21 Ibid., s3.
22 Defined as 'ordinary and complete' in *D v A* (1845) 1 Rob Ecc 279, which was further qualified as penetrative penile-vaginal sexual intercourse.
23 CPA 2004, s50.
24 Carl Stychin, 'Not (Quite) A Horse and Carriage: The Civil Partnership Act 2004' (2006) 14 *Feminist Legal Studies* 79.
25 Sarah Beresford, 'We're All Same (Sex) Now? Lesbian (Same) Sex; Consummation; Adultery and Marriage' (2016) *Journal of GLBT Family Studies* 1.
26 Chris Ashford, Alexander Maine and Giuseppe Zago, 'Normative Behaviour, Moral Boundaries, and the State' in Chris Ashford and Alexander Maine(eds), *Research Handbook on Gender, Sexuality and Law* (Forthcoming Edward Elgar 2020).
27 Notably, marriage's significance was emphasised in the *Wilkinson v Kitzinger* case: 'I want my marriage, and same-sex marriages more generally, to be recognised in Britain, and elsewhere, because I want to be able to refer to Celia as my wife and have that immediately and unproblematically understood as meaning that she is my life-partner with all the connotations and social consequences that using the term "wife" or "husband" has for a heterosexual couple. . . . This symbolic status of marriage as a fundamental social institution is, in many ways, as important as its formal legal status. It provides for social recognition of key relationships, and to have our relationship denied that symbolic status devalues it relative to the relationships of heterosexual couples.': (n 3) para 5.
28 Nicola Barker, *Not the Marrying Kind: A Feminist Critique of Same-Sex Marriage* (Palgrave Macmillan 2013); Rosemary Auchmuty, 'Same-Sex Marriage Revived: Feminist Critique and Legal Strategy' (2004) 14 *Feminism and Psychology* 101; Duggan (n 10).
29 The ex-Prime Minister, David Cameron, noted this as one of his favorite achievements in office: HC Deb 13 July 2016, vol 613, col 286.
30 Office for National Statistics, 'Marriages in England and Wales: 2015' (2018).
31 Martha Nussbaum, 'A Right to Marry?' (2010) 98 *California Law Review* 667.
32 Frances Hamilton, 'Strategies to Achieve Same-Sex Marriage and the Method of Incrementalist Change' (2016) 25 *Florida Journal of Transnational Law and Policy* 121.

33 Diane Richardson, 'Desiring Sameness? The Rise of a Neoliberal Politics of Normalisation' (2005) 37 *Antipodes* 519.
34 Rubin (n 9).
35 For instance, see *Burden v United Kingdom* App No. 13378/05 (ECtHR, 29 April 2008). In this case, a pair of elderly sisters sought to have the law changed regarding civil partnerships, in order to have their own caring relationship recognised in order to avoid paying inheritance tax. Kenneth McK Norrie, 'Inheritance Tax, Civil Partnership and the Rights of Spinster Sisters' (2008) 23 *Edinburgh Law Review* 438; Nancy Polikoff, 'Law That Values All Families: Beyond (Straight and Gay) Marriage' (2009) 22 *Journal of the American Academy of Matrimonial Lawyers* 85.
36 Samuel Fulli-Lemaire, 'Legal Recognition of Same-Sex Relationships in Central Europe: Steady Progress' in Katharina Boele-Woelki and Angelika Fuchs (eds), *Same-Sex Relationships and Beyond* (3rd edn, Intersentia 2017) 27.
37 Barlow, Duncan and James (n 2) 49.
38 'Equal Civil Partnerships' <http://equalcivilpartnerships.org.uk> accessed 28 November 2018.
39 *Steinfeld* (n 5).
40 CPA 2004, s 1.
41 Ibid., s 3(a).
42 *Schalk and Kopf v Austria* App No. 30141/04 (ECtHR, 24 June 2010).
43 *Oliari and Others v Italy* App Nos. 18766/11 and 36030/11 (ECtHR, 21 July 2015).
44 Eingetragene Partnerschaft-Gesetz 2009.
45 *Steinfeld* (n 5) 35 (Lord Kerr SCJ).
46 Ibid., 45.
47 Ibid., 35.
48 Ibid.
49 *Vallianatos v Greece* App Nos. 29381/09 and 32684/09 (ECtHR, 7 November 2013).
50 *Steinfeld* (n 5) 36 (Lord Kerr SCJ).
51 Ibid., 37.
52 Ibid., 49.
53 Women and Equality Unit, *Responses to Civil Partnerships: A Framework for the Legal Recognition of Same-Sex Couples* (2003) 19.
54 An Act to make provision about the registration of marriage, to make provision for the extension of civil partnerships to couples not of the same sex, to make provision for a report on the registration of pregnancy loss, to make provision about the investigation of still-births, and for connected purposes.
55 Civil Partnerships, Marriages and Deaths (Registration, Etc) Act 2019, s2.
56 Butler (n 6) 187; Lauren Berlant and Michael Warner, 'Sex in Public' (1998) 24 *Critical Inquiry* 547–548; Michael Warner, *The Trouble with Normal: Sex, Politics, and the Ethics of Queer Life* (2nd edn, Harvard University Press 2000).
57 Bernadette Hayes and John Nagle, 'Ethnonationalism and Attitudes Towards Same-Sex Marriage and Abortion in Northern Ireland' (2018) *International Political Science Review* 1; Jocelyn Evans and Jonathan Tonge, 'Partisan and Religious Drivers of Moral Conservatism: Same-Sex Marriage and Abortion in Northern Ireland' (2018) 24 *Party Politics* 335; Fulli-Lemaire (n 36) 30.
58 ONS (n 30).
59 Denise Levy and Corey Johnson, 'What Does the Q Mean? Including Queer Voices in Qualitative Research' (2011) 11 *Qualitative Social Work* 134.

60 Catherine Pope and Nick Mays, 'Qualitative Research: Reaching the Parts Other Methods Cannot Reach: An Introduction to Qualitative Methods in Health and Health Services Research' (1995) 311 *British Medical Journal* 4.
61 Brian Heaphy, Carol Smart and Anna Einarsdottir, *Same-Sex Marriages: New Generations, New Relationships* (Palgrave Macmillan 2013) 5.
62 Amy Hequembourg and Jorge Arditi, 'Fractured Resistances: The Debate Over Assimilationism Among Gays and Lesbians in the United States' (1999) 40 *The Sociological Quarterly* 667.
63 Hamilton (n 32).
64 Rubin (n 9).
65 Ken Plummer, 'Symbolic Interactionism and the Forms of Homosexuality' in Steven Seidman (ed), *Queer Theory/Sociology* (Blackwell 1996) 81.
66 Ibid.
67 Ibid.
68 Richardson (n 33).
69 Carl Stychin, 'Couplings: Civil Partnerships in the United Kingdom' (2005) 8 *New York City Law Review* 571.
70 Jeffrey Weeks, Brian Heaphy and Catherine Donovan, *Same Sex Intimacies: Families of Choice and Other Life Experiments* (Routledge 2001) 40.
71 Hequembourq and Arditi (n 62).
72 Stychin (n 69).
73 Clare Chambers, *Against Marriage: An Egalitarian Defence of the Marriage-Free State* (Oxford University Press 2017).
74 Nicola Barker, 'Sex and the Civil Partnership Act: The Future of (Non) Conjugality?' (2006) 14 *Feminist Legal Studies* 241; Stychin (n 24); Brian Heaphy, Catherine Donovan and Jeffrey Weeks, 'A Different Affair? Openness and Non-monogamy in Same Sex Relationships' in Jean Duncombe and others (eds), *The State of Affairs: Explorations in Infidelity and Commitment* (Routledge 2014); Lucy Crompton, 'Where's the Sex in Same-Sex Marriage?' (2013) 43 *Family Law* 564; Beresford (n 25).
75 Michael Warner, 'Homo-Narcissism; or, Heterosexuality' in Joseph Boone and Michael Cadden (eds), *Engendering Men* (Routledge 1990).
76 Kristoff Bonello and Malcolm Cross, 'Gay Monogamy: I Love You but I Can't Have Sex with Only You' (2009) 57 *Journal of Homosexuality* 117.
77 Heaphy, Donovan and Weeks (n 74) 168.
78 Warner (n 56) 96.
79 Provided in Schedule 4(3) Marriage (Same-Sex Couples) Act 2013, which amends section 12 of the Matrimonial Causes Act 1973 to state that consummation requirements and adultery do not apply to same-sex couples. Matrimonial Causes Act 1973, s12; *Dennis v Dennis* (1995) 2 All ER 51; Beresford (n 25); Crompton (n 74).
80 Michael Lasala, 'Monogamy of the Heart' (2004) 17 *Journal of Gay & Lesbian Social Services* 21.
81 Robin Bauer, 'Non-Monogamy in Queer BDSM Communities: Putting the Sex Back into Alternative Relationship Practices and Discourse' in Meg Barker and Darren Langdridge (eds), *Understanding Non-Monogamies* (Routledge 2010) 144.
82 Barker (n 28); Chambers (n 73).
83 *Burden* (n 35); Mck Norrie (n 35); Polikoff (n 35).
84 Michael Warner, 'Beyond Gay Marriage' in Wendy Brown and Janet Halley (eds), *Left Legalism/Left Critique* (Duke University Press 2002) 260; Janet Halley, 'Recognition, Rights, Regulation, Normalisation: Rhetorics of

Justification in the Same-Sex Marriage Debate' in Robert Wintermute and Mads Andenaes (eds), *Legal Recognition of Same-Sex Partnerships* (Hart Publishing 2001) 99.

85 Legalisation of same-sex marriage will take place automatically in Northern Ireland on 21 October 2019, unless the Northern Ireland devolved government no longer remains suspended following the Northern Ireland (Executive Formation) Bill 2017–19.

References

Primary sources

Burden v United Kingdom App No. 13378/05 (ECtHR, 29 April 2008).
Civil Partnership Act 2004.
Civil Partnerships, Marriages and Deaths (Registration, etc) Act 2019.
D v A (1845) 1 Rob Ecc 279.
Dennis v Dennis (1995) 2 All ER 51
Eingetragene Partnerschaft-Gesetz 2009 (Austria).
Marriage Act 1949.
Marriage (Same-Sex Couples) Act 2013.
Matrimonial Causes Act 1973.
Northern Ireland (Executive Formation) Bill 2017–19.
Oliari and Others v Italy App Nos. 18766/11 and 36030/11 (ECtHR, 21 July 2015).
R (Steinfeld and Keidan) v Secretary of State for International Development (2018) UKSC 32.
Schalk and Kopf v Austria App No. 30141/04 (ECtHR, 24 June 2010).
Vallianatos v Greece App Nos. 29381/09 and 32684/09 (ECtHR, 7 November 2013).
Wilkinson v Kitzinger (2006) EWHC 2022 (Fam).

Secondary sources

Ashford C, Maine A and Zago G, 'Normative Behaviour, Moral Boundaries, and the State' in Ashford C and Maine A (eds), *Research Handbook on Gender, Sexuality and Law* (Forthcoming Edward Elgar 2020).

Auchmuty R, 'Same-Sex Marriage Revived: Feminist Critique and Legal Strategy' (2004) 14 *Feminism and Psychology* 101.

Barker N, 'Sex and the Civil Partnership Act: The Future of (Non) Conjugality?' (2006) 14 *Feminist Legal Studies* 241.

———, *Not the Marrying Kind: A Feminist Critique of Same-Sex Marriage* (Palgrave Macmillan 2013).

Barlow A, Duncan S and James G, *Cohabitation, Marriage and the Law* (Hart Publishing 2005).

Bauer R, 'Non-Monogamy in Queer BDSM Communities: Putting the Sex Back into Alternative Relationship Practices and Discourse' in Barker M and Langdridge D (eds), *Understanding Non-Monogamies* (Routledge 2010).

Beresford S, 'We're All Same (Sex) Now? Lesbian (Same) Sex; Consummation; Adultery and Marriage' (2016) *Journal of GLBT Family Studies* 1.

Berlant L and Warner M, 'Sex in Public' (1998) 24 *Critical Inquiry* 547.
Bonello K and Cross M, 'Gay Monogamy: I Love You but I Can't Have Sex with Only You' (2009) 57 *Journal of Homosexuality* 117.
Butler J, *Gender Trouble: Feminism and the Subversion of Identity* (2nd edn, Routledge 1999).
Chambers C, *Against Marriage: An Egalitarian Defence of the Marriage-Free State* (Oxford University Press 2017).
Crompton L, 'Where's the Sex in Same-Sex Marriage?' (2013) 43 *Family Law* 564.
Do Mar Castro Varela M, Dhawan N and Engel A, 'Hegemony and Heteronormativity: Revisiting "The Political" in Queer Politics' in Do Mar Castro Varela M, Dhawan N and Engel A (eds), *Hegemony and Heteronormativity: Revisiting 'The Political' in Queer Politics* (Ashgate 2011).
Duggan L, 'The New Homonormativity: The Sexual Politics of Neoliberalism' in Nelson D and Castronovo R (eds), *Materializing Democracy: Toward a Revitalized Cultural Politics* (Duke University Press 2002).
———, *The Twilight of Equality? Neoliberalism, Cultural Politics and the Attack on Democracy* (Beacon Press 2003).
Evans J and Tonge J, 'Partisan and Religious Drivers of Moral Conservatism: Same-Sex Marriage and Abortion in Northern Ireland' (2018) 24 *Party Politics* 335.
Foucault M, *The History of Sexuality: An Introduction* (1st edn, Vintage Books 1978).
Fulli-Lemaire S, 'Legal Recognition of Same-Sex Relationships in Central Europe: Steady Progress' in Boele-Woelki K and Fuchs A (eds), *Same-Sex Relationships and Beyond* (3rd edn, Intersentia 2017).
Halley J, 'Recognition, Rights, Regulation, Normalisation: Rhetorics of Justification in the Same-Sex Marriage Debate' in Wintermute R and Andenaes M (eds), *Legal Recognition of Same-Sex Partnerships* (Hart Publishing 2001).
Hamilton F, 'Strategies to Achieve Same-Sex Marriage and the Method of Incrementalist Change' (2016) 25 *Florida Journal of Transnational Law and Policy* 121.
Hayes B and Nagle J, 'Ethnonationalism and Attitudes Towards Same-Sex Marriage and Abortion in Northern Ireland' (2018) *International Political Science Review* 1.
HC Deb 13 July 2016, vol 613, col 286.
Heaphy B, Donovan C and Weeks J, 'A Different Affair? Openness and Nonmonogamy in Same Sex Relationships' in Duncombe J and others (eds), *The State of Affairs: Explorations in Infidelity and Commitment* (Routledge 2014).
Heaphy B, Smart C and Einarsdottir A, *Same-Sex Marriages: New Generations, New Relationships* (Palgrave Macmillan 2013).
Hequembourg A and Arditi J, 'Fractured Resistances: The Debate Over Assimilationism Among Gays and Lesbians in the United States' (1999) 40 *The Sociological Quarterly* 667.
HL Deb 22 April 2004, vol 660, col 405.
Lasala M, 'Monogamy of the Heart' (2004) 17 *Journal of Gay & Lesbian Social Services* 21.
Levy D and Johnson C, 'What Does the Q mean? Including Queer Voices in Qualitative Research' (2011) 11 *Qualitative Social Work* 134.
McK Norrie K, 'Inheritance Tax, Civil Partnership and the Rights of Spinster Sisters' (2008) 23 *Edinburgh Law Review* 438.
———, 'The Changing Concept of "Family" and Challenges for Family Law in Scotland' in Scherpe J (ed), *European Family Law* (Edward Elgar 2016).

Murphy J, 'Straight Couples to Be Allowed to Enter Civil Partnerships, Theresa May Reveals' *Evening Standard* (London, 2 October 2018).

Nussbaum M, 'A Right to Marry?' (2010) 98 *California Law Review* 667.

Office for National Statistics, *Marriages in England and Wales* (2016).

———, *Marriages in England and Wales: 2015* (2018).

Plummer K, 'Symbolic Interactionism and the Forms of Homosexuality' in Seidman S (ed), *Queer Theory/Sociology* (Blackwell 1996).

Polikoff N, 'Law That Values All Families: Beyond (Straight and Gay) Marriage' (2009) 22 *Journal of the American Academy of Matrimonial Lawyers* 85.

Pope C and Mays N, 'Qualitative Research: Reaching the Parts Other Methods Cannot Reach: An Introduction to Qualitative Methods in Health and Health Services Research' (1995) 311 *British Medical Journal* 4.

Richardson D, 'Desiring Sameness? The Rise of a Neoliberal Politics of Normalisation' (2005) 37 *Antipodes* 519.

Rubin G, 'Thinking Sex: Notes for a Radical Theory of the Politics of Sexuality' in Vance CS (ed), *Pleasure and Danger: Exploring Female Sexuality* (Routledge 1984).

Stychin C, 'Couplings: Civil Partnerships in the United Kingdom' (2005) 8 *New York City Law Review* 571.

———, ' "Las Vegas Is Not Where We Are": Queer Readings of the Civil Partnership Act' (2006) 25 *Political Geography* 899.

———, 'Not (Quite) A Horse and Carriage: The Civil Partnership Act 2004' (2006) 14 *Feminist Legal Studies* 79.

Warner M, 'Homo-Narcissism; or, Heterosexuality' in Boone J and Cadden M (eds), *Engendering Men* (Routledge 1990).

———, *The Trouble with Normal: Sex, Politics, and the Ethics of Queer Life* (2nd edn, Harvard University Press 2000).

———, 'Beyond Gay Marriage' in Brown W and Halley J (eds), *Left Legalism/Left Critique* (Duke University Press 2002).

Weeks J, Heaphy B and Donovan C, *Same Sex Intimacies: Families of Choice and Other Life Experiments* (Routledge 2001).

Wintemute R, 'Civil Partnership and Discrimination in *R (Steinfeld) v Secretary of State for Education*: Should the Civil Partnership Act 2004 Be Extended to Different-Sex Couples or Repealed?' (2016) *Child and Family Law Quarterly* 265.

Women and Equality Unit, *Responses to Civil Partnerships: A Framework for the Legal Recognition of Same-Sex Couples* (2003).

Part 5

The heteronormative underpinnings of same-sex marriage

Chapter 12

Repackaged goods?

Interrogating the heteronormative underpinnings of marriage

Fergus Ryan

One of the most striking reforms in family law in the past half-century has been the extension of marriage to same-sex couples in several jurisdictions. In much of Western and Northern Europe, North and South America, South Africa, Australia, and New Zealand, states have overturned the well-worn legal understanding of marriage as the union of one man and one woman in favour of a model that opens marriage up to same-sex couples, as well.[1] Many jurisdictions have also adopted laws extending to unmarried same-sex couples in registered unions (such as civil partnerships, registered partnerships, and civil unions) various rights and obligations once reserved exclusively to marriage.[2] These laws give rise to a variety of different rights and obligations depending on the jurisdiction. Some of these regimes closely mirror marriage, while others are less extensive.

Marriage is now open to same-sex couples in England and Wales,[3] Scotland,[4] and the Republic of Ireland[5] (hereinafter Ireland). Civil partnership is also open to same-sex couples in the United Kingdom (UK).[6] By the end of 2019, in England and Wales, civil partnership should be open to opposite-sex couples, too.[7] In Ireland, between 2011 and 2016, same-sex couples could enter into civil partnerships. Since May 2016, however, it has not been possible for couples to form *new* civil partnerships in Ireland. Civil partnerships entered into before that date are still legally recognized, but civil partnership is now closed to new entrants. In Northern Ireland, which until very recently confined marriage to opposite-sex couples,[8] civil partnership was previously the sole means of formalising a union of a same-sex couple. The Northern Ireland (Executive Formation etc) Act 2019 (UK), however, mandated the extension of marriage to same-sex couples and of civil partnership to opposite-sex couples as the Northern Ireland Executive was not restored by 21 October 2019.

These marriage and civil partnership laws generally grant same-sex couples in such unions, to varying extents, rights and remedies formulated in the context of opposite-sex marriage. In fashioning civil partnership and in extending marriage, legislators have paid little regard to whether these regulatory models are best suited to addressing the dynamics of same-sex relationships and the needs of LGBTQ+ people.[9] The argument in this chapter is that, despite the extension of marriage to same-sex couples, marriage and civil partnership law remain overwhelmingly heteronormative in character.[10] While the law now allows same-sex couples to marry, its substance still presupposes that heterosexuality is the norm, the natural, default sexual orientation, the preferred way of being. Marriage law has evolved over centuries solely with a heterosexual model of family life in mind. Thus, although marriage and similar unions are now available to same-sex couples in many jurisdictions, the norms that regulate these unions have rarely been explicitly designed with same-sex couples in mind.

A classic example of this tendency arises in relation to laws that govern the sexual dimensions of marriage. In Ireland, for instance, laws that address sexual conduct in the context of marriage still implicitly presuppose that the spouses are of the opposite sex and heterosexual. Irish case law on the capacity to form and sustain a normal marriage makes a similar assumption, positing that a homosexual orientation may negate such capacity.[11] The purpose of this chapter is to examine these laws, with the broader aim of illustrating how marriage law is still fundamentally heteronormative, having been shaped with opposite-sex couples in mind. Given the former exclusion of same-sex couples from marriage, it is understandable that this should be so. Nonetheless, it poses a challenge to modern policy makers to address the diverse needs, expectations, and experiences of different couples and to cater in our laws to greater diversity within modern family life.

The evolution of legal recognition of same-sex couples

The introduction of marriage for same-sex couples in Ireland was the culmination of an extraordinary journey.[12] Victorian-era laws banning male homosexual sexual acts, even between consenting adults and in private, remained on the statute books until 1993.[13] Although once profoundly socially conservative, by the early 1990s, Irish attitudes to and laws relating to the LGBTQ+ community had begun to improve. From the late 1980s onwards, Ireland adopted various progressive policies and laws banning sexual orientation discrimination.[14] As late as the mid-2000s, however, the state remained deeply reticent about legal recognition of same-sex couples. This, in part, reflected the constitutionally embedded preference for the marital family, and a general reluctance to provide significant recognition for families outside marriage.[15]

The passage of the Civil Partnership and Certain Rights and Obligations of Cohabitants Act 2010 marked a notable turning point.[16] The Act gave same-sex couples[17] access to a significant registered status – that of civil partnership. It confers on registered civil partners substantial rights and obligations equivalent in most respects to those that arise on marriage. (Separately, the Act grants limited rights to cohabitants, both same-sex and opposite-sex.[18])

With the passage of time, the legal gaps that formerly existed between civil partnership and marriage have narrowed. For instance, while the 2010 Act *as originally enacted* generally avoided conferring additional rights or duties in respect to children, the Children and Family Relationships Act 2015 and the Adoption (Amendment) Act 2017 have largely remedied this gap.[19] There are, however, still some differences between marriage and civil partnership. The key distinction is that, unlike marriage, the household based on civil partnership (like any household not based on marriage) does not enjoy constitutional protection as a 'family' under Art.41 of the Irish Constitution.

Yet, in most other respects, the Irish State largely modelled civil partnership on marriage law. Most of the legislative provisions in the 2010 Act mirror (often identically) like provisions that already applied to marriage. The state put little effort into fashioning a bespoke regime for civil partners. Little thought was devoted to the possibility that the rules that addressed the position of married opposite-sex couples might not be well-tailored to the dynamics of same-sex relationships. The assumption underpinning the 2010 Act is that same-sex couples are, in the main, substantially like opposite-sex couples, a worthy signal of equality, but one that arguably demands assimilation to straight norms as a precondition for legal recognition. Indeed, many early critiques of civil partnership (including those by the present author) assessed its worth based on how similar it was to marriage; this benchmarking generally presupposed that similarity with marriage was a positive, difference from marriage a negative.[20]

The fact that civil partnership was never tailored to the specific needs of same-sex couples is implicitly confirmed by the UK Supreme Court decision in *Steinfeld and Keidan v Secretary of State for International Development*.[21] The Supreme Court ruled that the exclusion of opposite-sex couples from civil partnership in England and Wales was incompatible with Arts. 14 and 8 of the European Convention on Human Rights. In light of this decision, the UK Parliament has mandated the government to extend civil partnership to opposite-sex couples in England and Wales by the end of 2019.[22]

In Ireland, by contrast, the introduction of marriage for same-sex couples effectively closed off civil partnership to new entrants.[23] In 2015, the Thirty-fourth Amendment to the Constitution comfortably passed in a referendum approving the insertion of Art.41.4 into the Constitution. It stipulates, "Marriage may be contracted in accordance with law by two persons without distinction as to their sex." The Marriage Act 2015 thus removed the impediment to the marriage of same-sex couples, but simultaneously closed off the possibility of couples forming new civil partnerships (subject to transitional provisions that expired in May 2016). The government argued that allowing couples to choose between civil partnership and marriage would undermine constitutional safeguards for marriage, as some couples may favour civil partnership over marriage.[24] While existing civil partners who wish to remain in a previously formed civil partnership may do so indefinitely (civil partnerships entered into before May 2016 are still legally recognised), no couples may enter new civil partnerships with effect from May 2016.[25] Couples in an existing civil partnership with each other may marry each other, thus terminating their civil partnership.[26] As a result, the number of civil partners in Ireland is likely to decline significantly over time.

Adultery[27]

In England and Wales, as of September 2019, a divorce is available based on a single ground of irretrievable breakdown of marriage that the applicant must prove by demonstrating to the satisfaction of the court the existence of at least one of five facts.[28] One of these facts is that the respondent (the person against whom the divorce is sought) has committed adultery and the petitioner finds it intolerable to live with the respondent[29] (though it is not necessary to establish that this latter sentiment is necessarily due to the adultery.[30]) The remaining facts centre on the respondent's behaviour and desertion, as well as the fact of living apart (for two years, if both parties consent to the divorce; otherwise for five years). Notably, the Divorce, Dissolution and Separation Bill 2017–2019 proposed to remove the requirement to establish these facts and sought to adopt an entirely process-based, no-fault regime for divorce.[31]

In Ireland, by contrast, adultery is not a ground for divorce, the latter being based solely on no-fault conditions.[32] A court may take conduct into account in granting remedies following divorce where it would be unjust to ignore such conduct; nonetheless, the Irish courts generally do not consider incidents of adultery as sufficiently serious to merit attention in that context.[33] Adultery is, however, one of six alternative grounds for judicial separation in Ireland.[34]

Notably, a spouse cannot rely on his or her own adultery. Moreover, where spouses have lived with each other for a specified minimum period[35] after the applicant discovered the adultery, the applicant may not plead the adultery ground.[36] Ongoing cohabitation after the applicant's discovery of the act implies, the law suggests, that the parties have put the affair behind them.

Insofar as civil partners are concerned, adultery is legally irrelevant. In Ireland, judicial separation is not available to civil partners; hence the issue of adultery does not arise in this context. In the UK, the regime for civil partnership dissolution mirrors that for divorce in almost all respects, save that the fact of adultery is not a basis for dissolution of a civil partnership. Indeed, civil partnership law in both states tends generally to avoid addressing sexual matters.[37]

What does adultery mean in this context?

In English and Welsh law, adultery is understood to be an act of voluntary sexual intercourse between two people of the opposite sex, one or both of whom is married but not to the other participant.[38] The legal position is largely the same in Irish law. In respect of Ireland, Shatter states that while "[t]he commission of adultery does not require the complete act of sexual intercourse . . . there must be some penetration of the female vagina by the male organ."[39] In practice, a court may infer the fact of adultery from circumstances.[40]

The English case of *Dennis v Dennis*[41] establishes that, for adultery to arise, there must be some penetration by the male organ of the female organ. In that case, Singleton LJ remarked:

> I do not think that it can be said that adultery is proved unless there be some penetration. It is not necessary that the complete act of sexual intercourse should take place. If there is penetration by the man of the woman, adultery may be found, but if there is no more than an attempt, I do not think that a finding of adultery would be right.[42]

In *Dennis*, according to Morris LJ, "there was no penetration at all; there was therefore no sexual intercourse, and therefore no adultery."[43] In *Sapsford v Sapsford and Furtado*, Karminski J suggested that adultery requires at least some penetration involving "the introduction of the male organ into the female."[44] He continued, "[m]utual intercourse, in my view, means that there has to be intercourse in which both the man and the woman play what may be described as their normal role."[45]

In *MacLennan v MacLennan*, in the Scottish Court of Session, Lord Wheatley summarised the position in English law:[46]

1 For adultery to be committed there must be the two parties physically present and engaging in the sexual act at the same time.
2 To constitute the sexual act there must be an act of union involving some degree of penetration of the female organ by the male organ.
3 It is not a necessary concomitant of adultery that male seed should be deposited in the female's ovum.
4 The placing of the male seed in the female ovum need not necessarily result from the sexual act, and if it does not, but is placed there by some other means, there is no sexual intercourse.[47]

In that case, the Court concluded that artificial insemination using the sperm of a man other than the woman's husband was not adultery (though see *contra* the Canadian case of *Orford v Orford*).[48] A New Brunswick, Canada, decision suggests that bestiality does not constitute adultery.[49] In *Corbett v Corbett*, Ormrod J observed that "neither oral intercourse with a woman nor mutual masturbation will afford the wife the remedy of adultery."[50] By analogy with common law rape and the old offence of unlawful carnal knowledge, it appears that anal intercourse does not constitute adultery in this context.[51]

What happens when a same-sex married spouse engages in infidelity?

It is widely accepted in both the UK and Ireland that an extra-marital sexual liaison involving two persons of the same sex is not, as a matter of law, adultery.[52]

In relation to marriage, section 1(6) of the Matrimonial Causes Act 1973 makes it clear in the context of English and Welsh divorce law that "Only conduct between the respondent and a person of the opposite sex may constitute adultery for the purposes of this section." This leaves open the possibility that a spouse in a same-sex marriage may be found to have engaged in adultery, but it is only adultery if the other participant in the act is of the *opposite sex*. Section 1(3A) of the Divorce (Scotland) Act 1976 stipulates "For the avoidance of doubt, in relation to marriage between persons of the same sex, adultery has the same meaning as it has in relation to marriage between persons of different sexes." This seems to arrive at the same position as in English law; while a spouse in a same-sex marriage may be found to have committed adultery, only sexual intercourse with a person of the opposite sex constitutes adultery.

In Ireland, the Marriage Act 2015 is silent on the point, and made no amendment to judicial separation legislation. It is nonetheless likely that the position in Irish law is effectively the same as that in England and Wales. Certainly prior to the extension of marriage to same-sex couples, the understanding of adultery did not embrace infidelity with a person of the same sex. In Irish law, Shatter asserts, adultery does not arise when there is sexual activity between persons of the same sex.[53] Judicial separation legislation uses the gender-neutral term 'spouse' and thus applies equally to same-sex and opposite-sex spouses. Thus, in Irish law it appears that while a spouse in a marriage with a person of the same sex may be found to have engaged in adultery, this will only arise where the other party to the act is of the opposite sex.[54]

If this is indeed the case, a most curious situation arises. While a once-off casual act of sexual intercourse between a husband and a woman who is not his wife will expose the husband to a claim of adultery, a long-lasting, passionate affair between a husband and a man to whom he is not married will not. Admittedly, the man's aggrieved spouse could claim that the homosexual affair constitutes behaviour such that it is unreasonable to expect the petitioner to keep living with the respondent. This is a fact allowing divorce in England and Wales,[55] and is a ground for judicial separation in Ireland.[56] Nonetheless, while the former case will be judicially labelled with the weighty stigma of the title 'adultery,' the latter is lumped in with miscellaneous acts of intolerable conduct. The unmistakable implication is that the law regards infidelity with a person of the same sex as a less serious and pressing concern. An aggrieved spouse may justifiably condemn the legal sophistry that says that her husband's dalliance with a woman is adultery while a homosexual affair is simply behaviour that justifies her in leaving him, but not adultery in law. In the latter case, the emotional toll is at least as serious as in the case of infidelity with a person of the opposite sex.

A more expansive view?

In some jurisdictions, legislators and judges have expanded the definition of adultery, in some cases to include homosexual acts.[57] It is, of course, possible that the Irish courts, should the point arise, may also take a more expansive view based on the passage of the constitutional amendment permitting marriage by couples of the same sex. An Irish judge might argue that the common law understanding of adultery must also evolve to recognise the new constitutional reality.[58] Nonetheless, there are several reasons why this might not happen. First, a court may incline to the view that an alteration of the long-established legal understanding of adultery involves law-making, a function constitutionally reserved to the legislature.[59] Although the courts in Ireland have acknowledged an ongoing power to develop common law and equitable principles incrementally and by analogy,[60] they have disclaimed a right to develop "substantially new principles and policies,"[61] deferring to the legislature where a decisive change in the law is sought.[62] In *MH v GH*, Clarke J distinguished between a "proper evolution of the common law where the same fundamental principles are required to be applied, perhaps in quite a different way, because of new circumstances and conditions . . . and changes [that] require policy choices and detailed provisions."[63] While one might argue that extending adultery to homosexual acts is an evolution that flows logically from the Thirty-fourth Amendment, a court might be more likely to say that such a significant policy choice must be made in Parliament and not in the courts. A judge might equally prove reluctant to determine where the boundaries of adultery lie if the requirement of heterosexual sexual intercourse is to be abandoned. This is, indeed, a broader dilemma – if adultery is to be widened to embrace other sexual acts, then *what* sexual acts should constitute adultery? Expanding the definition of adultery, though possible, raises many questions as to where the boundaries should lie, particularly in the case of lesbian sexual acts.

Why is adultery a ground?

The law formerly permitted a husband to sue a man who had sex with the former's wife, under the tort of criminal conversation.[64] While the aforementioned tort has been abolished,[65] adultery, historically, was long considered a core requirement for divorce in the UK.[66] One possible rationale for this is that adultery may potentially result in extra-marital conception and births. This may explain why adultery is confined to acts of sexual intercourse, given the possibility of pregnancy arising. Monogamy ensures that there is certainty regarding a couple's offspring and clarity regarding paternity. The husband can be confident he is the father, and thus will (in principle) be more invested in his children's upbringing. The wife can be certain of the husband's exclusive attention to her offspring. As against that, however, adultery is not excluded where the participants are infertile, or where contraception is used. The age of the parties, moreover, is no bar to a claim of adultery, even when the female participant is beyond the age when pregnancy is likely. It is arguable also that penalising adultery specifically is born of a culture that formerly stigmatised births outside marriage (though it is not adultery if two unmarried persons have sex with each other).

Another possible rationale is that the ground is designed broadly to promote the ideal of monogamous marriage. Monogamy minimises the prospect of jealousy and rivalry within a marriage. In theory, it helps ensure a steady supply of mates for all suitors. If the aim is to ensure marital cohesion, however, it is unclear why the law on adultery stops short of categorising acts other than sexual intercourse as adultery. It also begs the question why sexual infidelity should be deserving of its own ground, while other, often more serious examples of intolerable conduct are lumped together in a catch-all behaviour ground.

The rationale for including adultery as a ground taps into a wider debate around the appropriateness of the current basis for divorce in England and Wales. Notably, the Divorce, Dissolution and Separation Bill 2017–2019 proposed to adopt an entirely process-based regime for divorce, removing the requirement to establish conduct-based facts such as adultery. There is a great deal of merit in this proposal.[67] There are many reasons to question the presence of adultery (or any other conduct-based fact) as a basis for divorce or judicial separation. First, there is the very real risk that parties may agree to claim adultery when it has not in fact occurred,[68] or may engineer an incident of adultery[69] with a view to obtaining a quick divorce. As the living apart facts in England and Wales require lengthy periods of separation, the temptation to do so may be high. Second, the adultery may be symptomatic of a marital breakdown rather than its direct cause. Indeed, there is nothing in either English or Irish law that requires that the adultery has *caused* the parties to part ways or is the primary reason for marital breakdown. In *JD v PD*,[70] for instance, a judicial separation was granted based on adultery that had only commenced after the husband had left the couple's home. As Lady Hale commented in *Owens v Owens* "[i]t is, for example, no answer to a petition based on adultery that the petitioner had been unfaithful and unloving for years or that the couple had not lived together for a long time."[71] Indeed, in some cases in England and Wales, spouses may rely on adultery simply to avoid the long waiting periods prescribed in cases involving desertion or living apart. Research by Trinder et al., for instance, suggests that the facts relied on by parties to a divorce do not always match the real reason for seeking a dissolution.[72] Correspondingly, an act of adultery may not, in fact, precipitate a relationship breakdown. The spouses may be willing to overlook incidents of adultery. They may, indeed, feasibly have formed an understanding that, provided certain limits are respected, acts of extra-marital sex will be tolerated. All of this being the case, the better approach may be to remove adultery entirely as a basis for divorce in England and Wales, and for judicial separation in Ireland.

Consummation

The inability to consummate a marriage is a ground for annulment of marriage in Ireland. Both inability to consummate and wilful refusal to do so are grounds for annulment in Northern Ireland,[73] and England and Wales.[74] These grounds render a marriage voidable rather than void, meaning that while a spouse may avoid the marriage, and thus have it declared invalid (retrospectively in Ireland, but prospectively only in Northern Ireland, and England and Wales), the marriage remains valid until avoided. In the UK, however, inability or refusal to consummate is not included as a ground for the annulment of a civil partnership[75] or in respect of nullity of marriage when a married couple are of the same sex.[76] Nor is it a ground for annulment of civil partnership in Ireland.[77] This has led to Beresford's perceptive observation that "the law only recognizes heterosexuals as sexual citizens, and does so by only recognizing sexual activity of a particular . . . type as legally relevant."[78] Ashford, too, has spoken, in this context, of a "careful de-sexing of the homosexual."[79]

Shatter describes consummation as " 'ordinary and complete' sexual intercourse after the solemnisation."[80] This, he continues, entails determining "whether a party is capable of *vera copula* i.e. capable of the natural sort of coitus."[81] He notes that the core question in such cases is whether there is the "practical possibility of full penetration by the male into the female."[82] In Irish law, however, ejaculation is not necessary for a marriage to be consummated; as McMahon J states in *MM v PM*, "it has long been accepted that penetration is sufficient to amount to consummation and that emission of seed is not necessary."[83]

It is reasonable, in general, to expect a minimum level of sexual capacity in one's marital partner. The ground, however, is not a guarantor of ongoing sexual satisfaction within marriage. The frequency and quality of the parties' ongoing sexual relationship is legally irrelevant in the context of this ground of nullity once the marriage has been consummated. Similarly, the ability to procreate is irrelevant; the parties may well be infertile, may be beyond the age at which child-bearing is possible, or may be consistently using contraception,[84] and the marriage may still be consummated. All this begs the question as to whether the ground continues to have a function relevant to modern times.

Clearly, a same-sex couple cannot consummate a marriage in the sense in which consummation has always been understood. They cannot have heterosexual sexual intercourse with each other. The fact that they could have sexual intercourse with other people of the opposite sex is irrelevant, as inability to consummate may render a marriage voidable even when it is only relative to one's spouse alone.[85] The matter is resolved in English law by s.12(2) of the Matrimonial Causes Act 1973, which stipulates that the consummation grounds do not apply to the marriages of same-sex couples. In this regard, at least some effort has been made in England and Wales to address the issue (though the result is a law that arguably erases the sexual character of same-sex unions). In Ireland, however, the legislation is silent. It would nonetheless be entirely illogical to allow the parties to a same-sex marriage to avoid the marriage on grounds of inability to consummate (as currently understood). Provided the parties are each aware that the other party is of the same sex, they must be regarded as having waived or approbated any right to avoid on this ground.

Inability to form and sustain a normal marital relationship

A curious Irish ground for annulment raises a further dilemma. In 1991, the Irish Supreme Court ruled in *UF v JC* that it is possible to avoid a marriage on the basis that the respondent, at the time of marriage, lacked the capacity to form and sustain a normal marital relationship.[86] Such incapacity may arise from either a psychiatric illness or disorder, or some other inherent quality or characteristic of a person's nature or personality that is not voluntary or self-induced. This affirmed a then-developing body of case law in the High Court suggesting that such a ground, by analogy with the ground of inability to consummate, could be invoked to avoid a marriage.[87]

In *UF*, the Supreme Court ruled that it was possible, in this context, for such lack of capacity to arise from a person's inherent and unalterable homosexual orientation. It therefore declared a marriage to be voidable and granted a decree of nullity on the basis that the husband's homosexual orientation prevented him from forming and sustaining a normal marital relationship with a person of the opposite sex. A similar outcome arose in *F v F*,[88] though that decision was based also on psychiatric evidence of severe personality and psychological disturbance. Likewise, in *C(G) v C* McKenzie J concluded that "an active and promiscuous homosexual is not capable of contracting a valid marriage."[89]

This is separate from the issue of consent. A party who marries in ignorance of a matter of substance relating to the inherent condition or mental stability of the respondent may claim the marriage is void for lack of consent. While concealment of past conduct and deception as to wealth, character, or experience will not invalidate a marriage,[90] there is clear authority that concealment of sexual orientation and gender identity will.[91]

The court in *UF* was careful not to assert that homosexuality in every case will render a marriage voidable. In *certain circumstances*, they say, a homosexual orientation *may* have that effect. As Byrne and Binchy remark:

> [i]t is less clear whether such a completely homosexual orientation, if established, inevitably comes within this ground. One can conceive of cases where the sexual dimension of a marriage may be of little or no importance to the parties, as where they both are very old or infirm.[92]

Notably in *McD v O'R*,[93] the High Court accepted that the respondent had engaged in a homosexual relationship before (though not after) marriage. On the facts, however, it rejected the proposition that he was incapable of forming a normal marital relationship. The marriage had lasted nearly 12 years, for much of which time the parties had what the court described as a "satisfactory and normal" sexual relationship with each other. In *AB v NC*,[94] the respondent had acknowledged homosexual feelings, on which he had never acted, though he claimed also to be attracted to women. The ground in that case was not established, O'Higgins J distinguishing the case, on its facts, from that of *UF*. This seems to establish that some homosexual attraction will not necessarily give rise to incapacity. One might tentatively draw the conclusion that bisexuality is not sufficient to render a marriage voidable.

The courts have emphasised that it is incapacity – rather than mere incompatibility – that gives rise to this ground. The incapacity, moreover, must arise from an inherent condition over which the person has no control. The courts have thus permitted parties to avoid marriages on this basis when a party suffers from bipolar disorder,[95] paranoid schizophrenia,[96] gross personality disorder,[97] severe emotional immaturity,[98] and paranoid psychosis.[99] The case law, therefore, establishes a clear dividing line differentiating 'normal' conditions from the 'abnormal.' Although the courts do not require the presence of a psychiatric illness, the conditions that give rise to the ground are characterised by a significant and pronounced departure from normal expectations as to emotional capacity. The Supreme Court in *UF* was careful not to categorise homosexual orientation as an illness or disorder. Nonetheless, homosexuality is associated and grouped with abnormal conditions; the ground presupposes the presence of something unusual in the respondent that prevents a 'normal' marital relationship from forming.

UF was admittedly decided at a time when male homosexual sexual acts were still unlawful in Ireland and was clearly predicated on the then confinement of marriage to opposite-sex couples. In the wake of the marriage referendum, it remains to be seen how the Irish courts will in the future address this precedent. Now that same-sex couples may marry, would an Irish court take a similar approach in a case in which one of two same-sex spouses had a concealed heterosexual orientation? By analogy, it must follow that when a person marries a partner of the same sex who is secretly heterosexual, the former should be allowed to avoid the marriage based on the capacity ground (independently of any issue as to whether the consent to marriage is valid in such circumstances). To say, however, that heterosexuality prevents a party from engaging in a 'normal' marital relationship would undoubtedly be radical. It is true to say that incapacity in this context can be relative to one's spouse alone.[100] In that sense, one might say that a heterosexual, while generally capable of conducting a normal marital relationship with a person of the opposite sex, may be incapable of such relative to a person of the same sex. It is nonetheless hard to envisage a court characterising heterosexuality as an 'abnormal' inherent quality or characteristic undermining capacity to form and sustain a normal marital relationship. The heteronormative dynamic would arguably lean heavily against such a verdict.

This view that homosexuality is inimical to the capacity of parties to care for each other within even an opposite-sex marriage is contestable. In *Norris v Attorney General*, the plaintiff claimed to be entirely immune to the charms of the opposite sex; an opposite-sex relationship was neither open nor possible, he claimed.[101] Yet, gay men often form profoundly close (albeit platonic) bonds with straight women; female celebrities often attain iconic status among gay males. This is not to suggest that such bonds would form the basis for a good marriage. Although it may not be wise for two persons of opposite sex, one or both of whom is gay, to marry each other, it is questionable whether one party's sexual orientation *per se* would always prevent a functioning marriage from developing. *UF v JC* seems to presuppose that an inclination towards and a preference for heterosexual intercourse is always a necessary foundation for a functioning opposite-sex marriage. The judgement might be said to foreground the quality of sexual activity as a predominant determinant of a marriage's success. In fact, some marriages exist and may function well without the parties engaging in regular sexual activity. In *Scott v Scott*,[102] Sachs J concluded that a pre-marital agreement to desist from sex during marriage was void,[103] but nonetheless refused to grant the husband an annulment, arguing that he had accepted the marriage without sexual intercourse.[104] This highlights the possibility of marriages wherein the parties have resolved not to have sexual intercourse with each other or to have children. It is equally possible that some very elderly or infirm parties will marry with no expectation of regular sexual activity. Over time, a couple's initial sexual ardour may diminish as passion makes way for companionship. Cohabitation law in Ireland, for instance, recognises that a relationship may be "intimate and committed" even when it is no longer sexual in nature.[105]

Conclusion

These are three very specific examples, though they are symptomatic of a wider phenomenon. Marriage for same-sex couples has generally been introduced without significant consideration as to whether the rules relating to marriage were well suited to the needs of same-sex couples. In Ireland, for instance, the Marriage Act 2015 largely confines itself to adapting marriage law so that, broadly, it applies equally to same-sex and opposite-sex couples.[106] The net effect is to apply to same-sex couples laws fashioned with only opposite-sex couples in mind and underpinned by heteronormative assumptions based on a traditional model of heterosexual marriage.

It is perhaps not entirely unreasonable to expect that marriage law will have been designed with opposite-sex couples in mind given that, for millennia, it was largely confined to such couples. There may be enough flexibility in family law remedies to allow judges to address the specific situation of each couple. The risk arises, nonetheless, that judges will apply heterosexual norms to same-sex couples, and that this may not necessarily result in appropriate outcomes for the latter. As Olivia Rundle has observed, same-sex couples have very particular experiences and perspectives that may demand a somewhat different approach:

> To truly achieve equality, it is necessary: first that judges perceive same-sex relationships as being of equal worth as heterosexual relationships and secondly, that the judiciary takes account of inherent differences between same-sex and heterosexual relationships when applying the law. If true equality is to

be achieved, the judiciary should not apply inappropriate hetero-normative assumptions to same-sex relationships when determining whether those relationships are "worthy of legal recognition."[107]

As marriage law evolves, one hopes that legislatures and courts will carefully consider the particular dynamics and needs of same-sex couples. Developments to date, however, leave the distinct impression that, at least for the time being, marriage law will struggle to break free of its heteronormative roots.

Notes

1 See generally Daniele Gallo, Luca Paladini and Pietro Pustorino (eds), *Same-Sex Couples Before National, Supranational and International Jurisdictions* (Springer-Verlag 2014).
2 Ibid.
3 Marriage (Same-Sex Couples) Act 2013 (E&W).
4 Marriage and Civil Partnership (Scotland) Act 2014 (Sc).
5 Thirty-fourth Amendment of the Constitution Act 2015 (Ir); Article 41.4 of the Constitution of Ireland 1937; and the Marriage Act 2015 (Ir).
6 Civil Partnership Act 2004 (UK). (CPA 2004).
7 Following the UK Supreme Court decision in *Steinfeld and Keidan v Secretary of State for International Development* (2018) UKSC 32, the UK Parliament enacted the Civil Partnerships, Marriages and Deaths (Registration etc) Act 2019 (E&W). This mandates the Government to extend civil partnership to opposite sex couples in England and Wales by the end of 2019.
8 Matrimonial Causes (Northern Ireland) Order 1978 (NI), art 13(1)(e).
9 On this point, see for instance, Ryan Conrad (ed), *Against Equality: Queer Critiques of Gay Marriage* (Against Equality Press 2010); Paula Ettelbrick, 'Since When Is Marriage a Path to Liberation?' in William Rubenstein (ed), *Lesbians, Gay Men and the Law* (New Press 1993).
10 There are multiple interpretations of the term 'heteronormativity' (see Joseph Marchia and Jamie M Sommer, '[Re]Defining Heteronormativity' [2019] 22 *Sexualities* 267). For the purpose of this chapter, the term describes the privileging of heterosexuality as the default, normal, and natural sexual orientation.
11 See *UF v JC* (1991) 2 IR 330, discussed further ahead.
12 On which see Fergus Ryan, 'Mapping a Transformed Landscape: Sexual Orientation and the Law in Ireland' in Lynsey Black and Peter Dunne (eds), *Law and Gender in Modern Ireland: Critique and Reform* (Hart Publishing 2019).
13 Offences against the Person Act 1861 (UK), ss.61 and 62; Criminal Law Amendment Act 1885 (UK), s.11. The Criminal Law (Sexual Offences) Act 1993 (Ir) brought about the decriminalisation of consensual homosexual acts between adult males. See also *Norris v Ireland* App No. 10581/83 (ECtHR, 26 October 1988).
14 See for instance, Department of Finance Circular 12/1988 (Ir), Prohibition of Incitement to Hatred Act 1989 (Ir), Video Recordings Act 1989 (Ir), Unfair Dismissals (Amendment) Act 1993 (Ir), Employment Equality Act 1998 (Ir), and Equal Status Act 2000 (Ir).
15 See for instance, *State (Nicolaou) v An Bord Uchtála* (1966) IR 567; and *JMcD v PL and BM* (2009) IESC 81. See also the Social Welfare (Miscellaneous Provisions) Act 2004, s19, which excluded recognition of same-sex couples in the context of certain social welfare schemes. There were, however, exceptions to

this trend: see for instance, the Parental Leave (Amendment) Act 2006 (Ir) and changes to immigration policy from 2006 onwards.

16 See generally Fergus Ryan, *The Civil Partnership and Certain Rights and Obligations of Cohabitants Act 2010 (Annotated)* (Round Hall 2011).

17 Civil Partnership and Certain Rights and Obligations of Cohabitants Act 2010 (Ir) (CPCROCA 2010), s.3 and s.107(e).

18 Ibid, Pt.15.

19 There are still some gaps, however, particularly in relation to parentage. See Fergus Ryan, 'Unfinished Business? Equality and Family Diversity in the Wake of the Irish Marriage Referendum' (2018) 21 *Irish Journal of Family Law* 59.

20 See for instance, Paula Fagan et al., *Missing Pieces* (Marriage Equality 2011); Fergus Ryan, 'The General Scheme of the Civil Partnership Bill 2008: Brave New Dawn or Missed Opportunity?' (2008) *Irish Journal of Family Law* 11.

21 *Steinfeld* (n 7).

22 Civil Partnerships, Marriages and Deaths (Registration etc) Act 2019 (E&W).

23 Marriage Act 2015 (Ir), Pt.4.

24 *Dáil Debates* Vol. 890, 23 September 2015.

25 Marriage Act 2015 (Ir), ss.8–10.

26 Ibid., s.6, 11; Civil Registration Act 2004 (Ir), s.2B; CPCROCA 2010 (n 17) s.109A.

27 See generally Fergus Ryan, '"Playing Away from Home on an Uneven Pitch?" Spouses, Civil Partners and Adultery in Irish and UK Law' (2014) 17 *Irish Journal of Family Law* 41–51.

28 Matrimonial Causes Act 1973 (E&W), (MCA 1973) s.1(1).

29 MCA 1973, s1(2)(a). In Northern Irish law, the added stipulation that the petitioner finds it intolerable to live with the respondent does not apply.

30 *Cleary v Cleary* (1994) 1 All ER 498.

31 The 2017–2019 bill had previously seemed to have fallen due to the prorogation of the UK Parliament in September 2019. On 24 September 2019, however, the UK Supreme Court in *R (on the application of Miller) v The Prime Minister; Cherry and others v Advocate General for Scotland* (2019) UKSC 41, declared the prorogation to be unlawful, null, and of no legal effect. The bill was subsequently introduced into Parliament in October 2019 as the Divorce, Dissolution and Separation Bill 2019–2020. This has subsequently fallen following the valid prorogation of Parliament in November 2019 for the 2019 general election.

32 The conditions for divorce in Ireland are contained in Art.41.3.2 of the Constitution of Ireland 1937, as amended by the 15th and 38th Amendments to the Constitution, and in the Family Law (Divorce) Act 1996.

33 S.20(2)(i) of the Family Law (Divorce) Act 1996; *DT v CT* (2002) 3 IR 334; *C v C* (2005) IEHC 276; *ES v DS* (2010) IEHC 474.

34 See s.2(1)(a) of the Judicial Separation and Family Law Reform Act 1989. (JSFLRA 1989).

35 More than one year in Ireland, and more than six months in England and Wales.

36 See JSFLRA 1989 (n 34) s4(1) and MCA 1973 s.2(1).

37 The sole exception being that a civil partner (A) may avoid a marriage in UK where her civil partner (B) was pregnant at the time of its formation by a person other than A and A was ignorant of that fact. See CPA 2004 s.50(1)(c) and 174(1)(c).

38 See *Dennis v Dennis* (1955) P 153 and MCA 1973 s1(6).

39 Alan Shatter, *Shatter's Family Law* (4th edn, LexisNexis Butterworth's 1997) 345.

40 *Woolf v Woolf* (1931) P 134; *JMH v JPH* (High Court, January 1983); *PF v GO'M* (High Court, 29 March 1999).
41 *Dennis* (n 38).
42 Ibid., 160.
43 Ibid., 163.
44 *Sapsford v Sapsford and Furtado* (1954) P 394 at 400.
45 Ibid.
46 Though the case, of course, concerned Scottish law.
47 *MacLennan v MacLennan* (1958) S.C. 105, 113.
48 *Orford v Orford* (1921) 58 DLR 251 (Ont.S.Ct).
49 *Babineau v Babineau* (1924) 51 NBR 501.
50 *Corbett v Corbett (1971) P 83*, 108.
51 See *Dennis* (n 38) 160. Cf *R v Gaston* (1981) 73 Crim App R. 164.
52 See Shatter (n 39) 345. See also Jonathan Herring, *Family Law* (4th edn, Pearson Longman 2009) 110. In *Dennis* (n 38) 163, Hodson LJ speaks of adultery as "natural copulation between the sexes."
53 Shatter (n 39) 345. Subject to narrow exceptions, s18 of the Gender Recognition Act 2015 recognises a person with a gender recognition certificate (GRC) as being, for all purposes, of their preferred binary gender. Nonetheless, difficult questions may arise in the context of adultery where, for instance, a person with a GRC still possesses the physical genitalia of their birth sex.
54 On the possible human rights implications of such a stance, see Department for Culture, Media and Sport, *Marriage (Same-Sex Couples) Bill 2013: Note for the Joint Committee on Human Rights* (2013) 26–27.
55 MCA 1973 s1(2)(b).
56 JSFLRA 1989 (n 34) s.2(1)(b).
57 See for instance *Patin v Patin,* 371 So 2d 682 (Fla CA 1979); *Bales v Hack,* 509 NE2d 95 (1986); *RGM v DEM,* 306 S.C. 145 (1991); *SB v SJB,* 609 A2d 124 (1992); *P(SE) v P(DD)* (2005) BCSC 1290. See generally Peter Nicolas, 'The Lavender Letter: Applying the Law of Adultery to Same-Sex Couples and Same-Sex Conduct' (2011) 63 *Florida Law Review* 97–127.
58 Cf. *McKinley v Minister for Defence* (1992) 2 IR 333.
59 Article 15.2 of the Constitution of Ireland 1937.
60 See, for instance, the Supreme Court decisions in *UF v JC* (n 11).
61 Per Clarke J in *R v An tArd Chláraitheoir* (2014) IESC 60 at [406].
62 See, for instance, *MM v PM* (1986) ILRM 515; *BL v ML* (1992) 2 IR 77; and *R v An tArd Chláraitheoir* (n 61).
63 *MH v GH* (2015) IESC 7 at [2.6].
64 See Niamh Howlin, 'Adultery in the Courts: Damages for Criminal Conversation in Ireland' in Niamh Howlin and Kevin Costello (eds), *Law and the Family in Ireland: 1800–1950* (Palgrave Macmillan 2017).
65 The Matrimonial Causes Act 1857 replaced the action in England and Wales with a suit for adultery, which was in turn abolished by the Law Reform (Miscellaneous Provisions) Act 1970 (E&W). In Ireland, see the Family Law Act 1981 (Ir), s.1.
66 On the history of divorce in England and Wales, and the role of adultery therein see Sybil Wolfram, 'Divorce in England 1700–1857' (1985) 5 *Oxford Journal of Legal Studies* 155. See also Diane Urquhart, 'Divorce Irish Style: Marriage Dissolution in Ireland, 1850–1950' in Howlin and Costello (n 64). Early English legislation maintained adultery as a central requirement for divorce: see the Matrimonial Causes Act 1857 (E&W), the Matrimonial Causes Act 1923 (E&W).
67 See generally the discussion in Catherine Fairbairn, 'No-Fault Divorce' (House of Commons Library 2019).

68 As Fairbairn, Ibid., 7, reports, a 2015 YouGov survey for Resolution "found that 27% of divorcing couples who asserted blame in their divorce petition admitted the allegation of fault was not true, but was the easiest option."
69 A court, however, may refuse a judicial separation when the adultery was committed with the connivance of the applicant: see JSFLRA 1989 (n 34) s44.
70 *JD v PD* (High Court, August 1994).
71 *Owens v Owens* (2018) UKSC 41, [48].
72 Liz Trinder et al., *Finding Fault? Divorce Law and Practice in England and Wales* (Nuffield Foundation 2017).
73 Matrimonial Causes (Northern Ireland) Order 1978 (NI), Art.14(a) and (b).
74 MCA 1973 s12(1)(a) and (b).
75 CPA 2004 ss.50 and 174.
76 MCA 1973, s12(2) as inserted by the Marriage (Same-Sex Couples) Act 2013 (E&W).
77 See CPCROCA 2010 (n 17) s107.
78 Sarah Beresford, 'We're All Same (Sex) Now? Lesbian (Same) Sex; Consummation; Adultery and Marriage' (2016) 12 *Journal of GLBT Family Studies* 468.
79 Chris Ashford, 'Same Sex Marriage and the De-Sexing of the Homosexual' (Law and Sexuality Blog 2012) <http://lawandsexuality.blogspot.com/2012/12/same-sex-marriage-and-de-sexing-of.html>
80 Shatter (n 39) 209.
81 Ibid.
82 Ibid., 210.
83 *MM v PM* (n 62).
84 *Baxter v Baxter* (1948) AC 274.
85 See *S v S* (1976–7) I.L.R.M. 156; *R (W) v W* (High Court, February 1980).
86 *UF v JC* (n 11).
87 *RSJ v JSJ* (1982) 2 ILRM 263; *D v C* (1984) ILRM 173.
88 *F v F* (1990) 1 IR 348.
89 *C(G) v C* (High Court, November 1989).
90 *PF v GO'M* (2000) IESC 81; *LB v TMacC* (2009) IESC 21.
91 *F v F* (n 88); *SB v FL* (2009) IEHC 623.
92 Raymond Byrne and William Binchy, *Annual Review of Irish Law 2006* (Thomson Round Hall 2007) 372.
93 *McD v O'R* (1984) WJSC-HC 2440.
94 *AB v NC* (2006) I.E.H.C. 127.
95 *D v C* (n 87).
96 *R v R* (High Court, December 1984); *DC v DW* (1987) ILRM 58; *WK v MC* (High Court, July 1992).
97 *W(C) v C* (1989) IR 696.
98 *W v P* (High Court, 7 June 1984).
99 *PK v MBN* (High Court, April 1995).
100 Cf. *S v S* (n 85); *R (W) v W* (n 85).
101 *Norris v Attorney General* (1984) IR 36.
102 *Scott v Scott* (1959) P. 103 (Note).
103 Cf *Brodie v Brodie* (1917) P. 271.
104 See also *Morgan v Morgan* (1959) 2 WLR 487.
105 See CPCROCA 2010 (n 17) s172(3).
106 This point is subject to some limited caveats relating, for instance, to religious solemnisers, and to the presumption of paternity.

107 Olivia Rundle, 'Following the Legislative Leaders: Judicial Recognition of Same Sex Couples in Australia and New Zealand' in Gallo, Paladini and Pustorino (n 1) 136.

References

Primary sources

AB v NC (2006) I.E.H.C. 127.
Adoption (Amendment) Act 2017 (Ir).
Babineau v Babineau (1924) 51 NBR 501.
Bales v Hack, 509 NE2d 95 (1986).
Baxter v Baxter (1948) AC 274.
BL v ML (1992) 2 IR 77.
Brodie v Brodie (1917) P. 271.
C v C (2005) IEHC 276.
C(G) v C (High Court, November 1989).
Children and Family Relationships Act 2015 (Ir).
Civil Partnership Act 2004 (UK).
Civil Partnership and Certain Rights and Obligations of Cohabitants Act 2010 (Ir).
Civil Partnerships, Marriages and Deaths (Registration etc) Act 2019 (E&W).
Civil Registration Act 2004 (Ir).
Cleary v Cleary (1994) 1 All ER 498.
The Constitution of Ireland (1937).
Corbett v Corbett (1971) P 83.
Criminal Law (Sexual Offences) Act 1993 (Ir).
Criminal Law Amendment Act 1885 (UK).
D v C (1984) ILRM 173.
DC v DW (1987) ILRM 58.
Dennis v Dennis (1955) P 153.
Department of Finance Circular 12/1988 (Ir).
Divorce (Scotland) Act 1976.
DT v CT (2002) 3 IR 334.
Employment Equality Act 1998 (Ir).
ES v DS (2010) IEHC 474.
Equal Status Act 2000 (Ir).
F v F (1990) 1 IR 348.
Family Law Act 1981 (Ir).
Family Law (Divorce) Act 1996.
Gender Recognition Act 2015 (Ir).
JD v PD (High Court, August 1994).
JMcD v PL and BM (2009) IESC 81.
JMH v JPH (High Court, January 1983).
Judicial Separation and Family Law Reform Act 1989 (Ir).
Law Reform (Miscellaneous Provisions) Act 1970 (E&W).
LB v TMacC (2009) IESC 21.
MacLennan v MacLennan (1958) S.C. 105.

Marriage (Same-Sex Couples) Act 2013 (E&W).
Marriage Act 2015 (Ir).
Marriage and Civil Partnership (Scotland) Act 2014 (Sc).
Matrimonial Causes Act 1857.
Matrimonial Causes Act 1857 (E&W).
Matrimonial Causes Act 1923 (E&W).
Matrimonial Causes Act 1973 (E&W).
Matrimonial Causes (Northern Ireland) Order 1978 (NI).
McD v O'R (1984) WJSC-HC 2440.
McKinley v Minister for Defence (1992) 2 IR 333.
MH v GH (2015) IESC 7.
MM v PM (1986) ILRM 515.
Morgan v Morgan (1959) 2 WLR 487.
Norris v Attorney General (1984) IR 36.
Norris v Ireland App No 10581/83 (ECtHR, 26 October 1988).
Offences Against the Person Act 1861 (UK).
Orford v Orford (1921) 58 DLR 251 (Ont.S.Ct.).
Owens v Owens (2018) UKSC 41.
P(SE) v P(DD) (2005) BCSC 1290.
Parental Leave (Amendment) Act 2006 (Ir).
Patin v Patin, 371 So 2d 682 (Fla CA 1979).
PF v GO'M (2000) IESC 81.
PF v GO'M (High Court, 29 March 1999).
PK v MBN (High Court, April 1995).
Prohibition of Incitement to Hatred Act 1989 (Ir).
R (on the application of Miller) v The Prime Minister; Cherry and others v Advocate General for Scotland (2019) UKSC 41.
R (W) v W (High Court, February 1980).
R v An tArd Chláraitheoir (2014) IESC 60.
R v Gaston (1981) 73 Crim App R. 164.
R v R (High Court, December 1984).
RGM v DEM, 306 S.C. 145 (1991).
RSJ v JSJ (1982) 2 ILRM 263.
S v S (1976–7) I.L.R.M. 156.
Sapsford v Sapsford and Furtado (1954) P 394.
SB v FL (2009) IEHC 623.
SB v SJB, 609 A2d 124 (1992).
Scott v Scott (1959) P. 103.
Social Welfare (Miscellaneous Provisions) Act 2004.
State (Nicolaou) v An Bord Uchtála (1966) IR 567.
Steinfeld and Keidan v Secretary of State for International Development (2018) UKSC 32.
Thirty-fourth Amendment of the Constitution Act 2015 (Ir).
UF v JC (1991) 2 IR 330.
Unfair Dismissals (Amendment) Act 1993 (Ir).
Video Recordings Act 1989 (Ir).
W v P (High Court, 7 June 1984).
W(C) v C (1989) IR 696.

WK v MC (High Court, July 1992).
Woolf v Woolf (1931) P 134.

Secondary sources

Ashford C, 'Same Sex Marriage and the De-Sexing of the Homosexual' (Law and Sexuality Blog 2012) <http://lawandsexuality.blogspot.com/2012/12/same-sex-marriage-and-de-sexing-of.html>

Beresford S, 'We're All Same (Sex) Now? Lesbian (Same) Sex; Consummation; Adultery and Marriage' (2016) 12(5) *Journal of GLBT Family Studies* 468.

Byrne R and Binchy W, *Annual Review of Irish Law 2006* (Thomson Round Hall 2007).

Conrad R (ed), *Against Equality: Queer Critiques of Gay Marriage* (Against Equality Press 2010).

Dáil Debates 23 September 2015, Col 890 (Ir).

Department for Culture, Media and Sport, *Marriage (Same-Sex Couples) Bill 2013: Note for the Joint Committee on Human Rights* (Department for Culture, Media and Sport 2013).

Ettelbrick P, 'Since When Is Marriage a Path to Liberation?' in Rubenstein W (ed), *Lesbians, Gay Men and the Law* (New Press 1993).

Fagan P et al., *Missing Pieces* (Marriage Equality 2011).

Fairbairn C, 'No-Fault Divorce' (House of Commons Library 2019).

Gallo D, Paladini L and Pustorino P (eds), *Same-Sex Couples Before National, Supranational and International Jurisdictions* (Springer-Verlag 2014).

Herring J, *Family Law* (4th edn., Pearson Longman 2009).

Howlin N, 'Adultery in the Courts: Damages for Criminal Conversation in Ireland' in Howlin N and Costello K (eds), *Law and the Family in Ireland: 1800–1950* (Palgrave Macmillan 2017).

Marchia J and Sommer JM, '(Re)defining Heteronormativity' (2019) 22(3) *Sexualities* 267.

Nicolas P, 'The Lavender Letter: Applying the Law of Adultery to Same-Sex Couples and Same-Sex Conduct' (2011) 63 *Florida Law Review* 97.

Rundle O, 'Following the Legislative Leaders: Judicial Recognition of Same Sex Couples in Australia and New Zealand' in Gallo D, Paladini L and Pustorino P (eds), *Same-Sex Couples Before National, Supranational and International Jurisdictions* (Springer-Verlag 2014).

Ryan F, 'The General Scheme of the Civil Partnership Bill 2008: Brave New Dawn or Missed Opportunity?' (2008) *Irish Journal of Family Law* 11.

———, *The Civil Partnership and Certain Rights and Obligations of Cohabitants Act 2010 (Annotated)* (Round Hall 2011).

———, '"Playing Away from Home on an Uneven Pitch?" Spouses, Civil Partners and Adultery in Irish and UK Law' (2014) 17(2) *Irish Journal of Family Law* 41.

———, 'Unfinished Business? Equality and Family Diversity in the Wake of the Irish Marriage Referendum' (2018) 21(3) *Irish Journal of Family Law* 59.

———, 'Mapping a Transformed Landscape: Sexual Orientation and the Law in Ireland' in Black L and Dunne P (eds), *Law and Gender in Modern Ireland: Critique and Reform* (Hart Publishing 2019).

Shatter A, *Shatter's Family Law* (4th edn, LexisNexis Butterworth's 1997).

Trinder L et al., *Finding Fault? Divorce Law and Practice in England and Wales* (Nuffield Foundation 2017).

Urquhart D, 'Divorce Irish Style: Marriage Dissolution in Ireland, 1850–1950' in Howlin N and Costello K (eds), *Law and the Family in Ireland: 1800–1950* (Palgrave Macmillan 2017).

Wolfram S, 'Divorce in England 1700–1857' (1985) 5(2) *Oxford Journal of Legal Studies* 155.

Part 6

Consideration of the necessity of both social and legal change, and the interaction between them

Chapter 13

Why legal equality is not enough

The case of domestic violence and abuse in the relationships of LGBTQ+ people

Catherine Donovan

Introduction

This chapter is concerned with how it is possible in a society where marriage is available to almost any adult couple,[1] so long as they identify with a recognised binaried gender identity, that LGBTQ+ people who are victimised by or enact domestic violence and abuse (DVA) rarely report to formal, mainstream statutory (e.g. police) or third sector specialist domestic violence organisations.[2] In exploring how this can be the case, what is meant by equality will be interrogated and the many ways in which structural and cultural inequalities shape and construct whether DVA might be recognised – let alone sought help for – will be explored. To do this, the discussion will first focus on equality and whether everybody being treated the same is sufficient to achieve equality. Subsequently, the impact of the public story of DVA will be explored in order to illustrate how a social problem such as violence and abuse between intimate partners can be constructed such that the problem is only recognised through particular heteronormative cisgendered presentations, practices and relationships. The implications of this are considered not only for LGBTQ+ people affected by DVA but also practitioners to whom LGBTQ+ people might take their concerns. However, before we begin this substantive discussion, there will be a brief discussion of language and a brief overview of the recent research on violence and abuse in the relationships of LGBTQ+ people.

Defining the terms for the debate

In order to make sense of the use of violence and abuse in an adult relationship, it is important to take into account the context, motives, meanings and impact, as this can include violent acts of self-defence as well as coercively controlling behaviour. The focus in this chapter is on DVA, which is defined by the England and Wales Home Office (2013)[3] as a pattern of incidents of violence and abuse (including physical, emotional, sexual and financial) that are enacted by one (ex-) partner over the other to exert power and control over them.

DVA in the relationships of LGBTQ+ people

It is difficult to get a consistent picture of the prevalence of DVA in the relationships of LGBTQ+ people for many reasons, not least because, as with research in this field more generally, reports of DVA to surveys, and certainly to the police, might not tally with the actual level of experiences of DVA in the population. In addition, methodologies, definition of terms used in research tools and different definitions of 'what counts' as DVA differ.[4] Overriding these concerns is the methodological problem of securing a random sample from which to extrapolate to the general population. It is extremely difficult to secure random samples of the population of LGBTQ+ people because it is difficult to know what the total population is. However, such work has been done in the United States of America (USA) and more recently in the United Kingdom (UK) and the prevalence rates are concerning.

Walter et al.'s[5] National Intimate Partner and Sexual Violence Survey (NISVS) in the USA show a slightly different set of findings from those we might expect: looking at lifetime prevalence, it is sexuality rather than gender that is associated with high rates of reporting: 61% of bisexual women, 44% of lesbians, 37% bisexual men, 35% of heterosexual women, 29% of heterosexual men and 26% of gay men reported experiencing rape, physical violence and/or stalking from an intimate partner. Unusually,[6] this study asked about the gender of the violent/abusive partner and shows that sexual violence reported by lesbian, gay male, bisexual women and men or heterosexual women was enacted mainly by male perpetrators; and that physical violence experienced by bisexual women was also largely from male perpetrators.[7]

In England and Wales there have been two analyses of the Crime Survey England and Wales (CSEW) partner abuse data looking specifically at how the sexuality of participants might shape prevalence. In 2010, Smith, Osbourne, Lau and Britton[8] reported that rates of partner abuse were higher for those identifying as lesbian, bisexual or gay male (13%) than those of heterosexual women and men (5%) (cisgender identity was assumed). In addition, the percentage of lesbians and bisexual women (12%), and gay and bisexual men (6%), reporting one or more instances of non-physical abuse, threats or force (not including sexual assault) in the year before the survey were three times and two times, respectively, higher than those reported by heterosexual women (4%) and men (3%).[9]

Neither the sexuality nor the gender identity of the perpetrator is asked about in the CSEW, which makes it difficult to do anything other than speculate about why these higher rates are reported. Smith et al.[10] suggest that those identifying as LGB in the CSEW are more likely than heterosexual respondents to be 16–24 years old (37% as opposed to 21%), which might explain the disparity in reporting rates since this is the age group generally most likely to report partner and sexual violence. Donovan and Hester[11] also speculated that the high rates for lesbians and bisexual women might be accounted for by previous male partners. Such high prevalence add force to the argument that data about the perpetrator should be collected but also that 'the problem' should not be understood only as a gendered one.

In the second analysis of the CSEW data conducted by the Office of National Statistics,[12] the focus was only on women respondents and indicates that, again, it is sexuality that might be more important than gender as a risk indicator for partner abuse. The rate of partner abuse reported by bisexual women (11%) is nearly double that of heterosexual women (6%) and lesbian/gay women are also more likely to report partner abuse than heterosexual women (8%). Looking at specific types of abuse, the differences are even starker, with, for example, bisexual women being five times more likely to report sexual assault (1.9%) than heterosexual women (0.4%), and lesbian/gay women (0.5%) also reporting more frequently than heterosexual women. Again, male partners or ex-partners might provide some explanation, yet it might also be worth considering other possibilities; for example, that because of the heteronormativity of the field of domestic violence and abuse – including cultural representations of it – those LGBTQ+ persons experiencing DVA from their (ex-) intimate partners might not recognise it, might not know what to do about it and might not know who to seek help from. This might result in them staying longer in DVA relationships. There might also be the impacts of the legacy of living in a society where LGBTQ+ people have been socially constructed as criminals, pathological or morally questionable.[13] This might lead some LGBTQ+ people to believe that their experiences are 'to be expected' and 'normal,' or that they would rather stay in a DVA relationships than face a solitary life – either because their experience tells them it is difficult to find other LGBTQ+ people who could be potential intimate partners, or because they expect that another relationship would not be any better.

Equality and diversity: the same but/or different?

Whilst the law has long been identified as one of the barriers to achieving (sex/gender) equality,[14] there has always also been an understanding that achieving legal equality between women and men or between other social groups should not be seen as the end of the struggle.[15] For one thing, some critiques argue,[16] the premise is wrong: why should LGBTQ+ people want to achieve equality with what heterosexual people have when that 'standard' of normality might be fundamentally flawed? Other critiques[17] have pointed to the fact that changing laws and policies do not necessarily change the attitudes, assumptions and hostility that led to the legal inequalities in the first place. Decriminalisation of discriminatory laws, laws instating equality of treatment – or, conversely, laws prohibiting discrimination and/or violence – can, it is argued, send ideological messages about the relative value and worth being ascribed to women and men, heterosexuals and LGBTQ+ people. The repeal of Section 28 of the Local Government Act (1988) is an example both of how its existence sent a message about the relative worth of the family lives of LGB people, they were characterised as 'pretended'; and of how its repeal sent a message of a change in attitudes towards them.[18]

However, it is not necessarily clear the extent to which such laws are able to promote culture change in the right direction, especially in light of the evidence of backlashes against such 'liberalism' or 'political correctness.'[19]

For LGBTQ+ people, the legal landscape is almost unrecognisable now compared to only twenty years ago with a range of legislation that both promotes equality (same-sex marriage, equal parenting opportunities through adoption or reproductive technologies) and prohibits discrimination (equalities legislation) and hate (hate crime guidance that identifies sexuality and transgender identity as protected strands).[20] Yet, as this chapter will argue, things are far from equal – and in relation to DVA and LGBTQ+ people, this can be seen as the result of the legacies for LGBTQ+ people of living in a society with social and cultural norms based on core concepts of binary thinking, social inequalities that result in hierarchies of social groups and the acceptance of power inequalities between both social groups and individuals within and across social groups.[21] Furthermore, the neoliberal turn in society has both economic and ideological consequences. Economically, the trend is towards unregulated capital and a small state[22]; and ideologically, the trend is to centre the 'responsibilised citizen'[23] as the agent of their own fate. In addition, heteronormative constructions of social problems affect how social problems are recognised, understood and acted upon by LGBTQ+ people.

The legacy of living in a heteronormative society

Heteronormativity is used to convey the multiple ways in which society is organised – structurally and culturally – to (re)produce a particular ideal of heterosexual living as the preferred way of living against which everybody else (including heterosexual women and men) can be compared and found wanting.[24] In order to really make sense of why legal equality is not enough, it is necessary to consider the extent to which the law is available to those who might benefit from it. Putting aside the cuts in legal aid and the resulting crisis of justice there now exists in the UK,[25] for those who are LGBTQ+, the use of the law to challenge discrimination or protect rights or even to take advantage of new entitlements to familial and parental relationships also relies on their willingness to be out enough to claim and enact those legal rights. For those who do come out, as well as those who struggle to come out or only come out in some settings with some people, there might still be personal, emotional and mental health costs attached.

There is a mistaken belief that young people coming out and/or questioning their sexuality and/or gender identities must be having a much easier time than their older counterparts born before the 1967 Homosexual Offences Act which decriminalised (male) homosexuality.[26] Yet, the Metro[27] research, the largest survey of – to use their terms – young LGBTQ+ (Questioning) people ever conducted in the UK (n = 6,514) suggests that homo-bi-transphobia – from family, school students, neighbours and friends – is quite ordinary. They found that 74% of young LGBTQ people reported 'name calling,' 45% reported 'harassment or threats and intimidation' and 23% reported 'physical assault.'[28] In addition, reporting of homophobic hate crime increased by 147% in the three months after the referendum on whether the UK should stay in the European Union or not,[29] indicating the way in which minoritised sexualities can be targeted for hate motivated behaviours.

There is also evidence in the UK[30] and Canada[31] that first same-sex relationships can heighten the risk of experiencing DVA. In their work, Donovan and Hester[32] argue that regardless of their age, those entering a first same-sex relationship often explained that their lack of knowledge about what to expect in such a relationship was a factor in their enduring DVA. Their lack of connectedness to LGBT scenes, venues, literature and media – oftentimes as a result of their abusive partner's isolating behaviour – facilitated their belief that their experiences were normal and/or that it was a bad relationship that they were at least partially responsible for. Donovan, Barnes and Nixon[33] talk about the 'experiential power' of an abusive LGB and/or intimate partner who takes advantage of their longer experience of being out and/or living as an LGBTQ+ person to exert control over their partner insisting, for example, that their behaviour is typical and to be expected in, for example, a gay male relationship; and/or dissuading their partner from seeking help by warning them of the homo-bi-transphobia they will endure.

Being almost invisible in the curricula of sex and relationships education enables these kinds of abuses to take place. At the time of writing, the Conservative government has, in early 2019, conducted a public consultation on new relationships and sex education guidance to replace the existing guidelines which warned schools not to 'promote' sexualities other than heterosexual.[34] However, this has been challenged by various, typically faith-led, groups of parents wanting to be given the right to withdraw their children from such teaching.[35] Objections are not only based on faith, but also on the belief that issues of sex and sexuality are sensitive and private and not suitable for the classroom. Richardson and Monro[36] argue that it is this individualising and reprivatising of sexuality that provides one of the barriers to rolling out sexualities equalities in the public sector.

Shame has been identified as shaping many LGBTQ+ lives,[37] the consequences of which include the rates of mental health problems, self-harming, suicides and substance use addictions reported.[38] Munt[39] has also argued that some white lesbians and gay men attempt to secure acceptance by making alliances based on their privileged backgrounds that run counter to the interests of other lesbians, gay men, bisexual and/or transpeople who might be poorer and/or Black and/or immigrant, and/or refugees. The latter provides evidence in itself of the difficulties of talking about LGBTQ+ people as if they might be all the same and/or as if they might share the same interests and/or as if they might all act in alliances with each other. This also reinforces the importance of approaching any analysis of the lives of LGBTQ+ people with an intersectional framework.

Reprivatising sexuality

Equal marriage legislation was secured by successfully arguing that: 'love between adults is a universal sentiment, goal and human right; and that marriage, being based on love, should, therefore, be open to any adult couple, regardless of sexuality or gender identity.'[40] Yet the human rights argument that underpins this has also resulted in an undermining of a social structural understanding of discrimination and oppression. Richardson and Monro,[41] in their study of the ways in which local authorities in England, Wales and Northern Ireland have implemented, or not, sexualities equalities, explicate the ways in which debates about LGBTQ+ equalities become contradictory around the binary of sameness/difference that exist in the human rights argument. The positive equalities duties expected in the public sector has led to the term 'equality and diversity' being used as the umbrella for the policies and practices guiding how all service users, employees and members of the public might expect to be treated. Fairness is part of this rationale and, they argue, an emphasis is emerging on individual rights to expect fairness and equality of treatment.

Richardson and Monro[42] argue that such processes lead to a depoliticisation of difference and a focus on 'the worth of every individual as an individual,' and enunciation of claims to citizenship as being about the sameness that every human shares rather than the differences that might exist between us. Here, difference is not assumed to be the result of essentialised understandings of biology, genetics or neuroscience, but differences that are the result of social, cultural and structural /material discrimination and oppression that position members of different social groups differently in terms of their potential opportunities and life outcomes.

What supports this approach to understanding human rights, which results in rendering invisible socially produced differences, is the broader neoliberal framework within which public (and private) services are being funded, organised, administered and experienced. Gedalof[43] criticises the emphasis placed on the individual in 'equality talk' because, she argues, this makes it difficult for 'difference' to be taken into account. Gedalof's analysis of the policy documents that led to the 2006 and 2010 Equality Acts illustrates the ways in which liberal exhortations to value the sameness that everybody shares ultimately means that everybody is assumed to be the same as a particular 'dominant group' with their 'particular interests and perspectives.'[44] Thus, the goal to treat everybody 'the same' results in them actually being treated in ways that reflect the needs of that dominant group, which may or may not be appropriate. Claims that this is not appropriate are difficult to challenge without evidence, which itself relies on processes of monitoring for protected characteristics – something practitioners often resist because of the reprivatised nature of sexuality. Specialist services are more difficult to argue for when it is believed that mainstream services are providing for everybody.[45]

Donovan and Barnes[46] illustrate the same argument in their analysis of qualitative interviews conducted with practitioners who provide both mandatory and voluntary perpetrator programmes. Existing programmes are based on research conducted with heterosexual (cisgender assumed) male perpetrators. The practitioners, whether situated in voluntary or statutory programme contexts, believed that DVA takes place in LGBTQ+ relationships and that LGBTQ+ perpetrators should have access to perpetrator programmes to address their behaviour. In discussing what programmes they might access, Donovan and Barnes identify an equalities discourse that reflects the human rights agenda of sameness: whilst most practitioners believe that perpetrators, regardless of gender or sexuality, are the same, that what they referred to as the shared perpetrator problems – for example, of attachment and dealing with anger – are the same; and/or that the abusive relationship dynamic whereby one partner exerts power and control – feminises – the other is the same.[47] The underlying problems with perpetrators such as attachment or anger problems are unproblematically presented as shared, 'human' problems regardless of the fact that they come from research with violent heterosexual men. Donovan and Barnes conclude that:

> The orthodoxy relying on discourses of sameness should be challenged to be better informed about the ways in which differences occur across sexualities and gender identities, between LGBTQ+ individuals, and across their relationships to better reflect the actual needs of these abusive partners'[48]

For some researchers exploring DVA in the relationships of LGBTQ+ people, the heteronormativity of the feminist explanatory framework is reason enough to reject it for its irrelevance.[49] The problem of DVA in the relationships of lesbians first, then gay men and – much more recently – bisexual and /or transpeople,[50] was originally articulated by those working within psychology, counselling or therapy.[51] This tradition has continued with the work of those who point to minority stress as an explanatory framework for understanding DVA in the relationships of LGBTQ+ people.[52] Minority stress is understood as the cumulative impact of the micro-aggressions that result from living in a society as a member of an oppressed group. Such stress, it is argued, can result in individual LGB people either being victimised or enacting violence and abuse in their intimate relationships. Researchers in this area identify 'measures' of stress: whether and to what degree an individual is out, whether and to what extent an individual has experienced homophobia (much of the research in this field has focussed on the experiences of lesbians and gay men)[53]; the degree to which somebody can be said to have internalised homophobia which is understood as a self-hatred about one's sexuality.[54] Different studies utilise different combinations of these measures, which poses problems of consistency and comparability across studies. It is also problematic when respondents only have to report either experiencing or enacting one incident of violence/abuse to be categorised as 'victim/survivors' or as 'perpetrators.' This goes counter to the Home Office definition of DVA as a pattern of behaviours, and does not account for the many motives for, meanings of and impact of using violence in an intimate relationship. For example, a single incident of violence reported as having been used by a respondent might actually have been their use of self-defence against an abusive partner.

Donovan and Hester[55] and Donovan[56] have questioned the utility of correlations between these various markers for minority stress and either victimisation or perpetration when the logic of the argument seems flawed. Were we to apply the same logic to other minoritised groups such as (cisgender, heterosexual) women, we might expect to see far more men being victimised by women who have experienced misogyny and far more white people being victimised by Black people who have experienced racism, yet this is not what is happening. It is also problematic when studies do not claim a causal relationship between minority stress and intimate partner violence, yet the correlations found are interpreted more broadly as if they are causal.[57]

Another problem with minority stress as an explanatory tool is its reliance on an individualistic approach to understanding the undoubted impacts of living in a homophobic (as well as a biphobic and transphobic) society. Scholars imply that it is individual maladaptation[58] to their sexuality and/or their experiences of homophobia or biphobia that leads to violence and abuse. Whilst there are negative consequences of living in a homo-bi-transphobic society that have been discussed previously, the question should be less about the failures of the individual to cope and more about the societal context that creates the conditions in which individuals are disproportionately disadvantaged, discriminated against and suffer hostility and hate.

Ironically, it might also be that some of the negative consequences being felt by LGBTQ+ people might be the result of the apparent celebratory atmosphere about the LGBTQ+ community having achieved equality. Richardson,[59] along with others, has problematised the construction of citizenship based on individual rights and concerns defined through a heteronormative neoliberal agenda 'emphasising consumption, rights and "family values."'[60] The consequences of this 'gold standard' of the 'responsibilised citizen,'[61] Richardson argues, is an emerging sexuality and gender fundamentalism which constitutes both 'good' and 'bad' gays, where the latter are those who either by design or as a result of socially exclusionary practices and processes live marginalised lives, transgressing the social norms associated with a heteronormative social order (e.g. monogamy, family life).[62]

The public story of DVA

Liang et al.[63] offer a three-stage, non-linear approach to thinking about help-seeking which involves recognising the problem, deciding to do something about it and choosing a source of help. At each point, there will be barriers and facilitators that enable or prevent achievement of that stage. For LGBTQ+ people experiencing DVA, being able to recognise and name their experiences as such can be prevented by what Donovan and Hester[64] call the public story of DVA. Public stories, as Jamieson[65] explains, are dominant shorthand stories that exist in society that can be drawn on to make sense of everyday lives. They can be seen as templates, basic and simple enough to confer strong messages about how social behaviours and phenomenon might be understood and constituted. They can be seen as necessary fictions that often reflect particular ideas originating from powerful interests in society. Donovan and Hester[66] argue that the public story of DVA is an unintended consequence of feminist successes in the domestic violence field, which has transformed DVA from being minimised and individualised as a 'domestic' – a private – trouble[67] to being understood as a profoundly important public problem requiring societal change to address it.

The public story of DVA presents the problem as that of (cisgender) heterosexual men for (cisgender) heterosexual women, a problem of, primarily, physical violence, and a problem of a particular presentation of (cis)gender: the 'big' 'strong' man being physically violent towards the 'small' 'weak' woman. They argue that this story can prevent LGBTQ+ people from being able to recognise their experiences as DVA, which makes it difficult for them to tell their stories. Conversely, the public story of DVA makes it difficult for informal or formal sources who are turned to for help, to hear those stories as recognisably DVA.

The public story has developed over many decades to capture the ways in which understandings have changed. In her analysis of how *Spare Rib* reported on DVA over the three decades the magazine was published, Donovan[68] shows how the terminology changed over time from stories about 'battered wives' to 'battered women' to 'domestic violence' and so on; always heterosexual but reflecting experience and research indicating that marriage was not the only context in which DVA took place, that physical violence was not the only violence inflicted and linking DVA along the continuum of men's violence against women and girls. The success of the feminist project in the field of violence against women and girls can be evidenced by the England and Wales Home Office having in their strategies' titled 'Violence Against Women and Girls' and by their stating that the highest risk for experiencing violence is being female.[69]

The public story of DVA does not only (re)produce a particular story about who might experience DVA, what DVA might consist of and who might enact DVA; it also (re)produces particular, binary (cis)gendered assumptions about victims and perpetrators that have an impact on how those who do not fit or cannot be seen in this public story of DVA. Thus it can be difficult for women to be understood as perpetrators and for men to be understood as victims; violence between women can be minimised because it cannot be comprehended that women might pose as high a risk to other women as men might pose to women; violence between men can be minimised because men, being used to violence, are able to defend themselves and the violence can be seen as a fair fight.[70] In any case, the violence of men towards women will typically be understood as far more potentially serious and pose higher risks of harm than any between two women or two men. Donovan and Hester[71] also report on women who explained that they did not report the violence they experienced from a female partner to the police because they were taller and/or bigger than their abusive partner; they assumed they would not be believed because they did not fit the public story that says the victim is smaller and weaker than the bigger, stronger abusive partner. Thus, epistemological knowledge about DVA is socially constructed through the public story of DVA.[72]

Other reasons why LGBTQ+ people might not report to any formal sources of help relate to the legacy of their historical structural positioning as potential criminals and/or 'sick' individuals in need of psychological (aversion) treatment. There exists a gap of trust[73] between LGBTQ+ people and the police, but also with professionals such as health practitioners.[74] Expectations exist that responses, far from being 'equal,' will be hostile and/or discriminatory, or that individuals' sexuality or gender identity will become the problem.[75]

The other source of evidence about the impact of the public story of DVA is the research that has been done exploring with different groups of practitioners their responses to DVA in different relationship scenarios. Most of this work has been conducted in the USA with refuge workers, the police, potential jurors and psychology students.[76] The latter might have a crucial part to play in providing support to LGBTQ+ people who are experiencing DVA, since it is to counsellors and therapists they turn rather than to the police or other mainstream DVA specialist agencies.[77] What these studies find is that practitioners tend to draw on heteronormative, binaried gender assumptions in order to make sense of the DVA they are being asked to consider. In a study of staff running a DVA refuge, they assessed DVA scenarios involving same-sex relationships as less serious than heterosexual relationships, that there was less likelihood of escalation in same-sex relationships and that they were less likely to recommend that the partner being victimised leave.[78]

Elsewhere, a study of the police found that, compared to female perpetrators in female same-sex relationships, male perpetrators in male same-sex relationships were only arrested when there had been a serious assault. The authors speculated that a certain level of violence between men might be tolerated and only acted on when it reaches or passes a certain threshold.[79] A study of university students – potential members of juries – were asked to consider DVA in different couple scenarios. Male violence against women was assessed as more serious than in same-sex relationships, respondents indicated they would be more likely to recommend a woman press charges against a male perpetrator than they would in same-sex relationships, participants perceived those victimised in same-sex relationships as less credible than heterosexual female victims and their perceptions about believability of the victim had sentencing implications.[80] In another study[81] that asked students to make decisions about a trial transcript relating to DVA in a female same-sex relationship, decisions were influenced by the extent to which the defendant and victim were perceived as more or less feminine/masculine.[82] The power of the public story is not just for those who do not see their experiences reflected in it and who might not, or might take longer to, realise and recognise their experiences as DVA. Its power is also in what the responses might be from those they seek help from which could have serious implications for people's safety.

Conclusion

There are many reasons why LGBTQ+ people who experience or enact DVA do not report to formal sources of help and/or support. In this chapter, I have attempted to take the focus away from any one individual's decision-making and look more broadly at what it is about the conditions in which those individuals live that might make seeking of help from formal sources a last, if ever, option. Whilst the legislative landscape suggests that equality is being legally achieved, the evidence explored in this chapter suggests that equality is not achieved through the law alone. In the early twenty-first century, several parallel trends continue to produce, reflect and reinforce the idea that the individual is at the centre of their own life, disconnected from the social groups and social structural hierarchies into which they have been born and the cultural contexts that have (re)produced public stories and values through which they might make meaning of their lives. The neoliberal turn to the individual responsibilised citizen, responsible for their successes and failures, is one such trend. This ideological trend has been bolstered and underpinned by successive governments since 2010 to impose austerity in the UK and cut publicly funded services that might be used by those who are victimised or those who perpetrate DVA, making it more difficult to secure funding for specialist LGBT DVA services and for mainstream DVA services to properly ensure their services are accessible to LGBTQ+ people. The equalities legislation and policies have been formed and implemented in ways that reflect neoliberal ideas; thus, sexualities have been reprivatised and rendered almost invisible in the public sector other than as an aspect of an individual they have a right to express (as long as this is heteronormatively). The specific problem for LGBTQ+ experiences of DVA is that the problem itself has been socially constructed as a heterosexual problem which affects both whether LGBTQ+ people are able to recognise their experiences as such, and also on how practitioners might respond.

Equality cannot be about treating everybody the same, nor can it be about unproblematically treating everybody as an individual. Aspiring for equality is about recognising the collective histories of minoritised groups – such as those who are LGBTQ+ – that position them in ways that lead to their stigmatised status in society: given less worth, being seen as threatening, being morally degenerate, having low expectations about their possibilities for living intimate lives. Aspiring for equality in responses to and prevention of DVA is about understanding the ways in which the public story of DVA has socially constructed a particular kind of authentic victim and perpetrator of a particular kind of violence. It is also about understanding the implications for those whose experiences do not fit within this public story. This can result in non-recognition of DVA by those who are victimised, practitioners and policy makers with potentially serious consequences following from not being understood as in need of access to public services.

Notes

1 Any adult couple that does not contravene law about consanguity in the Marriage (Prohibited Degrees of Relationship) Act 1986.
2 Catherine Donovan and Marianne Hester, 'Seeking Help from the Enemy: Help-Seeking Strategies of Those in Same-Sex Relationships Who Have Experienced Domestic Abuse' (2011) 23 *Child and Family Law Quarterly* 26; Damien Riggs and others, 'Domestic Violence Service Providers' Capacity for Supporting Transgender Women: Findings from an Australian Workshop' (2016) 46 *British Journal of Social Work* 2374.
3 Home Office, *Circular 003/2013: New Government Domestic Violence and Abuse Definition* (2013) <www.gov.uk/government/publications/new-government-domestic-violence-and-abuse-definition/circular-0032013-new-government-domestic-violence-and-abuse-definition> accessed 20 July 2019.
4 Catherine Donovan and Marianne Hester, *Domestic Violence and Sexuality: What's Love Got to Do with It?* (Policy Press 2014); Adam Messinger, *LGBTQ Intimate Partner Violence: Lessons for Policy, Practice, and Research* (University of California Press 2017).
5 Mikel Walters, Jieru Chen and Matthew Breiding, *The National Intimate Partner and Sexual Violence Survey (NISVS): 2010 Findings on Victimization by Sexual Orientation* (National Center for Injury Prevention and Control 2013).
6 Sylvia Walby and others, *The Concept and Measurement of Violence Against Women and Men* (Policy Press 2017).
7 For similar discussion about data collected in the Canadian context, see Janice Ristock, 'Introduction: Intimate Partner Violence in LGBTQ Lives' in Janice Ristock (ed), *Intimate Partner Violence in LGBTQ Lives* (Routledge 2011).
8 Kevin Smith and others, *Homicides, Firearm Offences and Intimate Violence 2010/11, (Supplementary Volume 2 to Crime in England and Wales)* (Home Office 2012).
9 Ibid.
10 Ibid.
11 Donovan and Hester (n 5).
12 Office for National Statistics (ONS), 'Women Most at Risk of Experiencing Partner Abuse in England and Wales: Years Ending March 2015 to 2017' (ONS 2018).
13 For example, Catherine Donovan and Rebecca Barnes, 'Being "Ideal" or Falling Short? The Legitimacy of Lesbian, Gay, Bisexual and/or Transgender Victims of Domestic Violence and Hate Crime' in Marian Duggan (ed), *Revisiting the Ideal Victim Concept* (Policy Press 2018).
14 For example, Carol Smart, *The Ties the Bind: Law, Marriage and the Reproduction of Patriarchal Relations* (Routledge 1984).
15 For example, Robert Leckey, *After Legal Equality: Family, Sex, Kinship* (Routledge 2015).
16 For example, Rosemary Auchmuty, 'What's so Special About Marriage? The Impact of Wilkinson v Kitzinger' (2008) 20 *Child and Family Quarterly* 475.
17 For example, Ilan Meyer, 'The Elusive Promise of LGBT Equality' (2016) 106 *American Journal of Public Health* 1356.

18 For example, Robert Vanderbeck and Paul Johnson, 'Homosexuality, Religion and the Contested Legal Framework Governing Sex Education in England' (2015) 37 *Journal of Social Welfare & Family Law* 161.
19 For example, Susan Faludi, *Backlash: The Undeclared War Against American Women* (Three Rivers Press 1991).
20 Catherine Donovan, John Clayton and Stephen Macdonald, 'New Directions in Hate Reporting Research: Agency, Heterogeneity and Relationality' (2018) 24 *Sociological Research Online* 185.
21 Sylvia Walby, 'Complexity Theory, Systems Theory and Multiple Intersecting Social Inequalities' (2007) 22 *Philosophy of the Social Sciences* 449.
22 For example, Simon Clarke, 'The Neoliberal Theory of Society' in Alfredo Saad-Filho and Deborah Johnston (eds), *Neoliberalism: A Critical Reader* (Pluto Press 2005).
23 Nikolas Rose, 'Government and Control' (2000) 40 *British Journal of Criminology* 321.
24 For example, Lauren Berlant and Michael Warner, 'Sex in Public' (1998) 24 *Critical Inquiry* 547.
25 For example, Asher Flynn and Jacqueline Hodgson (eds), *Access to Justice and Legal Aid: Comparative Perspectives on Unmet Legal Aid* (Hart Publishing 2017).
26 For an argument that homophobia is in decline among young heterosexual men, see Mark McCormack, *The Declining Significance of Homophobia: How Teenage Boys Are Redefining Masculinity and Heterosexuality* (Oxford University Press 2012).
27 Metro, 'Youth Chances: Integrated Report' *Metro Charity* (2016) <https://metrocharity.org.uk/sites/default/files/2017-04/National%20Youth%20Chances%20Intergrated%20Report%202016.pdf> accessed 20 July 2019.
28 Ibid., A2.
29 Adam Lusher, 'Homophobic Attacks Rose 147 Per Cent After the Brexit Vote' *The Independent* (London, 9 October 2016) <www.independent.co.uk/news/uk/home-news/brexit-hate-crime-hatred-homophobia-lgbt-147-per-cent-rise-double-attacks-on-gays-lesbians-a7352411.html> accessed 20 July 2019.
30 Catherine Donovan and Marianne Hester, ' "Because She Was My First Girlfriend, I Didn't Know Any Different": Making the Case for Mainstreaming Same-Sex Sex/Relationship Education' (2008) 8 *Journal of Sex Education* 277; Donovan and Hester (n 5).
31 Janice Ristock, *No More Secrets: Violence in Lesbian Relationships* (Routledge 2002).
32 Donovan and Hester (n 31).
33 Catherine Donovan, Rebecca Barnes and Catherine Nixon, *The Coral Project: Exploring Abusive Behaviours in Lesbian, Gay, Bisexual and/or Transgender Relationships: Interim Report* (Universities of Sunderland and Leicester 2014).
34 See Donovan and Hester (n 31).
35 Simon Jenkins, 'Sex Education Is Not a Matter for Ministers' *The Guardian* (London, 1 March 2019) <www.theguardian.com/commentisfree/2019/mar/01/ministers-sex-education-schools> accessed 30 March 2019; Simon Rocker, 'Sex Education Plans Will "Limit" Parents' Religious Rights, Say Opponents' *The Jewish Chronicle* (London, 8 March 2019) <www.thejc.com/education/education-news/sex-education-proposals-opposed-1.481183> accessed 30 March 2019.
36 Diane Richardson and Surya Monro, 'Public Duty and Private Prejudice: Sexualities Equalities and Local Government' (2013) 61 *The Sociological Review* 131.

37 Matthew Todd, *Straight Jacket: How to Be Gay and Happy* (Black Swann 2018); Sally Munt, 'Gay Shame in a Geopolitical Context' (2019) 33 *Cultural Studies* 223.
38 Stephen Whittle, Lewis Turner and Maryam Al-Alami, *Engendered Penalties, Transgender and Transsexual People's Experiences of Inequality and Discrimination* (Press for Change, Manchester Metropolitan University 2007); Ruth Hunt and Julie Fish, *Prescription for Change: Lesbian and Bisexual Women's Health Check* (Stonewall 2008); and specifically looking at young people, Ian Rivers and Nausicaa Noret, 'Well-Being Among Same-Sex and Opposite-Sex Attracted Youth at School' (2008) 37 *School Psychology Review* 174; Elizabeth McDermott and Katrina Roen, *Queer Youth, Suicide and Self-Harm: Troubled Subjects, Troubling Norms* (Palgrave Macmillan 2016).
39 Munt (n 38).
40 Catherine Donovan, 'Tackling Inequality in the Intimate Sphere: Problematizing Love and Violence in Same-Sex Relationships' in Robert Leckey (ed), *After Legal Equality* (Routledge 2015) 167–183.
41 Richardson and Monro (n 37); Surya Monro, 'Sexuality, Space and Intersectionality: The Case of Lesbian, Gay and Bisexual Equalities Initiatives in UK Local Government' (2012) 44 *Sociology* 996.
42 Richardson and Monro (n 37) 134.
43 Irene Gedalof, 'Sameness and Difference in Government Equality Talk' (2013) 36 *Ethnic and Racial Studies* 117.
44 Ibid., 120.
45 Catherine Donovan and Matt Durey, '"Well That Would Be Nice, but We Can't Do That in the Current Climate"' in Peter Rushton and Catherine Donovan (eds), *Austerity Policies: Bad Ideas in Practice* (Palgrave Macmillan 2018) 197–220.
46 Catherine Donovan and Rebecca Barnes, 'Making Sense of Discourses of Sameness and Difference in Agency Responses to LGBTQ+ Abusive Partners' (2017) *Sexualities* (online).
47 Ibid.
48 Ibid., 16.
49 David Island and Patrick Letellier, *Men Who Beat the Men Who Love Them: Battered Gay Men and Domestic Violence* (Routledge 1991).
50 Messinger (n 5).
51 Rebecca Barnes and Catherine Donovan, 'Domestic Violence in Lesbian, Gay, Bisexual and/or Transgender Relationships' in Nancy Lonbard (ed), *Gender and Violence Research Companion* (Routledge 2018).
52 Kimberly Balsam, 'Nowhere to Hide: Lesbian Battering, Homophobia, and Minority Stress' in Ellyn Kaschak (ed), *Intimate Betrayal: Domestic Violence in Lesbian Relationships* (The Howarth Press 2001) 25–37; Kimberly Balsam and Dawn Szymanski, 'Relationship Quality and Domestic Violence in Women's Same-Sex Relationships: The Role of Minority Stress' (2005) 29 *Psychology of Women Quarterly* 258; Jesmen Mendoza, 'The Impact of Minority Stress on Gay Male Partner Abuse' in Janice Ristock (ed), *Intimate Partner Violence in LGBTQ Lives* (Routledge 2011); Rob Stephenson and Catherine Finneran, 'Minority Stress and Intimate Partner Violence Among Gay and Bisexual Men in Atlanta' (2017) 11 *American Journal of Men's Health* 952.
53 Lisa Langenderfer-Magruder and others, 'Experiences of Intimate Partner Violence and Subsequent Police Reporting Among Lesbian, Gay, Bisexual, Transgender, and Queer Adults in Colorado: Comparing Rates of Cisgender and Transgender Victimization' (2016) 31 *Journal of Interpersonal Violence* 855.
54 Mendoza (n 53); Balsam (n 53); Balsam and Szymanski (n 53).

55 Donovan and Hester (n 5).
56 Donovan (n 41).
57 See, for example, Mendoza (n 53).
58 Ibid.
59 Diane Richardson, 'Desiring Sameness? The Rise of a Neoliberal Politics of Normalisation' (2005) 37 *Antipode* 515; Diane Richardson, 'Rethinking Sexual Citizenship' (2017) 51 *Sociology* 208.
60 Richardson (2017) (n 60) 214.
61 Rose (n 24).
62 See also Todd (n 38).
63 Belle Liang and others, 'A Theoretical Framework for Understanding Help-Seeking Processes Among Survivors of Intimate Partner Violence' (2005) 36 *American Journal of Community Psychology* 71.
64 Catherine Donovan and Marianne Hester, '"I Hate the Word Victim": An Exploration of Recognition of Domestic Violence in Same-Sex Relationships' (2010) 9 *Social Policy and Society* 279; Donovan and Hester (n 5).
65 Lynn Jamieson, *Intimacy and Personal Relationships in Modern Society* (Polity Press 1998).
66 Donovan and Hester (n 65); Donovan and Hester (n 5).
67 C. Wright-Mills, *The Sociological Imagination* (Oxford University Press 1959).
68 Catherine Donovan, 'An Exploration of Spare Rib's Treatment of Violence Between Women in Same-Sex Relationships' in Angela Smith (ed), *Re-Reading Spare Rib* (Palgrave Macmillan 2017).
69 Home Office, *Call to End Violence Against Woman and Girls: Action Plan* (HMSO 2011); Home Office, *Violence Against Women and Girls: Action Plan: Strategy 2016–2010* (HMSO 2016).
70 See also, Donovan and Barnes (n 14) 83–102.
71 Donovan and Hester (n 5).
72 See Donovan and Barnes (n 14) for a broader discussion about how victimisation and perpetration more generally are also (cis) binary gendered.
73 Donovan and Hester (n 3).
74 Julie Fish, 'Conceptualising Social Exclusion and Lesbian, Gay, Bisexual and Transgender People: The Implications for Promoting Equity in Nursing Policy and Practice' (2010) 15 *Journal of Research in Nursing* 303.
75 Donovan, Barnes and Nixon (n 34).
76 Michael J Brown and Jennifer Groscup, 'Perceptions of Same-Sex Domestic Violence Among Crisis Centre Staff' (2009) 24 *Journal of Family Violence* 87; April Pattavina and others, 'A Comparison of the Police Response to Heterosexual Versus Same-Sex Intimate Partner Violence' (2007) 13 *Violence Against Women* 374; Paula Poorman, Eric Seelau and Shelia Seelau, 'Perceptions of Domestic Abuse in Same-Sex Relationships and Implications for Criminal Justice and Mental Health Responses' (2003) 18 *Violence and Victims* 659.
77 Donovan and Hester (n 5).
78 Brown and Groscup (n 77) 87–93.
79 Pattavina and others (n 77).
80 Poorman, Seelau and Seelau (n 77).
81 Nesa Wasarhaley and others, 'The Impact of Gender Stereotypes on Legal Perceptions of Lesbian Intimate Partner Violence' (2017) 32 *Journal of Interpersonal Violence* 635.
82 See Betsi Little and Cheryl Terrance, 'Perceptions of Domestic Violence in Lesbian Relationships: Stereotypes and Gender Role Expectations' (2010) 57 *Journal of Homosexuality* 429, for similar findings with psychology students.

References

Primary sources

Marriage (Prohibited Degrees of Relationship) Act 1986.

Secondary sources

Auchmuty R, 'What's so Special About Marriage? The Impact of Wilkinson v Kitzinger' (2008) 20 *Child and Family Quarterly* 475.

Balsam K, 'Nowhere to Hide: Lesbian Battering, Homophobia, and Minority Stress' in Kaschak E (ed), *Intimate Betrayal: Domestic Violence in Lesbian Relationships* (The Howarth Press 2001).

Balsam K and Szymanski D, 'Relationship Quality and Domestic Violence in Women's Same-Sex Relationships: The Role of Minority Stress' (2005) 29 *Psychology of Women Quarterly* 258.

Barnes R and Donovan C, 'Domestic Violence in Lesbian, Gay, Bisexual and/or Transgender Relationships' in Lonbard N (ed), *Gender and Violence Research Companion* (Routledge 2018).

Berlant L and Warner M, 'Sex in Public' (1998) 24 *Critical Inquiry* 547.

Brown MJ and Groscup J, 'Perceptions of Same-Sex Domestic Violence Among Crisis Centre Staff' (2009) 24 *Journal of Family Violence* 87.

Clarke S, 'The Neoliberal Theory of Society' in Saad-Filho A and Johnston D (eds), *Neoliberalism: A Critical Reader* (Pluto Press 2005).

Donovan C, 'Tackling Inequality in the Intimate Sphere: Problematizing Love and Violence in Same-Sex Relationships' in Leckey R (ed), *After Legal Equality* (Routledge 2015), 167–183.

———, 'An Exploration of Spare Rib's Treatment of Violence Between Women in Same-Sex Relationships' in Smith A (ed), *Re-Reading Spare Rib* (Palgrave Macmillan 2017).

Donovan C and Barnes R, 'Making Sense of Discourses of Sameness and Difference in Agency Responses to LGBTQ+ Abusive Partners' (2017) *Sexualities* (online).

———, 'Being "Ideal" or Falling Short? The Legitimacy of Lesbian, Gay, Bisexual and/or Transgender Victims of Domestic Violence and Hate Crime' in Duggan M (ed), *Revisiting the Ideal Victim Concept* (Policy Press 2018) 83–102.

Donovan C, Barnes R and Nixon C, *The Coral Project: Exploring Abusive Behaviours in Lesbian, Gay, Bisexual and/or Transgender Relationships: Interim Report* (Universities of Sunderland and Leicester 2014).

Donovan C, Clayton J and Macdonald S, 'New Directions in Hate Reporting Research: Agency, Heterogeneity and Relationality' (2018) 24 *Sociological Research Online* 185.

Donovan C and Durey M, 'Well That Would Be Nice, but We Can't Do That in the Current Climate' in Rushton P and Donovan C (eds), *Austerity Policies: Bad Ideas in Practice* (Palgrave Macmillan 2018), 197–220.

Donovan C and Hester M, '"Because She Was My First Girlfriend, I Didn't Know Any Different": Making the Case for Mainstreaming Same-Sex Sex/Relationship Education' (2008) 8 *Journal of Sex Education* 277.

———, '"I Hate the Word Victim": An Exploration of Recognition of Domestic Violence in Same-Sex Relationships' (2010) 9 *Social Policy and Society* 279.

———, 'Seeking Help from the Enemy: Help-Seeking Strategies of Those in Same-Sex Relationships Who Have Experienced Domestic Abuse' (2011) 23 *Child and Family Law Quarterly* 26.

———, *Domestic Violence and Sexuality: What's Love Got to Do with It?* (Policy Press 2014).

Faludi S, *Backlash: The Undeclared War Against American Women* (Three Rivers Press 1991).

Fish J, 'Conceptualising Social Exclusion and Lesbian, Gay, Bisexual and Transgender People: The Implications for Promoting Equity in Nursing Policy and Practice' (2010) 15 *Journal of Research in Nursing* 303.

Flynn A and Hodgson J (eds), *Access to Justice and Legal Aid: Comparative Perspectives on Unmet Legal Aid* (Hart Publishing 2017).

Gedalof I, 'Sameness and Difference in Government Equality Talk' (2013) 36 *Ethnic and Racial Studies* 117.

Home Office, *Circular 003/2013: New Government Domestic Violence and Abuse Definition* (2013) <www.gov.uk/government/publications/new-government-domestic-violence-and-abuse-definition/circular-0032013-new-government-domestic-violence-and-abuse-definition> accessed 20 July 2019.

———, *Call to End Violence Against Woman and Girls: Action Plan* (HMSO 2011); Home Office, *Violence Against Women and Girls: Action Plan: Strategy 2016–2010* (HMSO 2016).

Hunt R and Fish J, *Prescription for Change: Lesbian and Bisexual Women's Health Check* (Stonewall 2008).

Island D and Letellier P, *Men Who Beat the Men Who Love Them: Battered Gay Men and Domestic Violence* (Routledge 1991).

Jamieson L, *Intimacy and Personal Relationships in Modern Society* (Polity Press 1998).

Jenkins S, 'Sex Education Is Not a Matter for Ministers' *The Guardian* (London, 1 March 2019) <www.theguardian.com/commentisfree/2019/mar/01/ministers-sex-education-schools> accessed 30 March 2019.

Langenderfer-Magruder L and others, 'Experiences of Intimate Partner Violence and Subsequent Police Reporting Among Lesbian, Gay, Bisexual, Transgender, and Queer Adults in Colorado: Comparing Rates of Cisgender and Transgender Victimization' (2016) 31 *Journal of Interpersonal Violence* 855.

Leckey R, *After Legal Equality: Family, Sex, Kinship* (Routledge 2015).

Liang B and others, 'A Theoretical Framework for Understanding Help-Seeking Processes Among Survivors of Intimate Partner Violence' (2005) 36 *American Journal of Community Psychology* 71.

Little B and Terrance C, 'Perceptions of Domestic Violence in Lesbian Relationships: Stereotypes and Gender Role Expectations' (2010) 57 *Journal of Homosexuality* 429.

Lusher L, 'Homophobic Attacks Rose 147 Per Cent After the Brexit Vote' *The Independent* (London, 9 October 2016) <www.independent.co.uk/news/uk/home-news/brexit-hate-crime-hatred-homophobia-lgbt-147-per-cent-rise-double-attacks-on-gays-lesbians-a7352411.html> accessed 20 July 2019.

McCormack M, *The Declining Significance of Homophobia: How Teenage Boys Are Redefining Masculinity and Heterosexuality* (Oxford University Press 2012).

McDermott E and Roen K, *Queer Youth, Suicide and Self-Harm: Troubled Subjects, Troubling Norms* (Palgrave Macmillan 2016).

Mendoza J, 'The Impact of Minority Stress on Gay Male Partner Abuse' in Ristock J (ed), *Intimate Partner Violence in LGBTQ Lives* (Routledge 2011).

Messinger A, *LGBTQ Intimate Partner Violence: Lessons for Policy, Practice, and Research* (University of California Press 2017).

Metro, 'Youth Chances: Integrated Report' *Metro Charity* (2016) <https://metrocharity.org.uk/sites/default/files/2017-04/National%20Youth%20Chances%20Intergrated%20Report%202016.pdf> accessed 20 July 2019.

Meyer I, 'The Elusive Promise of LGBT Equality' (2016) 106 *American Journal of Public Health* 1356.

Monro S, 'Sexuality, Space and Intersectionality: The Case of Lesbian, Gay and Bisexual Equalities Initiatives in UK Local Government' (2012) 44 *Sociology* 996.

Munt S, 'Gay Shame in a Geopolitical Context' (2019) 33 *Cultural Studies* 223.

Office for National Statistics (ONS) 'Women Most at Risk of Experiencing Partner Abuse in England and Wales: Years Ending March 2015 to 2017' (ONS 2018).

Pattavina A and others, 'A Comparison of the Police Response to Heterosexual Versus Same-Sex Intimate Partner Violence' (2007) 13 *Violence Against Women* 374.

Poorman P, Seelau E and Seelau S, 'Perceptions of Domestic Abuse in Same-Sex Relationships and Implications for Criminal Justice and Mental Health Responses' (2003) 18 *Violence and Victims* 659.

Richardson D, 'Desiring Sameness? The Rise of a Neoliberal Politics of Normalisation' (2005) 37 *Antipode* 515.

———, 'Rethinking Sexual Citizenship' (2017) 51 *Sociology* 208.

Richardson D and Monro S, 'Public Duty and Private Prejudice: Sexualities Equalities and Local Government' (2013) 61 *The Sociological Review* 131.

Riggs D and others, 'Domestic Violence Service Providers' Capacity for Supporting Transgender Women: Findings from an Australian Workshop' (2016) 46 *British Journal of Social Work* 2374.

Ristock J, *No More Secrets: Violence in Lesbian Relationships* (Routledge 2002).

———, 'Introduction: Intimate Partner Violence in LGBTQ Lives' in Ristock J (ed), *Intimate Partner Violence in LGBTQ Lives* (Routledge 2011).

Rivers I and Noret N, 'Well-Being Among Same-Sex and Opposite-Sex Attracted Youth at School' (2008) 37 *School Psychology Review* 174.

Rocker S, 'Sex Education Plans Will "Limit" Parents' Religious Rights, Say Opponents' *The Jewish Chronicle* (London, 8 March 2019) <www.thejc.com/education/education-news/sex-education-proposals-opposed-1.481183> accessed 30 March 2019.

Rose N, 'Government and Control' (2000) 40 *British Journal of Criminology* 321.

Smart C, *The Ties the Bind: Law, Marriage and the Reproduction of Patriarchal Relations* (Routledge 1984).

Smith K and others, *Homicides, Firearm Offences and Intimate Violence 2010/11, (Supplementary Volume 2 to Crime in England and Wales)* (Home Office 2012).

Stephenson R and Finneran C, 'Minority Stress and Intimate Partner Violence Among Gay and Bisexual Men in Atlanta' (2017) 11 *American Journal of Men's Health* 952.

Todd M, *Straight Jacket: How to Be Gay and Happy* (Black Swann, 2018).

Vanderbeck R and Johnson P, 'Homosexuality, Religion and the Contested Legal Framework Governing Sex Education in England' (2015) 37 *Journal of Social Welfare & Family Law* 161.

Walby S, 'Complexity Theory, Systems Theory and Multiple Intersecting Social Inequalities' (2007) 22 *Philosophy of the Social Sciences* 449.

Walby S and others, *The Concept and Measurement of Violence Against Women and Men* (Policy Press 2017).

Walters M, Chen J and Breiding M, *The National Intimate Partner and Sexual Violence Survey (NISVS): 2010 Findings on Victimization by Sexual Orientation* (National Center for Injury Prevention and Control 2013).

Wasarhaley N and others, 'The Impact of Gender Stereotypes on Legal Perceptions of Lesbian Intimate Partner Violence' (2017) 32 *Journal of Interpersonal Violence* 635.

Whittle S, Turner L and Al-Alami M, *Engendered Penalties, Transgender and Transsexual People's Experiences of Inequality and Discrimination* (Press for Change, Manchester Metropolitan University 2007).

Wright-Mills C, *The Sociological Imagination* (Oxford University Press 1959).

Chapter 14

Incrementalism in same-sex marriage legalization

Erez Aloni

Introduction

Incrementalist framework in same-sex marriage advocacy – the idea that the legal progress toward recognition of same-sex marriage follows piecemeal and predictable steps – is prevalent and widely accepted among commentators, legal scholars, advocates, and policymakers. The notion of incrementalism in this context posits that legal change is contingent upon a concurrent and steady change of public opinion. Accordingly, legal change occurs gradually in small steps while each of these steps occurs only when public opinion is ready for the next stage. Thus, each small legal change makes the public more ready for and receptive to the next legal step.

The incrementalist paradigm, or the "law of small change," a depiction first coined by Dutch Law Professor Kees Waaldijk, has won great influence in legal scholarship.[1] This framework has descriptive, predictive (or prescriptive), and normative elements.[2] Incrementalist frameworks document the steps which most countries that reached same-sex marriage have followed, they predict which countries will be next to legalize same-sex marriage, they propose advocacy and policy plans that minimize backlash, and they also postulate marriage as the final frontier on the path to LGBTQ+ equality. Supporters of incrementalism thus advocate a policy of compromise: waiting for the right moment before claiming the final goal of marriage equality. Reaching the next stage too quickly, the incrementalist strategy warns, is likely to result in backlash – a political reaction that takes the movement a few steps back.

Although the incrementalist path is corroborated by the experience of many nations, particularly the Nordic states, some scholars have offered a sustained critique of the paradigm.[3] First, descriptively, even though most nations did follow the sequences laid out in the incrementalist paradigm, the few exceptions raise questions about the universal nature of the paradigm. Second, as a plan for advocacy purposes, the paradigm fails to provide material information, such as the time that it takes to move between stages.[4] Third, the strategy centers on the belief that progress is dependent on, or at least connected to, public readiness for change, and thus trivializes the harm of those who are harmed by the ban on same-sex marriage.[5] Finally, by upholding marriage equality as the final stage, proponents of incrementalism, explicitly or impliedly, divert attention from other alternative and innovative advocacy strategies that can advance substantive equality beyond marriage.

In what follows, I first canvass the fundamental character of the incrementalist model as pertaining to same-sex marriage, its rationales, and its broad scholarly support. I then turn to examine the applicability of incrementalism as reflected in the experience of select countries. Finally, I discuss the aforementioned critiques of incrementalism.

Incrementalism in same-sex marriage advocacy

Incrementalist progress, as a preferred political strategy to advance social change, is a cornerstone of liberal democracies.[6] According to political scientist Michael Hayes, "public policies necessarily evolve gradually through a pluralistic and highly conflictual process," making incrementalism "a superior form of policy-making."[7] Among the benefits of incrementalism, Hayes enumerates the facilitation of "majority-building by minimizing disruption to established practices" since "minimizing the scope of the reform will minimize opposition."[8] Additionally, incremental changes enable process of learning from mistakes and allow smart and measured policy changes. Dramatic changes that include multiple moving parts are harder to measure, for it is difficult to evaluate which part did not go well. Conversely, "piecemeal policy proposals make changes at the margins of existing policy, enabling policy analysts to trace consequences to their true causes."[9]

The benefits of incrementalism were quickly adopted in the context of same-sex marriage.

The first scholar to identify and advance a paradigm of small change in the recognition of same-sex partnerships was Waaldijk, who posits predicting legalization of same-sex marriage based on a series of steps leading toward legal recognition almost as a "law of nature."[10] To determine when a nation is likely to legalize same-sex marriage, Waaldijk asserts it is merely a matter of identifying what stage the state in question is currently at on the pre-determined path to marriage equality.[11]

According to Waaldijk, based on the experience of the Netherlands (the first nation to legalize same-sex marriage), as well as other nations that followed a similar path, the legal history of the recognition of LGBTQ+ rights in European countries reveals a pattern of steady incremental progress leading to the legalization of same-sex marriage. This process consists of three major stages, each of which consists of several sub-steps. Step one consists of the decriminalization of sodomy, after which the age of consent for same-sex relationships is made the same as that for different-sex relationships. Step two includes the enactment of legislation prohibiting discrimination on the basis of sexual orientation in the workplace and housing, and the inclusion of sexual orientation as a protected category in hate crime laws. Finally, step three culminates in the state recognizing same-sex partnerships and parental rights, typically first by enacting marriage-alternative schemes (such as domestic partnership or civil unions), and then lifting the ban on marriage altogether.

Waaldijk suggests that the European experience teaches that progress to the next step is contingent on the previous one. That is, each step facilitates the next one. To justify incremental progress, Waaldijk asserts that any legal change that advances legal recognition and acceptance of same-sex partnerships can only be enacted and accepted by the public if this change is perceived as small or insignificant.[12] This way, each small change leads to the next one, until they reach the final goal of marriage equality and parentage rights for same-sex couples.

U.S. Law Professor William Eskridge endorses and advances the premises of Waaldijk's incrementalist approach by addressing the important component of social attitudes.[13] He proposes that the "law cannot move unless public opinion moves, but public attitudes can be influenced by changes in the law."[14] Ultimately, Eskridge attempts to tackle the chicken-before-the-egg issue whereby legislative change tends to follow social change, but legislative change is often cited as a means of catalyzing social change. To get around this paradox, Eskridge uses incrementalism as a way to break the cycle. As incremental legal changes give greater visibility to LGBTQ+ issues, so social attitudes can become more accepting of the LGBTQ+ community, thus making further legal changes more possible and palatable.[15] "Human beings rarely change their fundamental attitudes overnight," Eskridge explains, but exposure to LGBTQ+ individuals might change their minds gradually, making them supportive of the next stage.[16] Accordingly, each stage creates more visibility to LGBTQ+ individuals, and society thus becomes more accepting of them. Eskridge warns that moving to the next step too quickly, without the societal and grassroots preparations, is likely to result in backlash.[17]

English Senior Lecturer in Law Frances Hamilton introduces another strong endorsement of the principles of incrementalism in same-sex marriage advocacy, along with an elaborated account of the role of the interconnection between public opinion and legal change.[18] Hamilton employs comparative constitutionalism, which reveals that the optimal method to achieve same-sex marriage recognition in countries is via a process of slow, incremental change. Derived from this approach is the proposition that change should arrive from the legislative branches, as court-based interventions are likely to cause public opinion backlash and potential legislative reversal, such as the passing of amendments to the law to restrict marriage to different-sex couples by popular vote. Indeed, in many instances in the United States, backlash resulted in LGBTQ+ rights being eroded or truncated in referenda. Hamilton submits that court-initiated recognition of same-sex marriage without sufficient public support may lead to substantive social inequality and to backlash. Responding to critics of incrementalism who are concerned that small change might be too slow, she asserts that incremental shifts are actually advantageous, as they are more likely to lead to lasting, substantively effective and enduring change.[19] Favorable public opinion is therefore vital to ensuring effective and long-lasting change and, in turn, is cultivated by small, incremental change.

Supporters of incrementalism not only describe the past and sketch a plan for the future. Incrementalist progress also validates some controversial policies and advocacy strategies. Fundamentally, the incrementalist approach promotes compromises and endorses intermediate solutions on the path toward same-sex marriage.

The clearest example of bolstering a compromise in the name of a piecemeal process is the case of civil unions. Civil unions and domestic partnerships are often regarded as registration schemes that were created as a compromise, to provide partnership rights to same-sex couples, while still excluding them from the marriage institution itself.[20] Although some argue that these civil unions short of marriage possess symbolic status in their own right, they provoked debate among supporters of LGBTQ+ rights as to whether they constitute a "separate-but-equal" type of institution that should be rejected or a middle-ground compromise on the path to same-sex marriage that will accelerate and facilitate the legalization of same-sex marriage. Incrementalists have been strong proponents of civil unions.[21] Waaldijk, for instance, clarifies that the registered partnership scheme in the Netherlands only emphasized the unfairness of the ban on same-sex marriage because it highlighted that same-sex couples were being discriminated against and demonstrated that there are no good policy reasons to ban them from marriage itself.[22] Eskridge acknowledges that civil unions pose a challenge to equality, as they treat same-sex couples different from others "for reasons that are hard to justify without resort to arguments grounded in state denigration or even prejudices."[23] Yet, Eskridge defends civil unions as "equality practice," because they remedy inequality in treatment of LGBTQ+ couples and are a necessary temporary stage on the way to same-sex marriage.[24] Namely, civil unions highlight the lack of justification for the discriminatory treatment of different-sex and same-sex couples by the state. Civil unions also demonstrate that recognition of same-sex relationships does not create the sorts of harmful consequences that opponents of LGBTQ+ equality often predict, thus further undermining justification for discriminatory treatment. Similarly, Hamilton contends that: "Intermediate stage legislation allows public opinion to adjust and develop."[25]

The incrementalist approach also advises achieving change through legislative means rather than through the courts. Incrementalists favor legislative rather than court action in bringing about incremental change because it allows for public opinion to adapt and change gradually.[26] Although courts may seem the quickest way to achieve marriage equality, the outcomes may be confused and/or inconsistently applied. Moving too quickly and using the courts to instigate change is also likely to cause backlash. Legislative change, conversely, "is more likely to facilitate mutual accommodation" in a way that is more "politically acceptable."[27] Legislative change will always be deemed "more legitimate" than court change.[28] Incrementalism in this context, again, sanctions compromise by suggesting that, to avoid backlash, courts will do well if they "adopt a compromise approach by suspending their judgment to give the legislature time to canvas public opinion on the topic and amend legislation."[29]

Scholars have largely subscribed to the incremental model as the ideal path toward reaching same-sex marriage. The next section examines the lessons we can derive from the experiences of selected countries that legalized same-sex marriage.

Incrementalism in practice – what we learn from experience

The framework for the incrementalist approach is grounded in the experiences of the nations that first recognized same-sex marriage, and largely proves itself to be the general pattern that countries still on this path are following. At the same time, the few exceptions call for pause and contemplation of the weaknesses in generalizations. In the following paragraphs, I first outline a few major examples of nations that followed the descriptive component of the incremental process. I analyze only some examples, although other sources have studied the incrementalist paths in several nations more thoroughly.[30]

The first country to legalize same-sex marriage was the Netherlands in 2001. Most of the countries of Northern Europe soon after adopted domestic partnership schemes (and eventually marriage equality), and can be said to have followed the stages espoused by frameworks of incrementalism.[31] This is understandable, as these are the countries, particularly the Netherlands, that Waaldijk initially studied to generate his framework. Western Europe is another good example of incrementalism being followed, eventually culminating in the recognition of same-sex marriage.[32] France, Germany, and the United Kingdom all followed the steps outlined by the theory of small change, although their different paces and different paths are worthy of a separate discussion which I cannot offer here.

The United States is a commonly studied country for the paradigm of incrementalism, although it tells a complex story. Some of the legal history of individual states provides strong ground for the conclusion that incrementalism is a better policy to follow, since those states that did not follow the gradual approach often experienced more significant backlash. Vermont is a paradigmatic example of a state that followed the incrementalist approach and is often depicted by proponents as an indicator of the virtues of incrementalism. In 2000, the Vermont Supreme Court held that the state must bestow on same-sex couples the same rights and privileges that married different-sex couples receive.[33] The final implementation, however, was left to the state legislature, which, in turn, embraced the idea of civil unions – a gradual move, classic to incremental change.[34] Almost ten years later, the legislature voted to allow marriage between members of the same sex.[35] Yet, even Vermont's incremental change was not free of backlash, as a large number of legislators and judges were voted out of office that year, perceived to be partly as a result of their support for same-sex civil unions.[36] However, this can be said to be a weaker form of backlash when compared with the experiences of other states.

A prime example of a state moving too quickly with LGBTQ+ rights is Hawaii's 1993 *Baehr* decision. In *Baehr v. Lewin*, the Hawaiian Supreme Court became the first in the United States to recognize that excluding same-sex couples from marriage amounts to sex-based discrimination.[37] The Hawaiian Supreme Court remanded the case to the lower court and by the time the case returned to the Supreme Court, Hawaiian voters had, by a 69% majority, ratified a constitutional amendment through a state referendum that gave the Hawaiian legislature the authority to limit marriage to being between a man and a woman only. The reaction to Hawaii's Supreme Court decision, throughout the United States, was an example of a powerful backlash. The *Baehr* decision triggered a very strong political reaction, which led in part to the enactment of the federal Defense of Marriage Act (DOMA), a law that defined marriage, for federal purposes, as between a man and a woman only, thus denying same-sex couples over a thousand benefits and protections from the federal government that are awarded to recognized marriages. Moreover, by the end of 1996, 15 states had passed versions of DOMA, which later expanded to over 30 states legislating provisions prohibiting the recognition of same-sex relationships.[38] Proponents of incrementalism often attribute DOMA and the other "mini-DOMAs" to the public's response to *Baehr*, a case that brought up anger and fear for opponents of same-sex marriage. Achieving marriage equality through the courts too early, without public readiness, resulted in a severe legislative response that harmed the LGBTQ+ community.

The US path toward marriage equality at the federal level complicates the incremental paradigm. Factually speaking, it seems like the United States did not follow the "necessary process" (as Law Professor Yuval Merin calls the incremental framework),[39] as many states do not provide protection from employment discrimination, and the federal law does not explicitly provide such protection, either.[40] Hence, when the US Supreme Court invalidated the nationwide ban on same-sex marriage as unconstitutional in *Obergefell v. Hodges*, the second step of the incremental process had not been fully completed.[41] Moreover, as Hamilton argues, *Obergefell* raises another challenge to the incrementalist approach as it represents a court-based order rather than legislative action. Additionally, this case was reached rather early and without sufficient public support, especially considering the fact that approximately a quarter of the states at the time still banned same-sex marriage. Finally, per Hamilton, this early decision prevented "a full democratic debate" on same-sex marriage.[42] As such, *Obergefell* would be expected to "raise concerns about the possibility of a backlash in public opinion or a lack of substantive support in some of the U.S. states."[43] However, the backlash that resulted from the decision was weak, and did not live up to the grim predictions of incrementalist supporters.[44] The United States thus challenges the notion that countries must follow the sequence in the order prescribed by incrementalists, as well as the inevitability of backlash when courts rule in favor of same-sex marriage.

Canada is a textbook example of a country following the incremental approach. In 2005, Canada was the first country outside Europe and the fourth country in the world to legalize same-sex marriage nationwide. Prior to the Federal Marriage Act, there were many protections offered to sexual minorities and same-sex couples and, indeed, the majority of provinces and territories already recognized same-sex marriage.[45] Additionally, a majority of Canadians supported same-sex marriage, thus ensuring that there was popular support for marriage equality.[46]

The incremental model shows applicability outside of Europe and North America, and describes the path that nations in South America and Australasia have taken. For example, in 2013, Uruguay legalized same-sex marriage following the incremental paradigm.[47] New Zealand's path to same-sex marriage, legalized in 2013, also conforms to the three-stages pattern.

However, the experience of a few countries, especially those that are not from the Global North, complicates the paradigm of incremental stages, exposing variations and nuances in the path to same-sex marriage. For example, in 2010, Argentina became the first Latin American country to legalize same-sex marriage.[48] However, it did not follow the incremental path, as Argentina's first Penal Code in 1887 made no reference to same-sex sexual activity and, other than in Buenos Aires, Argentina does not have an anti-discrimination law that protects sexual minorities. Brazil is another nation that legalized same-sex marriage while not having employment discrimination protections. After surveying the different paths that Argentina and Brazil took toward same-sex marriage, political scientist Omar Encarnación calls to:

> "de-center" gay politics when looking at the experiences outside of the developed West . . . [in order to] get a broader understanding of the historical factors at work in the emergence of gay rights movements, together with a deeper perspective on how different social and political environments are shaping divergent outcomes with respect to the embrace of gay rights in the developing South.[49]

Similarly, the experience of the only country in Asia that has legalized same-sex marriage, Taiwan, serves as another example that complicates the incremental framework, because it also legalized same-sex marriage without following the steps enumerated in the incrementalist model. Taiwan never had any anti-sodomy laws (in fact, it never previously had any mention of homosexuality in any of its laws).[50] While this may seem in accordance with the paradigm, whereby Taiwan can skip the first step of Waaldijk's framework of incrementalism, in reality it rendered the LGBTQ+ community legally invisible and thus highly vulnerable.[51] Moreover, Taiwan has no anti-discrimination protections, nor civil rights formally extended to sexual minorities.[52] In fact, discrimination and hate speech are not particularly recognized by Taiwanese law as warranting protection against.[53] Thus, Taiwanese members of the LGBTQ+ community face prejudice and discrimination (sometimes even from state actors and police) without legal recourse.[54] Therefore, Taiwan has achieved neither of the initial steps articulated in the pattern of incrementalism. Yet, on 24 May 2019, Taiwan became the first country in Asia to legalize same-sex marriage. The bill passed by the government not only allows same-sex partners to create a "permanent union of intimate and exclusive nature for the committed purpose of managing a life together to realise the equal protection of the freedom of marriage," but also offers some adoption rights.[55]

The bill is partly a result of a Taiwan Constitutional Court ruling in 2017 which held that a statutory ban on same-sex marriage in Taiwan's Civil Code was "in violation of the Constitution's guarantees of both the people's freedom of marriage under Article 22 and the people's right to equality under Article 7" and which gave the government two years to amend existing laws or create new laws compliant to the ruling.[56] Article 7 guarantees that "all citizens of the Republic of China, irrespective of sex, religion, race, class, or party affiliation, shall be equal before the law."[57] Although sexual orientation is not a listed classification of impermissible discrimination, the Court ruled that the list was "only illustrative, rather than exhaustive," and thus, sexual orientation should also be governed by Article 7.[58] This essentially reads sexual orientation into the list of prohibited grounds of discrimination, but whether that will be upheld robustly in future rulings is yet to be seen. Ultimately, the ruling paved the way for Taiwan to legislate a recognition of same-sex marriage without addressing discrimination of LGBTQ+ persons in other situations.

Taiwan's example demonstrates that the paradigm of incrementalism is not always so scrupulously followed, even in liberal democracies. Elaine Jeffereys and Pan Wang argue that a "combination of an active LGBT movement, multiparty strategizing and government efforts to differentiate Taiwan from the PRC [People's Republic of China] in international arenas" are the major factors in Taiwan's recent recognition of same-sex marriage.[59] This suggests that there are other factors that may be just as important in analyzing the likelihood of marriage equality recognition in a state as those enumerated in theories of incrementalism.

The supranational courts of Europe and the Americas offer another opportunity to assess theories of incrementalism. While the European Court of Human Rights (ECtHR) and the Court of Justice of the European Union (CJEU) have taken a slower, more incremental approach in recognizing same-sex marriage (and encouraging their Member States to do the same), the Inter-American Court of Human Rights (CIDH) has taken a more radical approach, generating backlash from some member states. Although the ECHR has held twice that Member States are under no obligation to legalize same-sex marriage, it has also held that its Member States have a positive obligation to provide a legal framework to protect the rights of same-sex couples.[60] Prior to this, the ECHR also ruled that bans on same-sex sexual activity violate Article 8 and that discrimination on the basis of sexual orientation is impermissible.

The Court of Justice of the European Union has been slower to move toward recognition of marriage equality. The CJEU ruled in 2018 that European Union countries must protect and recognize the rights of same-sex married couples (particularly in relation to free movement and citizenship), even if same-sex unions are not legally recognized in the state in question.[61] While this certainly extends the legal benefits of marriage to same-sex couples who are married in states where same-sex unions are legal, it falls short of requiring all EU states to legalize same-sex marriage themselves. This is an example of an incremental pace toward marriage equality – one that would, presumably, be applauded by incrementalists and used as an indicator that recognition of same-sex marriage is soon to follow.

Indeed, legal experts justify the incremental process of the European supranational tribunals as the tribunals taking a cautious approach that reflects the diversity of the states that are bound by their rulings. Finnish Law Professor Massimo Fichera maintains that:

> Because the ECtHR does not enjoy an overarching federal framework – unlike in the United States – this is probably as far as the ECtHR can currently go. It cannot proclaim the existence of a right to same-sex marriage unless the overwhelming majority of states decide to come to a consensus via similar legislation.[62]

This compromising approach is consistent with the incrementalist logic of slow change and concurrent shifting public opinion, although whether at some stage the ECtHR will require full legalization remains to be seen.

The Inter-American Court of Human Rights took a marked departure from its European counterparts in 2018 by mandating that same-sex marriages (and not a separate legal institution) be recognized by all member states.[63] Although previously the CIDH ruled that sexual orientation is a suspect classification for discrimination, it has not ruled on decriminalizing same-sex sexual activity (despite Guyana continuing to hold anti-sodomy laws) nor has it ruled directly on its member states legislating LGBTQ+ discrimination protections. Thus, the decision binding on all member states to legalize full marriage equality comes quite abruptly. Moreover, the Court clarified that it would not be sufficient for member states to create a marriage alternative (like civil unions), because separate institutions with different names would constitute a form of discrimination on the basis of sexual orientation. Unsurprisingly, there is substantial backlash from many member states where majorities of their populations do not support same-sex marriage, with some states like Paraguay vowing not to uphold the ruling. Peru has also failed to recognize marriage equality as of the date of writing.[64] Ultimately, the case of the CIDH raises questions about the role of supranational courts in same-sex marriage, especially when a majority of member states have not legalized same-sex marriage.

Finally, the incremental model also helps to explain the lack of, or very slow, progress toward partnership rights in Asia and Africa, where most nations still criminalize same-sex intimacy.[65]

In conclusion, the legal history of liberal democracies that reached same-sex marriage often complies with the incremental accounts, especially if the stages are read broadly and substantively. Yet, the experiences of some states also show diversity and nuance often becoming lost in the incremental framework. The next section will analyze some criticisms based on these broad generalizations of incrementalism.

Critiques of the incrementalist framework

Although most academics have accepted the incrementalist framework with broad support, others have offered valuable critiques of the paradigm. In this part, I divide critiques of the incrementalist framework into three areas: first, criticisms about the generalization, universalization, and lack of clear information about how to move between the stages of incrementalism; second, a substantive critique about the compromise that incrementalism advocates and challenges to the backlash that incrementalists predict; and third, criticism about the normative glorification of marriage that incrementalism implies through its teleological logic.

Imprecision, generalizations, and limited data

At the basic level, the fixation on three stages, as a framework, misses variations that states have taken on the path to same-sex marriage. As I have written elsewhere,

> [g]enerally speaking, while some states . . . have followed the theory of small change, other states have followed very different paths. In fact, many states have legalized same-sex marriage without ever passing civil unions or following the path proscribed by Waaldjik.[66]

Consider, for example, that, as mentioned earlier, the United States (at the federal level) has never met the second stage of enacting LGBTQ+ discrimination protections. Law Professor Jeremiah Ho creatively argues that the United States did pass through the incremental process, although the second stage looks different than the conventional second stage.[67] To understand the US trajectory as following the prescribed sequences, he asserts we need to revise our understanding of what these stages consist of by looking at them substantively.[68] Rather than examining the particular three steps in the incremental paradigm, Ho analyzes how the US jurisprudence represents a gradual progress from anti-gay essentialism toward animus-focused jurisprudence. While Ho's analysis is compelling, his suggestions create a much more complex and rich theoretical framework than that which the incremental paradigm offers.

The generalizations of the experience of nations – the imprecision of grouping diverse experiences into one universal path – are not merely nit-picky errors in descriptions. Rather, they paint the road to same-sex marriage as one uniform path, distracting from the role of other important factors such as culture, politics, and legal systems. The paradigm further undercuts the effect of different levels of religion, tradition, importance of marriage, and LGBTQ+ advocacy, to name just a few factors that are neglected. This is not surprising, because while the incremental framework has proven itself relatively reliable descriptively, it makes a universal claim that ignores the differences between nations and overgeneralizes the experience of recognizing same-sex relationships. As Badgett puts it, "[t]ransferring political lessons and experiences from one continent to another runs the risk of ignoring important cultural or social differences between countries and continents."[69] Indeed, the legal experience that helps to generate the incrementalist paradigm relies on the experience of liberal democracies, and it is much less clear how it would be helpful to explain the experience of nations with different cultures and structures of governance. Incrementalism is too entrenched within a specific socio-political paradigm to be broadly generalizable.

Because of the generalization, Fichera concludes quite directly that:

> The theory of small change is attractive but not entirely convincing. As a pseudo-scientific theory, it smacks of immodesty; it fails to find reassuring and well-tested schemes to explain contemporary phenomena. Aside from a few cases . . . there is little empirical or statistical data to support this approach's allegedly universal applicability.[70]

Further, political scientist Michael Yarbrough criticizes the incrementalist model as overly emphatic on the heteronormative institution of marriage, asserting that "[a] closer look reveals that conjugal-law reforms have appeared in diverse chronologies and combinations, and in ways that do not always neatly follow local practices."[71] He further points out that the paradigm is focused on equality, to the neglect of important questions about legal recognition of diverse family forms. Thus, he adds,

> [f]actors related to other conjugal behaviors and attitudes are mentioned only in passing, however, as are questions about the character of the recognition extended to same-sex couples – for example, why the substantive rights conferred with recognition vary, often significantly, from one jurisdiction to the next, in ways that do not always neatly track the rights offered different-sex couples. The question is presumed simply to be: Are same-sex couples recognized or not? And the answer is presumed to relate exclusively to LGBT politics rather than also to broader conjugal issues.[72]

Finding deviations from the general pattern that incrementalists offer does not merely constitute a "Gotcha!" moment. Rather, the simplification of the ways to achieve equality limit our imaginative ability to think about attentive facts, nuances, and catalysts for change. In particular, the shortcoming of the purported universality of the paradigm then is that it fails to provide knowledge and direction for each step. How long does it take to move to the next one? When should advocates for same-sex marriage aim at challenging the current regime? When and how is readiness for the next stage tested? And is there any point by which advocates can move to the next stage, even in the absence of readiness? As Badgett states, "Not surprisingly, the incrementalists offer no clear idea about how long each incremental step should or will take. However, each step might require significant political mobilization and could generate increasing practical and symbolic opposition."[73] Thus, the incrementalist paradigm presents a roadmap that purports to predict next steps, but leaves far too much guesswork involved.

Justice as dependent on the change of public opinion

The most compelling critique against incremental process, in my opinion, is that justice delayed is justice denied.[74] In the case of same-sex marriage, like in other cases of civil rights, the delay occurs while discrimination continues, and is likely to be accompanied by harm to the same-sex couples who are denied access to marriage. Asking people who suffer unlawful discrimination to wait until the time is right in order to vindicate their rights – that is, until the public is ready to accept their claim – is contradictory to the basic principles of justice.[75] The price of waiting for the time the public will be ready is borne by the people who suffer as second-class citizens unable to achieve equality before the law. As Ted Olson, who litigated a few of the major same-sex marriage cases in the United States stated: "If people are suffering and being hurt by discrimination, and their children and families are . . . then who are we as lawyers to say, 'Wait ten years?'"[76] The Supreme Court's majority decision in *Obergefell* acknowledged a similar sentiment in holding that "[a]n individual can invoke a right to constitutional protection when he or she is harmed, even if the broader public disagrees and even if the legislature refuses to act."[77] The right to equality, the majority continued, "holds true even when protecting individual rights affects issues of the utmost importance and sensitivity." To the argument that ruling on issues like same-sex marriage should be held to the legislative authorities and not the courts, the Court answered sharply that "there has been far more deliberation than this argument acknowledges."[78]

The presumption that the incrementalist paradigm mitigates backlash also requires more scrutiny. For one, although *Obergefell* is depicted as non-incremental, it did not result in broad countermobilizations.[79] Further, the backlash that resulted from previous successes in litigation through courts has not only been a setback, but has also gained victories for LGBTQ+ people. Often, asking for more at once results in a better compromise. Hence, despite the setbacks in early litigations, it often accelerated the process toward the creation of other institutions for legal recognition of relationships.[80] Losses can also serve as fuel to mobilize, inspire, and energize the movement. Hawaii's litigation resulted in a backlash, but also galvanized the movement and accelerated the enactment of a "reciprocal beneficiary" scheme – a legal institution with limited partnership rights open to same-sex couples. Further, social scientists have called into question the assumption that incremental legislative changes provoke weaker backlash.[81] Although the backlash theory that serves as the major rationale for adopting the incremental process has strong appeal, it should also be treated with a grain of salt.

Normative critique of marriage as the final goal

The law of small change is not just a descriptive account and not merely an advocacy plan. Rather, "[t]he incrementalist account of same-sex marriage legalization is manifestly teleological – it presents marriage as the end, both literal and normative, of the LGB movement."[82] By upholding marriage as the end goal, it portrays it as the holy grail of the LGBTQ+ equality. As Critical Law Professor Adler contends,

> [b]y instilling the sense of a march down a clear path toward a well-lit destination, the speakers tell us what progress is. This in turn produces gays' desire for progress within the terms of the discourse. The small steps theory describes reality accurately because it is making reality. . . . As a consequence, all eyes turn toward marriage not because it is the only wish that the law can grant, but because runway lights point in that direction.[83]

Hence, it is not surprising that many nations followed the sequence of small changes as espoused by incrementalism, as this was the discourse and narrative that was transferred among LGBTQ+ movements along the globe. So, the incrementalist approach became not only a descriptive and predictive framework, but also a normative one and a self-fulfilling prophecy.

Furthermore, by placing marriage, a highly gendered legal institution, at the end of the path toward equality, and by focusing on the achievement of this goal, the LGBTQ+ community has ignored other advocacy options and other avenues for equality. Adler argues that marriage advocacy embraced a neoliberal politics that neglected other battles that could have assisted LGBTQ+ individuals that are not part of the mainstream movement. For instance, the movement could have supported disaggregating marriage from the benefits that are attendant to it, or universal rights – regardless of marriage – like health care for everyone. Instead, the LGBTQ+ community subscribed to marriage as the ultimate equality, entrenching a homonormative ideal.[84]

The argument that the incremental political process limits innovation and imagination is far from being exclusive to the same-sex marriage arena. As political scientist William Berry puts forward, "at the heart of the initial conceptualization of incrementalism by Lindblom is the requirement that the decision maker limit 'policy comparisons to those policies that differ in relatively small degree from policies presently in effect.'"[85] Looking at a limited number of options, and restricting the assessment of solutions to issues in the margins, will inevitably lead to adopting cautious mainstream policies. As Law Professor Michael D. Gilbert explains, incrementalism works in a cycle. Once society is ready for the next change, the lawmakers will likely address it. When society gets used to the change again, the law "becomes too conservative for citizens' tastes, and legislators change it. However, the incrementalism principle confines that change to small steps, and small steps mean the newly amended law hardly differs from its predecessor."[86] Incrementalism, then, is essentially a non-radical strategy that rarely leads to significant change of the status quo.

One clear way in which the incrementalist account missed an opportunity to catalyze broader societal change is in its advocacy for civil unions. Incrementalists portray civil unions as a necessary evil that has to be tolerated as a step on the path to same-sex marriage. As a stage, it serves to highlight how same-sex couples are still being discriminated against without rationale. When marriage advocates argued in courts that civil unions are different from marriage, they often portrayed it as an inferior institution to marriage. Civil unions in the United States, Katherine Franke documents, were "vilified from within the gay community as a meager step in the right direction," a temporary compromise on the road to marriage equality.[87] Moreover, as a strategy to convince courts that civil unions are discriminatory, same-sex advocates in the United States also emphasized the abnormality and stigma associated with living outside marriage, including in marriage alternatives. As Melissa Murry puts it,

> [t]hroughout the country, efforts to secure marriage equality have necessarily focused on marriage as the paradigm model. In so doing, they have characterized marriage alternatives, like domestic partnerships and civil unions, as cut-rate counterfeits that may serve as interim measures in the struggle to secure marriage equality, but not as ends unto themselves.[88]

But there are other ways to treat civil unions that better serve justice. For example, while acknowledging that civil unions are born as a "separate -but equal" institution, they have the potential to offer a fresh new legal institution that is helpful to individuals regardless of sexual orientation. First, symbolically, civil unions could have offered a legal institution that is free of the patriarchal history of marriage. Many ideological cohabitants could have enjoyed the benefits of such an alternative. Second, if civil unions were not designed to be "marriage by a different name," they could have represented an alternative legal institution that is different from marriage and suitable for couples that do not want the full extent of obligations that marriage offers.[89] However, as civil unions and their likes are perceived only as a step toward marriage, they are portrayed as inferior and harmful. Thus, the idea of an incremental move toward marriage is one of the reasons that civil unions have typically been abolished after marriage legalization and are barely used by opposite-sex couples even when they are an option. They are viewed as institutions that are meant for compromise – and nothing more. The innovative potential of such institutions is therefore lost due to the narrow politics of some incrementalists.

Conclusion

Incrementalist framework gained strong support within academia and advocacy groups, and proved itself to be a useful descriptive and predictive tool, for the most part. At the same time, a nuanced examination of the history of several countries, especially those of Europe and North America, portrays a more complex question that advises to treat the universal theory of gradual process with caution. Nations have taken different approaches to advocacy, as well as to the question of how gradual progress should be. And some experiences teach that reaching too far too quickly can result in progress along with this backlash.

In some places in the world where same-sex marriage is already achieved, members of the LGBTQ+ community will do well if they think about marriage as merely one goal along a path toward a more substantive equality. That is, they should challenge the premise that marriage is the end, or the near-end, of the fight for LGBTQ+ equality. Additionally, even in places where marriage is already a fact, it is important to challenge the paradigm of incremental process, especially in the context of importing lessons into other rights struggles. The incremental way might be safer, but it also has the potential to limit policy options and do too little to challenge the status quo, particularly for minorities within the LGBTQ+ community. For other places, where marriage equality is not yet achieved, it is important to challenge the universality of the incremental paradigm and dig deeper into the path toward marriage, particularly when building on the success of other places. While incrementalism is sometimes a viable and even necessary political policy, other options should not be off the table. Each nation needs to consider its own way, in its own time, based on its specific political, social, and legal situation, and not to subscribe to the appeal of a purportedly universal and predictable path.

Notes

1 Libby Adler, *Gay Priori: A Queer Critical Legal Studies Approach to Law Reform* (Duke University Press 2018) 102.

2 Kees Waaldijk, 'Small Change: How the Road to Same-Sex Marriage Got Paved in the Netherlands' in Robert Wintermute and Mads Andenæs (eds), *Legal Recognition of Same-Sex Partnerships: A Study of Nation, Europe, and International Law* (Hart Publishing 2001).

3 Adler (n 1); MV Lee Badgett, 'Predicting Partnership Rights: Applying the European Experience in the United States' (2005) 17 *Yale Journal of Law & Feminism* 71.

4 Ibid., 75.
5 John M Broder and Katharine Q Seelye, 'Groups Debate Slower Strategy on Gay Rights' *New York Times* (New York, 9 December 2004) A1.
6 Michael T Hayes, *The Limits of Policy Change: Incrementalism, Worldview, and the Rule of Law* (Georgetown University Press 2001).
7 Ibid., 4–5.
8 Ibid., 42.
9 Ibid.
10 Waaldijk (n 2) 439.
11 Ibid., 427.
12 Ibid., 440.
13 William N Eskridge Jr, *Equality Practice: Civil Unions and the Future of Gay Rights* (Routledge 2002).
14 Ibid., 115.
15 Ibid.
16 William N Eskridge Jr and Darren R Spedale, *Gay Marriage: For Better or Worse? What We've Learned from the Evidence* (Oxford University Press 2006) 230.
17 Ibid., 228.
18 Frances Hamilton, 'Strategies to Achieve Same-Sex Marriage and the Method of Incrementalist Change' (2015–2016) 25 *Journal of Transnational Law & Policy* 121, 152.
19 Hamilton (n 18).
20 Erez Aloni, 'Registering Relationships' (2013) 87 *Tulane Law Review* 573, 626, 633–634; Eskridge and Spedale (n 13) 229–230.
21 Misha Isaak, '"What's in a Name?" Civil Unions and the Constitutional Significance of "Marriage"' (2008) 10 *University of Pennsylvania Journal of Constitutional Law* 607, 642; Thomas M Keck, 'Beyond Backlash: Assessing the Impact of Judicial Decisions on LGBT Rights' (2009) 43 *Law & Society Review* 151, 171.
22 Waaldijk (n 2) 447.
23 William N Eskridge Jr, 'Equality Practice: Liberal Reflections on the Jurisprudence of Civil Unions' (2001) 64 *Albany Law Review* 853–854.
24 Eskridge, *Equality Practice* (n 13) 144.
25 Ibid., 138.
26 Hamilton (n 18) 140–144.
27 Eskridge and Spedale (n 16) 236.
28 Ibid., 237.
29 Hamilton (n 18) 142.
30 Erez Aloni, 'Incrementalism, Civil Unions and the Possibility of Predicting Legal Recognition of Same-Sex Marriage' (2010–2011) 18 *Duke Journal of Gender Law & Policy* 105; Kees Waaldijk, 'Others May Follow: The Introduction of Marriage, Quasi-Marriage, and Semi-Marriage for Same-Sex Couples in European Countries' (2004) 38 *New England Law Review* 569–571; Yuval Merin, *Equality for Same-Sex Couples: The Legal Recognition of Gay Partnerships in Europe and the United States* (University of Chicago Press 2002); Hamilton (n 18).
31 Aloni (n 29) 117–118.
32 Hamilton (n 18) 152–153.
33 *Baker v Vermont* 170 Vt 194, 744 A 2d 864 (VT 1999).
34 Eskridge and Spedale (n 16) 239.
35 An Act to Protect Religious Freedom and Recognize Equality in Civil Marriage 2009 (VT).
36 Keck (n 20) 153.
37 *Baehr v Lewin* 74 Haw 530, 852 P 2d 44 (Hawaii, 1993).

38 Carlos A Ball, *The First Amendment and LGBT Equality: A Contentious History* (Harvard University Press 2017).
39 Merin (n 29).
40 William N Eskridge Jr, 'Title VII's Statutory History and the Sex Discrimination Argument for LGBT Workplace Protections' (2017) 127 *Yale Law Journal* 322, 325.
41 *Obergefell v Hodges* 576 US, 135 S Ct 2584 (2015).
42 Hamilton (n 18) 150.
43 Ibid., 135.
44 Katherine Franke, *Wedlocked: The Perils of Marriage Equality* (New York University Press 2015). ("The backlash against married same-sex couples that I expected has not taken place").
45 Ibid., 39.
46 Ibid., 38.
47 Tyler Valiquette and Daniel Waring, 'A Tale of Two Congresses: Sex, Institutions, and Evangelicals in Brazil and Chile' in Bronwyn Winter, Maxime Forest and Réjane Sénac (eds), *Global Perspectives on Same-Sex Marriage: A Neo-Institutional Approach* (Global Queer Politics 2018).
48 Shawn Schulenberg, 'The Construction and Enactment of Same-Sex Marriage in Argentina' in Charles A Smith (ed), *Globalizing Human Rights: Emerging Issues and Approaches* (Routledge 2014).
49 Omar G Encarnación, 'International Influence, Domestic Activism, and Gay Rights in Argentina' (2013) 128 *Political Science Quarterly* 687, 715.
50 Chen Yu-Rong and Wang Ping, 'Obstacles to LGBT Human Rights Development in Taiwan' (2010) 18 *Positions: East Asia Cultures Critique* 399.
51 Ibid.
52 Ibid., 400.
53 Ibid.
54 Josephine CJ Ho, 'Queer Existence Under Global Governance: A Taiwan Exemplar' (2010) 18 *Positions: East Asia Cultures Critique* 537, 540.
55 The Enforcement Act of Judicial Yuan Interpretation No. 748.
56 Ibid.
57 Constitution of the Republic of China, art 7.
58 The Enforcement Act of Judicial Yuan Interpretation No. 748.
59 Elaine Jeffereys and Pan Wang, 'Pathways to Legalizing Same-Sex Marriage in China and Taiwan: Globalization and "Chinese Values"' in Bronwyn Winter, Maxime Forest and Réjane Sénac (eds), *Global Perspectives on Same-Sex Marriage: A Neo-Institutional Approach* (Global Queer Politics 2018).
60 *Oliari and Others v Italy* App Nos. 18766/11 and 36030/11 (ECtHR, 21 July 2015).
61 Case C-673/16 *Relu Adrian Coman, Robert Clabourn Hamilton, Asociaţia Accept v Inspectoratul General pentru Imigrări, Ministerul Afacerilor Interne* ECLI:EU:C:2018:2.
62 Massimo Fichera, 'Same-Sex Marriage and the Role of Transnational Law: Changes in the European Landscape' (2016) 17 *German Law Journal* 383, 395.
63 Norma Gutierrez, *Costa Rica/OAS: Inter-American Court of Human Rights Declares Right to Marry Should Be Extended to Same-Sex Couples* (Library of Congress, 9 February 2018).
64 Anastasia Moloney, *Peru Gay Marriage Bill "Doomed" This Year – Congressman* (Thompson Reuters Foundation, 17 May 2019).
65 Aengus Carroll and Lucas R Mendos, 'State-Sponsored Homophobia: A World Survey of Sexual Orientation Laws: Criminalisation, Protection and Recognition'

(ILGA, May 2017). <https://ilga.org/ilga-state-sponsored-homophobia-report-2017> accessed 3 September 2019.
66 Waaldijk (n 2) 127–128.
67 Jeremiah A Ho, 'Weather Permitting: Incrementalism, Animus, and the Art of Forecasting Marriage Equality After U.S. v. Windsor' (2014) 62 *Cleveland State Law Review* 1, 10.
68 Ibid., 134–155.
69 Badgett (n 3) 85.
70 Fichera (n 61) 413.
71 Michael W Yarbrough, *Toward a Political Sociology of Conjugal-Recognition Regimes: Gendered Multiculturalism in South African Marriage Law* (CUNY Academic Works 2015) 5.
72 Ibid., 11.
73 Badgett (n 3) 75.
74 *Baker v Vermont* (n 32), Johnson, J., dissenting, in part: "While the laudatory goals of preserving institutional credibility and public confidence in our government may require elected bodies to wait for changing attitudes concerning public morals, those same goals require courts to act independently and decisively to protect civil rights guaranteed by our Constitution."
75 Kathryn L Marshall, 'Strategic Pragmatism or Radical Idealism? The Same-Sex Marriage and Civil Rights Movements Juxtaposed' (2010) 2 *William and Mary Policy Review* 194, 198.
76 Margaret Talbot, 'A Risky Proposal: Is It Too Soon to Petition SCOTUS on Gay Marriage?' *The New Yorker* (New York, 18 January 2010).
77 *Obergefell* (n 40).
78 Ibid.
79 Franke (n 43) 5.
80 Keck (n 20) 169.
81 Ibid., 179–181.
82 Aloni, 'Registering Relationships' (n 19) 155.
83 Adler (n 1) 104.
84 Ibid., 105–106.
85 William D Berry, 'The Confusing Case of Budgetary Incrementalism: Too Many Meanings for a Single Concept' (1990) 52 *The Journal of Politics* 167, 169 (citing from Charles E Lindblom, 'The Science of Muddling Through' [1959] 19 *Public Administration Review* 79, 84).
86 Michael D Gilbert, 'Entrenchment, Incrementalism, and Constitutional Collapse' (2017) 103 *Virginia Law Review* 631, 636.
87 Franke (n 43) 106–109.
88 Melissa Murray, 'Paradigms Lost: How Domestic Partnership Went from Innovation to Injury' (2013) 37 *New York University Review of Law and Social Change* 291, 293.
89 Aloni, 'Registering Relationships' (n 19) 627–628.

References

Primary sources

An Act to Protect Religious Freedom and Recognize Equality in Civil Marriage 2009 (VT).

Baehr v Lewin 74 Haw 530, 852 P 2d 44 (Hawaii, 1993).

Baker v Vermont 170 Vt 194, 744 A 2d 864 (VT 1999)
Constitution of the Republic of China.
The Enforcement Act of Judicial Yuan Interpretation No. 748.
Obergefell v Hodges 576 US, 135 S Ct 2584 (2015).
Oliari and Others v Italy App Nos. 18766/11 and 36030/11 (ECtHR, 21 July 2015).
Relu Adrian Coman, Robert Clabourn Hamilton, Asociaţia Accept v Inspectoratul General pentru Imigrări, Ministerul Afacerilor Interne (C-673/16) ECLI:EU:C:2018:2.

Secondary sources

Adler L, *Gay Priori: A Queer Critical Legal Studies Approach to Law Reform* (Duke University Press 2018).

Aloni E, 'Incrementalism, Civil Unions and the Possibility of Predicting Legal Recognition of Same-Sex Marriage' (2010–2011) 18 *Duke Journal of Gender Law & Policy* 105.

———, 'Registering Relationships' (2013) 87 *Tulane Law Review* 573.

Badgett MVL, 'Predicting Partnership Rights: Applying the European Experience in the United States' (2005) 17 *Yale Journal of Law & Feminism* 71.

Ball CA, *The First Amendment and LGBT Equality: A Contentious History* (Harvard University Press 2017).

Berry WD, 'The Confusing Case of Budgetary Incrementalism: Too Many Meanings for a Single Concept' (1990) 52 *The Journal of Politics* 167.

Broder JM and Seelye KQ, 'Groups Debate Slower Strategy on Gay Rights' *New York Times* (New York, 9 December 2004).

Carroll A and Mendos LR, 'State-Sponsored Homophobia: A World Survey of Sexual Orientation Laws: Criminalisation, Protection and Recognition' (ILGA, May 2017) <https://ilga.org/ilga-state-sponsored-homophobia-report-2017> accessed 3 September 2019.

Encarnación OG, 'International Influence, Domestic Activism, and Gay Rights in Argentina' (2013) 128 *Political Science Quarterly* 687.

Eskridge WN, 'Equality Practice: Liberal Reflections on the Jurisprudence of Civil Unions' (2001) 64 *Albany Law Review* 853.

———, *Equality Practice: Civil Unions and the Future of Gay Rights* (Routledge 2002).

———, 'Title VII's Statutory History and the Sex Discrimination Argument for LGBT Workplace Protections' (2017) 127 *Yale Law Journal* 322.

Eskridge WN and Spedale DR, *Gay Marriage: For Better or Worse? What We've Learned from the Evidence* (Oxford University Press 2006).

Fichera M, 'Same-Sex Marriage and the Role of Transnational Law: Changes in the European Landscape' (2016) 17 *German Law Journal* 383.

Franke K, *Wedlocked: The Perils of Marriage Equality* (New York University Press 2015).

Gilbert MD, 'Entrenchment, Incrementalism, and Constitutional Collapse' (2017) 103 *Virginia Law Review* 631.

Gutierrez N, *Costa Rica/OAS: Inter-American Court of Human Rights Declares Right to Marry Should Be Extended to Same-Sex Couples* (Library of Congress, 9 February 2018).

Hamilton F, 'Strategies to Achieve Same-Sex Marriage and the Method of Incrementalist Change' (2015–2016) 25 *Journal of Transnational Law & Policy* 121.

Hayes MT, *The Limits of Policy Change: Incrementalism, Worldview, and the Rule of Law* (Georgetown University Press 2001).

Ho JA, 'Weather Permitting: Incrementalism, Animus, and the Art of Forecasting Marriage Equality After U.S. v. Windsor' (2014) 62 *Cleveland State Law Review* 1.

Ho JCJ, 'Queer Existence Under Global Governance: A Taiwan Exemplar' (2010) 18 *Positions: East Asia Cultures Critique* 537.

Isaak M, '"What's in a Name?" Civil Unions and the Constitutional Significance of "Marriage"' (2008) 10 *University of Pennsylvania Journal of Constitutional Law* 607.

Jeffereys E and Wang P, 'Pathways to Legalizing Same-Sex Marriage in China and Taiwan: Globalization and "Chinese Values"' in Winter B, Forest M and Sénac R (eds), *Global Perspectives on Same-Sex Marriage: A Neo-Institutional Approach* (Global Queer Politics 2018).

Keck TM, 'Beyond Backlash: Assessing the Impact of Judicial Decisions on LGBT Rights' (2009) 43 *Law & Society Review* 151.

Lindblom CE, 'The Science of Muddling Through' (1959) 19 *Public Administration Review* 79.

Marshall KL, 'Strategic Pragmatism or Radical Idealism? The Same-Sex Marriage and Civil Rights Movements Juxtaposed' (2010) 2 *William and Mary Policy Review* 194.

Merin Y, *Equality for Same-Sex Couples: The Legal Recognition of Gay Partnerships in Europe and the United States* (University of Chicago Press 2002).

Moloney A, *Peru Gay Marriage Bill "Doomed" This Year – Congressman* (Thompson Reuters Foundation, 17 May 2019).

Murray M, 'Paradigms Lost: How Domestic Partnership Went from Innovation to Injury' (2013) 37 *New York University Review of Law and Social Change* 291.

Schulenberg S, 'The Construction and Enactment of Same-Sex Marriage in Argentina' in Smith CA (ed), *Globalizing Human Rights: Emerging Issues and Approaches* (Routledge 2014).

Talbot M, 'A Risky Proposal: Is It Too Soon to Petition SCOTUS on Gay Marriage?' *The New Yorker* (New York, 18 January 2010).

Valiquette T and Waring D, 'A Tale of Two Congresses: Sex, Institutions, and Evangelicals in Brazil and Chile' in Winter B, Forest M and Sénac R (eds), *Global Perspectives on Same-Sex Marriage: A Neo-Institutional Approach* (Global Queer Politics 2018).

Waaldijk K, 'Small Change: How the Road to Same-Sex Marriage Got Paved in the Netherlands' in Wintermute R and Andenæs M (eds), *Legal Recognition of Same-Sex Partnerships: A Study of Nation, Europe, and International Law* (Hart Publishing 2001).

———, 'Others May Follow: The Introduction of Marriage, Quasi-Marriage, and Semi-Marriage for Same-Sex Couples in European Countries' (2004) 38 *New England Law Review* 569.

Yarbrough MW, *Toward a Political Sociology of Conjugal-Recognition Regimes: Gendered Multiculturalism in South African Marriage Law* (CUNY Academic Works 2015).

Yu-Rong C and Ping W, 'Obstacles to LGBT Human Rights Development in Taiwan' (2010) 18 *Positions: East Asia Cultures Critique* 399.

Conclusions

Frances Hamilton

Analysis

This book has involved a series of inter-locking themes, including the role of the ECtHR and the EU in relation to the treatment of same-sex couples' relationships (Part 1), differing paths towards legalisation of same-sex marriage (Part 2), rainbow families (Part 3), the importance of civil partnership in an era of same-sex marriage (Part 4), the heteronormative underpinnings of same-sex marriage (Part 5) and the interaction between social change and legal change (Part 6). Many chapters in this volume investigate the potential opportunities open to the EU in protecting the rights of LGBTQ+ persons and same-sex couples and the consequent potential impact of Brexit for these persons based in the UK.[1] Whilst traditionally the EU was even stricter than the ECtHR in recognising non-conventional family types,[2] Hamilton's chapter has demonstrated that EU law has potential to further advance LGBTQ+ persons and same-sex couples' rights.[3] The EU concept of citizenship, which proceeds on the basis of an ever-expanding array of practical rights, has recently stressed free movement and non-discrimination rights, offering many opportunities for the groups studied.[4] Both the *Coman*[5] and *MB*[6] case studies included in Hamilton's chapter exemplify the importance of EU action.[7] In *Coman*, subsidiarity concerns were over-ridden in preference for the principle of free movement.[8] Similarly in *MB*, non-discrimination rights were given prominence as opposed to Member States' public policy concerns.[9] Whilst the CJEU sought to confine both *Coman* and *MB* case strictly to their facts,[10] these cases are symbolically important[11] and may signal further developments from the CJEU.

In contrast, the ECtHR continues to stress concerns about a lack of consensus.[12] The Council of Europe's 47 states are more divergent[13] than the arguably more homogeneous currently EU28 (although differences should not be ignored here).[14] The EU can rely on stronger enforcement mechanisms than the ECtHR through use of EU concepts of supremacy[15] and state liability.[16] If, as anticipated, Brexit were to affect free movement of persons, UK LGBTQ+ persons and same-sex couples will have to rely on whatever rights their country of destination sees fit to grant them. Further, if Brexit affects the remit of the CJEU, UK LGBTQ+

persons and same-sex couples will miss out on important developments in relation to expanding EU law.

Noto La Diega and Clayton-Helm grapple with conflicts of law questions concerning whether and how a foreign same-sex relationship will be recognised, following relocation of the couple to a new jurisdiction. Noto La Diega, after conducting empirical research[17] on the response to the *Coman* judgment,[18] concluded that European countries could be placed into three groups, which he terms recognition, downgrading and erasure.[19] Whilst some countries went further than required by *Coman* and recognised same-sex marriages as marriages for all purposes,[20] others in Noto La Diega's terminology 'downgraded' a foreign same-sex marriage and recognised this as a civil partnership only.[21] Whilst Hayward analyses whether a civil partnership should be considered a 'downgrade,'[22] countries in Noto La Diega's second denoted group did not recognise foreign same-sex marriage in their original form.[23] Still other states contravened EU and ECtHR law entirely[24] by refusing to recognise foreign same-sex marriages at all, thereby falling into Noto La Diega's erasure group.[25] This divergence of practical response serves to illustrate that legal change will never suffice, if in practice lack of social acceptance results in a lack of enforcement.

Clayton-Helm's chapter considers the potential power of a unified conflicts of law system under an EU umbrella.[26] Clayton-Helm proceeds by comparative law analysis with the US following *Obergefell*.[27] Whilst following *Coman* the EU determined that same-sex marriages had to be recognised cross-border for the purpose of free movement and residency rights,[28] in *Obergefell* the US Supreme Court required full legalisation of same-sex marriage across the US.[29] US federal unity was achieved despite traditional lack of involvement by the Supreme Court in family law[30] and many divergent approaches between US states as to the status of legal recognition of same-sex marriage.[31] Clayton-Helm argues that the US Supreme Court set a precedent[32] for the EU, and concludes that a unified federal approach is the 'only way to achieve certainty.'[33] This conclusion should be properly balanced against Noto La Diega's research, which already demonstrates a more divergent response to *Coman* across the EU than is actually required by law. The historically narrow competence of the CJEU to deal with family law is also relevant.[34] However, Clayton-Helm's chapter does demonstrate the potential impact of EU law.[35] Once again, following the likely impact of Brexit, UK citizens would no longer be able to benefit from these potential further advances by EU law.

Further chapters analyse different methods of introducing same-sex marriage. Aloni explains that incrementalists[36] prefer legislative to judicial methods as they allow 'public opinion to adapt and change gradually'[37] and mitigate the potential of a backlash following a far-reaching court judgment.[38] However, Aloni argues that 'grim' concerns following *Obergefell* have largely been unfounded, and backlash has been weak.[39] Sperti's chapter demonstrates that the 'apparent contrast' between legislative and court-based methods should not be exaggerated.[40] In fact, she considers that the similarity in synergy between national legislatures and constitutional courts needs to be acknowledged.'[41] Prior to the far-reaching judgements of the US and Canada, which introduced same-sex marriage through constitutional courts by declaring violations of human rights,[42] earlier work had already been done. Earlier case law had created important relationships between movements, government officials and citizens, thereby developing public opinion.[43] European constitutional courts, in deferring to national legislatures, should also not be depicted as overly deferent.[44] In fact, Sperti argues that the strategy of European legislatures was not dissimilar to that of countries taking court-based approaches. European legislatures were only able to act following earlier court cases which developed issues such as defining key terms such as family and challenging stereotypes about LGBTQ+ persons, thereby opening up public debate and allowing space for action.[45]

Tobin and Richardson-Self et al. analyse the introduction of same-sex marriage by means of votes from the population.[46] Whilst Tobin rightly acknowledges the 'milestone'[47] achievement of same-sex marriage in the Republic of Ireland (ROI), he considers that the referendum was only chosen as a method of legalisation due to political expediency. His chapter relates 'on-going circuitousness' between the Oireachtas (the Irish Parliament)[48] and the courts, neither of wished to expressly support the cause of marriage equality for . . . 'fear of backlash.'[49] Instead, they selected to pass the matter to a constitutional convention (consisting of 33 Members of the Irish Parliament and 66 citizens representing a cross-section of Irish society) who recommended a referendum. Although the referendum was ultimately successful by a huge margin,[50] Tobin considered this to a be a high-risk strategy because of the history of failed referendums in the ROI.[51]

Richardson-Self et al.'s analysis of the Australian non-compulsory Marriage Law Postal Survey demonstrates that this also followed a long drawn out history of debate and deadlock between conservatives and progressives in both major parties and following proposals for a referendum being blocked.[52] There had been myriad attempts to introduce bills at federal level[53] and instances of backlash from the federal government following advances by individual Australian states.[54] Ultimately, 79.5% of the population voted, with a high margin of 61.6% in favour of change. Richardson-Self et al.'s analysis of data obtained through nine qualitative interviews with LGBTQ+ Tasmanians working in government funded religious organisations and schools[55] demonstrates that the referendum also entailed negative consequences.[56] The 'No' campaign, unhampered by the 'stringent advertising restrictions which apply to federal elections,' consequently spread 'deliberately misleading' misinformation about the LGBTQ+ community,[57] leading to 'prejudicial public scrutiny' and consequent pain and suffering to the LGBTQ+ community.[58] Richardson-Self et al. also critique the 'Yes' campaign,[59] which proceeded on the basis of advocacy emphasising sameness[60] resulting in heteronormativity.[61] This approach resonates with other campaigns across the Western world.[62] Whilst it may 'explain the high voter turnout,'[63] the achievement of marriage 'equality' in Australia on this analysis was bought at a cost. Richardson-Self et al. refer to other authors who suggest that marriage equality 'privilege[s] the most "central" member of the LGBTQ+ community – namely cisgender, white, middle- and upper-class gays and, to an extent, lesbians [but on the other hand] – it leaves its most vulnerable members' concerns on the sidelines.'[64] Following marriage 'equality' in Australia, clear-cut conclusions have not been reached. Questions remain, particularly in light of proposals from some faith-based organisations to introduce a 'right to discriminate' on grounds of religious belief.[65]

Burton's chapter utilises examples from contemporary culture to outline a number of new legal questions raised by changes in society when considering same-sex couples and transpersons whose children form rainbow families. She highlights issues concerned with surrogacy[66] and the case of male transpersons who have retained their female reproductive organs and subsequently given birth to the children.[67] Burton's chapter also serves to illustrate that legal change is far from complete, and that social changes concerning rainbow families continue to challenge judges and legislators in a series of ever-expanding and novel contexts.[68] Further complexities are brought into play by rainbow families who cross international borders. Tryfonidou critically analyses EU treatment of rainbow families and stresses the need for EU judges and institutions to 'fashion rules and principles that reflect the reality of the lives of rainbow families, when such families move between EU Member States.'[69] Her chapter again exemplifies the continued need for legal development in this area, particularly on a pan-EU level, given the diversity of treatment across EU states when considering same-sex couples' parental rights[70] and limited access to surrogacy and medically assisted reproduction.[71] Like Hamilton and Clayton-Helm's chapters, Tryfonidou's chapter demonstrates the opportunities for future development by the EU. Schuster considers the ECtHR's notion of 'family life' as the cornerstone of a pan-European standard of family. Despite the EU not having competence to harmonise family law, it has enacted laws that refer to the concepts of spouse and child. He notes that EU law can self-define the notion of family life (Article 7 of the Charter of Fundamental Rights of the EU), as well as the rights to family and found a family. Their meaning and scope must be the same as the European Convention, although EU law can provide a stronger protection.[72] Schuster argues that the EU standard of 'family' should not result from the commonalities between Member States; some of them are in breach of EU fundamental rights because of their narrow idea of family. Constitutional definitions of 'family' and 'marriage' shall not shape the relevant EU standard; indeed, European fundamental rights shall prevail also on national constitutional principles.[73] He concludes that the EU should not impose a EU-wide definition of family and that '[p]luralism and respect for the diversity of Europe's family patterns is the only viable common standard to ensure free movement.'

Hayward explores the status of civil partnership in an era of same-sex marriage. He refers to sources who describe marriage as a 'cornerstone'[74] and emphasise the 'historical role . . . ceremonial rites and . . . symbolism'[75] associated with marriage. The status ascribed to civil partnership is less certain. In many nations, as Ryan corroborates in an ROI context,[76] civil partnership has been treated as a 'stepping stone' and is abolished following the introduction of same-sex marriage.[77] Noto La Diega's analysis also considers civil partnership to be a 'downgrade,' when on relocation a same-sex couple's marriage is not recognised and they are instead provided with civil partnership as an alternative status.[78] In a UK context, at the time of the Civil Partnership Act 2004, leading gay rights movement Stonewall, considered civil partnership to be 'preferable to marriage.'[79] However, this contentment soon dissolved and Burton points out that the equal marriage campaign quickly stepped up its demand for same-sex marriage.[80] Yet the accuracy of seeing civil partnership as a 'stepping stone' only or as inferior to marriage is debatable. Ryan explains that the reason the ROI abolished civil partnership as a status was because of government concerns that its continued existence, thereby allowing individuals a choice between civil partnership and marriage, 'would undermine constitutional safeguards for marriage as some couples may favour civil partnership over marriage.'[81] The ECtHR also considers civil partnership as having an 'intrinsic value.'[82] Maine and Aloni's analysis also emphasises the importance of a 'a fresh new legal institution,'[83] echoing sentiments expressed by the opposite-sex partners behind the *Steinfeld* litigation as presenting an opportunity to break free from the institution of marriage with its traditional religious and patriarchal connotations.[84] Hayward concludes optimistically that civil partnership has developed a 'nascent ideology'[85] which needs full consideration whereby the future of civil partnership is concerned.

Following analysis of twenty semi-structured interviews with LGBTQ+ persons aged 20–67 in Newcastle in 2016, Maine concludes that despite the legalisation of same-sex marriage, and the achievement of hetereosexual civil partnership, relationship recognition in the UK still reinforces Rubin's sexual hierarchy.[86] The latter concept determines how '[m]odern Western societies appraise sex acts according to a hierarchical system of sexual value. Marital, reproductive, heterosexuals are alone at the top erotic pyramid.'[87] Maine's analysis demonstrates that heteronormativity is privileged and that the new regimes promote coupled, domestic same-sex and different-sex relationships. He concludes that this means that 'non-marital relationships . . . are still excluded.'[88] Individuals which do not fit the prism of monogamous relationships such as homoradicals (those participants who wish to engage in non-monogamous, kink or public sex) are side-lined and do not receive any legal protection, or even criminalised.[89] Donovan also attaches the caveat that whilst marriage is available to almost any adult couple in England and Wales this is providing 'they identify with a recognised binary gender identity.'[90] This provides another example demonstrating that legal change is not all encompassing, and the law needs to continually evaluate the needs of the population in its regulation of recognised relationship statuses.

Ryan interrogates the heteronormative underpinnings of marriage. He explains that until recent legalisation of same-sex marriage in some jurisdictions, throughout history, marriage law was 'solely with a heterosexual model of family life in mind.'[91] Consequently, his chapter considers that as a result marriage law is 'fundamentally heteronormative.'[92] This ties in to Hayward's reference to Norrie, who considers that '[e]quality is granted, but only on heterosexual terms.'[93] Richardson-Self et al. also refer to the further important factor of feminist, leftist and queer criticisms of the marriage equality.[94] They refer to Daniel Thomas, who considers that whilst issues with gender and sexual diversity are framed in '[cis]heteronormative terms . . . [this means] that it ultimately . . . positions gender and sexually diverse people within a hierarchically inferior position to [cis]heterosexuals.'[95] Donovan also considers that pursuit of equality is a flawed agenda raising concerns of other feminists and queer theorists about the sameness and difference debate, considering that legal equality may not be a desirable goal, because 'why should LGBTQ+ people want to achieve equality with what heterosexual people have when that 'standard' of normality might be fundamentally flawed?'[96] Whilst this criticism of lack of real equality calls for future and ongoing legal and social reform, in the context of this debate, it should not be forgotten that some individuals are passionate believers in a right to enter into same-sex marriage. Hamilton, referring to others, argues that for some proponents of same-sex marriage, this is seen as a 'right central to citizenship.'[97] Recognition of same-sex marriage allows a choice for those such as petitioner Sue Wilkinson in the *Wilkinson v Kritzinger* case, who considered marriage as a 'gold-standard.'[98] This accords with research from Pew which demonstrates growing public opinion in favour of same-sex marriage across liberal democracies worldwide,[99] the result of the ROI referendum,[100] leading cases[101] and the changing position of gay rights movements to adopt a more positive view towards same-sex marriage.[102]

Ryan uses examples from both England and Wales, and the ROI, to illustrate differences in legal regulation of same-sex relationships as opposed to heterosexual relationships, therefore on his analysis demonstrating the heteronormativity of marriage equality.[103] At present and until no-fault divorce legislation is re-introduced into Westminster, adultery is a ground for divorce for heterosexual couples in England and Wales but not for same-sex couples. The Matrimonial Causes Act 1973 states that '[o]nly conduct between the respondent and a person of the opposite sex may constitute adultery.'[104] In Irish law, although the Marriage Act 2015 is technically silent on the point,[105] Ryan refers to Shatter's definition of adultery to include 'some penetration of the female vagina by the male organ.'[106] There is also a difference in treatment between same-sex and opposite-sex couples, in the law's treatment of whether the lack of ability consummate a marriage remains a ground for annulment. Law in the ROI, Northern Ireland[107] and England and Wales[108] allows a marriage to be voidable on those grounds for opposite-sex couples.[109] However, for same-sex couples, the inability or refusal to consummate is not a ground for dissolution of English and Welsh civil partnerships[110] or same-sex marriages.[111] With reference to the ROI, Ryan refers to consummation as being 'ordinary and complete' sexual intercourse after the solemnisation'[112] with the core question in such cases is whether there is the 'practical possibility of full penetration by the male into the female.'[113]

Ultimately, Ryan concludes that this difference in treatment leads to the '[t]he unmistakable implication that the law regards homosexual infidelity as less serious and pressing a concern.'[114] His analysis demonstrates a continued lack of equality in the actual legal provisions in place in England and Wales and ROI. Ryan considers that care needs to be taken regarding risks that judges will apply 'heterosexual norms.'[115] He refers to Rundle in observing that 'same-sex couples have very particular experiences and perspectives that may demand a somewhat different approach,'[116] therefore requiring 'flexibility' to accommodate different couples.[117] Once again, the achievement of marriage 'equality' in England and Wales and ROI is not the end of the story.

Donovan's chapter demonstrates that despite extensive legal reform and the introduction of same-sex marriage, there remains a distinct lack of equality for LGBTQ+ people experiencing domestic violence and abuse (DVA). LGBTQ+ persons experiencing DVA may not recognise it as such, may stay in DVA relationships for longer periods[118] and still rarely report to formal, mainstream statutory (e.g. police) or third-sector specialist domestic violence organisations.[119] She considers that this lack of lived equality for LGBTQ+ persons experiencing DVA is a result of three main factors. Firstly, because of the historical portrayal of LGBTQ+ persons as 'deviant' having been 'socially constructed as criminals, pathological or morally questionable.'[120] Secondly because of the impact of 'neoliberalism'[121] on sexualities equalities policies and finally because of the social construction of DVA in a heteronormative fashion. This may result in vulnerable LGBTQ+ individuals experiencing DVA being disenfranchised.

Donovan, referencing Richardson,[122] portrays citizenship as based on a 'heteronormative neoliberal agenda'[123] which promotes the 'responsibilised citizen' who can action their own rights.[124] This analysis of citizenship results in a divide between 'good' and 'bad' gays.[125] The primary category comply with the 'heteronormative social order,' including monogamy and family life.[126] The latter category, either by choice or as a result of being socially excluded, become marginalised and despite myriad law reforms, including same-sex relationships recognition and equal parenting opportunities, become unable to access any legal rights, thereby impeding their citizenship.[127] This leads Donovan, referencing others, to state that 'law has long been identified as one of the barriers to achieving sex/gender equality.[128] On this view, marriage 'equality' – if seen as a conclusion, where this contributes to the creation of 'sexual hierarchies'[129] and the marginalisation of others – could actually prevents the citizenship of LGBTQ+ persons being fully realised.'[130]

Equality goals are therefore questioned, and 'legal equality' cannot be seen as the end of the struggle.[131] Hamilton, referencing others, considers that perhaps citizenship theorists should move away from 'contested understandings of equality.'[132] Instead, wider conceptions of citizenship could be considered to include considerations of responsibilities towards the wider community and social processes through which individuals and social groups engage in claiming, expanding or losing rights.[133] This view of citizenship includes the drive to question what it means to be included and to belong.[134] This entails a sociologically informed definition of citizenship in which the emphasis is less on legal rules and more on normal practices, meanings and identities.[135] There would no longer be total reliance on the 'formal relationship between the individual and the state,' but instead there should be 'a more total relationship inflected by identity, social positioning, cultural assumptions, institutional practices and a sense of belonging.'[136] Hamilton considers that this accords with the EU's aspiration to engage with citizens in a 'more meaningful and direct way,'[137] and for EU citizens to feel a sense of belonging to the EU.[138] This is arguably of essential importance for the EU in a Brexit era. Hamilton accords with authors who consider citizenship as an aspirational ideal which is 'less than complete.'[139] One of the driving forces of change is the need to accommodate new populations.[140] As this book has demonstrated, a key question is to continually evaluate how to include otherwise 'disenfranchised' LGBTQ+ groups.[141]

Donovan reflects points made by Ryan that ultimately legal change alone will not 'change the attitudes, assumptions and hostility that led to the legal inequalities in the first place.'[142] Whilst legal change is credited in providing 'ideological messages,' it continues to raise concern about the possibility of 'backlash.'[143] In considering the inter-relationship between public opinion and legal change, incrementalist scholars set out a step-by-step process, otherwise known as the theory of small change, which allows change over time[144]; therefore 'permitting gradual adjustment of antigay mind-sets, slowly empower[ing] . . . gay right advocates and . . . discredit[ing] antigay arguments.'[145] Proponents of this theory argue that this is supported by statistics which demonstrate the correlation between favourable public opinion and legal change in order to achieve long-term successful change.[146] Aloni comments that the 'incrementalist path is corroborated by the experience of many nations,'[147] and advocates consider that it results in a 'policy which minimizes backlash.'[148] Many of the chapters in this edited collection have endorsed an incrementalist method of change, not least Clayton-Helm, Noto La Diega and Sperti.[149] Maine's data analysis demonstrates that his interviewees did 'posit civil partnerships as a stepping-stone towards same-sex marriage,' arguably therefore supporting the incrementalist paradigm.[150] Yet Aloni critiques the actual steps set out in the incrementalist model.[151] He argues that although the experience of most nations was to follow the incrementalist steps, high-profile exceptions remain.[152] He also raises questions about the time taken to move between stages. In a policy that prefers 'compromise,' this could arguably 'trivialize the harm of those who are harmed by the ban.'[153] He explains that the incrementalist model could help to explain the very slow progress made in Asia and Africa, where many nations still criminalise same-sex intimacy.[154] He refers to Badgett, who explains that one of the problems here is that incrementalists 'offer no clear idea about how long each incremental step should take.'[155] He also argues that the focus on marriage equality as a goal is a false one, as it means that attention is 'explicitly or impliedly diver[ted] . . . from other alternative and innovative innovation strategies that can advance substantive equality beyond marriage.'[156]

Conclusion

Although 28 states worldwide now recognise same-sex marriage,[157] and others some level of civil partnership, many countries continue to 'other' same-sex relationships either by leaving them unrecognised or by criminalising them.[158] At a pan- European level, both the CJEU and the ECtHR are at a crossroads with regards to future development. Whilst different European countries have had varying responses to advances in EU law, many of the chapters in this book are optimistic about the potential role of the EU in expanding rights for LGBTQ+ persons, same-sex couples and rainbow families.[159] The EU concept of citizenship offers an ever-expanding array of practical rights offering opportunities for new groups in society, including LGBTQ+ persons and same-sex couples. Of prominence within the expanding group of rights include those of free movement and non-discrimination rights. Further, the EU offers the possibility of a unified conflicts of law system. A consequent effect of Brexit could also mean that UK LGBTQ+ persons and same-sex couples will not benefit from these expanding rights. When considering the road of individual countries to recognising same-sex legal relationships, the methods of court-based, legislative and public vote analysed within this edited collection all entail the necessity of both legal and social change to ensure the long-term success and acceptance of same-sex relationships. Differences between court-based and legislative methods should not be overstated, as prior to leading court judgements, earlier work had already been done in advancing public opinion and creating the 'necessary relationships between movements, governments officials and citizens.'[160] Whilst legalisation of same-sex marriage by means of a public vote in ROI and Australia perhaps entailed the ultimate attempt at public engagement, both these instances have been critiqued by the authors in the collection on the basis that they only took place due to deadlock between different branches of government.[161] The status of civil partnership is disputed between those who see it as having an 'intrinsic status'[162] and those who see it as a 'downgrade.'[163] In any event, further reform of civil partnership should not be without necessary consultation.[164]

However, even for those countries which have achieved same-sex marriage, many of the chapters in this edited collection demonstrate that this is not a conclusion in itself. Legal and social change need to work together with regard to future development of legal regulation of same-sex relationships and rainbow families, the status of civil partnership and the lived reality of equality of LGBTQ+ persons. Whilst incrementalism allows a model of 'small change,'[165] this is subject to critique.[166] There remain ongoing issues for LGBTQ+ persons who do not fit into the monogamous categories which are given legal protection.[167] Other marginalised individuals, such as LGBTQ+ individuals experiencing DVA, may simply not be able to bring forwards claims to rights if they are disconnected from appropriate social groups and without support in a society which values individualism and characterises DVA in heteronormative terms.[168] Other issues include the contested status of LGBTQ+ education in schools and continued high levels of homo-bi-transphobia[169] and the high level of homophobic hate crime.[170] New challenges constantly need to be considered, not least the issue of certain Australian states bringing forward a right to discriminate on religious grounds.[171] For proponents of same-sex marriage, the legalisation of same-sex marriage in 28 jurisdictions should be represented in an optimistic light. Perhaps this could result in a 'beneficial reappraisal of the role of marriage in society'[172] for everyone, regardless of sexual orientation. There remains much work to be done to be a truly globally LGBTQ+ inclusive society.

Notes

1 See chapters 1–3 and 8.
2 Frances Hamilton, 'Strategies to Achieve Same-Sex Marriage and the Method of Incrementalist Change' (2015–2016) 25 *Journal of Transnational Law & Policy* 121, 140–144.
3 Hamilton.
4 Ibid.
5 Case C-673/16 *Relu Adrian Coman, Robert Clabourn Hamilton, Asociaţia Accept v Inspectoratul General pentru Imigrări, Ministerul Afacerilor Interne* ECLI:EU:C:2018:2.
6 Case C-451/16 *MB v Secretary of State for Work and Pensions* ECLI:EU:C:2018:492.
7 Hamilton (n 2).
8 *Coman* (n 5).
9 *MB* (n 6).
10 *Coman* (n 5); *MB* (n 6).
11 Alina Tryfonidou, 'The EU Top Court Rules that Married Same-Sex Couples Can Move Freely Between EU Member States as "Spouses": Case C-673/16, Relu Adrian Coman Robert Clabourn Hamilton, Asociaţia Accept v Inspectoratul General pentru Imigrări, Ministerul Afacerilor Interne' (2019) *Feminist Legal Studies* 1.
12 *Schalk and Kopf v Austria* App No. 30141/04 (ECtHR, 24 June 2010).
13 Including countries such as Russia, where gay propaganda laws are still in force. See Paul Johnson, 'Homosexual Propaganda' in the Russian Federation: Are They in Violation of the European Convention on Human Rights?' (2015) 3 *Russian Law Journal* 37.
14 For instance, with Eastern European countries.
15 See Tryfonidou (n 11) for discussion.
16 The state liability principle was established in Case C-6/60 and C-9/90 *Francovich v Italy* ECLI:EU:C:1991:428.
17 Noto La Diega carried out 20 semi-structured email interviews with lawyers representing LGBTQ+ persons, LGBTQ+ organisations and police officers.
18 *Coman* (n 5).
19 Noto La Diega.
20 *Coman* (n 5) only requires the receiving country to recognise same-sex marriages for the purposes of free movement and residency, and does not require the receiving country to legalise same-sex marriage.
21 An example here is Italy.
22 Hayward.
23 Noto La Diega.
24 Ibid.

25 Example here is Hungary.
26 Clayton-Helm.
27 *Obergefell v Hodges* 576 US, 135 S Ct 2584 (2015).
28 *Coman* (n 5).
29 *Obergefell* (n 27).
30 Clayton-Helm (n 26).
31 Sheldon D Pollock, 'Same-Sex Marriage and the Conflict of Law: The "Other" Constitutional Issue' (2015) 13 *Georgetown Journal of Law and Public Policy* 477.
32 Clayton-Helm referring to *Obergefell* (n 27).
33 Clayton-Helm (n 26).
34 Aude Fiorini, 'Rome III – Choice of Law in Divorce: Is the Europeanization of Family Law Going Too Far?' (2008) 22 *International Journal of Law, Policy and the Family* 178.
35 Clayton-Helm (n 26).
36 See Aloni referring to Kees Waaldijk, 'Small Change: How the Road to Same-Sex Marriage Got Paved in the Netherlands' in Robert Wintermute and Mads Andenæs (eds), *Legal Recognition of Same-Sex Partnerships: A Study of Nation, Europe, and International Law* (Hart Publishing 2001).
37 Hamilton (n 2).
38 Erez Aloni, 'Incrementalism, Civil Unions and the Possibility of Predicting Legal Recognition of Same-Sex Marriage'(2010–2011) 18 *Duke Journal of Gender Law & Policy* 105, 156.
39 Aloni referring to Katherine Franke, *Wedlocked: The Perils of Marriage Equality* (New York University Press 2015).
40 Angioletta Sperti, *Constitutional Courts, Gay Rights and Sexual Orientation Equality* (Hart Publishing 2017).
41 Ibid.
42 Sperti referring to *Obergefell* (n 27) and Canadian examples such as *M v H* (1999) 2 SCR 3 (Canada).
43 See Sperti referring to Reva B Siegel, 'Community in Conflict: Same-Sex Marriage and Backlash' (2017) 64 *UCLA Law Review* 1728.
44 Sperti referring to examples from Spain, Portugal, France and Germany.
45 Sperti.
46 Tobin and Richardson-Self.
47 Tobin referring to Omar Encarnacion, 'There's Something About Marriage' *Foreign Affairs* (31 May 2015) <www.foreignaffairs.com/articles/ireland/2015-05-31/theres-something-about-marriage> accessed 11 February 2019.
48 Tobin.
49 Ibid.
50 In ROI, the referendum was successful by 62.07% to 37.93%.
51 Tobin referring to Census 2011, *This is Ireland: Part 1* (CSO 2012).
52 Richardson-Self et al.
53 Richardson-Self et al. refer to Deirdre McKeown, 'Chronology of Same-Sex Marriage Bills Introduced into the Federal Parliament: A Quick Guide' *Parliament of Australia* (15 February 2018) <www.aph.gov.au/About_Parliament/Parliamentary_Departments/Parliamentary_Library/pubs/rp/rp1718/Quick_Guides/SSMarriageBills> accessed 2 January 2019.
54 Richardson-Self et al. who refer to the example of Tasmania.
55 Richardson-Self et al. explain that '[t]he recruitment of employees from faith-based organisations was driven by the possibility that changes to *federal* legislation could mean that LGBTQ+ employees in Tasmanian religious organisations

may be discriminated against in the future, if a right to discriminate on religious grounds is introduced. (This would not be the case in secular organisations.)'

56 Richardson-Self et al.

57 Richardson-Self et al. referring to Matt Connellan, '"Deliberately Misleading": First "Vote No" to Same-Sex Marriage Advertisement Airs' *SBS News* (30 August 2017) <www.sbs.com.au/news/deliberately-misleading-first-vote-no-to-same-sex-marriage-advertisement-airs> accessed 4 January 2018.

58 Richardson-Self referring to Quinn Eades and Son Vivienne (eds), *Going Postal: More Than 'Yes' or 'No'. One Year On: Writings from the Marriage Equality Survey* (Brow Books 2018).

59 Of which the most visible organisation was Australian Marriage Equality.

60 Richardson-Self et al.

61 Ibid.

62 Richardson-Self et al. referring to Louise Richardson-Self, *Justifying Same-Sex Marriage: A Philosophical Investigation* (Rowman & Littlefield International 2015). See also Donovan.

63 Richard-Self et al.

64 Richardson-Self et al. referring to Gorrie and Ison's in Quinn Eades and Son Vivienne (n 58).

65 Richardson-Self et al.

66 Burton.

67 Ibid.

68 Ibid.

69 Tryfonidou (n 11).

70 Tryfonidou referring to ILGA, 'Europe Rainbow Europe Package: Annual Review and Rainbow Europe Map' (2019) <https://rainbow-europe.org> last accessed 13 May 2019.

71 Tryfonidou for further detail.

72 Article 52(3) of the Charter of Fundamental Rights of the European Union.

73 Case C-285/98 *Tanja Kreil v Bundesrepublik Deutschland* ECLI:EU:C:2000:2.

74 Hayward referring to Sebastian Poulter, 'The Definition of Marriage in English Law' (1979) 42 *Modern Law Review* 409; Rebecca Probert, '*Hyde v Hyde*: Defining or Defending Marriage?' (2007) *Child and Family Law Quarterly* 322.

75 Hayward.

76 Ryan.

77 See referring to Jens M Scherpe and Andy Hayward, *The Future of Registered Partnerships: Family Recognition Beyond Marriage?* (Intersentia 2017).

78 Noto La Diega.

79 Aloni (n 38) referring to Beccy Shipman and Carol Smart, 'It's Made a Huge Difference: Recognition, Rights and the Personal Significance of Civil Partnership' 12 *Social Research Online* (2007) para 2.5.

80 Burton (n 66).

81 Ryan referring to *Dáil Debates* vol. 890, 23 September 2015.

82 See *Vallianatos v Greece* (2013) 59 EHRR 519, [81] and *Oliari and Others v Italy* (2015) 65 EHRR 957 [174].

83 Aloni and Maine.

84 *R (Steinfeld and Keidan) v Secretary of State for International Development (2018) UKSC 32.*

85 Hayward.

86 Maine referring to Gayle Rubin, 'Thinking Sex: Notes for a Radical Theory of the Politics of Sexuality' in Carole S Vance (ed), *Pleasure and Danger: Exploring Female Sexuality* (Routledge 1984) 151.

87 See Ibid.
88 Maine.
89 Ibid.
90 Donovan.
91 Ryan.
92 Ibid.
93 Hayward referring to Kenneth McK Norrie, 'Marriage Is for Heterosexuals – May the Rest of Us Be Saved from It' (2000) *Child and Family Law Quarterly* 363.
94 Louise Richardson-Self, 'Questioning the Goal of Same-Sex Marriage' (2012) 27 *Australian Feminist Studies* 205.
95 Richardson-Self et al. referring to Daniel Jay Thompson, 'Your Parents Will Read This: Reading (as) Parents in Journalistic Coverage of the Safe Schools Coalition Australia Controversy' (2018) *Journalism* <https://journals.sagepub.com/doi/pdf/10.1177/1464884918755638> accessed 30 June 2019.
96 Donovan referring as an example to Rosemary Auchmuty, 'What's So Special About Marriage? The Impact of Wilkinson v Kitzinger' (2008) 20 *Child and Family Quarterly* 475.
97 Hamilton referring as an example to example Nicholas Bamforth, 'Sexuality and Citizenship in Contemporary Constitutional Argument' (2012) 10 *International Journal of Constitutional Law* 477; Michel Rosenfeld, 'Introduction: Gender, Sexual Orientation and Equal Citizenship' (2012) 10 *International Journal of Constitutional Law* 340; David Bradley, 'Comparative Law, Family Law and Common Law' (2003) 33 *Oxford Journal of Legal Studies* 127.
98 Sue Wilkinson in her Witness Statement contained in *Wilkinson v Kitzinger* (2006) EWHC 2022 (Fam), para 6.
99 See Pew Research Center, 'Attitudes on Same-Sex Marriage' (14 May 2019) <www.pewforum.org/fact-sheet/changing-attitudes-on-gay-marriage/> accessed 16 September 2019. Pew Research Center has surveyed public opinion on same-sex marriage since 2001 and documents increasing support for this.
100 In the ROI referendum (n 50).
101 See, for example, *Goodridge v Department of Public Health*, 798 NE 2d 941 (Mass 2003); *Loving v Virginia*, 388 US 1 (1967) and *Obergefell* (n 27).
102 See, for example, Yvonne Zylan, *States of Passion, Identity and Social Construction of Desire* (Oxford University Press 2011) 205, referring to Evan Wolfson, 'Crossing the Threshold: Equal Marriage Rights for Lesbians and Gay Men and the Intra-Community Critique' (1994) 21 *New York University Review of Law and Social Change* 567 at 611.
103 Ryan.
104 Ryan referring to section 1(6) of the Matrimonial Causes Act 1973.
105 Ryan.
106 Ryan referring to Alan Shatter, *Shatter's Family Law* (4th edn, LexisNexis Butterworth's 1997) 345.
107 Matrimonial Causes (Northern Ireland) Order 1978 (NI), Art.14(a).
108 Matrimonial Causes Act 1973, s12(1)(a).
109 Ryan explains that 'The consequence of this is that the marriage is 'voidable rather than void,' meaning that the marriage is technically continuing, but providing a spouse the ability to avoid a marriage.'
110 Civil Partnership Act 2004 (UK), ss 50 and 174. See also s 107 of the Civil Partnership and Certain Rights and Obligations of Cohabitants Act 2010 (Ir).
111 Matrimonial Causes Act 1973 (E&W), s.12(2) as inserted by the Marriage (Same-Sex Couples) Act 2013 (E&W).

112 Ryan referring to Shatter (n 106) 209.
113 Ryan referring to Ibid, 210.
114 Ryan.
115 Ibid.
116 Ryan referring to Olivia Rundle, 'Following the Legislative Leaders: Judicial Recognition of Same Sex Couples in Australia and New Zealand' in Daniele Gallo, Luca Paladini and Pietro Pustorino (eds), *Same-Sex Couples Before National, Supranational and International Jurisdictions* (Springer-Verlag 2014) 136.
117 Ryan.
118 Donovan.
119 Donovan referring to Catherine Donovan and Marianne Hester, 'Seeking Help from the Enemy: Help-Seeking Strategies of Those in Same-Sex Relationships Who Have Experienced Domestic Abuse' (2011) 23 *Child and Family Law Quarterly* 26; Damien Riggs and others, 'Domestic Violence Service Providers' Capacity for Supporting Transgender Women: Findings from an Australian Workshop' (2016) 46 *British Journal of Social Work* 2374.
120 Donovan referring as an example to Catherine Donovan and Rebecca Barnes, 'Being "Ideal" or Falling Short? The Legitimacy of Lesbian, Gay, Bisexual and/or Transgender Victims of Domestic Violence and Hate Crime' in Marian Duggan (ed), *Revisiting the Ideal Victim Concept* (Policy Press 2018).
121 Donovan refers to 'the neoliberal [concept of the] responsibilised citizen, responsible for their successes and failures is one such trend' as further conceptuatlised by Diane Richardson, 'Desiring Sameness? The Rise of a Neoliberal Politics of Normalisation' (2005) 37 *Antipode* 515; Diane Richardson, 'Rethinking Sexual Citizenship' (2017) 51 *Sociology* 208.
122 Donovan referring to Richardson (n 121) and Richardson (n 121).
123 Donovan.
124 Ibid.
125 Ibid.
126 Donovan referring to Matthew Todd, *Straight Jacket: How to Be Gay and Happy* (Black Swann, 2018).
127 Donovan.
128 Donovan referring to, for example, Carol Smart, *The Ties the Bind: Law, Marriage and the Reproduction of Patriarchal Relations* (Routledge 1984).
129 Brian Heaphy, Carol Smart and Anna Einarsdottir (eds), *Same Sex Marriages: New Generations, New Relationships* (Palgrave Macmillan 2013) 132.
130 As also discussed by Jyl Josephson, 'Citizenship, Same-Sex Marriage and Feminist Criitques of Marriage' (2005) 3 *Perspectives on Politics* 269.
131 Donovan also referring to Robert Leckey, *After Legal Equality: Family, Sex, Kinship* (Routledge 2015).
132 Hamilton (n 2).
133 Hamilton referring to Ruth Lister, 'Why Citizenship: Where, How and Why Children' (2007) 8 *Theoretical Inquiries in Law* 693; Engin F. Isin and Bryan S Turner, 'Citizenship Studies: An Introduction' in Engin F Isin and Bryan Turner (eds), *Handbook of Citizenship Studies* (Sage 2002).
134 Hamilton referring to Brenda Cossman, *Sexual Citizens: The Legal and Cultural Regulation of Sex and Belonging* (Stanford University Press 2007).
135 Hamilton referring to Lister (n 133).
136 Pnina Werbner and Nira Yuval-Davis, 'Introduction: Women and the New Discourse of Citizenship' in Pnina Werbner and Nira Yuval-Davis (eds), *Women, Citizenship and Difference* (Zed 1999).

137 Hamilton referring to Helen Stalford, 'Concepts of Family Under EU Law – Lessons from the ECHR' (2002) 16 *International Journal of Law, Policy and the Family* 410, 413. See also Frances Hamilton, 'The Differing Treatment of Same Sex Couples by European Union Law and the European Convention on Human Rights: The European Union Concept of Citizenship' (2015) 2 *Journal of International and Comparative Law* 87.
138 See Hamilton referring to Kate Nash, 'Between Citizenship and Human Rights' (2004) 43 *Sociology* 1067–1068; Craig Calhoun, *Nations Matter: Culture, History and the Cosmopolitan Dream* (Routledge 2007).
139 Hamilton referring to Lydia Morris, 'Citizenship and Human Rights: Ideals and Actualities (2012) 63 *British Journal of Sociology* 39; David Lockwood, 'Civil Integration and Class Formation' (1996) 47 *British Journal of Sociology* 531, 536.
140 Hamilton referring to Gershon Shafir and Alison Brysk, 'The Globalization of Rights: From Citizenship to Human Rights' (2006) 10 *Citizenship Studies* 275, 279; Will Kymlicka, *Multicultural Citizenship: A Liberal Theory of Minority Rights* (Oxford University Press 1995).
141 Shafir and Byrsk (n 140) 279.
142 Donovan and Ryan.
143 Donovan referring to Susan Faludi, *Backlash: The Undeclared War Against American Women* (Three Rivers Press 1991).
144 Waaldijk (n 36) 437.
145 William Eskridge Jr, *Equality Practice: Civil Unions and the Future of Gay Rights* (Routledge 2002).
146 See David Masci and Drew Desilver, 'A Global Snapshot of Same-Sex Marriage' (Pew Research Center, 21 June 2019) <www.pewresearch.org/fact-tank/2013/06/04/global-snapshot-sex-marriage/> accessed 16 September 2019. The Pew Research Center conducts surveys annually in 17 nations on this subject.
147 Aloni (n 38).
148 Aloni.
149 Clayton-Helm, Noto La Diega and Sperti.
150 Maine.
151 Aloni (n 38).
152 Aloni.
153 Ibid.
154 Ibid.
155 Aloni referring to MV Lee Badgett, 'Predicting Partnership Rights: Applying the European Experience in the United States' (2005) 17 *Yale Journal of Law & Feminism* 71, 75.
156 Aloni referring to Libby Adler, *Gay Priori: A Queer Critical Legal Studies Approach to Law Reform* (Duke University Press 2018) 104.
157 See introduction n 2.
158 See '72 Countries Where Homosexuality Is Illegal' *76 Crimes* (11 June 2019) <https://76crimes.com/76-countries-where-homosexuality-is-illegal/> accessed 16 September 2019.
159 See Hamilton, Noto La Diega, Clayton-Helm, Tryfonidou and Schuster.
160 Sperti referring to Siegel (n 43) 1731.
161 Tobin and Richardson-Self et al.
162 ECtHR in *Oliari and Others v Italy* (n 82).
163 Noto La Diega.
164 Hayward.

165 Waaldijk (n 36).
166 Aloni (n 38).
167 Maine and Donovan.
168 Donovan.
169 Donovan referring to Metro, 'Youth Chances: Integrated Report' *Metro Charity* (2016) <https://metrocharity.org.uk/sites/default/files/2017-04/National%20Youth%20Chances%20Intergrated%20Report%202016.pdf> accessed 20 July 2019.
170 Donovan referring to Adam Lusher, 'Homophobic Attacks Rose 147 Per Cent After the Brexit Vote' *The Independent* (London, 9 October 2016) <www.independent.co.uk/news/uk/home-news/brexit-hate-crime-hatred-homophobia-lgbt-147-per-cent-rise-double-attacks-on-gays-lesbians-a7352411.html> accessed 20 July 2019.
171 Richardson-Self et al. referring to New South Wales currently considering the Anti-Discrimination Amendment (Religious Freedoms) Bill 2018 (NSW), 'which would allow broad ranging discrimination on the basis of religious belief.'
172 Hayward referring to *Obergefell v Hodges* (n 27).

References

Primary sources

Anti-Discrimination Amendment (Religious Freedoms) Bill 2018 (NSW).
Charter Fundamental Rights of the European Union.
Civil Partnership Act 2004 (UK).
Civil Partnership and Certain Rights and Obligations of Cohabitants Act 2010 (Ir).
Dáil Debates 23 September 2015, vol. 890.
Francovich v Italy (Case C-6/60 and C-9/90) ECLI:EU:C:1991:428.
Goodridge v Department of Public Health, 798 NE 2d 941 (Mass 2003).
Loving v Virginia 388 US 1 (1967).
Marriage (Same-Sex Couples) Act 2013 (E&W).
Matrimonial Causes Act 1973.
Matrimonial Causes Act 1973 (E&W).
Matrimonial Causes (Northern Ireland) Order 1978 (NI), Art.14(a).
MB v Secretary of State for Work and Pensions (Case C-451/16) ECLI:EU:C:2018:492.
M v H (1999) 2 SCR 3 (Canada).
Obergefell v Hodges 576 US, 135 S Ct 2584 (2015).
Oliari and Others v Italy (2015) 65 EHRR 957 [174].
Relu Adrian Coman, Robert Clabourn Hamilton, Asociaţia Accept v Inspectoratul General pentru Imigrări, Ministerul Afacerilor Interne (Case C-673/16) ECLI:EU:C:2018:2.
R (Steinfeld and Keidan) v Secretary of State for International Development (2018) UKSC 32.
Schalk and Kopf v Austria App No. 30141/04 (ECtHR, 24 June 2010).
Tanja Kreil v Bundesrepublik Deutschland (Case C-285/98) ECLI:EU:C:2000:2.
Vallianatos v Greece (2013) 59 EHRR 519.
Wilkinson v Kitzinger (2006) EWHC 2022 (Fam).

Secondary sources

'72 Countries Where Homosexuality Is Illegal' *76 Crimes* (11 June 2019) <https://76crimes.com/76-countries-where-homosexuality-is-illegal/> accessed 16 September 2019.

Adler L, *Gay Priori: A Queer Critical Legal Studies Approach to Law Reform* (Duke University Press 2018) 104.

Aloni E, 'Incrementalism, Civil Unions and the Possibility of Predicting Legal Recognition of Same-Sex Marriage'(2010–2011) 18 *Duke Journal of Gender Law & Policy* 105.

Auchmuty R, 'What's So Special About Marriage? The Impact of Wilkinson v Kitzinger' (2008) 20 *Child and Family Quarterly* 475.

Badgett MV, 'Predicting Partnership Rights: Applying the European Experience in the United States' (2005) 17 *Yale Journal of Law & Feminism* 71.

Bamforth N, 'Sexuality and Citizenship in Contemporary Constitutional Argument' (2012) 10 *International Journal of Constitutional Law* 477.

Bradley D, 'Comparative Law, Family Law and Common Law' (2003) 33 *Oxford Journal of Legal Studies* 127.

Calhoun C, *Nations Matter: Culture, History and the Cosmopolitan Dream* (Routledge 2007).

Census 2011, *This is Ireland: Part 1* (CSO 2012).

Connellan M, '"Deliberately Misleading": First "Vote No" to Same-Sex Marriage Advertisement Airs' *SBS News* (30 August 2017) <www.sbs.com.au/news/deliberately-misleading-first-vote-no-to-same-sex-marriage-advertisement-airs> accessed 4 January 2018.

Cossman B, *Sexual Citizens: The Legal and Cultural Regulation of Sex and Belonging* (Stanford University Press 2007).

Donovan C and Barnes RM, 'Being "Ideal" or Falling Short? The Legitimacy of Lesbian, Gay, Bisexual and/or Transgender Victims of Domestic Violence and Hate Crime' in Marian Duggan (ed), *Revisiting the Ideal Victim Concept* (Policy Press 2018).

Donovan C and Hester M, 'Seeking Help from the Enemy: Help-Seeking Strategies of Those in Same-Sex Relationships Who Have Experienced Domestic Abuse' (2011) 23 *Child and Family Law Quarterly* 26.

Eades Q and Vivienne S (eds), *Going Postal: More Than 'Yes' or 'No'. One Year On: Writings from the Marriage Equality Survey* (Brow Books 2018).

Encarnacion O, 'There's Something About Marriage' *Foreign Affairs* (31 May 2015) <www.foreignaffairs.com/articles/ireland/2015-05-31/theres-something-about-marriage> accessed 11 February 2019.

Eskridge Jr W, *Equality Practice: Civil Unions and the Future of Gay Rights* (Routledge 2002).

Faludi S, *Backlash: The Undeclared War Against American Women* (Three Rivers Press 1991).

Fiorini A, 'Rome III – Choice of Law in Divorce: Is the Europeanization of Family Law Going Too Far?' (2008) 22 *International Journal of Law, Policy and the Family* 178.

Franke K, *Wedlocked: The Perils of Marriage Equality* (New York University Press 2015).

Hamilton F, 'The Differing Treatment of Same Sex Couples by European Union Law and the European Convention on Human Rights: The European Union Concept of Citizenship' (2015) 2 *Journal of International and Comparative Law* 87.

Hamilton F, 'Strategies to Achieve Same-Sex Marriage and the Method of Incrementalist Change' (2015–2016) 25 *Journal of Transnational Law & Policy* 121.

Heaphy B, Smart C and Einarsdottir A, (eds), *Same Sex Marriages: New Generations, New Relationships* (Palgrave Macmillan 2013) 132.

ILGA, 'Europe Rainbow Europe Package: Annual Review and Rainbow Europe Map' (2019) <https://rainbow-europe.org> last accessed 13 May 2019.

Isin EF and Turner BS, 'Citizenship Studies: An Introduction' in Isin EF and Turner B (eds), *Handbook of Citizenship Studies* (Sage 2002).

Johnson P, 'Homosexual Propaganda' in the Russian Federation: Are They in Violation of the European Convention on Human Rights?' (2015) 3 *Russian Law Journal* 37.

Josephson J, 'Citizenship, Same-Sex Marriage and Feminist Criitques of Marriage' (2005) 3 *Perspectives on Politics* 269.

Kymlicka W, *Multicultural Citizenship: A Liberal Theory of Minority Rights* (Oxford University Press 1995).

Leckey R, *After Legal Equality: Family, Sex, Kinship* (Routledge 2015).

Lister R, 'Why Citizenship: Where, How and Why Children' (2007) 8 *Theoretical Inquiries in Law* 693.

Lockwood D, 'Civil Integration and Class Formation' (1996) 47 *British Journal of Sociology* 531.

Lusher A, 'Homophobic Attacks Rose 147 Per Cent After the Brexit Vote' *The Independent* (London, 9 October 2016) <www.independent.co.uk/news/uk/home-news/brexit-hate-crime-hatred-homophobia-lgbt-147-per-cent-rise-double-attacks-on-gays-lesbians-a7352411.html> accessed 20 July 2019.

Masci D and Desilver D,'A Global Snapshot of Same-Sex Marriage' (Pew Research Center, 21 June 2019) <www.pewresearch.org/fact-tank/2013/06/04/global-snapshot-sex-marriage/> accessed 16 September 2019.

McKeown D, 'Chronology of Same-Sex Marriage Bills Introduced into the Federal Parliament: A Quick Guide' *Parliament of Australia* (15 February 2018) <www.aph.gov.au/About_Parliament/Parliamentary_Departments/Parliamentary_Library/pubs/rp/rp1718/Quick_Guides/SSMarriageBills> accessed 2 January 2019.

Metro, 'Youth Chances: Integrated Report' *Metro Charity* (2016) <https://metro-charity.org.uk/sites/default/files/2017-04/National%20Youth%20Chances%20Intergrated%20Report%202016.pdf> accessed 20 July 2019.

Morris L, 'Citizenship and Human Rights: Ideals and Actualities (2012) 63 *British Journal of Sociology* 39.

Nash K, 'Between Citizenship and Human Rights' (2004) 43 *Sociology* 1067–1068.

Norrie McK, 'Marriage Is for Heterosexuals – May the Rest of Us Be Saved from It' (2000) *Child and Family Law Quarterly* 363.

Pew Research Center, 'Attitudes on Same-Sex Marriage' (14 May 2019) <www.pewforum.org/fact-sheet/changing-attitudes-on-gay-marriage/> accessed 16 September 2019.

Pollock SD, 'Same-Sex Marriage and the Conflict of Law: The "Other" Constitutional Issue' (2015) 13 *Georgetown Journal of Law and Public Policy* 477.

Poulter S, 'The Definition of Marriage in English Law' (1979) 42 *Modern Law Review* 409.
Probert R, '*Hyde v Hyde*: Defining or Defending Marriage?' (2007) *Child and Family Law Quarterly* 322.
Richardson D, 'Desiring Sameness? The Rise of a Neoliberal Politics of Normalisation' (2005) 37 *Antipode* 515.
Richardson D, 'Rethinking Sexual Citizenship' (2017) 51 *Sociology* 208.
Richardson-Self L, 'Questioning the Goal of Same-Sex Marriage' (2012) 27 *Australian Feminist Studies* 205.
Richardson-Self L, *Justifying Same-Sex Marriage: A Philosophical Investigation* (Rowman & Littlefield International 2015).
Riggs D et al. 'Domestic Violence Service Providers' Capacity for Supporting Transgender Women: Findings from an Australian Workshop' (2016) 46 *British Journal of Social Work* 2374.
Rosenfeld M, 'Introduction: Gender, Sexual Orientation and Equal Citizenship' (2012) 10 *International Journal of Constitutional Law* 340.
Rubin G, 'Thinking Sex: Notes for a Radical Theory of the Politics of Sexuality' in Vance CS (ed), *Pleasure and Danger: Exploring Female Sexuality* (Routledge 1984) 151.
Rundle O, 'Following the Legislative Leaders: Judicial Recognition of Same Sex Couples in Australia and New Zealand' in Gallo D, Paladini L and Pustorino P (eds), *Same-Sex Couples Before National, Supranational and International Jurisdictions* (Springer-Verlag 2014) 136.
Scherpe JM and Hayward A, *The Future of Registered Partnerships: Family Recognition Beyond Marriage?* (Intersentia 2017).
Shafir G and Brysk A, 'The Globalization of Rights: From Citizenship to Human Rights' (2006) 10 *Citizenship Studies* 275.
Shatter A, *Shatter's Family Law* (4th edn, LexisNexis Butterworth's 1997).
Shipman B and Smart C, 'It's Made a Huge Difference: Recognition, Rights and the Personal Significance of Civil Partnership' 12 *Social Research Online* (2007) para 2.5.
Siegel RB, 'Community in Conflict: Same-Sex Marriage and Backlash' (2017) 64 *UCLA Law Review* 1728.
Smart C, *The Ties the Bind: Law, Marriage and the Reproduction of Patriarchal Relations* (Routledge 1984).
Sperti A, *Constitutional Courts, Gay Rights and Sexual Orientation Equality* (Hart Publishing 2017).
Stalford H, 'Concepts of Family Under EU Law – Lessons from the ECHR' (2002) 16 *International Journal of Law, Policy and the Family* 410.
Thompson DJ, 'Your Parents Will Read This: Reading (as) Parents in Journalistic Coverage of the Safe Schools Coalition Australia Controversy' (2018) *Journalism* <https://journals.sagepub.com/doi/pdf/10.1177/1464884918755638> accessed 30 June 2019.
Todd M, *Straight Jacket: How to Be Gay and Happy* (Black Swann, 2018).
Tryfonidou A., 'The EU Top Court Rules that Married Same-Sex Couples Can Move Freely Between EU Member States as "Spouses": Case C-673/16, Relu Adrian Coman Robert Clabourn Hamilton, Asociaţia Accept v Inspectoratul General pentru Imigrări, Ministerul Afacerilor Interne' (2019) *Feminist Legal* Studies 1.

Waaldijk K, 'Small Change: How the Road to Same-Sex Marriage Got Paved in the Netherlands' in Wintermute R and Andenæs M (eds), *Legal Recognition of Same-Sex Partnerships: A Study of Nation, Europe, and International Law* (Hart Publishing 2001).

Werbner P and Yuval-Davis N, 'Introduction: Women and the New Discourse of Citizenship' in Werbner P and Yuval-Davis N (eds), *Women, Citizenship and Difference* (Zed 1999).

Wolfson E, 'Crossing the Threshold: Equal Marriage Rights for Lesbians and Gay Men and the Intra-Community Critique' (1994) 21 *New York University Review of Law and Social Change* 567.

Zylan Y, *States of Passion, Identity and Social Construction of Desire* (Oxford University Press 2011).

Index

Note: **Boldface** page references indicate tables.